MW00446487

THE PALACE

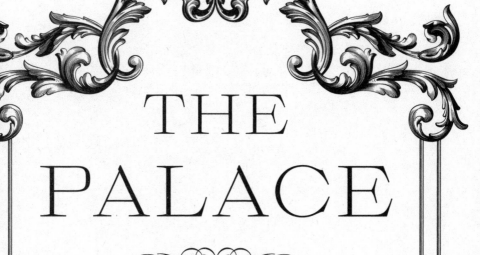

THE
PALACE

FROM THE TUDORS
TO THE WINDSORS,
500 YEARS OF
BRITISH HISTORY
AT HAMPTON COURT

GARETH RUSSELL

ATRIA BOOKS
New York · London · Toronto · Sydney · New Delhi

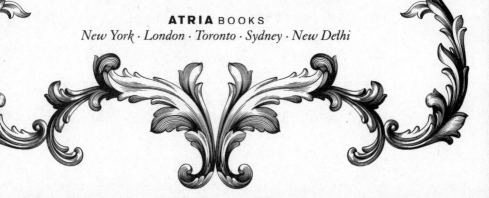

ATRIA
BOOKS

An Imprint of Simon & Schuster, Inc.
1230 Avenue of the Americas
New York, NY 10020

Copyright © 2023 by Gareth Russell

Originally published in Great Britain in 2023 by William Collins

First Atria Books hardcover edition December 2023

ATRIA BOOKS and colophon are trademarks of Simon & Schuster, Inc.

For information about special discounts for bulk purchases, please contact Simon & Schuster Special Sales at 1-866-506-1949 or business@simonandschuster.com.

The Simon & Schuster Speakers Bureau can bring authors to your live event. For more information or to book an event, contact the Simon & Schuster Speakers Bureau at 1-866-248-3049 or visit our website at www.simonspeakers.com.

Interior design by Dana Sloan

Manufactured in the United States of America

1 3 5 7 9 10 8 6 4 2

Library of Congress Cataloging-in-Publication Data has been applied for.

ISBN 978-1-9821-6906-0
ISBN 978-1-9821-6908-4 (ebook)

To

My godson Alexander,

On his christening

And to Laura, Tom, and Raife

With the end of each generation, the lives that submerged here were absorbed again. With each death, the air of the place had thickened.

—ELIZABETH BOWEN, *BOWEN'S COURT* (1942)

CONTENTS

Part III

THE HOUSE OF HANOVER

Part IV

THE HOUSE OF WINDSOR

FAMILY TREES

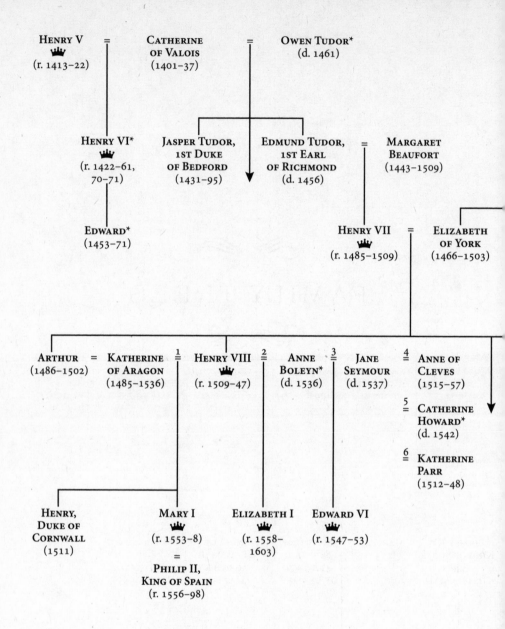

The House of Tudor

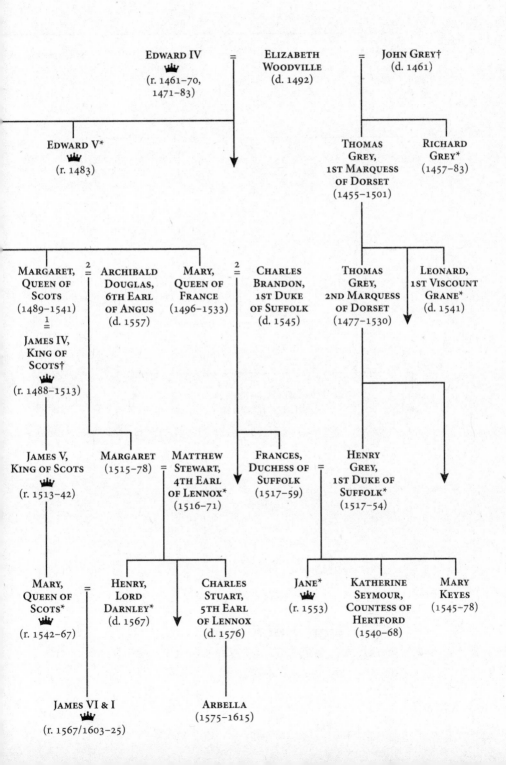

EDWARD IV
♔
(r. 1461–70,
1471–83)

ELIZABETH
WOODVILLE
(d. 1492)

JOHN GREY†
(d. 1461)

EDWARD V*
♔
(r. 1483)

THOMAS
GREY,
1ST MARQUESS
OF DORSET
(1455–1501)

RICHARD
GREY*
(1457–83)

MARGARET,
QUEEN OF
SCOTS
(1489–1541)

²

ARCHIBALD
DOUGLAS,
6TH EARL
OF ANGUS
(d. 1557)

MARY,
QUEEN OF
FRANCE
(1496–1533)

²

CHARLES
BRANDON,
1ST DUKE
OF SUFFOLK
(d. 1545)

THOMAS
GREY,
2ND MARQUESS
OF DORSET
(1477–1530)

LEONARD,
1ST VISCOUNT
GRANE*
(d. 1541)

JAMES IV,
KING OF
SCOTS†
♔
(r. 1488–1513)

JAMES V,
KING OF SCOTS
♔
(r. 1513–42)

MARGARET
(1515–78)

MATTHEW
STEWART,
4TH EARL
OF LENNOX*
(1516–71)

FRANCES,
DUCHESS OF
SUFFOLK
(1517–59)

HENRY
GREY,
1ST DUKE OF
SUFFOLK*
(1517–54)

MARY,
QUEEN OF
SCOTS*
♔
(r. 1542–67)

HENRY,
LORD
DARNLEY*
(d. 1567)

CHARLES
STUART,
5TH EARL
OF LENNOX
(d. 1576)

JANE*
♔
(r. 1553)

KATHERINE
SEYMOUR,
COUNTESS OF
HERTFORD
(1540–68)

MARY
KEYES
(1545–78)

JAMES VI & I
♔
(r. 1567/1603–25)

ARBELLA
(1575–1615)

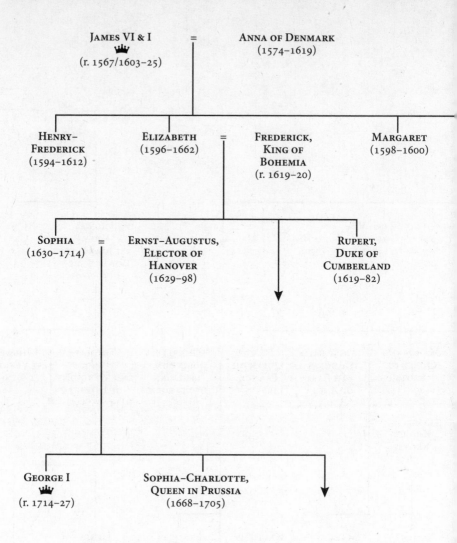

The House of Stuart

 Monarchs in the British Isles

* Executed or murdered

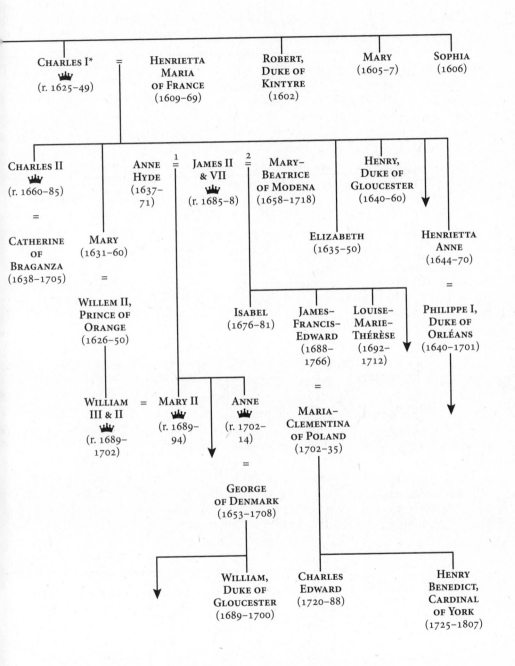

CHARLES I*
👑
(r. 1625–49)

=

HENRIETTA
MARIA
OF FRANCE
(1609–69)

ROBERT,
DUKE OF
KINTYRE
(1602)

MARY
(1605–7)

SOPHIA
(1606)

CHARLES II
👑
(r. 1660–85)

=

CATHERINE
OF
BRAGANZA
(1638–1705)

ANNE
HYDE
(1637–71)

= ¹

JAMES II
& VII
👑
(r. 1685–8)

= ²

MARY-
BEATRICE
OF MODENA
(1658–1718)

HENRY,
DUKE OF
GLOUCESTER
(1640–60)

MARY
(1631–60)

=

WILLEM II,
PRINCE OF
ORANGE
(1626–50)

ELIZABETH
(1635–50)

HENRIETTA
ANNE
(1644–70)

=

ISABEL
(1676–81)

JAMES-
FRANCIS-
EDWARD
(1688–
1766)

LOUISE-
MARIE-
THÉRÈSE
(1692–
1712)

PHILIPPE I,
DUKE OF
ORLÉANS
(1640–1701)

WILLIAM
III & II
👑
(r. 1689–
1702)

=

MARY II
👑
(r. 1689–
94)

ANNE
👑
(r. 1702–
14)

MARIA-
CLEMENTINA
OF POLAND
(1702–35)

=

GEORGE
OF DENMARK
(1653–1708)

WILLIAM,
DUKE OF
GLOUCESTER
(1689–1700)

CHARLES
EDWARD
(1720–88)

HENRY
BENEDICT,
CARDINAL
OF YORK
(1725–1807)

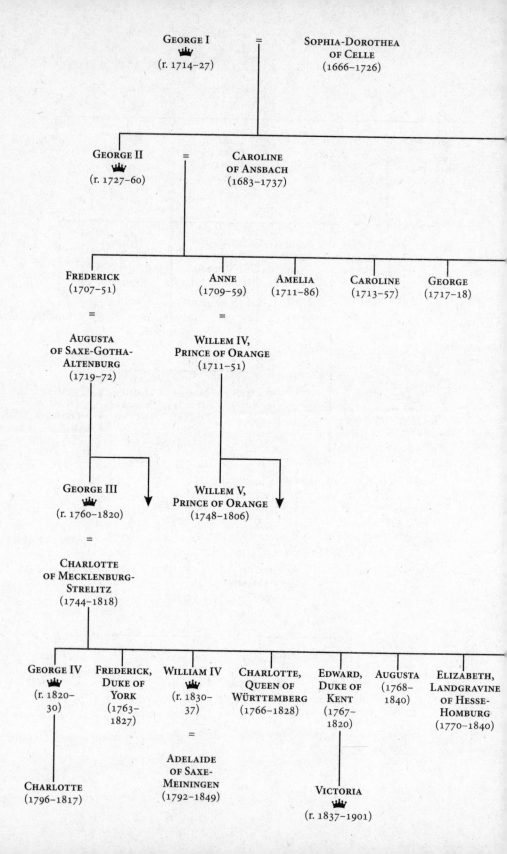

The House of Hanover

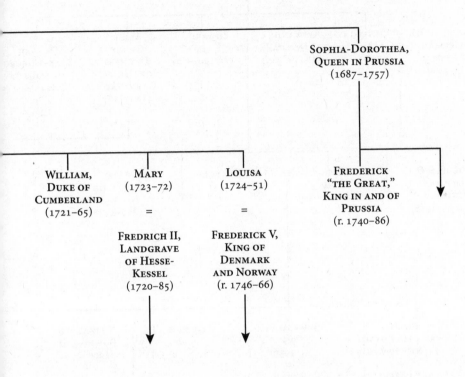

Monarchs in the British Isles

SOPHIA-DOROTHEA,
QUEEN IN PRUSSIA
(1687–1757)

WILLIAM,
DUKE OF
CUMBERLAND
(1721–65)

MARY
(1723–72)

=

FREDRICH II,
LANDGRAVE
OF HESSE-
KESSEL
(1720–85)

LOUISA
(1724–51)

=

FREDERICK V,
KING OF
DENMARK
AND NORWAY
(r. 1746–66)

FREDERICK
"THE GREAT,"
KING IN AND OF
PRUSSIA
(r. 1740–86)

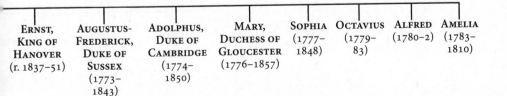

ERNST,
KING OF
HANOVER
(r. 1837–51)

AUGUSTUS-
FREDERICK,
DUKE OF
SUSSEX
(1773–
1843)

ADOLPHUS,
DUKE OF
CAMBRIDGE
(1774–
1850)

MARY,
DUCHESS OF
GLOUCESTER
(1776–1857)

SOPHIA
(1777–
1848)

OCTAVIUS
(1779–
83)

ALFRED
(1780–2)

AMELIA
(1783–
1810)

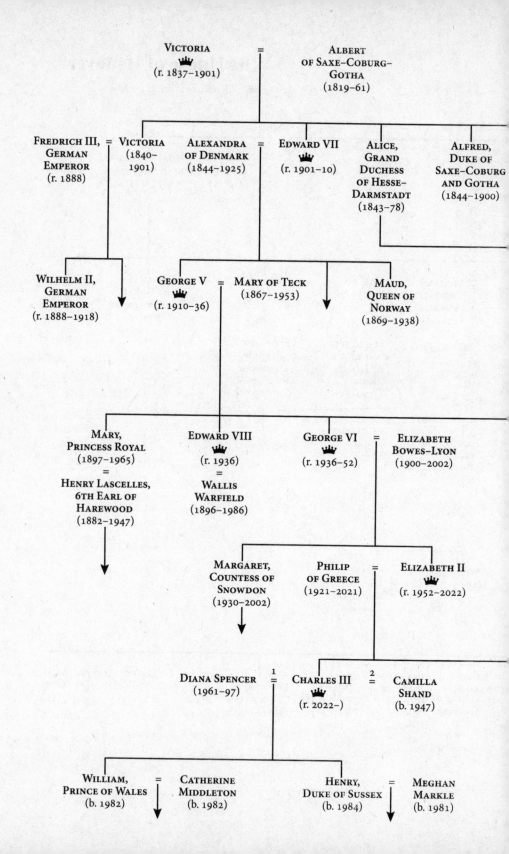

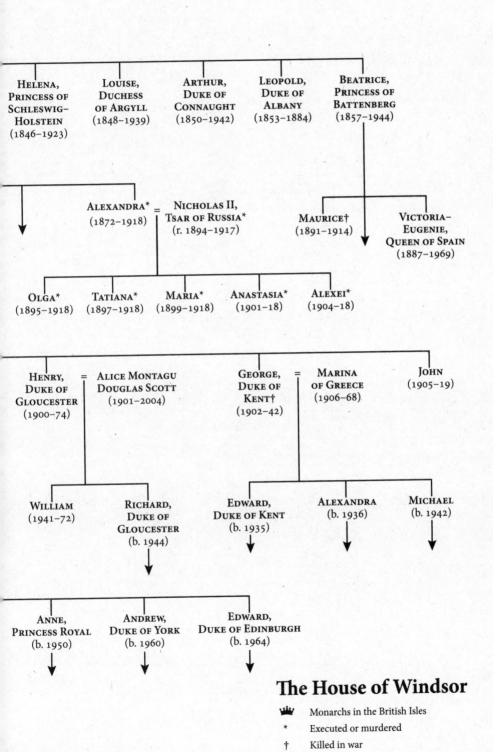

HELENA,
PRINCESS OF
SCHLESWIG-
HOLSTEIN
(1846–1923)

LOUISE,
DUCHESS
OF ARGYLL
(1848–1939)

ARTHUR,
DUKE OF
CONNAUGHT
(1850–1942)

LEOPOLD,
DUKE OF
ALBANY
(1853–1884)

BEATRICE,
PRINCESS OF
BATTENBERG
(1857–1944)

ALEXANDRA* = **NICHOLAS II,**
(1872–1918)   **TSAR OF RUSSIA***
             (r. 1894–1917)

MAURICE†
(1891–1914)

VICTORIA-
EUGENIE,
QUEEN OF SPAIN
(1887–1969)

OLGA*
(1895–1918)

TATIANA*
(1897–1918)

MARIA*
(1899–1918)

ANASTASIA*
(1901–18)

ALEXEI*
(1904–18)

HENRY,
DUKE OF
GLOUCESTER
(1900–74)

= **ALICE MONTAGU**
DOUGLAS SCOTT
(1901–2004)

GEORGE,
DUKE OF
KENT†
(1902–42)

= **MARINA**
OF GREECE
(1906–68)

JOHN
(1905–19)

WILLIAM
(1941–72)

RICHARD,
DUKE OF
GLOUCESTER
(b. 1944)

EDWARD,
DUKE OF KENT
(b. 1935)

ALEXANDRA
(b. 1936)

MICHAEL
(b. 1942)

ANNE,
PRINCESS ROYAL
(b. 1950)

ANDREW,
DUKE OF YORK
(b. 1960)

EDWARD,
DUKE OF EDINBURGH
(b. 1964)

The House of Windsor

👑   Monarchs in the British Isles

*   Executed or murdered

†   Killed in war

INTRODUCTION

As it has done for centuries, Hampton Court Palace draws thousands of visitors every year—as far back as the reign of Elizabeth I, staff were supplementing their incomes by offering tours to visitors, and the fascination shows no signs of dwindling. I began this account of Hampton Court during the lockdowns of 2020 and, as soon as it was possible to do so, I returned to visiting it in 2021 and 2022. In writing about Hampton Court and the different people who lived there, or visited, in the decades between 1495 and 2016, I fell a little in love with this extraordinary place. There were so many important and interesting moments at Hampton Court that it would be unfeasible to include them all without producing a book hefty enough to perform double duty as a door stopper. Some, however, could not be excluded. Having previously written a biography of Henry VIII's fifth wife, Queen Catherine Howard, whose downfall began at Hampton Court in 1541, I wanted to avoid repeating too much of what I had already covered. However, Catherine's tragedy is so inextricably linked to the history—and mythology—of Hampton Court that it would have been absurd to leave it out. Where the relevant sections in that biography, *Young and Damned and Fair*, look closely at the actions of the accused and the accusers, this book's chapter on 1541 shifts the focus to explore how those two weeks appeared to the palace's other residents—those outside the scandal, such as Lady

1

Margaret Douglas, who tried to piece together what was happening as the arrests and rumors multiplied.

The aesthetics and construction of Hampton Court play an important part in this narrative. When referring to buildings or locations in the palace, I have used the name most familiar to modern visitors—such as the Anne Boleyn Gate, an eighteenth-century name for a sixteenth-century tower. However, this is not an architectural history; that was done twenty years ago with Simon Thurley's brilliant *Hampton Court: A Social and Architectural History. The Palace* is a history of the people who lived and died at Hampton Court, of the monarchy and countries that they shaped, the glories they achieved, and the horrors that they inflicted.

After spending two and a half years on this book, I left with a greater sense of awe at how far-reaching Hampton Court's impact has been. Reflecting on the personal importance of history to the historian is difficult, and many do not think it has a place in works of nonfiction. Generally, but not absolutely, I agree. While writing chapter 12, it occurred to me that the Hampton Court Conference of 1604—at which King James commissioned the translation of the Bible that now bears his name—has shaped, or had an influence on, many of the major milestones of my life and many others. Its translations were the words read out at my christening, at the christenings of my siblings, and at the funerals of our loved ones. The precise grammar and wording chosen by the translators for their translation of the Epistle to the Ephesians were the last words we chose to be read aloud to my grandfather as he lay on his deathbed in the hospital, and his firm squeezing of my mother's hand as he heard them was the last unambiguous sign of consciousness he gave before he passed away. In a Sunday school eleven miles outside Belfast, my early concept of religion was shaped by the King James Bible, as we memorized its words along with the catechism. Dr. John Rainolds, the Jacobean theologian who features in this book, would have despaired at my student theater days; he also sat on the committee that translated the book of Job into the version my grandmother read when she was unwell. Lastly, the words of the King James translation were the last I read to my father, who was ill before and throughout the writing of this book, and who passed away shortly before it was edited. From a king sitting among a group of bishops in a drawing room at Hampton Court in 1604 sprang a translation of an ancient text that has shaped countless millions of lives in the centuries since. It is that sense of history, flowing in and out of Hampton Court, that remains the strongest impression that I have taken from writing its story.

From 1529 to 1760, Hampton Court was an ark of monarchy, revolution, politics, and religious turmoil, with the Tudor, Stuart, and Hanoverian dynasties using it to augment their prestige. Through its people, the palace offers the opportunity to study power, faith, hubris, courage, brilliance, cruelty, and folly as the British state and the Anglican Church emerged—and the royal line changed four times. The country's torturous experiment with the Divine Right of Kings was born and buried at Hampton Court, and the only English republic started its march into the grave there. Its apartments, halls, orchards, gardens, chapels, kitchens, and drawing rooms have been home to sexual scandals, controversies, and personal drama as much as they have been to royalty, Welsh ladies-in-waiting, English page boys, Scottish knights, Irish barons, chocolatiers, exhausted mathematicians, Spiritualists, divorced marchionesses, clergymen, and retired jesters.

PROLOGUE

The Queen and The Duke of Edinburgh, accompanied by The Princess Margaret, were present this evening at a Ball at Hampton Court given by Officers of the Household Brigade.

—Court Circular, May 30, 1953

In the late afternoon of May 29, 1953, in one of the 775 rooms of Buckingham Palace, Elizabeth II dressed in a rose-colored crinoline gown to attend a ball at Hampton Court. Five feet four inches in height, with her mother's "wonderful blue eyes," her father's dark hair, and a chin and cheekbones that advertised her descent from the House of Teck via her paternal grandmother, Elizabeth had not changed much in temperament since a journalist described her as a child who was "happy natured but serious."[1] She was helped into her ballgown by her dresser Margaret MacDonald, the forty-nine-year-old daughter of a Scottish railway worker. MacDonald— nicknamed Bobo by Elizabeth—had joined royal service as nursery maid when Elizabeth was born in 1926 and never left.[2] A dresser's title was "a bit misleading," thought one of MacDonald's successors. With corsets and hoops consigned to the past, a dresser's job was, by 1953, comparable to a stylist's: "[our] role is to lay everything out for her and sometimes help zip her up or fasten a tricky piece of jewellery."[3] Outside, from just beyond the palace perimeters, the Queen and MacDonald could hear the sounds of revellers celebrating Elizabeth's forthcoming coronation, due to take place three days later.

The twenty-six-year-old Elizabeth II, who had acceded to the throne following her father's death from cancer fifteen months earlier, had spent the first part of her day with a bedsheet tied to her shoulders as a stand-in for the robes she would wear on June 2. Her movements—the coronation was as much choreography as it was theology—were perfected with the help of tape on the Buckingham Palace floors, marking out the space she would process through in Westminster Abbey. As she rehearsed, Elizabeth listened, over and over again, to audio recordings of her father's coronation sixteen years before. Afterward, the Queen held two audiences. First, she welcomed Haiti's new ambassador to Britain, who was accompanied to the palace by his secretary, Gerard Baptiste, and his attaché, Adaline Maximilien; afterward, the Queen met with Sir William Strang, Permanent Under-Secretary of State for Foreign Affairs.[4] Then it was upstairs for a change of dress, which ended with MacDonald fastening the clasp of "a heavy diamond and ruby" necklace and fixing a diamond tiara into Elizabeth's hair.[5] The ball was being thrown in the Queen's honor by officers of the Household Brigade, the army cavalry units responsible for guarding state occasions in London, to celebrate her imminent coronation. It would also be the first time in 193 years that Hampton Court Palace had hosted its sovereign for a major event.[6]

Both of the palaces that hosted Elizabeth II that evening owed their current status to the actions of her four-times great-grandfather, King George III. Buckingham Palace had become indelibly associated with the public image of the British monarchy after George III bought it for £21,000 from the Duke of Buckingham's son in 1761 as a wedding gift for his German wife, Charlotte of Mecklenburg-Strelitz.[7] At the same time as he was turning Buckingham House into a palace, George III consigned Hampton Court to oblivion as a royal residence. He opened its gardens to the public and subdivided its abandoned apartments into living quarters for revolution-fleeing royal cousins, down-on-their-luck bishops' widows, and retired servants.

Dressed for the ball, the Queen joined her husband, Philip, and her sister, Margaret, in a Rolls-Royce that drove out the gates of Buckingham Palace. Following in a second car was Elizabeth's lady-in-waiting for the evening, Lady Margaret Hay, accompanied by her equerry*, twenty-nine-year-old Captain Johnny Spencer, Viscount Althorp, who three decades later would become father-in-law to Elizabeth's eldest son, Charles, through the marriage of his daughter Lady Diana Spencer. In her car, Elizabeth sat next to her twenty-two-year-old sister, described by their mother as having "large blue eyes and a will of iron."[8] Their grandmother judged Margaret "more complicated and difficult" than Elizabeth, summarizing her as *espiègle*, meaning intelligent and wild without necessarily intending to be bad; one of her mother's friends called Margaret "naughty but amusing." Writer Gore Vidal thought she was "too intelligent for her role in life" as a member of the royal family, as did the Conservative Party politician Norman St. John-Stevas, who considered the princess "one of the cleverest women I've ever met." Far less impressed was a courtier's wife, who thought that Margaret's "nature was to make everything go wrong. Nice one day— nasty the next. . . . She had everything, and then she destroyed herself."[9] In the decades ahead, Princess Margaret would become one of the most unpopular members of the royal family, nicknamed "Her Royal Lowness," criticized by politicians and journalists for her extravagance, then pilloried and impersonated by comedians who lampooned her as haughty, arrogant, and useless.[10] But as of 1953, she was still admired as young, beautiful, and stylish, and there was a great deal of sympathy for her at the grief she felt after her father's sudden death.

Ahead of the sisters in the car sat Elizabeth's husband, Philip, Duke of Edinburgh, who thirty years earlier had been born on a kitchen table in Corfu as his parents fled a coup that pushed his uncle off the Greek throne. Boarding at a school in Germany run by a reliable royalist who had served as secretary to the last chancellor under the old German monarchy, Prince Philip had come to Britain when his Jewish headmaster had

---

* A military officer who assists members of the British royal family at certain official functions.

to flee a Nazi arrest warrant in 1933.[11] He completed his education at the
school his headmaster founded in Scotland, joined the Royal Navy, served
in the Second World War, became a British citizen, and fell in love with
the King's eldest daughter not long after victory.[12] Their wedding took
place in November 1947, just after Philip was created Duke of Edinburgh,
Earl of Merioneth, and Baron Greenwich by his future father-in-law, King
George VI. The Duke of Edinburgh was tall, blond, energetic, handsome,
and eye-wateringly tactless. In conversation with a friend, Elizabeth's
private secretary, Sir Alan ("Tommy") Lascelles, summarized Philip as
"rough, ill-mannered, uneducated, and would probably not be faithful."[13]
The swipe about his education was made because Philip had attended the
newly established Gordonstoun boarding school in Scotland rather than
the sacred bastions of old money at Eton, Harrow, Winchester, or Marlborough (Lascelles's alma mater).[14]

Philip, who regarded Lascelles as chief in the cabal of insufferable palace snobs—the grim-faced "men with moustaches," as Margaret dubbed
them—proved how prepared he was to ruffle feathers in his quest to mod-
ernize the monarchy, particularly after he was appointed to the chair of the
committee that organized his wife's coronation. In that capacity, he had
waged a successful campaign to allow cameras into Westminster Abbey to
make the ceremony the first televised coronation in history. The BBC was
so thrilled by the decision that it installed two new television transmitters—
one in the north of England in County Durham, the other just outside Belfast in Northern Ireland—to improve coverage across the United Kingdom
for the big day. It proved a worthwhile investment: the coronation inspired
a revolution in British television ownership, which surged from 1.2 million
to 3 million households, enabling an estimated 27 million—in a population
of 50 million—to watch the ceremony's live broadcast.[15]

In the hour or so that it took Elizabeth, Philip, and Margaret to travel
from the newer Buckingham Palace to the older Hampton Court, Elizabeth's image gazed back at them again and again. They drove beneath celebratory arches, tons of red, white, and blue bunting, and past shop windows,
lampposts, private homes, factories, and government buildings decorated

with royalist slogans such as "Happy and Glorious," "God Save Our Gracious Queen," "God Save the Queen," "Rule Britannia," "Vivat Regina," "Long Live the Queen," and "God Bless You, Ma'am." Tabloids were posting front-page countdowns to the ceremony—even the left-leaning *Daily Mirror*, which on the day of the coronation itself would break the record for daily sales of a British newspaper with 7 million copies.[16]

The monarchy's critics were either bemused or offended by the intensity of the public's devotion to Elizabeth II. Few skeptics were concerned with criticizing the Queen directly, since, at that stage, she was largely an unknown quantity. Criticism tended instead to focus on attitudes toward the monarchy itself, which they felt had been elevated into something approaching an ersatz religion. The British former-spy-turned-journalist Malcolm Muggeridge argued that, regardless of the monarch's personality, the monarch, as an idea, upheld the class system: "The impulses out of which snobbishness is born descend from the Queen at the apex of the social pyramid, right down to the base. . . . If it is considered—as I consider—that such a social setup is obsolete and disadvantageous in the contemporary world, then the Monarchy is to that extent undesirable."[17] For others, like the playwright John Osborne, the spectacle of monarchy was being used as a grotesque opiate for the British people to distract themselves from economic difficulties, diplomatic decline, and political stagnation. Eight years earlier, the United Kingdom had emerged from the Second World War victorious yet bankrupt. Far from the promised land of plenty, living standards had fallen in victory's aftermath; rationing had still been in place two years later when Princess Elizabeth married Prince Philip. The empire was dead by the time Elizabeth II came to the throne—a fact obvious to all but its most blinkered supporters, some of whom gravitated to far-right pressure groups such as the League of Empire Loyalists, founded two years after the coronation.[18] The economy was only just beginning to stabilize and was a long way from prospering, and Britain had been eclipsed in terms of global power by her former allies the United States and the Soviet Union. To Osborne, the millions celebrating the coronation and cheering the royal family were performers

in the last circus of a civilisation that has lost faith in itself and sold itself
for a splendid triviality, for the beauty of the ceremonial. . . . When the
Roman crowds gather outside St. Peter's [at the Vatican], they are taking
part in a moral system, however detestable it may be. My objection to
the Royal symbol is that it is dead; it is a gold filling in a mouth full of
decay. . . . It distresses me that there should be so many empty minds,
so many empty lives in Britain to sustain this fatuous industry; that no
one should have the wit to laugh [the monarchy] out of existence or the
honesty to resist it.[19]

Equally philosophical were some of the monarchy's supporters, such as psychoanalyst Ernest Jones and author C. S. Lewis, the Oxford professor and theologian best known for his seven-part biblical allegories for children, *The Chronicles of Narnia.*[20] Defenders of monarchy in Britain typically identified the institution as a constitutional bulwark against dictatorship, a custodian of stability and nationhood, and a preventative against party politics infecting the role of head of state as much as they did day-to-day government. For Jones and Lewis, as much as for Muggeridge and Osborne on the opposite side of the issue, the question of monarchy ran deeper. Where those like Osborne saw the Crown as a distracting and harmful panacea that got the crowds punch-drunk on patriotism and tacky sentiment to distract them from issues that mattered, Lewis presented the monarchy as not just constitutionally but also culturally essential—almost an evolutionary necessity—by giving people something to focus natural human emotions on that was more edifying and less harmful than the emerging craze for celebrities or the cults of personalities surrounding elected demagogues. In his 1943 article "Equality," Lewis argued, "We Britons should rejoice that we have contrived to reach much legal democracy (we still need more of the economic) without losing our ceremonial Monarchy. For there, right in the midst of our lives, is that which satisfies the craving. . . . Monarchy can easily be 'debunked,' but watch the faces, mark well the accents of the debunkers." Lewis characterized anti-monarchists as "men to whom pebbles laid in a row are more beautiful than an arch. . . . Where men are forbidden to honour a king, they honour millionaires, athletes, or film-stars instead— even famous prostitutes or gangsters. For spiritual nature, like bodily nature, will be served—deny it food, and it will gobble poison."[21]

Yet the monarchy could no longer be as separate from the media as Lewis might have liked. For better and for worse, Elizabeth II's reign was illuminated by a camera flash; the Queen understood that, or, as she put it, "I have to be seen to be believed."[22] A crowd—some of them waiting for more than two hours to see her—had gathered to cheer as Elizabeth's car reached the bridge that linked Hampton Court to the local train station. The Queen ordered the car's interior light switched on so that they could see her—a technique pioneered by her mother, whose detractors nick-named her "Grinning Liz," thanks to her seemingly insatiable appetite for public applause. Elizabeth II waved, the crowd cheered, and a photographer for the *Daily Mirror* caught the moment for tomorrow's front page with its headline "The Queen Goes to an All-Night Ball." The *Mirror*'s usual banner, in socialist red, had temporarily been replaced with monarchial gold to announce, "Three Golden Days to June 2!" The accompanying photo of the Queen and Princess Margaret covered more than half the front page, sharing space with adverts for a special *Mirror* commemorative book on the coronation and another for Cadbury's Milk Tray chocolates.[23]

After crossing the bridge, the Queen's car turned right, passing through the gates of Hampton Court and driving toward the palace that loomed ahead of them—a colossus in red brick at the heart of a large estate, with the River Thames to the right. In its heyday, Hampton Court had been as inextricably linked to the monarchy as Buckingham Palace would be after it. For a brief moment in 1953, it looked as if those days had returned. Every room, even those seldom used and emptied to their fragile floorboards, was illuminated for the ball as Hampton Court's reflection shone over the river. One reveller wrote, "A world that had vanished . . . lived again for the night."[24] The royals were driven across the palace's stone bridge, dating from the reign of Henry VIII and traversing a now-drained moat. From their car windows, the Queen, the Duke,* and the Princess could see the bridge's stone yales†, panthers, unicorns, lions, and dragons, in the respective hoofs, paws, and claws of which were clasped the heraldic shields of the Beaufort, Plantagenet, Seymour, Stuart, and Tudor families. These carved beasts had the appearance of antiquity; in fact, they were a tasteful restoration carried out under the auspices of Elizabeth II's grandmother Queen Mary, Britain's queen consort from 1910 until the death of her husband, King George V, in 1936.[25] Queen Mary had passed away two months before the Hampton Court ball, with specific instructions that her death was not to disrupt the scheduled coronation.

The royals passed under a large redbrick gatehouse erected on the orders of the sixteenth-century churchman Cardinal Thomas Wolsey and into a large courtyard that they crossed before passing through the Anne Boleyn Gate, a clocktower named in honor of Henry VIII's second wife. It sported a famous clock showing a pre-Galilean solar system with Earth at its center; around it spun the hours of the day, days of the week, months of the year, signs of the zodiac, cycles of the Moon, and tides of the Thames. The two cars came to a halt in the smaller courtyard on the other side of the gate. The Queen—after gathering the white fox-fur wrap selected by Margaret MacDonald—stepped out onto the cobblestones, turned left with her husband, and walked up a flight of stone steps. Her sister followed. Their mother was not with them. The fifty-two-year-old Queen Elizabeth the Queen Mother had stayed in London to be guest of honor at the Royal Auxiliary Air Force Officers' Coronation Dinner and Ball at the Savoy Hotel.[26] The Queen Mother's absence also meant that another figure was missing from Hampton Court, as she had requested that one of the two people to accompany her to the Savoy was the comptroller of her

---

* Philip was not referred to as a prince between 1947 and 1957. He ceased using his title as a Greek prince after becoming a naturalized British subject. He was created a Prince of the United Kingdom by his wife in February 1957, after which he was officially His Royal Highness The Prince Philip, Duke of Edinburgh.

† A mythical beast with the body of an antelope or goat, and tusks. In some legends, fire-breathing.

household, Group Captain Peter Townsend.[27] Choosing him as one of her attendants made sense, since Townsend was a handsome and well-liked Royal Air Force veteran who had been decorated for his bravery, "leadership, determination, and skill of the highest order" against the German Luftwaffe at the Battle of Britain in 1940. After leaving the forces, he had become an equerry to King George VI. The family liked Townsend so much that, following the King's death, the new Queen Mother asked him if he would become her comptroller as she established her household as a widow. However, the Queen, the Duke of Edinburgh, and Princess Margaret might have been forgiven if they suspected that the Queen Mother had requested Townsend's presence at the Savoy to make sure he was not dancing at Hampton Court with the Princess.

A few months earlier, Margaret and Townsend had told her mother that they were in love and that Townsend had sued to divorce his wife, Rosemary, so that he and the Princess could marry.[28] Up until that point, the Queen Mother, like most of Townsend's colleagues in the royal household, assumed that the breakdown in the Townsends' marriage had been a consequence of Rosemary's affair with businessman John de László, son of the famous portraitist Philip de László. The Queen Mother worried that Margaret would be required to renounce her place in the succession, which would mean sacrificing her income from the government-approved Civil List, followed by a possible stint of living abroad—all for a match that seemed forged in the midst of grief. After the initial shock wore off, the Queen Mother fell back on her default position of acting as if nothing unpleasant had happened—and hoping that things would soon resolve themselves. If nobody caused a fuss it would speed along the point where the romance would fizzle out—or "peter out," as one wag put it.

At the top of the stone stairs, the royal party stepped into the Great Hall. King James I's three-century-long ban on smoking had been rescinded to suit Margaret, who was seldom seen at parties without her fashionable cigarette holder. An official struck his staff on the floor to announce, "Her Majesty The Queen and His Royal Highness The Duke of Edinburgh."

It had been 600 years since the first monarch—Elizabeth's nineteen-times great-grandfather King Edward III—arrived at Hampton, and 450 years since her fourteen-times great-grandmother, Elizabeth of York, had been entertained on the spot where Elizabeth II entered ahead of her husband and sister.[29]

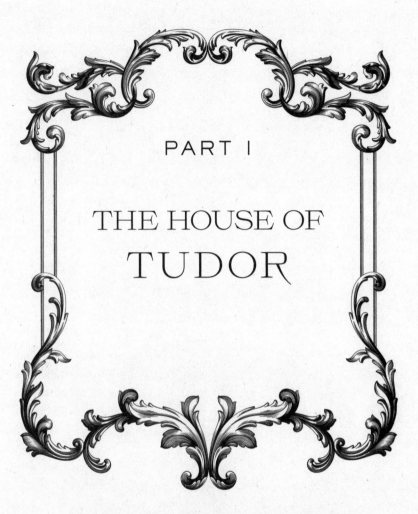

PART I

THE HOUSE OF
TUDOR

*"Well," said the King, "let make a cry, that all the lords,
knights, and gentlemen of arms, should draw unto a
castle called Camelot."*

—Sir Thomas Malory, *Le Morte d'Arthur* (1485)

CHAPTER I

STAR OF THE SEA

God is where He was.

—Elizabeth of York, Queen of England (1502)

Five centuries before the Tudors climbed onto the English throne, Hampton had been Hammtonne (Anglo-Saxon for "the place/settlement on the bend of the river"). There had been settlements in the area since the Bronze Age (c. 2000–700 BC) and aristocratic estates during Roman Britain (AD 43–410). The site's early importance derived from its convenience to the river, its correspondingly fertile soil, and later its proximity to significant royal events—such as a Church synod in 838 attended by the King of the pre-unification southern kingdom of Wessex, and the coronation at nearby Kingston in 925 of Æthelstan as the first king of a united England.[1] Prior to his death in 1062, the manor of Hammtonne had been held by Ælfgar, Earl of Mercia, courtier to the saint-king Edward the Confessor and son of Lady Godiva, the noblewoman who entered English popular culture thanks to the colorful—and almost certainly apocryphal—legend that she rode naked through the streets of Coventry to shame her avaricious husband into lowering taxes on the beleaguered townsfolk.* Ælfgar of Mercia had the good luck

---

* We also owe the phrase "Peeping Tom" to the legend of Lady Godiva, or Godgifu, to use her original Anglo-Saxon name. The story runs that the people of Coventry, touched by Godiva's gesture to humiliate herself on their behalf, agreed to turn away or keep indoors as she rode by, with the exception of a curious adolescent, Tom, who peeked from an upstairs window. Variations on the legend have him being stricken blind by God in punishment or murdered by his enraged neighbors.

to shuffle off the mortal coil four years before the invading Norman armies swept through England, all but obliterating the Anglo-Saxon nobility as a class.[2] In the land redistribution free-for-all that followed, William the Conqueror, England's king from 1066 to 1087, granted Hampton to his cousin and companion in arms, Walter de St.-Valery.[3] Later generations of the St.-Valerys served successive Norman and Plantagenet kings and fought in the Crusades, where Reginald de St.-Valery encountered the warrior-monks of the Order of the Knights Hospitaller of St. John of Jerusalem.[4] Under the protection of the wealthy St.-Valerys, the Knights Hospitaller began renting land at Hampton for an English chapter of their order.[5]

In the long run, those monks proved more enduring than their patrons-cum-landlords. Bernard de St.-Valery, who fell fighting for the Third Crusade at the siege of Acre, was called *dilecto familiari nostro* ("a beloved familiar of ours") by King Richard the Lionheart, but Bernard's son and heir Thomas eventually joined the insurrections against the Lionheart's brother and nephew, kings John and Henry III, supporting the rebellions against them until defeat in 1217. In a desperate scramble to save Hampton before it was confiscated in retaliation by the Crown, Thomas's daughter Annora took half of the estate with the help of her husband, while the rest was tactically gifted to a family friend, a merchant named Henry of St. Albans. Two generations later, the Knights Hospitaller bought the estate from their descendants; they were to hold Hampton for the next two and a half centuries.

The Hospitallers beautified the manor to serve as a place of ecclesiastical hospitality for courtiers, who could take advantage of the Church's hospitality as they traveled but who were expected to make some sort of financial gesture when they continued on their way. This practice became particularly lucrative for Hampton in the early fourteenth century when aristocratic footfall increased thanks to Byfleet, a riverside residence belonging to Edward II, who ruled from 1307 to 1327. Hampton was en route to Byfleet, which made it a natural spot for well-heeled visitors to halt their journey for a night or two. A long-standing legend has it that Byfleet was built on King Edward's orders as a gift to the man he loved, Piers Gaveston, Earl of Cornwall.[6] Unfortunately, there is no extant documentary evidence confirming that Byfleet was created for Gaveston, although he did own it; Edward seems to have spent a significant amount of time near Hampton only after 1312, the year Gaveston was lynched by his enemies.[7] His son Edward III, king from 1327 to 1377, possessed the happy combination of his father's good looks with none of his bad luck.[8] The King stayed at Hampton himself, as evidenced by the royal household's payment for a roof damaged by fire that broke out when the court was in residence. However, after Edward III's great-grandson Henry V dismantled Byfleet as a royal manor, Hampton slipped into decline.

For the rest of the fifteenth century, the manor was lucky to escape much of the chaos that engulfed England during the Wars of the Roses, the name given later to a series of civil wars fought over disputed successions to the throne. The conflict began with the mental breakdown of King Henry VI, head of the royal House of Lancaster, and the resultant bid for the crown by a distant kinsman (his second cousin, once removed), the Duke of York.[9] Over the next three decades, the conflict scythed through the royal family tree—leaving one king, a prince of Wales, and a duke of York dead on different battlefields, along with thousands of their countrymen. Kings Henry VI and Edward V were murdered in the Tower of London, as was the latter's younger brother, likewise after being moved there ostensibly for his own safety.[10] A queen died in exile; a king was forced to publicly deny accusations that he intended to poison his wife in order to marry his niece; noblemen were dragged from council meetings to be murdered on the spot; unpopular advisers were lynched; women of the royal line were accused of adultery, witchcraft, or both in order to conveniently disinherit their children and thereby clear the path for whichever relative wanted to replace them in the line of succession; and royal men were targeted with arrows of bastardy and bigamy to the same purpose.* Pliant parliaments performed legislative acrobatics to legitimize the latest rear-

---

* A common trope in discrediting a royal was to spread the story that he or she was the illegitimate child of a lowlyborn foreigner. With subtle alterations, the rumors were reinvented for Richard II, Henry IV, Edward IV, and Elizabeth I—the occupation of the putative father shifting from a French clerk, to a Dutch butcher, an archer based in the French town of Rouen, and a Flemish musician.

rangement of the dynastic chessboard, the last of which came when Henry
Tudor, Henry VI's nephew, emerged as King Henry VII over Richard III's
corpse at the Battle of Bosworth in 1485.[11] This would have spelled disaster
for Hampton Court's most recent lessee, Sir John Wode, a loyal supporter of
the Yorkist cause. He had been Speaker of the House of Commons* under
King Edward IV and later a vice admiral for King Richard III. Like Earl
Ælfgar long before him, Wode died with perfect timing, twelve months
before his benefactor King Richard was killed at Bosworth.[12]

For the last year of Richard III's rule and the first ten of Henry VII's,
the prior† of the Knights Hospitaller in England seems to have used Hampton Court as his country retreat. During that decade or so, the order does
not appear to have invested much of its own money into Hampton, allowing
the house to go a little to seed. An opportunity then presented itself for the
order to make the manor as profitable as it had been in days gone by. Like
Edward II two centuries earlier, Henry VII upped Hampton Court's value
on the property market by building a new royal residence farther upriver.
This was the palace of Richmond, described by an admiring contemporary as an "earthly and second paradise of our region of England."[13] With
the creation of Richmond Palace, Hampton Court again became useful to
courtiers. The two palaces were built on the banks of the Thames—given
the state of late medieval roads, those who could preferred to travel by water.

Its revived appeal brought Hampton Court to the attention of one of
Henry VII's favorites, Giles Daubeney, 1st Baron Daubeney, who, in 1495,
began renting the estate from the Knights Hospitaller. Under the terms of
the lease, Daubeney had to maintain the order's chapel at Hampton, including funding a priest to celebrate Mass and sing requiems on the absent Knights' behalf. Since it was an eighty-year lease, in practical terms
it functioned more like a freehold, empowering Daubeney to "take, alter,
transpose, break, change, make and new build at their proper cost any
houses, walls, moats, ditches, works, or other things within or about the

---

* The lower chamber of the English Parliament.

† Head of male religious orders or monastic houses.

said manor." Armed with this permission, Daubeney halted Hampton's slow rot through his series of renovations, the majority of which seem to have been carried out from 1495 to 1500.

Tall, thin, in his early forties, and described by another courtier as "a good man, prudent, just, honest, and loved," Daubeney had served the Yorkist kings during the Wars of the Roses before crossing the floor, and the English Channel, to join Henry Tudor's cause while the future monarch was still in exile.[14] After having participated in a failed plot against Richard III, Daubeney admittedly had very little choice. It was either flight or death. About a half dozen of his servants had sensibly absconded with him.[15] Since pledging his loyalty to Tudor, Daubeney had proved so devoted that his notoriously suspicious master never doubted him, refusing to credit tall tales of tentative treason concocted by Daubeney's few enemies. He had returned to the British Isles with Tudor's armies, triumphed with them at the Battle of Bosworth, helped dress Henry on his coronation day, and become a privy councillor, then co–Master of the Mint, Master of the Hart Hounds, and Lieutenant of Calais, the city on the northern French coast that remained under English control as the rump of its once-vast medieval empire in Europe. Henry VII had Daubeney inducted into the Order of the Garter, the highest chivalric honor in England, and raised him to the peerage as a baron. He became Lord Chamberlain, the most senior official in the running of the royal household, and he returned to the battlefield to help suppress early uprisings against Tudor rule. Daubeney acquired a fortune through royal grants of land that gave him estates in Devon, Dorset, Hampshire, Wiltshire, and especially in Somerset, his family's ancestral county.[16] Through this, Giles Daubeney became the greatest landowner in the southwest. In 1497 the Duchy of Milan's ambassador to England identified Daubeney as one of the three most influential men in the country, a view seconded by the Princess of Wales, who told her father that Daubeney was the courtier who possessed the greatest private sway with King Henry.[17]

Unquestionably and unquestioningly loyal, Lord Daubeney's competence was, regrettably, a more fruitful topic for critique. Earlier in his career, his bravery had been exceptional, even by the standards of a martial age. While leading his men to attack the Flemish siege lines at Dixmude in 1489, Daubeney launched himself into the thick of battle rather than command from a distance, wading through ditches until the water reached his armpits. But he did not always successfully navigate the proverbial tight-rope between bravery and foolishness. At the Battle of Blackheath in 1497, Daubeney nearly lost the day for the Tudor armies by leading the charge too early and getting himself captured by the rebels, until his own men rescued him.[18] That embarrassment may have stymied Daubeney's valor in the field because, two years after Blackheath, he allegedly proved "slack" in dispersing another rebel force.[19] He continued to enjoy Henry VII's trust, however; after he completed his first major set of changes to Hampton Court, Daubeney received the honor of hosting the King for several days in October 1500. Aware of how much it cost nobles to host a royal visit, Henry VII sometimes attempted to ameliorate the expense by contributing with a grand version of "bring your own bottle." In preparation for his stay at Hampton Court in 1500, 312 barrels of expensive malmsey wine had rolled into the manor, all paid for by the royal household. Once the barrels were drained and the King had left, Daubeney embarked upon eighteen months of further modifications to the house.

So much has changed at Hampton Court in the intervening centuries that it is hard to imagine it as it was in Lord Daubeney's lifetime. We can gain some limited visual idea of how it might have looked from its surviving near contemporaries, English houses such as Oxburgh Hall in the county of Norfolk or Layer Marney Tower in the county of Essex, both of which also display the architectural aesthetics popular in the early Tudor period.[20] Set within a grand yet comfortable medium-sized country estate, bifurcated by the River Thames with recently imparked fields on one side and its redbrick manor house on the other, Hampton Court's garderobe (lavatory) turrets, its chimneys, and the roof of Lord Daubeney's new Great Hall were visible to the river traffic shuttling between palaces, manors, and the capital. The manor bore witness to the prosperity and influence that had accrued to Daubeney in the long peace following the Wars of the Roses. Another testament was the number of servants needed to run the household; the man who had once fled for his life with six retainers had come to employ dozens.

Most of his servants were at Hampton Court as its chapel bell tolled to wake them in the chilly second week of January 1503. Or, as most of the manor's residents would have dated it, 1502. Prior to 1752, the British Isles piously started the new calendar year on March 25, in homage to the great beginning marked on that day by the Feast of the Annunciation, when the Archangel Gabriel had appeared to the Blessèd Virgin Mary with the gospel that she would give birth to the Messiah.[21] England was a country shaped by its Catholicism, even more so than by its recent experiences of civil war. Whether under Henry VI, Edward IV, Edward V, Richard III, or Henry VII, the cock crowed at dawn's first light as servants rose from their bedding to say the Our Father, the Hail Mary, the Glory Be, or the Apostles' Creed—or, as they were referred to in Latin even by those who did not speak it, the Pater Noster, the Ave Maria, the Gloria, and the Credo.

Staff in Hampton Court and most other great English houses slept in communal spaces, with pillows and blankets on top of rushes, cut and dried reeds that were scattered across the floors. Our understanding of this way of life has been immeasurably improved in recent years by the research of British social historian Ruth Goodman, who decided to test our certainty that the lives of those in the 1500s must have been an unending litany of the uncomfortable and the foul. By re-creating the recommendations from contemporary guides to domesticity, Goodman found that the rushes would most likely have been gathered in bundles. Once laid about six inches deep, they prove comfortable enough as places to sleep. Arranged thus, they also fail to snag on the hems of robes or gowns. If sprinkled with water, very lightly and occasionally, they retain a "fresh, cucumberish smell" for months.[22] This also prevents the rushes from becoming too much of a hazard via an errant spark from a candle or a fireplace. Even at the bottom layer of the rushes, after a half year of heavy use, Goodman found "there was no mould, mildew, slime, or gunge of any sort."[23]

After the servants' sleeping mats, covers, and headrests were tidied away, they cleaned themselves with clear, cold water. Most people used wet cloths to wash their bodies, and privacy in the servants' sleeping quarters was almost nonexistent. After that, they slipped into their linen undergarments, which were to be sent regularly to the laundresses, because they acted as protective barriers between the body's sweat and less frequently cleaned outer outfits.[24] Dental hygiene was typically taken care of with another cloth or with the finger. Clean soot was the most effective; chalk or salt could be used in a pinch.[25] At the time, many English Christians wore, for talismanic protection, roundels bearing the words *In Principio erat Verbum et Verbum erat apud Deum et Deus erat Verum*, the opening verse of Saint John's Gospel.[26] Besides these and medallions bearing the images of saints, other popular devotional tokens were coins bent in half in promise that the grateful bearer would one day make a pilgrimage to a particular shrine where they would offer the coin to the interceding saint.[27]

Washed in water, soot, and prayer, the male servants streamed into the manor's courtyard. Women, then the minority in domestic service, arrived from their separate sleeping quarters while the household priests bustled to the chapel to celebrate Prime, the first service of the day.[28] The maintenance of these priests was among Lord Daubeney's contractual obligations, and so, whether he was in residence or not, this Liturgy of the First Hour was the first of eight canonical "hours" that framed the day through religious services, as it did in churches throughout England.[29] Within Hampton Court's chapel, the gentle face of the Virgin Mary, rendered in wood, gazed out in the carved company of her Son, with Saint John the Evangelist and Saint Nicholas the Wonderworker nearby.[30] Two pews faced a painting of the crucifixion and the small red glow cast by the tabernacle light, flickering in fulfilment of instructions given by God to Moses.[31] The tabernacle's illumination could be augmented by that of the votive candles lit in supplication before the statue of the Virgin. Devotion to the Mother of God bit deeply into the souls of English Christians—Richard II had consecrated his kingdom to Mary, Henry V had begged for her protection of his armies on the eve of the Battle of Agincourt, and the whole country was popularly nicknamed "Our Lady's Dowry."[32] Mariology had kept active the minds of Christianity's most gifted theologians since the dawn of the Church, as well as inspiring widespread popular devotion, the latter reflected in the many sobriquets accorded the Virgin. One of those, *Stella Maris*, "Star of the Sea," was inscribed onto the twenty-four-year-old chapel bell that roused Hampton Court's servants from their sleep. The bell-imprinted prayer read *Stella Maria Maris Succurre Piisima Nobis* ("Mary, Most Gracious, Star of the Sea, come to our assistance"). It is unclear how a bell carrying a prayer to the Virgin more obviously associated with sailors or fishing villages ended up at a manor house in a landlocked county.[33] As the morning Psalms wafted heavenward from the manor's chapel, the other servants made their way to their duties, many of them wearing the Daubeneys' livery of a red shield with four silver lozenges.*

Some of the staff crossed over to the kitchens, which, of all the buildings constructed on Lord Daubeney's orders at Hampton Court, are the ones that survive and can be visited today.[34] The Great Kitchen was a bustling place, hot on cold days and suffocating on warm ones; according to a later Spanish visitor, the Great Kitchen in full working order on a summer's day was as close to the open gates of hell as he could imagine.[35] The Hampton Court kitchens were a place of effort and sweat. Servants turned the spits, roasting meats in one of the two cavernous fireplaces, while in a smaller one nearby, their colleagues boiled fish and meat, made stews, and marinated sauces. The pots and cauldrons used in the latter were scrubbed clean, "both within and without," by the scullions in the scullery, while the buttery helped dispense the food, ale, and wine to staff, the differing amounts allocated on the basis of the recipient's rank in the household's hierarchy.[36] Administrative offices were nearby, from which the officers were supposed to keep a careful record of the kitchens' bills, since aristocratic households at the time spent nearly one-quarter of their considerable expenditure on food.[37] For the servants working there in January 1503, their workload was about to increase hugely thanks to the weeklong visit to Hampton Court of Henry VII's wife, Elizabeth of York. She arrived on January 7 aboard her "great boat," commanded by her bargemaster Lewis Waltier.[38] Waltier and his rowers had brought the Queen from a Christmas at nearby Richmond Palace, which, with her interest in architecture, she had a hand in designing.[39]

---

* A diamond shape on heraldic shields.

Elizabeth of York was beloved by many of her husband's subjects. In part, her popularity stood as testament to the Queen's personal virtues. The contemporary chronicle *The Annals of Ulster* records Elizabeth's continent-wide reputation as "a woman that was of the greatest charity and humanity from Italy to Ireland."[40] It also reflected public gratitude for the role her marriage had played in ending the Wars of the Roses after Bosworth. Elizabeth was the eldest daughter of Edward IV, the king who had overthrown Henry VI. The lasting dynastic realignment in the Tudors' favor was supported by many former Yorkists after their senior princess, Elizabeth, married the new king, thereby uniting the two previously warring sides of the royal line. At the time of her wedding in 1486, Elizabeth was considered the most beautiful princess in Europe—hardly surprising given that her late father was remembered as a man "of visage lovely, of body mighty," while her mother, Queen Elizabeth Woodville, was once described as "the most beautiful woman in the island of Britain."[41]

In the seventeen years since becoming queen consort, Elizabeth of York had continued to prove herself invaluable to the nascent Tudor regime, often by balancing some of her husband's weaknesses. Elizabeth had seen her father and brother deposed and had twice fled into sanctuary with her mother, while Henry VII had also endured a childhood brutally shaped by the Wars of the Roses. Unlike Elizabeth, who never travelled outside England, those vicissitudes had compelled Henry to a maturity acquired abroad. Born in Wales in 1457 two months after his father died of plague in a Yorkist prison, Henry's birth had nearly killed his thirteen-year-old mother; as her confessor had put it, "It seemed a miracle that of so little a personage anyone should have been born at all."[42] The wars saw him separated from his mother as a child and then entrusted to the care of a guardian who was himself beheaded in the aftermath of yet another battle.[43] After his uncle Henry VI lost the throne for the second and final time, young Henry, then aged fourteen, was evacuated through secret passageways running beneath the streets of the Welsh port of Tenby to be bundled into a fishing boat. He and his uncle Jasper escaped on the vessel into the Celtic Sea, where storms drove them to the temporary safety of a harbor in Brittany.[44] Henry spent the next fourteen years down on his luck as an exile in Europe, returning to the British Isles in 1485 after having spent half his life—and all of his adulthood—in foreign countries. In some important ways, this proved of benefit to him after he became king. His education abroad had given him the strength of an outsider's gaze. Not only was Henry VII attuned to the nuances of international politics, but also he shrewdly and dispassionately analyzed his English and Welsh nobles' scheming. That was one of the reasons why he knew that plotters would concoct lies to try to separate him from loyal men such as Lord Daubeney. In other areas, the years spent in exile had given the King less helpful attitudes: for example, the Spanish ambassador to London, Don Pedro de Ayala, thought that, left to his own devices, Henry VII would have dispensed with Parliament altogether to rule like the French autocrats who had sheltered him as a young man and from whom he descended on his father's side.[45]

His queen seems to have softened some of those impulses. In partnership with her remarkable mother-in-law, Margaret Beaufort, Elizabeth of York helped turn Henry's court into a theater of monarchy. Both women understood the utility of splendor and the importance of pomp in conveying a sense of political stability, which, in turn, was interpreted by onlookers as proof of the providential. In an era when God spoke through the events of men, Henry VII's cause was regarded as having first been blessed by the victory given to him at the Battle of Bosworth, then by his defeating every rebellion subsequently mounted against him. Heaven's blessing had been confirmed by some helpful paperwork courtesy of Pope Innocent VIII, who sanctioned Henry's peace-buying wedding to Elizabeth, which he followed with a helpful supplementary threat of excommunication against anyone who challenged Tudor rule.[46] Having won peace for her compatriots in this life, Queen Elizabeth then set herself to winning similar blessings for them in the next; she interceded with the Pope to grant English Christians a pardon if, each time they heard a church bell toll the Angelus,* they recited the

---

* A prayer commemorating the incarnation of Christ, traditionally accompanied by a ringing of the church bell at six o'clock in the morning, at noon, and at six o'clock in the evening. In practice, the Angelus could often function like a call to prayer for Catholics.

words uttered in the Bible by the Queen's patron saint, Elisabeth, when she first beheld the pregnant Virgin Mary: "Blessèd art thou amongst women and blessèd is the fruit of thy womb."[47]

Celestial approval for the devout queen and the victorious king again expressed itself through the many children that God sent into their royal nursery. By the time she disembarked at Hampton Court's wharf on January 7, 1503, the thirty-six-year-old Elizabeth was seven months pregnant with her eighth child—among the staff accompanying her was one of her midwives, Alice Massey.[48] The Portuguese ambassador described Elizabeth as stout and large breasted, while a Venetian traveller in London wrote home that the Queen of England was "a very handsome woman."[49] She was not, however, a happy woman. True, she had just successfully delayed the wedding of her eldest daughter to the King of Scots on the grounds that the princess, having just celebrated her thirteenth birthday, was too young for wedlock. In this, Elizabeth had again allied with her mother-in-law, who knew from personal experience the agony inflicted by labor at thirteen. However, this triumph came not long after the Queen had buried her youngest and eldest sons within two years of each other. Baby Edmund had died during a summer outbreak of the plague in 1500, and in 1502 the Queen had been awoken by her servants in the dead of night to the devastating news that the heir, fifteen-year-old Prince Arthur, had also died, just six months after his wedding. What caused Arthur's passing is still debated, with undiagnosed cancer or tuberculosis suggested by different historians. The plague had also been active in the countryside around Ludlow Castle, where Arthur had been in residence, and his Spanish widow was ill enough that she had to be moved back to London in a slow-moving litter.[50] Queen Elizabeth tried to remain strong in the face of her husband's grief, rushing to his bedchamber where she urged him to trust in God who "had left him yet a fair Prince, two fair Princesses, and that God is where He was, and we are both young." She had held herself together until she returned to her own apartments, where "natural and motherly remembrance of that great loss smote her so sorrowful" that her ladies-in-waiting sent for the King, who comforted Elizabeth with the "true gentle and faithful love" she had just shown him.[51]

She conceived again within a few months of her eldest son's death. There were signs—not least in her decision to retire to Hampton Court the day after festivities for the twelve days of Christmas ended at Richmond— that the Queen was finding her latest pregnancy particularly difficult. She and her husband shared a devotion to the Virgin Mary, and an anxious Elizabeth had sent for a relic of the Virgin to be brought from Westminster Abbey to accompany her during her forthcoming labor.[52] She dispatched one of her chaplains, Father William Barton, on pilgrimage to the great shrine to Our Lady of Walsingham in Norfolk, to make offerings on the Queen's behalf.[53] She sought refuge, too, in astrology. Although later generations of Christians would more often regard astrology as essentially pagan, Elizabeth of York's contemporaries believed that God indicated His intentions through the stars as clearly as He did through battles and bloodlines, citing the star-guided journey of the Magi to Bethlehem as biblical proof that astrology was a decipherable code from the heavens.[54] That Christmas, the royal astrologer had tried to soothe Queen Elizabeth's nerves by predicting that she would live into her eighties.[55]

As wine was decanted and meats shorn from the kitchen spits, musicians and minstrels performed for the Queen and her ladies. It was not her first visit to the Hampton Court estate—that had taken place in 1501, eighteen months after her husband's stay and Daubeney's second set of improvements. In 1503 she stayed for a week. Each day, the chapel bell tolled the eight canonical hours, winning remission of a sin for those souls who, upon hearing it, recited Saint Elisabeth's words to the Virgin Mary and thereby took advantage of the indulgence won for them by their queen. Each night, the bell fell silent, and the pregnant Elizabeth retired to her chambers while the servants unfurled their sleeping bags in the halls and dormitories. After an uneventful seven days—which, as it transpired, would be Elizabeth of York's last as a guest in a private home—she and her retinue boarded her "great boat," which slipped into the current to carry her back to Richmond; from there, after a few days, it would bring her to London and the labor that would kill her on her thirty-seventh birthday.

CHAPTER 2

TURRETS AND TOWERS

Building royally,
Their mansions curiously
With turrets and with towers,
With halls and with bowers,
Stretching to the stars
With glass windows and bars;
Hanging about the walls,
Cloths of gold.

—Father John Skelton, "Colin Clout" (1522)

James Butler had a limp. The young Irish nobleman had taken a French bullet in the thigh fighting in the wars of Elizabeth of York's second son, who succeeded to the throne as Henry VIII aged seventeen in 1509 when tuberculosis ended the life of Elizabeth's widower, Henry VII.[1] The same war that testified to the increasing popularity of artillery in battle, which limited James Butler's mobility, had also launched into orbit the career of Butler's future master, Oxford graduate and priest Father Thomas Wolsey. England's campaigns against Scotland and France allowed Wolsey to show-case his extraordinary organizational skills, for which Henry VIII, who was bored by the minutiae of such things, proved gratefully impressed and impressively grateful. According to a palace servant, it was after the wars of 1513–14 that Henry "called [Wolsey] more unto him and esteemed him so highly that his estimation and favor put all councillors out of their accustomed favor that they were in before."[2]

Prior to that, Wolsey's trajectory had been respectable if comparatively unremarkable: bursar at his former University of Oxford college, Magdalen,* tutor to two of Elizabeth of York's nephews, then a chaplain to Henry VII.[3] He had helped organize an archbishop of Canterbury's funeral in 1503 and was an occasional member of diplomatic missions to Scotland and the Hapsburg Empire for the old king. Among the courtiers Wolsey had served on his way up the social ladder was Sir Richard Nanfan, a deputy of Lord Daubeney. It is unclear if Wolsey saw Hampton Court while he was on Nanfan's payroll, but in January 1515, not long after his rapid rise in Henry VIII's favor, Wolsey secured the transfer of Hampton Court's lease from Giles Daubeney's son, Henry. The old Lord Daubeney had passed away in May 1507, whereupon his loyalty to the Tudors received its final reward with the honor of a tomb at Westminster Abbey.[4] The new Lord Daubeney came of legal age in December 1514, and the speed with which he sold Hampton's lease to Wolsey suggests either a desire for the money or a lack of affection for the manor.[5]

Thomas Wolsey felt neither ambivalence toward his new home nor any timidity about spending money. He could certainly afford it. A cavalcade of honors, sacred and secular, flowed from the young King's favor. Wolsey became Bishop of Lincoln for a few months in 1514 before the death of the Archbishop of York created a more prestigious prize, which became Wolsey's—along with a cardinal's hat from Pope Leo X—in 1515.[6] Hampton Court was transformed as magnificently and quickly as its new occupant's career, to the point that the splendor of one became symbiotic with the success of the other.[7]

Usually a master in the art of networking, Wolsey leaned on his friend Thomas Docwra, Prior of the Knights Hospitaller, who approved the trans-

---

* Pronounced like the modern *maudlin* and dedicated to Saint Mary Magdalene. All three words are linked. The evolution of Magdalene/Magdalen/maudlin lay with the legend of Mary Magdalene's sorrowful tears at the feet of Christ.

fer of the lease from the Daubeneys but would not yield to the Cardinal's desire to make the manor a freehold. The Church's newest prince had to content himself with a ninety-nine-year lease, which, like Giles Daubeney's tenancy before him, left him free to transform the manor as he saw fit. Wolsey was especially pleased with Hampton Court's performance in a game of architectural tit for tat with his rival William Warham, Archbishop of Canterbury, who, around the same time as Wolsey started his refurbishments, began a similarly expensive series of changes to the archiepiscopal palace at Otford.[8] The transformation of Otford may have commenced first, and the two competing palaces quickly became surrogates for the clergymen's politesse-laced feud, in which they tried unconvincingly to mask their one-upmanship with Christian concern for each other. Once Warham was satisfied that his palace had been "magnificently enlarged," he humbly invited Wolsey to visit him at "my poor house at Otford."[9] Wolsey, on discovering that Otford had a reputation for mild damp, professed worry about Warham's health—surely it would be better if Warham spent some time at Wolsey's "most wholesome Manor of Hampton Court," with its "high and dry grounds."[10] Warham installed a new courtyard that was larger than Hampton Court's.[11] Wolsey spent more money on artisans and architects.

By 1522, Hampton Court had definitively outsparkled its southeastern rival. Otford may have been sufficiently splendid four years earlier to host a visiting Italian cardinal, but it was Hampton Court that was picked to entertain the Hapsburg Emperor, Charles V, in June 1522, at the end of his second state visit to England.[12] A contemporary thought that Hampton Court had become one of the "great palaces without comparison, most glorious of outward sight, and within . . . more like unto a paradise than an earthly habitation."[13] Eight emperors had appeared in the palace's courtyards since Wolsey took over the lease, but Charles V would be the first to be present in person. The previous summer, Tuscan sculptor Giovanni da Maiano had submitted his expenses for completing work on gilded terracotta heads of eight Roman emperors, as well as separate pieces depicting Julius Caesar and Cleopatra VII.[14] The terracotta pharaoh, the dictator, and the eight emperors seem to have been installed in Hampton Court's new and second courtyard, subsequently called its Base* Court.[15] The creation of this new courtyard was part of a transformation that also saw a new westward-looking entry, capped by a five-story gatehouse that opened onto the Base Court.[16] The manor's original courtyard, henceforth accessed through the Base, was extended with bricks in the same red hue as those used by Lord Daubeney's men.

The Base was ringed by new lodgings that could accommodate many more guests than had been possible in Daubeney's lifetime. South-facing, sun-catching gardens bloomed on the land reclaimed through the relocation of the gatehouse and its correspondingly obsolete moat. Two orchards were planted, surrounding tiled banqueting houses for summer entertainments. Hampton Court's well-stocked fishponds proved useful for its residents' dietary needs when eating meat was forbidden by the Church, such as on Fridays and Saturdays, on the eves preceding the major feast days dedicated to the Virgin Mary and to any of the Twelve Apostles, as well as during the four weeks of Advent preceding Christmas or the forty days of Lent preceding Easter.† The Hampton Court carp and shrimp were apparently delicious enough to be appreciated as gifts by members of the elite.[17]

With its bell bearing the invocation to the Virgin Mary as Star of the Sea reinstalled in a new belltower, the old chapel had been demolished to make way for a much larger replacement, with room for four side altars and a great organ.[18] There, every day when he was in residence at his favorite home, Wolsey's household chapel celebrated a High Mass, devoted to whichever feast day or commemoration was prescribed in the Church calendar, along with the daily Lady Mass in honor of the Virgin Mary, sunrise's Prime, and sunset's Vespers with Compline. It was possibly only on holy days that Matins and Lauds, services held between dusk and dawn, were sung by Wolsey's choir, which was judged by some to be in finer collective voice than the King's.[19] Although the Cardinal attended all of a day's devo-

---

* From the French *basse*, "low."

† The less devout could make an exception for the meat of a heron, on the stretched-to-its-limit technicality that heron eat only fish themselves.

tions only infrequently, he was present for at least one church service daily. At Hampton Court, he prayed in a chapel dominated by a large crucifix and the stained glass he had commissioned depicting the crucifixion. Saint Mary Magdalene, patroness of Wolsey's alma mater, was shown weeping at the foot of the cross, while adoring in prayer were stained glass images of Wolsey himself, Saint Thomas Becket, Saint Paul, and Saint Peter, the latter of whom, according to Catholic tradition, had been the first Pope and Prince of the Apostles.[20] On the opposite side of the great window knelt King Henry VIII, his Spanish wife, Katherine of Aragon, and their daughter, Princess Mary, ushered into Christ's presence by their patron saints and, in the King's case, also by England's patron Saint George.[21]

Wolsey's changes employed teams of architects, masons, carpenters, gardeners, and bricklayers, all of whom were overseen by the best and brightest in their respective fields. Among those who transformed Hampton Court were men who had worked on Henry VII and Elizabeth of York's tomb; on completing Eton College and King's College, Cambridge; or on the royal renovations at the Palace of Westminster and Windsor Castle. The little town of Hampton, just outside the estate's walls, had become one of the most cosmopolitan places in Tudor England. Craftsmen from the Italian states, the Netherlands, France, and the Holy Roman Empire* settled there while they worked on the many alterations to Hampton Court between 1515 and 1522. The chapel's stained glass windows, for instance, were installed by a team headed by Wolsey's master glazier, Englishman James Nicolson, and probably designed by Erhard Schön, the Nuremberg-born protégé of Albrecht Dürer.[22]

A large house required a robust staff, and Hampton Court, in Wolsey's time, ran on a princely scale. The chapel alone retained a dean and his

---

* The Holy Roman Empire was an elective federal monarchy that lasted from 800 until 1806. Having originally had lands in France and Italy, its borders changed often. By the sixteenth century, the empire's member states broadly correlated to what is now Germany, where it is sometimes referred to as the First Reich. Charles V was the third consecutive member of his family to be elected Holy Roman emperor, after which it became a custom. Between 1440 and 1740, and again from 1764 until the empire's disintegration, every emperor was a Hapsburg.

deputy, ten chaplains, ten clerks, and ten choristers, who went with Wolsey as he moved from one house to the next.[23] Its Master of the Choristers, Richard Pygott, was an admired composer in his own right whose works were performed at Hampton Court, where the Cardinal gave Pygott time and space to develop his own music while in service. Frustratingly, only one of Pygott's works survives intact. The devotional *Quid petis, o fili?* ("What are you seeking, O Son?"), a reflection on the Nativity and specifically on the Virgin Mary's maternal love for the Christ Child, has been recorded by modern choirs whose work gives us an idea of what Pygott's audiences heard at Hampton Court in the 1520s. Among the choirmaster-composer's pieces that survive in fragmentary form are a hymn to the Virgin Mary, one about Saint Thomas Becket, a lullaby, and a hymnal prayer for the dead.[24]

On the secular side, the estate required many more gardeners, cooks, scullions, and cleaners than it had in the previous generation. Wolsey was also attended by many young men from the English, Irish, and Welsh elites, whose parents sent them to live in the chief minister's household in the hope that he would promote them when they were older—or, at the very least, afford them the chance to make valuable connections with other prominent families. James Butler was one such satellite. After his war wound, they called him Séamas Bacach ("James the Lame") back home in Ireland, a nickname that exaggerated the extent of his injury. Another was the Earl of Northumberland's eldest and heir, Lord Henry Percy. The greater the number of young blue bloods attached to a household, the greater the importance of the household's head. Their attendance was a testament to Wolsey's influence, and they were expected to enhance his current prestige as much as he would their future prospects. Clergymen, inspired partly by how they interpreted verses in the Bible that exhorted "any one [who] aspires to the office of bishop" to be "dignified, hospitable . . . and [manage] his own household well," were held to have a duty to show hospitality to those who crossed their threshold.[25] As did many of his churchly contemporaries, Wolsey took that point and ran with it, and he expected everyone in his establishment to augment his glory through hospitality. One of his gentlemen-ushers in 1522—who had the job of standing in attendance to announce visitors or turn away the unwelcome—was twenty-eight-year-old George Cavendish, a Cambridge dropout, a talented writer, and son of one of the court's financial officials. His devotion to his employer lasted beyond Wolsey's death: thirty years later, Cavendish wrote one of the first biographies of Wolsey, an invaluable albeit partisan source on the Cardinal's later years, in which he recalls the Cardinal's attention to detail when welcoming foreign guests. In preparation, "my lord [the Cardinal] called for his principal officers of his house [such] as his Steward, Controller, and the Clerks of his Kitchen, whom he commanded to prepare for this banquet at Hampton Court and neither to spare for expenses . . . to make [for] them such triumphant cheer as they may not only wonder at it here but also make a glorious report in their Country to the king's honour and of this Realm."[26]

Having received their instructions from the Cardinal, the officers of the household

> *sent forth all their Cators [caterers], purveyors and other persons to prepare of the finest viands [fine food] that they could get either for money or friendship from my lord's friends. Also they sent for all the expertest Cooks, besides my lord's, that they could get in England where they might be gotten to serve to garnish this Feast. The purveyors brought and sent in such plenty of Costly provision as ye would wonder at. . . . The Cooks wrought both night and day. . . . The Yeomen and Grooms of the Wardrobe were busy in hanging of the Chambers with costly hangings and furnishing the same with beds of silk and other furniture [that was] apt for the same in every degree.*[*27]

Cavendish and his fellow gentlemen-ushers then had to inspect every room to make sure it met Wolsey's standards—"our pains were not small or light," he recalled of another state visit, later in the same decade.[28] Nor were the pre-visit labors of "the Carpenters, the Joiners, the Masons, the painters, and

---

*. Cavendish here refers to the accommodation being furnished with furniture appropriate to the guest's rank.

all other Artificers [artisans] necessary to glorify the house."[29] For everybody who lived in a large household—be they aristocratic wards, priests, kitchen staff, or guards—it was busy, sometimes exciting, and stressful in varying degrees when they hosted another large establishment such as the visiting Emperor's. It is unclear how many of the twenty-two-year-old Hapsburg monarch's entourage of 2,044 aristocrats, gentlemen, and servants joined him at Hampton Court.[30] This large group had been well treated throughout the rest of its six-week visit to England, which had included jousts and tourneys, a parade through the streets of London, as well as feasts and banquets at the King's palaces of Greenwich and Richmond. They had been let down only by the food and the weather, both of which proved leaden.[31]

Physically, the best feature of Hampton Court's imperial guest was his "beautiful light-blue eyes," according to one of his sister's servants. The same observer thought Charles V was "a graceful man in very good shape," but conceded that "his mouth and chin [are] not as beautiful as his other features." This view was confirmed by an Italian diplomat who, after meeting Charles for the first time, wrote home describing him as "tall and splendidly built" with "a lopsided mouth (which drops open when he is not on his guard) and a drooping lower lip."[32] The Emperor's parents bore the contrasting sobriquets of Philip the Handsome and Juana the Mad—Juana likely suffered from depression exacerbated first by her husband's adulteries and then by his death. The latter caused a nervous breakdown that was exploited to have Juana labelled insane, placed under a glorified form of house arrest, and sidelined from her inheritance, which was co-opted by her father, who then passed it to her eldest son.* Along with this kingdom purloined from his Spanish mother, Charles inherited the territories of his Burgundian† grandmother and Austrian grandfather, which, in combination, effectively made him master of central Europe, as well as of what is

---

* Henry VII, who met Queen Juana during a state visit, doubted that she was ever insane, noting that although "her husband and those with him made her out to be mad, to me she seemed sane."

† Now part of eastern and central France, the Duchy of Burgundy was a wealthy independent state from 880 until 1477.

now Belgium, Luxembourg, the Netherlands, Naples, Spain, Sicily, and Sardinia. Before he turned twenty, Charles V ruled more land than any European since the days of ancient Rome.

Given the logistics of sixteenth-century travel, it was not at all clear that the pieces of this dynastic jigsaw were meant to fit together as an ad hoc empire and its difficulties had left Charles dependent on English support. Its consequences in part were the reasons for his visit to Hampton Court. His Spanish grandparents might have hesitated at marrying their daughter Juana to a Hapsburg archduke had they known that it would drive her "mad" and that her childless brother would predecease her, thus leaving Charles to inherit both empires, separated from each other by a hostile sea and an even more hostile French government. Charles resorted to ruling his dominions by oscillating devolution, constantly travelling between the different provinces, leaving relatives or friends behind as governors when he moved on. By the end of his life, Charles told a group of his subjects, "I have been nine times to Germany, six times to Spain, and seven to Italy; I have come here to Flanders ten times and have been four times to France in war and peace, twice to England, and twice to Africa . . . without mentioning the other lesser journeys. I have made eight voyages in the Mediterranean and three in the seas of Spain."[33]

Cardinal Wolsey excelled at foreign policy, and he had kept a close eye on the new Emperor. In assessing his youth and the problems facing his empires, many contemporaries had underestimated Charles V when he first came to power, aged nineteen, in 1519, not least the English diplomat Richard Pace, who had told Wolsey in a secret letter not to worry too much about the new emperor, since he was "but an idiot" surrounded by corrupt advisers.[34] When they had first met in person, during one of Charles's earlier trips to English territory, Wolsey disagreed with his underling's advice and had shrewdly concluded of the Emperor: "For his age, [he] is very wise and well understanding his affairs right; cold and temperate in speech, with assured manner touching his words right well and to good purpose when he doth speak. And undoubtedly by all appearance he shall prove a very wise man."[35] Shortly before the 1522 sojourn to Hampton Court, Charles's chief minister, the Marquis of Chièvres, had died, after which the young Emperor was more obviously in command of his government. Revealingly, as regards his own political priorities, when Wolsey had heard a rumor that the Marquis planned to retire shortly before he became ill, he dismissed it, saying, "You do not understand the nature of men who hold such responsibilities."[36]

As his comment on the Marquis of Chièvres indicates, Cardinal Wolsey relished power and its accompanying pomp. That was evident as he showed Charles around Hampton Court. The palace glittered, thanks in part to the twenty-five thousand ducats' worth of gold plate Wolsey kept on display wherever he went, much of which was the work of Robert Adamas, one of the Cardinal's favorite craftsmen. Amadas, the son, nephew, and grandson-in-law of prominent London goldsmiths, was a man whose skills also attracted patronage from King Henry and Queen Katherine.[37] Wolsey's crest, topped by his cardinal's galero and surrounded by the galero's red tassels, was everywhere in Hampton Court, in glass, masonry, in the Cardinal's hugely expensive imported rugs that went with him from palace to palace, or woven into some of the palace's 136 new tapestries.[38] Servants had finished hanging them only two months before the Emperor arrived. Their installation brought the Cardinal's tapestry tally to just over six hundred, at a time when they were so expensive that an aristocrat would be considered a person of great wealth if he owned fifty.[39] Charles V may have recognized the craftsmanship when he saw Hampton Court's tapestries; many had been imported from his Dutch dominions. Wolsey was also very proud of his new two-hundred-foot gallery, built in brick and with glass windows— another substantial expense—through which the Cardinal could show his guests his newly designed and planted gardens.[40]

George Cavendish wrote that the Cardinal liked to walk, talk, and conduct business in his galleries. Officially, the reason for the young Emperor's arrival had been to see Katherine of Aragon—"my good aunt," as Charles V called her—and he had knelt on arrival to receive her blessing, which, as a Member of Parliament noted, "is the fashion of Spain, between aunt and nephew."[41] In reality, his visit had more to do with solidifying the Anglo-Hapsburg alliance promoted by Queen Katherine and negotiated by Wolsey, which included yet another generous loan from Henry VIII that Charles V needed after the hole inflicted in his treasury by a recent uprising against him in Spain. This was accompanied by an anti-French treaty between the two dynasties that would be sealed with the Emperor's marriage to his English cousin, Princess Mary.[42] Wolsey likely guessed that Charles V had no intention of going through with that clause, since his subjects' representatives had recently urged the Emperor to prioritize the succession, arguing that the empire was not secure "until you are married and have heirs."[43] Charles's younger brother had recently married a Hungarian princess, and it was considered odd that the senior sibling remained a bachelor. Given that Princess Mary had turned only six in 1522, it would be years before she and Charles could legally marry and even longer before they could safely start a family. If he honored his betrothal to Mary of England, the Emperor might wait more than a decade before he had a legitimate son. Shortly before he arrived at Hampton Court, Charles had proved himself capable of producing heirs when, during his preceding residency in the Netherlands, he had affairs with two women—a Dutch servant and a "very beautiful" Italian upper-class widow—both of whom conceived his illegitimate children.[44]

Wolsey was unlikely to be offended, much less shocked, by this news. Despite his own priestly vows of celibacy, the Cardinal had two illegitimate children, Thomas and Dorothy, whom he had fathered with his confessor's sister.[45] What happened in an emperor's bedroom was more important, and, having proved his ability to procreate, Charles was bound to face renewed pressure to marry a princess of childbearing age. Doubts about the long-term viability of the engagement provision in the treaty were justified. Charles V was only paying lip service to a future marriage with Princess Mary. He wanted to please Henry VIII and Katherine of Aragon, and thus secure their promised loan. Five months before his visit to Hampton Court, the Emperor had secretly written to King João the Pious of Portugal, proposing to his sister.[46]

The spinning roulette of royal betrothals, made and broken with alacrity, was par for the course in sixteenth-century European diplomacy. So, too, were dreams of restarting the Crusades, an idea with which Henry VIII toyed throughout his life, encouraged by Charles V.[47] A year earlier, worryingly for the Hapsburgs, the Balkan city of Belgrade had fallen to the armies of the new Ottoman Sultan, Süleyman the Magnificent, whose late father Selim I had increased their empire's size by nearly 70 percent and pointedly sent war galleys to sail past Barcelona while Charles and his sisters were in residence.[48] France was the only major Christian government in the West that enjoyed cordial diplomatic relations with the Sultan, a fact exploited by Charles V and Henry VIII to depict the French king as a duplicitous traitor to his own religion.

Grandiose visits such as the Emperor's were the perfect opportunity for statesmen to discuss such issues privately and immediately without worrying that their letters might be intercepted or delivered by messengers who were delayed by bad roads or poor weather. It also gave them a chance to test how accurate their informants' assessments were. There was much for Charles and Wolsey to discuss in June 1522, apart from the Sultan's wars, the fall of Belgrade, the Spanish uprising, and Charles's maybe-marriage plans. Pope Leo X had died at the calends of the previous year, after which Charles V's boyhood tutor, Adrian of Utrecht, had been elected Pope Adrian VI. It was rumored that Wolsey had dreamed of winning the papal tiara for himself until it went to the erudite Dutchman. Among the other developments Charles brought with him to England in 1522 was information on a continent that was new to Europeans and a religion that was new to everybody. The accuracy of the terms "the New World" and "the New Religion" were, of course, to be hotly contested. Both would be the harbinger of many lives lost and ruined.

Earlier in his English visit, Charles had shown King Henry and Queen Katherine a selection of treasures that had once belonged to Emperor Moctezuma Xocoyotzin, the late ruler of the Aztec Empire that had fallen to the Spanish invasion of Mesoamerica.[49] Two years before that, Charles himself had met his first American, who had crossed the ocean for an audience in Brussels. Noticing that the man was shivering, the Emperor ordered that he be given a cloak. The American in Brussels quickly revealed that

Charles's conquistador subjects were turning the ruins of the Aztec and Inca empires, and the Caribbean islands, into a wasteland in which thousands upon thousands of Americans were coerced into servile labor or de facto slavery in gold or emerald mines, significantly expanding the number of slaves beyond those ensnared during the Aztec Era, as well as introducing the institution to the Caribbean.

The Catholic hierarchy's recent teaching on enslavement was inconsistent. It had been permitted by popes Nicholas V, Callixtus III, and Alexander VI, but condemned by Martin V and Pius II. The latter had specifically prohibited the enslavement of Africans by European Christians, a ruling that Pope Paul III would later extend to the indigenous populations in America and Asia.[50] Charles V, a devout Catholic who accepted the interpretations of Martin V and Pius II, writhed in moral agony when he found out how many people in Cuba and Hispaniola* had been enslaved and then died in the conquerors' mines. The Emperor became convinced that God would cast his soul into Hell if he permitted slavery to flourish in his domains.[51] However, in the Americas, the Spanish soldiers and their superiors joked that it took longer for commands to come from Madrid than they did from Heaven, and any of the Emperor's edicts that Americans should be treated fairly were ignored. By 1522, Spanish colonial policies had all but wiped out at least one indigenous race in the Americas—the Taíno people of the Caribbean—whose culture Christopher Columbus had summarized as "affectionate and without malice."[52] As Charles V dined at Hampton Court in 1522 and showed off his treasures imported from the Americas, his empire included eleven thousand Taíno subjects—95 percent fewer than had existed thirty years earlier.[53] Until very recently, the decimation of the American population by the Spanish invasion has erroneously been attributed to the soldiers' and sailors' accidental importation of diseases, principally smallpox, to which the Americans had no natural immunity. A closer examination of the population collapse does not support that. The initial and greatest cause of the implosion was Spanish-implemented violence. Within

---

* Today the island of Hispaniola is Haiti and the Dominican Republic.

a decade of their invasion, a Spanish missionary wrote home in horror that the Taíno people, having initially shown neither aggression nor fear toward the Spanish arrivals, had been enslaved by the conquerors, who executed "anyone and everyone who has shown the slightest sign of resistance." Survivors were treated "worse than animals" as their overseers deliberately forced them "to carry excessive workloads until they broke them down."[54] When the Spanish ships first arrived in the Caribbean, the Taíno consisted of about three hundred thousand people; within sixteen years—and ten years before the first smallpox epidemic hit the region—that population had fallen to about sixty thousand. The Spanish responded by doubling down and rounding up communities from places such as Florida and Cuba, transporting them to Hispaniola, Puerto Rico, Jamaica, and Trinidad to replace the dying Taíno workforce. When the same hideous pattern repeated itself—as of 1522, almost the entire native population of Barbados and the Bahamas had also been obliterated—the Spanish and Portuguese colonial authorities decided to replicate the same policy of enslaving communities that they would then transport to the pulverized Caribbean and the Americas. With so few American communities left, the Spanish colonialists turned their eyes and shackles eastward across the Atlantic to Africa.

Cardinal Wolsey favored English involvement in the Americas. To his frustration, he could not stimulate his compatriots' interest in it at this stage. Five years earlier, he had supported an expedition to the Americas with the express mission of colonization, which reached Waterford in southeastern Ireland before it gave up and turned back.[55] Wolsey had subsequently tried to lure Venetian navigators to England to lead future voyages to North America to locate, as was still believed possible, a northern route through to trade more easily with India and China.[56] The guilds of London merchants who were asked to invest in the expeditions declined, on the grounds that the desired passage to Asia through the Americas was an unknown, and colonization was expensive. The well-armed Spanish and Portuguese had established themselves there, and the cautious moneymen of London thus felt that there was more tangible benefit in focusing their investments on the existing English trade networks with the Netherlands.[57]

It was another part of the Emperor's dominions—the German states— that dominated the conversation in 1522, specifically their religious tensions, which Wolsey and the King feared had started to seep into England, thanks to merchants travelling back and forth on those trade networks to the Netherlands. Around the time that Wolsey's abortive American colonization enterprise shrugged shoulders and dropped anchor in County Waterford, Martin Luther, then a professor of theology at the German University of Wittenberg, published his ninety-five theses objecting to practices in the Church. Some of Luther's points targeted the Church's bureaucracy and corruption; others, more seriously, unpicked its theologies. Luther's spiritual *cri de guerre* struck a chord with many Christians in the German states. Much of his early success was facilitated by the Vatican's inept response, which lurched between sloth and wrath—both failing, with equal aplomb, to tackle the issue. When the papacy published a rebuttal, three years later and too late, it did so with the document *Exsurge Domine*, which did not comment on all of Luther's points. With several of the issues that the Church did critique in *Exsurge Domine*, it was apparent that it either had not understood what Luther was saying or was willfully misrepresenting it.

The papacy's dim-witted sanguinity about Luther appears baffling in hindsight. The impact of Protestantism on European history—and, later, world history—is almost incalculable. Initially, however, many of the devout did not believe that Protestantism would prove more tenacious than the other myriad heresies that had, over the centuries, intermittently plucked at the fabric of Church unity. From the earliest days of their faith, Christians had fought over points of doctrinal disagreement. There was rioting in some early Christian cities over the question of whether Christ had a divine soul or a human soul; a human mind or a divine mind. Early generations of Christian bishops had torn out their hair over whether there even could be a Christianity that accepted Jesus as God without the Virgin Mary being referred to as "Mother of God," because to refer to her as "Mother of Jesus," as some theologians wanted initially, implied the heresy that Jesus had not always been co-eternal with God.[58] Faith was central, and passions inevitably ran high.

However, apart from the great schism between the Eastern and Western branches of the Church in 1054, Christianity had proved remarkably hardy in weathering its self-generating disputes. Why should the ramblings of an unhappy defrocked German monk like Martin Luther prove more enduring than Docetism, Marcionism, Arianism, Donatism, Audianism, Apollinarianism, Nestorianism, or Monophysitism? All of them, by 1522, were fragments of half-remembered philosophies, more or less confined to the pages of obscure histories and theologies, of interest to the occasional inquisitor or curious academic. Wolsey would have learned about them as he trained for the priesthood. They were presented as errors that had justly been condemned to the dustbin of history. Even theological deviations closer to Wolsey and Luther's time, such as Catharism, Lollardy, Hussitism, and Utraquism, stood as paradoxical testament to the Church's resilience. All these heresies, antique or contemporary, had been successfully debated back to orthodoxy, contained to rural backwaters, anathematized into a silence that bred the next generation's amnesia or, in rare yet hideously memorable cases, scorched from the face of the Earth by the tribunals of the Inquisition.

Since this latest threat to Christian unity originated in his empire, Charles V was expected to help the Vatican deal with the problem. The year before his visit to Hampton Court, Charles had invited Martin Luther—or, as the Emperor publicly and politely called him, "our dear Reverend Dr. Martin Luther of the Augustinian Order"—to an imperial audience in the western German city of Worms, with the promise of safe conduct.[59] Charles V's hope was to use charm and the hopefully discombobulating glamor of a royal audience to bounce Luther back into obedience. A religious quarrel in his empire was the last thing that Charles, as a statesman, wanted. He was also sincerely religious, like many of his family: his Austrian grandfather, Emperor Maximilian I, had left instructions that, as a sign to his people of the sins of the flesh, he wanted his corpse flagellated, shorn of its hair, and its teeth smashed out of its skull before it was buried in Vienna.[60] Catholicism permeated the Hapsburg dynasty's sense of purpose, perhaps even more so than it did Cardinal Wolsey's, and the head of the family's style included the honorific His Sacred, Imperial, and Catholic Majesty.

If His Most Catholic Majesty harbored any doubt about Martin Luther's popularity with the German people, he was disabused by what he saw in Worms, where icons circulated in the city streets conflating Luther's face with that of Saint Paul. Lutherans kissed cheap printed pictures showing the preacher's head ringed by an angelic halo. The Emperor treated Luther with great honor at their meetings in Worms, but he had not brought him there to negotiate. Charles told his "dear Reverend Dr. Martin Luther" that he came from a long line of men and women who had been "defenders at all times of the Catholic Faith, its sacred ceremonies, decrees, and ordinances, and its holy rites," and that he had no intention of being the first Hapsburg to break that covenant.[61] Luther, for his part, stalwartly refused to retract any of his teachings, which increasingly articulated the view that not only was the Catholic Church corrupt to its very core but also that her teachings were scripturally unsustainable, a hodgepodge of quasi-Christianity mixed with residuals of paganism, superstition, and, worst of all from Luther's ferociously anti-Semitic perspective, Judaism. In a chilling microcosm of what would happen to Europe in the decades ahead, Luther was carried from the audience on the shoulders of his cheering supporters, while Spanish delegates in the same room screamed, "Burn him! Burn him!"[62]

From there, Lutheranism spread westward to the Hapsburg-controlled Netherlands, whose aforementioned trade links to England were among the busiest in early modern Europe. At the same time that Charles had been in his Dutch territories, having his affairs with the servant Jeanne van der Gheynst and the widowed Ursolina della Penna, English merchants to the Netherlands were discussing Luther's controversial ideas with their Dutch and German colleagues. The Emperor ordered that every copy of a book by Luther be tracked down in the Netherlands and burned publicly, but by then, English traders had already bought many of them and smuggled them home.

The fight had come to Wolsey's doorstep. In May 1521 he imitated Charles V's actions by seizing every copy of Luther's works that his agents could find and condemning them all to a public bonfire outside London's St. Paul's Cathedral.[63] Spurred to pious polemic, King Henry wrote a defense of Catholic theology, *Assertio Septem Sacramentorum*, a copy of which, bound

in gold, had been sent to Rome to be laid at the feet of Pope Leo.[64] Thomas
More, a lawyer and courtier who composed some of the speeches welcoming
the Emperor to England, was also working on his own next book *Responsio
ad Lutherum*, in which he referred to Martin Luther as "truly the shitpool of
all shit" and described his protests as "all the muck and shit which your dam-
nable rottenness has vomited up."* Luther's followers were called "the most
absurd race of heretics, the dregs of impiety, of crimes and filth," and their
fellow protesters were accused of having sex in churches so that they could
"bespatter the most holy image of Christ crucified with the most foul excrement of their bodies [which are] destined to be burned." More complained of
the mental and spiritual exhaustion of attacking Luther because it required
engaging with his writings—or, to quote the author, "while I clean out this
fellow's shit-filled mouth, I see my own fingers covered with shit."[65] More was
later sufficiently embarrassed by the vim and vigor of this book, as were King
Henry and Cardinal Wolsey, that he tried to deny authorship, and it was
published under the pseudonym William Ross.[66]

As night fell during the Emperor's stay, Hampton Court must have glittered
in reflection on the dark river waters outside. Torches would have flickered
in the evening air as the sound of music, conversation, entertainment, the
trumpets used to announce a banquet, and the many languages spoken by
the Emperor's entourage carried out over the redbrick walls along with the
smell of food. Inside, Wolsey's crest of arms would likely have been joined
by the Hapsburgs' double-headed eagle, Henry VIII's lions, unicorns, and
roses, and Katherine of Aragon's heraldic pomegranates. Hampton Court's
metamorphosis from manor to palace under Thomas Wolsey is almost as
remarkable a feat as Wolsey's life. His talents took him far from his humble
origins; as his many detractors never tired of reminding themselves, Wolsey

---

* Ironically, Thomas More shared this penchant for scatological scourges with Martin Luther,
who once woke up from a nightmare in which he had been pursued by demons and told the
Devil, "Lick my arse!"

had come from "low origins." He spent his childhood in the east English town of Ipswich—some said as the son of an innkeeper-cum-butcher; others, as the son of a moderately wealthy farmer, or grazier.[67] Yet he had risen until he was entertaining an emperor in his palace, where his own most private rooms were decorated with cloth of gold.*[68]

The Cardinal's critics argued that such grandiosity was unseemly, especially when they were excluded from it. As he watched the army of workers and artisans transform Hampton Court between 1515 and 1522, Wolsey's fellow clergyman Father John Skelton was furious. In contrast to Wolsey the Oxonian, Skelton was probably educated at England's only other university at the time; in the fabulously florid phrasing of the sixteenth century, he had "first suckled the breast of learning at Cambridge."[69] The contemporary philosopher Erasmus of Rotterdam regarded Skelton as "a light and glory of English letters," although the poetry that Skelton wrote when not engaged in his priestly duties included pieces that read like manuals on seduction, affectionate reminiscences of prostitutes who frequented a local tavern, and puns that stable-hands were bound to be good at riding.[70] Having been retained briefly by Elizabeth of York to tutor the future Henry VIII, Skelton was familiar enough with the royal court to have witnessed Thomas Wolsey's rise through its ranks.[71] By the early 1520s, Skelton had turned his quill to mocking the Cardinal. Polemic's relationship with accuracy has never been particularly intimate, and Skelton was quite prepared to lie to his readers by presenting an eye infection suffered by the Cardinal as proof that he had syphilis. He mocked, too, Wolsey's lower-class birth and his ambition, alliterating them in references to the "bragging butcher."

Skelton focused much of his ire on Hampton Court, presenting its expansion as symptomatic of the "abuses of the age," and suggesting that Wolsey was guilty of architectural lèse-majesté in creating a residence that rivalled the King's. Wolsey's new palace made him seem like an *alter rex*: the other king. Wolsey had spent more on expanding and beautifying his homes than had either Henry VIII or Henry VII, including the latter's creation of the "second

---

* Silk wrapped with a band or strip containing a high proportion of gold.

paradise" at Richmond.[72] As Skelton put it in the poem "Why Come Ye Not to Court?," which was probably completed sometime around November 1522:

> Why come ye not to court?—
> *To which court?*
> *To the king's court,*
> *Or to Hampton Court?*
> Nay, to the king's court:
> *The king's court*
> *Should have the excellence;*
> *But Hampton Court*
> *Hath the preeminence.*

The palace, Skelton argued, was a manifestation of the Cardinal's towering ambition. He warned that Hampton Court

> *Sets up a wretch on high,*
> *In a throne triumphantly,*
> *Make him of great estate*
> *And he will play check mate*
> *With royal majesty*
> *Count himself as good as he.*[73]

"Why come ye not to court?" seems to have been a culmination to the satirical series of anti-Wolsey poems written by Skelton in 1521 and 1522, which included "Speak, Parrot" and "Colin Clout," an extract from which, with modernized spelling, forms the epigraph to this chapter.[74] Fortunately for Skelton, the Cardinal seems to have accepted that being written about unpleasantly, even dishonestly, is an unavoidable irritant for those in positions of power, privilege, or prominence. He developed a thick skin when it came to insults and got on with his job. In time, Skelton proved the truth of the Oscar Wilde quip that those who speak most disparagingly of high society are sometimes those with a frustrated desire to enter it. The minute Wolsey decided to silence Skelton by hiring him, the poet-priest replaced his stanzas of character assassination with missives in which Wolsey converses with the allegorical figure of the Queen of Fame, who assures the great Cardinal that he need not worry about posterity, for his place of honor is ensured in her halls.[75]

Wolsey was sometimes equally forgiving of aristocrats who got in his way. He had first tussled with the landowning elite not long after he graduated from Oxford.[76] As an obscure cleric, he had somehow irritated a local gentleman, Sir Amyas Paulet, who, according to a colorful although probably accurate story, used his influence to have Wolsey put in the stocks.* When he came to power, Wolsey had not visited any vengeance on the curmudgeonly Paulet. As Henry VIII's chief minister, however, Wolsey was detested by most of the great families. A few resented his hypocrisy in reforming the royal household, a process through which he had cunningly limited the power of the King's favorites and urged Henry VIII to be less generous to those around him—except to Wolsey himself. In 1521 Henry VIII had shocked the nobility by signing the death warrant of his pompous cousin Edward Stafford, 3rd Duke of Buckingham†, who was condemned after a show trial for which Wolsey, unfairly, was blamed by outraged aristocrats who could not openly criticize the King.[77] The Cardinal was also preparing himself for a forthcoming contretemps with Parliament, where he knew many of the members held him responsible for the Crown's frequent requests for higher taxes. On this point, Wolsey again took the blame even though he did not deserve it. Henry VIII's mismanagement of the economy changed in form but remained consistent in impact over the thirty-eight years of his reign. He was extravagant, expansionist, and pro-war, three

---

* A genial disposition did not, regrettably, seem to gallop through the Paulet family: Amyas's grandson and namesake was jailer to the deposed Mary, Queen of Scots, who described him as "one of the most zealous and pitiless men I have ever known."

† Each time a noble title is created, the incumbents are numbered. If the title falls into disuse and is subsequently revived or passes to another family, the numbering starts anew. The only exceptions are when the titles are held by immediate members of the royal family, in which case numbers are not attached. The 3rd Duke of Buckingham did not count as an immediate member of the royal family because he was related to Henry on the maternal side.

combined policies that had seen him already blow through the fortune his father had left him in 1509. Wolsey was expected to find the money and bear the brunt for the tax hikes needed to keep Henry solvent.

Despite this and his own sybaritic lifestyle, Wolsey was praised in a private letter by a contemporary abbot as being "the especial help of the poor" during his time as Lord Chancellor.[78] He organized committees to hear the legal petitions of poor men who were being squeezed out of their ancient rights to arable fields by landowners bent on increasing their own incomes through the enclosure of common land. He had spent the past five years trying to tackle poverty in England, setting up investigative commissions in the countryside and liaising with local authorities in towns and cites such as London, Coventry, Lincoln, Leicester, and Shrewsbury. During the plague outbreak of 1518, Wolsey had also attempted to create a quarantine system for marking and isolating infected houses.[79]

Wolsey was above all a pragmatist. He believed that effective government needed both the good and the bad, as well as the truthful and the mendacious, a view which is expressed in the choice of terracotta heads he commissioned for his new courtyard. The emperors Wolsey picked were unusual subjects. It was common to focus artistically on the "Five Good Emperors" of Rome—and some of the emperors gazing down on Hampton Court, such as Trajan and Hadrian, were used by Tudor-era educators as examples of "good emperors." Others, however, like Nero and Vitellius, were "bad," held up to warn of the dangers of tyranny, treason, or, in the case of Cleopatra VII, scheming and extravagance.[80] By commissioning images of Cleopatra, Julius Caesar, and varyingly successful emperors, Wolsey acknowledged the complexity of what it took to make politics work.

As Charles V returned to his empire, Wolsey turned his attention to a crisis building in Ireland, which he was trying to manage from his household at Hampton Court. It was that emergency that had brought James Butler, or Séamas Bacach, into Wolsey's establishment—quite unwillingly, for the young man made no secret of his desire to go home to southern Ireland as soon as he received the Cardinal's permission. That would not be granted until James had married his English cousin Anne Boleyn, in a match arranged by Wolsey to stop their two competing families from tipping eastern and southern Ireland into chaos. Anne, who had been completing her education in the household of Queen Claude of France, had been fetched home under pressure from Wolsey.[81] Anne's father, the diplomat Sir Thomas Boleyn, was the senior living grandson of the late Earl of Ormond,* who had died without sons in 1515. The Ormond earldom, with its base in Kilkenny, Ireland, was one of the largest, oldest, and wealthiest noble titles in northern Europe, and the old earl—and nearly everyone who mattered—had expected his title, vast estates, and castles to pass to his grandson and namesake, Thomas.[82] Everybody, that is, except James Butler's father, Sir Piers, nicknamed Piaras Ruadh—Piers the Red—in Ireland, a junior cousin of the family who, having run the Butlers' lands during the previous earl's later years, argued that he should inherit them, as opposed to his English kinsman. Armed with a significant military following in Ireland and having cleverly married his daughters into neighboring aristocratic families, Piers had made sure that he had feudal soldiers and allies to support him.[83] However, the archbishopric of Dublin, its law courts, its surrounding counties, and aristocratic precedent, favored Thomas Boleyn.[84] Wolsey had been watching throughout his time as Lord Chancellor as the crisis built and family relations deteriorated.[85] A century earlier, when the Butlers had descended into a feud, they had dragged down with them most of the Irish economy, law, order, and Crown income. The ancient earldom of Ormond must not be allowed to go into freefall again.

Wolsey proposed that the earldom go to Piers Butler, on the condition that his eldest son, James, marry Thomas Boleyn's eldest daughter, Mary.[86] This arrangement clearly favored Piers's might over Thomas's right, since it meant that Piers would get the earldom because the government knew it would take too much manpower to dislodge him. The Boleyns were understandably nonplussed. They deserved medals for the inventiveness of

---

* Thomas Butler, 7th Earl of Ormond, had spent much of his time in England, where he served as Lord Chamberlain in the household of Queen Katherine of Aragon.

their foot-dragging, and it is tempting to wonder if Mary Boleyn's 1520 wedding to an English courtier was one such move.[87] Outright refusal was, however, impossible once Wolsey issued explicit orders. Since Mary Boleyn had married, her younger sister, Anne, was brought back from France and into Queen Katherine's household, while James came from Ireland and into Wolsey's.[88]

Then, sometime in the summer of 1522 or shortly after, Wolsey's match-making briefly looked about to unravel, thanks to one of his most irritating wards. He had never particularly liked Lord Henry Percy, noticing earlier than anybody else the privileged young man's financial incompetence. Years later, when Percy succeeded his father to the earldom of Northumberland, he earned the sobriquet "the Unthrifty Earl." Percy, about nineteen years old that summer, was possibly bisexual; even allowing for the hyperbolic way sentiments within the sexes were expressed in the sixteenth century, his subsequent language to and about his companion Sir Thomas Arundell seems at times too intimate to be convincingly explained as platonic.[89] Arundell, too, served in Wolsey's household in the early 1520s, where it is likely that he and Percy initially shared the luxury of a bed at Hampton Court. There was nothing unusual about this; it was common practice in large households. Far less common was Percy's persistence in referring to Arundell affectionately and nostalgically in his letters as "my dearest bed-fellow," long after they had ceased sharing that bed.[90] In 1522–23, Wolsey was less interested in Percy and Arundell and more in the rumor that Percy had fallen in love with Anne Boleyn and wanted to marry her. Not only had Percy been betrothed, aged fourteen, to Lord Shrewsbury's daughter, Lady Mary Talbot—a union that would facilitate smoother relations between the great families in the north of England—but Percy's interest threatened to derail Wolsey's solution to the Ormond problem. His already low opinion of Percy's intellect and self-control was stretched and he considered contacting the young man's father to hurry along Percy's wedding to Lady Mary. Wolsey was determined to grant James Butler's petition that he be allowed to leave Hampton Court to return to Ireland only if he did so with Anne Boleyn beside him as his wife and future Countess of Ormond.

CHAPTER 3

THE ANNE BOLEYN GATE

The royal estate of princes . . . doth represent and
outwardly show unto us the glorious and celestial
monarchy which God, the governor of all things,
doth exercise in the firmament.

—Anne Boleyn, Queen of England (c. 1533)

Anne Boleyn never made it to Ireland. Instead, on July 2, 1533, just over eleven years after Wolsey had hosted Charles V, she became the first queen of England to stay at Hampton Court as a Crown property.[1] Of medium height, a brunette with dark "eyes always most attractive," which some observers considered to be her best feature, and entering the third trimester of her first pregnancy, she arrived by barge with her husband.[2] The marriage negotiations for her hand to James Butler had stalled, shrivelled, then died, in part because of the Boleyns' delay-inspiring distaste for the plan. The final nail in the coffin, possibly, was Henry VIII's own romantic interest in Anne, which developed around 1526. Instead, Cousin James entered into an arranged match with another Irish aristocrat, the Earl and Countess of Desmond's daughter Lady Joan Fitzgerald.[3] James and Joan had since welcomed their first child, a son christened Tomás, and Henry VIII was hoping for similarly happy Y-chromosome-containing news for his nursery.

At Hampton Court, the new Queen occupied a suite overlooking the palace's smaller Clock Court; through its windows was directly visible the new gateway that, centuries later, would be renamed the Anne Boleyn Gate. In her rooms, Anne sat on her throne beneath a cloth of estate woven from cloth of gold and fringed with silk, or another in purple velvet.[4] There were two new chairs for honored guests, also upholstered in cloth of gold, and more soon arrived finished in silk—some crimson; others a regal purple—while carpets imported from the Ottoman Empire were delivered, as were green silk ribbons to decorate the clavichords she loved to play.[5] These rooms were not technically a queen's apartments, although they had been designed as accommodation for Anne's predecessor, Katherine of Aragon, on the infrequent occasions when she had visited Hampton Court as Cardinal Wolsey's guest. Wolsey had died in disgrace two years earlier, after being dismissed by the King in retribution for his failure to secure an annulment of Henry's twenty-two-year marriage to Queen Katherine. Before and after Wolsey's downfall, Anne had stayed at Hampton Court on several occasions. She sent the Cardinal a thank-you note for the carp he had gifted her from its estate during Lent, and it may have been at Hampton Court that she was exposed to plague, which nearly killed her in 1528. She stayed there again in the spring and summer of 1529, not long after her recovery, but she had her own estate at the nearby manor of Haworth, which perhaps explains the infrequency of her stays at Hampton Court until she became queen.[6]

For nine days after the King and Queen's arrival, Hampton Court hosted celebrations for Anne's coronation, which had taken place in London the previous week. The King of France sent Anne the gift of a litter pulled by three mules, which meant a slower but more comfortable journey for her, especially during her pregnancy.[7] There was hunting during the day—the royal falconers were worried about an aggressive new merlin who still needed to be broken in—and balls and banquets in the evenings.[8] Due to her pregnancy, the Queen could not partake in much of the dancing or hunting; nonetheless, those who saw her remarked on her contentment.[9] King Henry did not even allow the death of his youngest and favorite sister,* which occurred a week before his return to Hampton Court, to cast a pall over his "merry spirits."[10] A French diplomat recalled how the entertainments for Anne Boleyn's coronation "were notable as the English sought, unceasingly, to honour their new princess. . . . The lords and ladies set to dances, sports of various kinds, hunting expeditions, and pleasures without parallel. Numerous tournaments were held in her honour . . . and everything was a success. And as well as magnificent and joyful celebrations, everyone strove to be as attentive and solicitous as possible to their new mistress."[11]

Anne's father, the Earl of Ormond, was present, as was her mother, Elizabeth, to whom the Queen was particularly close and who had once been the object of poetry written by John Skelton celebrating her beauty. As Anne rose to prominence, she had used her influence to finally settle the earldom dispute in her family's favor and broker a deal with Piers, who relinquished his claim to the Ormond earldom in return for a newly—and tactically—created earldom of Ossory. Anne's father was now an earl twice over; Henry VIII had also made him Earl of Wiltshire in the English nobility. The two earldoms—Ormond and Wiltshire—had been tied to each other in the previous century, until Edward IV separated them in punishment for the then-earl's support for the opposing side of the Wars of the Roses.

Another Irish peer at court that summer was "young and wilful" Thomas FitzGerald, Lord Offaly, the nineteen-year-old heir to his father, the Earl of Kildare. Lord Kildare was in frequent correspondence with the Queen's father, as their estates neighbored one another's. Offaly, an acclaimed harpist, was fluent in English and Irish, thanks to childhood lessons from his bilingual English mother; he was also a dapper dresser, for which his opponents mocked him with the nickname "Silken Thomas." Before long, though, his supporters turned it into a term of endearment,

---

* Mary Tudor the Elder, Dowager Queen of France and Duchess of Suffolk (1496–1533), had been the third wife of France's King Louis XII (d. 1515). After his death, she had married Charles Brandon, 1st Duke of Suffolk (d. 1545). It is through Mary that her granddaughter, Lady Jane Grey (ex. 1554), acquired her claim to the throne.

shouting it when they saw him ride through the streets of Dublin.[12] Clothes and music played a major part in life at Anne Boleyn and Henry VIII's court. One of the Queen's harshest critics conceded that she was "unrivalled in the gracefulness of her attire, and the fertility of her invention in devising new patterns, which were imitated by all the court belles, by whom she was regarded as the glass of fashion."[13]

The Queen's paternal grandmother, Lady Margaret Boleyn, was one of the highest-ranking female Irish aristocrats, but sadly she was not among those celebrating with her granddaughter that summer, as she had been battling with dementia for the past few years, when her son had brought her to live safely with them at Hever Castle.[14] Other absentees from the post-coronation court were the Queen's brother Lord Rochford and their uncle the Duke of Norfolk, both of whom were on a diplomatic mission to Paris.

There was work to do in making Hampton Court suitable as a royal residence. After Cardinal Wolsey lost royal favor, the estate had passed to the King, who assumed responsibility for its upkeep in 1529. In 1531 Henry VIII persuaded William Weston, the new prior of the Knights Hospitaller, to grant him the estate's freehold as part of a property exchange through which the order received the Priory of St. Mary Magdalene in Stanesgate in the eastern county of Essex.[15] How gently Henry persuaded Prior Weston is debatable; how fair the exchange was seems less ambiguous. Several changes had since been made at Hampton Court to suit Henry's needs. A meeting room was hastily added for the Privy Council, whose members, all appointed by the King, travelled with him as the principal form of daily government in England, and the palace's "downstairs" had been expanded to suit the greater number of servants working for the royal household. Henry VIII's father had been an enthusiastic tennis player, and it is possible that Lord Daubeney had built Hampton Court's first tennis court in preparation for Henry VII's visit in 1500.[16] It needed improving by the 1530s, as Henry VIII, who had been very athletic in his youth, turned to tennis and bowling to keep fit as he entered his forties. A new indoor tennis court was built for him, with a viewing gallery added in the spring of 1533.[17] The game became very popular with courtiers in the 1530s, with

Henry's brother-in-law, George Boleyn, Lord Rochford, being one of the best players.

Henry had shown relatively little interest in architecture for the first twenty years of his reign. When the royal apartments at the old Palace of Westminster burned down, he was quite content to "make do" by borrowing accommodation from the Archbishop of Canterbury, whose London residence of Lambeth Palace was conveniently located on the opposite side of the river from the fire-damaged palace. His second wife came from two families—the Butlers and the Boleyns—with a long history of interest in architecture.[18] It is therefore almost certainly no coincidence that the next major building phases at Hampton Court commenced the week of Anne Boleyn's first residency there as queen. Like her late mother-in-law at Richmond, Anne took a leading role in designing the new palace.[19] It would grow and display a unified aesthetic, smoothing the architectural styles of Daubeney, Wolsey, and Henry VIII into a whole that looked deliberate. Inspired in part by the French palaces Anne had known during her education there, and by the architectural projects the Boleyns had undertaken on their private estates—her father had extensively expanded, modernized, and beautified their homes at Blickling Hall, Hever Castle, and Beaulieu Palace*—Hampton Court would have a new wing to the east and south. This would connect to, and incorporate, the private quarters in the tower erected for Henry after 1529, which included his bedchamber, with an en suite bathroom (the building was called the Bayne—meaning "bath"—Tower); his privy closet, which functioned much like a modern study; the King's personal library, curtained heavily to protect the books from damaging sunlight; and his jewel house, or vault. There was also a smaller dining room, a guard chamber, a presence chamber, and a withdrawing chamber. Henry's tower would henceforth also border Anne Boleyn's greatest change to Hampton Court: the addition of the third courtyard, expanding the palace to almost half again its original size and forming the center of the new wing containing the Queen's apartments. Gal-

---

* Previously New Hall in Essex. Thomas Boleyn had "flipped" the property by selling it to the King in 1516 for the substantial sum of £1,000.

leries linking the Queen's rooms to the King's were planned, both of which would also stretch to face south toward the hunting grounds and forests. The Florentine artist Toto del Nunziata was among those commissioned to decorate the King and Queen's private apartments with works including paintings of Christ washing the feet of the Apostles at the Last Supper, portraits of each of the four Evangelists, and a pietà.[*]

Along with the Presence Chamber, where Anne would receive guests and petitioners, there would be more private spaces, including her bedroom, a withdrawing room, a dressing room, and a separate privy kitchen installed nearby solely to cook meals that could be delivered safely and warmly to the Queen.[20] A private oratory for prayers, two garderobes for the convenience of her ladies-in-waiting, a secured jewel house, and a private room known as a Closet from where the Queen could write letters, were also designed. The decorators of the rooms' moldings included two German artists named Rupprecht and Heinrich—their names are anglicized in the records to Robert Shynk and Henry Blankston, respectively—who worked with their English colleague John Hethe. Their projects included a nursery for Anne's expected children. A coal house was built in the palace grounds to guard the expensive sea coal that was exclusively for use in the King and Queen's fireplaces. Soon Queen Anne's designs inspired Henry to revamp his rooms. A vast storage facility for Anne's wardrobe would be constructed, conveniently, beneath her new lodgings; also planned were bathrooms with hot and cold running water, heated by unseen servants on the other side of the wall, a luxury that Henry VIII already enjoyed in his private apartments with his copper bathtub.

These royal bathrooms were the height of luxury in terms of private dwellings in the 1530s, and they feature in one of the many legends inspired by Anne Boleyn's career. Centuries after her death, the French novelist Alexandre Dumas claimed to have read a contemporary source stating that Anne had been so beautiful that the noblemen of England fought duels to possess a vial of her bath water. As with so many of Dumas's "missing sources,"

---

[*] The Virgin Mary, cradling the crucified body of her son Jesus Christ in her arms.

it is highly likely that it existed only in his imagination. Contemporary estimations of Anne's appearance vary, although none of the eyewitnesses mention the legendary sixth finger or a vestigial one, nor a deformed nail.[21] The most frequently cited account today is the notoriously dismissive assessment of Francesco Sanuto, a Venetian diplomat who, upon seeing Boleyn for the first time in 1532, wrote, "Madam Anne is not one of the handsomest women in the world; she is of middling stature, swarthy complexion, long neck, wide mouth, bosom not much raised, and in fact has nothing but the English king's great appetite and her eyes, which are black and beautiful, and take great effect."[22] Sanuto seems to have been dramatically dismissive when compared with nearly all the other eyewitness testimonies, such as that of the Cambridge scholar who described Anne as "competent belle" ("beautiful enough"); the residents at the French court, where she was remembered as "very beautiful"; and the English courtier who did describe her as very attractive—with the caveat that one of the King's earlier romantic interests, his former mistress Bessie Blount, had been more beautiful. While the other details of Anne's appearance remain subjective, there was consensus on the more important issues of her intelligence, humor, and bravery. A diplomat stationed at the English court compared her courage to that of a lion.[23]

She had needed courage in the half decade and more it had taken her to become queen. When Henry VIII first attempted to seduce her in the mid-1520s, Anne had declined to become his mistress. Later, her enemies accused her of deliberately playing "hard to get" in order to manipulate Henry into falling even more in love with her. That reads as history unduly influenced by hindsight, especially in view of the lengths to which Anne initially went to escape Henry's attention. She left court by retreating, with her parents' blessing, to the family's estate at Hever Castle, two days' ride from London and not easily accessible, especially for a man in charge of the government and watched by everybody. Instead, messengers had arrived at Hever with a series of letters to Anne from Henry, each one showcasing a different mood to the one before. Henry's emotional roulette wheel spun from adoration to cloying desperation, to recrimination at her failure to respond in a way sufficiently loving to bring him joy, then to distress at her refusal to return to court even after he gave permission for her to be constantly chaperoned by her mother. The letters' tones are united solely by Henry's obsession. Then he proposed marriage, which Anne accepted on the promise that he would soon end his marriage to Queen Katherine. The chess pieces of the struggle had largely been set by 1527, for what nobody initially suspected would prove a particularly long game. The papacy had liquidated many marriages, especially royal ones, on grounds far more dubious than those underpinning Henry VIII's petition. He insisted belatedly that his wife's previous marriage to his late brother, Arthur, constituted a contravention of biblical law, citing as evidence God's failure to bless their union with healthy sons. Queen Katherine countered that her first marriage had never been consummated, a detail that she and many theologians believed discounted it as a full union. Katherine received the backing of her nephew, Emperor Charles V.

Pope Clement VII, faced with the unappealing prospect of offending either the Hapsburgs or the Tudors, dithered in the hope that somehow the matter would resolve itself. Henry might lose interest in Anne, she might fall sick and die, as might Queen Katherine. Henry vented his rage on Cardinal Wolsey, who lost his power and his palaces in retribution for having failed to persuade the Pope to grant the annulment. Anne, already interested in the Reformation ideas percolating through society, began to promote its writings to her fiancé, who, at the tail end of 1532, married her after they returned from a state visit to France. The new Archbishop of Canterbury, Thomas Cranmer, ruled in the King's favor, annulled the marriage to Katherine of Aragon, and retrospectively blessed the new Queen, who was crowned at Westminster and afterward decamped with the royal household to Hampton Court. By which point, Clement VII had not yet contradicted the Archbishop's decision.

Anne's residency at Hampton Court in July 1533 proved to be the Rubicon moment. On July 11 news arrived from Rome. The Pope had tried to lock the stable door after the horse had bolted. After seven years of indecision, Clement VII ruled in Katherine of Aragon's favor, declaring her to be Henry's rightful wife and threatening Henry VIII with excommunication if he did not banish Anne from court. Henry and his advisers decided to keep the news from Queen Anne in case it induced a miscarriage.[24] With the papal ruling in Katherine's favor arriving at the same time as Anne's pregnancy and after her coronation and consecration as queen consort, there was no longer any easy route back from creating a national Church. A Church of England, separate from Rome, had *de facto* come into existence.

Henry's concern about how his wife would take the news of the Pope's decision raises an interesting query about Anne Boleyn's supposed religious and political views. Why was Henry worried that it might prove so distressing to her that it could damage her health? While Anne had, for the past few years, promoted books critiquing and belittling the papacy, the fact that Clement VII's ruling was initially kept from her raises the possibility that, even at this late stage—she had privately hoped for a different outcome, whereby a full schism with Rome might be avoided. Queen Anne was incorporated into subsequent histories as a Protestant heroine—and is still regularly described as such even today—yet there is almost nothing by way of evidence to support that claim. Well read and highly intelligent, Anne was interested in the theological debates surrounding the Protestant cause and even sympathetic to many of their points. However, with the sole exception of her anti-papalism, every single one of her religious beliefs would today be classified as Catholic, if not necessarily as Roman Catholic. She supported pilgrimages and veneration of the Virgin Mary, which she confirmed in her desire to make pilgrimage to the miraculous shrine of Our Lady of Walsingham in Norfolk. She kept prayer books featuring Catholic imagery such as the Assumption of Mary into Heaven, and, even in the last year of her life, she declined to fund philosophers who supported a Protestant interpretation of Holy Communion against the traditionalist Catholic teachings on the subject.[25] Admittedly, she was passionately committed to supporting those who defied the ban on the Bible being published in English, a cause that she adopted relatively early in her career and at considerable risk to herself. Later attempts to present this as the action of someone who believed in allowing the majority to make up their own minds by reading the Scriptures in English are perhaps solipsistic when one considers how many people in Henrician England were illiterate or quasi-literate.

An English-language Bible was, at this stage, an initiative that would be of value predominantly to Anne's fellow members of the elite; while there is no justification for dismissing the bravery and tenacity with which she pursued her support for the Bible in English, it is worth tempering it by understanding just how few people it would benefit directly.

A similar caveat cannot fairly be applied to her charitable donations, which were efficient, extensive, and generous. Anne's Christian faith does not easily fall into the later categories of Catholic or Protestant, in which one might expect a person who shared her beliefs to also be loyal to the Vatican or to oppose the dissemination of the English-language Bible. Anne was of a generation born immediately before the start of the Reformation and who grew up as it developed. It was a process, rather than a conclusion, and it did not seem obvious that there needed to be a schism within western European Christianity, or Christendom, as it was then called. As the conflict crystallized, many of those who lived later and longer than Anne Boleyn eventually picked a side, but in the early 1530s it was still hoped that the Church could be reformed rather than divided. It was the question of how far those reforms should go, and whether or not they could be achieved within the Church, that eventually proved a point of no return.

Political theories in the 1530s were changing along with the religious. Recollections from Anne's chaplains, particularly Father William Latymer, who served as the Queen's almoner (the household priest responsible for her charitable donations) and who accompanied her as she moved from Hampton Court to the other favored Tudor palaces—Whitehall, Richmond, Greenwich, and Windsor—or to the many smaller hunting lodges where the royals spent much of their autumns, indicate Anne's strong support for the Divine Right of Kings. This political theory, which promoted the belief that monarchs were intended by God to hold power above all earthly institutions, including the Church's hierarchy, was not a product of the Middle Ages, when kings had often been held in hock to the elaborate reciprocity of loyalty and obedience, service and protection, encased within feudalism. However imperfectly that theory was applied, it remained the prevailing ideal, augmented by the papacy's rights as underscored by the Donation of

Constantine, a probably forged document in which the first Christian emperor, Constantine the Great, had allegedly given the bishops of Rome political supremacy over secular rulers. In contrast, the Divine Right of Kings theory gained momentum amid the vigorous cultural and intellectual chaos unleashed by the Reformation. Kings and princes who rejected Catholicism, and with it papal supremacy, typically installed their monarchies as custodians of the local church in lieu of the Vatican. Even those sovereigns who remained Catholic began to question and erode papal absolutism over local matters. Critics of the papacy cited the example of Emperor Constantine's attending the early ecclesiastical councils as proof that kings and emperors had a historical right to be involved in the governance of the Church.

These ideas had an obvious utility to Henry VIII, since they told him what he wanted to hear at a time when he was frustrated by the Pope's refusal to support his second marriage. They fed the emerging philosophical principle that kings were not, as they had been seen in the Middle Ages, God's servants but rather God's lieutenants on Earth. They were still answerable to God, but only to God, not to noble assemblies, nor to any ecclesiastic. On Judgement Day, monarchs would be called to give an account before the Throne of God as to how they had ruled their subjects in a Christian manner, so God and God alone would be their judge. The entire system of monarchy had been deliberately created by Almighty God to give people on Earth their closest possible glimpse of the hierarchy of Heaven. Anne Boleyn articulated and supported this view unambiguously in a conversation with Father Latymer, when she argued that "The royal estate of princes . . . doth represent and outwardly show unto us the glorious and celestial monarchy which God, the governor of all things, doth exercise in the firmament." Henry presented his newfound position as Supreme Head of a separate Church of England as a restoration, not a revolution, and he showed no real enthusiasm to radically alter the theological nature of his church. Spiritually, he was still the man who had written *Assertio Septem Sacramentorum*, attacking Martin Luther's critique of Catholic sacramentary theology.

The Royal Supremacy over the Church was in practice in England by
the time the Queen and King returned to Hampton Court in the winter of 1533. One reason for their visit was to inspect the building work.
The workmen on site were paid overtime to be ready for them, which
they managed, barely, by running around holding charcoal braziers under
still-drying paint hours before the royals arrived. One of the most impressive of the many projects that had been completed was the dismantling of
Lord Daubeney's hall and replacing it with a new Great Hall, decorated
with Anne's heraldic leopard, griffin, and falcon, and Henry's rose, lion,
and dragon, capped by a magnificent hammer beam roof facing a tiled
floor.[26] An oak screen at the lower end of the hall was decorated with the
King's and Queen's insignia. Cavernous new cellars were created beneath
the hall for storing beer. Much like Henry's religious policy, the Great Hall
was a new construct with an antique spirit. Stylistically, it was a throwback
to the halcyon days Henry imagined as having existed under his favorite
predecessors, Edward III and Henry V. It was designed to look like a traditional medieval hall—the French royal family installed similar rooms
at their new palaces of Fontainebleau and Saint-Germain-en-Laye.[27] A
log-burning open hearth was installed at the center of the room, as it
had been in older halls. Tests conducted in 1924 on the Great Hall's roof
showed no traces of soot, indicating that a fire was almost certainly never
lit in it. The hall became both the most and the least useful room in the
palace. Despite its size, Henry VIII hardly ever used it for formal recep-
tions or banquets; instead, it functioned more often as the Hampton Court
cafeteria, where servants gathered to eat on long trestle tables, enjoying
their bouche (mouth) of the court: the daily meals they were entitled to
under court etiquette.

   In the intervening months between her first visit as queen and seeing
the new Great Hall, Anne had given birth to their first child. Any disappointment at Princess Elizabeth's gender had not visibly knocked the
Queen off course. Publicly, she remained confident about the future. She
continued to take a great interest in the work on her wings and the changes
to Hampton Court, where she twice hosted banquets and entertainments

for ambassadors from the German Hanseatic League.* Having spent almost all of her education at courts—first at the Hapsburg, then the French, and, finally, the English—this was the milieu in which Queen Anne was most comfortable; she was an excellent hostess, a witty conversationalist, and, as an ambassador's daughter who had spent so much of her childhood abroad, she was interested in international diplomacy.

Tragically, the next summer, a year to the day since she had arrived at Hampton Court from her coronation, Anne almost certainly suffered her first miscarriage there. It probably took place in her rooms overlooking the Clock Court, as her apartments remained under construction. We know from the sources that Anne arrived at the palace with a "goodly belly," after which her pregnancy vanishes from the records.[28] Horribly, court itineraries reveal that, on July 2, 1534, the King departed suddenly, leaving the Queen to recuperate without him.[29] They resided at the palace again, briefly, the following summer, to inspect the Queen's nearly finished apartments. A few months later, Anne lost another pregnancy, and a few months after that, she was dead on the scaffold—for a crime she had allegedly committed at Hampton Court.

On December 3, 1533, during her visit to inspect the Great Hall, Anne allegedly committed adultery at the palace with William Brereton, an ornery Anglo-Welsh landowner whose charms were apparent only to her and to his devoted, now betrayed, wife.[30] Five days later, on the Feast of the Immaculate Conception, the couple again avoided detection when they met somewhere in the palace to have sex. The affair had begun a week earlier at Greenwich Palace, and, after the royal household moved to Hampton Court, the Queen apparently lost little time in arranging another rendezvous. Brereton was the second lover Anne had secretly taken since her wedding to King Henry less than a year before.[31] Her first had been the recently widowed Henry Norris, a well-liked and very wealthy courtier in his early forties who was, ostensibly, one of her husband's confidants. Anne had seduced Norris that autumn, only a few weeks after giving birth to Princess

---

* A confederation of prosperous northern and central European trading towns and ports.

Elizabeth. All this was revealed at their trials two and a half years later, along with the information that these liaisons had begun a pattern of increasingly depraved libidinousness on the part of the new Queen. Her roll call of lovers had expanded to include a young musician named Mark Smeaton, whom she "procured" at Westminster in the spring of 1534; three and a half weeks later, she slept with the promiscuous and athletic Sir Francis Weston, who became her preferred sexual partner that spring and summer.[32] The Queen's escalating lust degenerated to the point where she made the hideous decision to seduce her brother George, Lord Rochford, in the winter of 1535. The Boleyn siblings' last incestuous interaction took place only nine days before a pregnant Anne summoned all her lovers, bar the low-born Smeaton, to her apartments at Greenwich Palace, where they promised to help achieve her latest desire: her husband's murder. Once Henry VIII was safely dead and either little Elizabeth or the child in Anne's womb was on the throne with their widowed mother installed as regent[*], she would, after a decent interval and a convincing performance of mourning, marry one of her paramours. The front-runner was Henry Norris: Lord Rochford was a nonstarter because their incest would have to remain a permanent secret; Mark Smeaton was disqualified because he was a servant. William Brereton and Francis Weston were both married, although, if the cabal was willing to kill their king, then successfully disposing of their spouses would not presumably pose an insuperable logistical, or moral, problem.[33] In the two years between the adultery at Hampton Court and the murder conference at Greenwich, Queen Anne had ruthlessly played the five men off against one another, manipulating them through jealousy, as well as using sex and lavish gifts to buy their loyalty.

They almost got away with it, until Anne made a joke about their marriage plans to Norris that was overheard by other courtiers, while poor

---

[*] Temporary caretaker of the government during a time of kingly incapacity or absence. Two of Henry's wives—Katherine of Aragon and Katherine Parr—briefly served as regent when he was invading France. If a king was still a child when he or she acceded, a close relative was often chosen to serve as regent—sometimes known as their Protector—until the young monarch reached legal adulthood in their mid-to-late teens.

Smeaton, no longer able to mask his love for the Queen, was detained by the King's suspicious chief minister, Thomas Cromwell. Under questioning, the musician Smeaton confessed everything. Once the arrests began, the mind-boggling details of the Queen's private life tumbled forth to the public, who, predictably, were both repulsed and enthralled by the cocktail of rumored murder, sex, perversion, and intrigue. A merchant working in London at the time was almost embarrassed to write to his employer's wife with the details, since "I think verily that, if all the books and chronicles were totally revolved, and to the uttermost persecuted and tried, which against women hath been penned, contrived, and written since Adam and Eve, those same were, I think, verily nothing in comparison of that which hath been done and committed by Anne the Queen . . . so abominable and detestable that I am ashamed that any good woman should give ear thereunto."[34]

By the time the Queen stood trial, thirteen days after her arrest, different suspicions had taken root. Ballads in Anne's defense were being written, printed, and sung in the capital.[35] A local legal expert was not the only person to question the credibility of the evidence against her after he noticed that the prosecution seemed to hope that smut would serve as a distracting substitute for specifics.[36] Any details it did offer weakened its case. Did a joke between the Queen and Sir Francis Weston about why he was flirting with one of her ladies-in-waiting really indicate they were in love with each other? Who could fairly see Anne's decision to tell her brother that she was pregnant as credible proof of an incestuous relationship? How could the prosecution know the logistics of Anne's first sexual encounter with her brother in such detail as to describe in the indictments how the Queen had persuaded him "to violate her, alluring him with her tongue in the said George's mouth, and the said George's tongue in hers"?[37] Where did this information come from? Neither Anne nor George wavered in their protestations of innocence, so they could not have been the source for this vignette of what their tongues were doing in late 1535. Treason and adultery are not usually spectator events. Since the two participants were not the witnesses, and none of the Queen's ladies-in-waiting was tried for facilitating her adulteries, who, exactly, had provided this excruciatingly vivid testimony? The answer was: nobody.[38] And so, in what febrile underbelly of a prosecutor's mind had there been the inclination to imagine, and then pen, these details of incest?

Was it the same minds who accused Anne of first committing adultery with Henry Norris at Westminster on two dates when she had, in fact, been in post-childbirth seclusion at Greenwich, watched and attended by a large entourage? It was also at Greenwich that Anne had kept the Feast of the Immaculate Conception in 1533, not Hampton Court, where she had supposedly been sleeping with William Brereton.[39] The locations' roles in vice were reversed for the claims about that summer, in which a heavily pregnant Queen had been in residence at Hampton Court when her affair with Francis Weston was commencing at Greenwich. The prosecution alleged she first had sex with Mark Smeaton a year later at Greenwich on a day when she had been staying miles away at Richmond—a closer margin of geographical error than their claim that she had plotted her husband's assassination at Greenwich in January 1536, on dates when she had been in residence at Windsor Castle.[40] None of Anne's accused "lovers" would confess, except Smeaton, and credible rumors at court soon had it that he, as the only commoner in the group, had not simply been questioned but "grievously wracked" until he had brokenly babbled whatever his accusers wanted.[41] The Queen articulated the closest thing we have to an irrefutable truth about the case when she remarked at her trial that whatever she had done to cause her downfall, it clearly had nothing to do with the tissue of pornographic absurdities presented in the courtroom.

It is difficult not to be transfixed by the tragedy of Anne Boleyn, with its gradient of catastrophe that took her from Greenwich Palace to kneeling alone seventeen days later on a scaffold at the Tower of London, praying, while she waited for an expert swordsman to strike off her head. Her contemporaries' skepticism about Anne's guilt is shared by the overwhelming majority of modern historians.[42] However, that is the last point of something resembling a consensus, since debate continues about what actually motivated the coup of 1536. It has been argued by some scholars that the Queen was the victim of a plot organized by her political enemies, possibly prompted by her ideological swing that Easter toward a more theologically conservative position.[43] Her final miscarriage perhaps turned her husband permanently against her, since he subsequently regarded their marriage as cursed.[44] The King's chief minister, Thomas Cromwell, resentful of Anne's power, may have framed her, manufactured the evidence, tricked the King into believing it, accused some of his main political rivals of being the Queen's lovers to get rid of them at the same time, and then pushed the trial and executions through before there was time for Anne's supporters to organize a counterattack.[45] The Queen's risqué sense of humor perhaps collided with mounting palace paranoia, the two being woven together to sweep her off the throne in one of history's most horrible misunderstandings.[46] Others have argued that the key to the riddle is Henry VIII, whose obsessive attitude toward his second wife turned to murderous loathing in something that very much resembles a narcissistic rage attack.[47]

The case of William Brereton, Anne's alleged lover at Hampton Court, is particularly interesting, since there was almost unanimous agreement at the time that he was innocent.[48] There was almost equal consensus as to how personally unlikable Brereton was; moreover, with his temper and arrogance, he had attracted the enmity of Thomas Cromwell several years earlier, when Brereton used his influence in Wales to hang an enemy who was under Cromwell's protection.[49] In 1536, Cromwell and Henry VIII were planning to introduce at the next session of Parliament the country's first Act of Union, under which Wales would be legally fully unified with England. The two countries had been ruled by the same monarchy since the late thirteenth century, but they had continued to use distinctly different legal codes. The 1536 Act of Union planned to change this, among other things. The King and his chief minister intended to see English emerge as the preferred language instead of Welsh, and they planned to subdivide the principality into English-style counties, each of which would henceforth be entitled to send representatives to Parliament. The same laws were to be enforced in both countries.[50] Several major landowners in Wales were expected to obstruct Cromwell's plans; William Brereton being anticipated as the most truculent and effective. With the caveat that it remains circumstantial, the possibility that Brereton was selected both to settle an old score between him and Cromwell and to get him out of the way of the government's plans regarding the future of Wales, has been suggested by at least one study of Anne's life and one of Brereton's career.[51]

Two of Anne Boleyn's other co-accused had links of their own to Hampton Court. There is a long-standing legend that the musician Mark Smeaton was the son of a carpenter who may or may not have been from the Dutch province of Flanders.[52] While that has been dismissed recently as lacking in corroborating evidence, it is noteworthy that Hampton Court's warden carpenter, during Cardinal Wolsey's time, was a man listed as Thomas Smeton or Thomas Smeyton—and that many Dutch or Flemish artisans were enticed to England to work on Hampton Court. Given the fluidity of sixteenth-century spelling, it is possible that Smeton was related to Mark Smeaton; Thomas Smeton remained in his post as warden carpenter of the palace until 1536, the year of Mark Smeaton's execution.[53] William Weston, the prior of the Knights Hospitaller, who surrendered the palace to Henry VIII, was an uncle of Sir Francis, whose links to the palace went deeper through his family seat at Sutton Place in Surrey, built by his father, Sir Richard Weston, in imitation of Wolsey's alterations to Hampton Court; Sir Richard even hired some of the same craftsmen.[54]

Work had finished on the Queen's apartments by the spring of 1536. In poor health following her final miscarriage, Anne never saw the rooms she had helped design, and they remained unoccupied at the time of her execution. The accounts outstanding at her death included payments to Mr. Baven, her bedmaker; Mr. Floyd, who was in charge of her wardrobe; her saddler; and her tailor, for a green silk gown she had commissioned as a gift for her court jester, known as her Fool, and for forty yards of Venetian gold for a nightgown for herself. There were bills for the measurements for caps for Anne's daughter, Princess Elizabeth, which the Queen wanted made in purple satin, white satin, gold, and crimson satin; a receipt for the red fringe to a harness made for the mule she had received as a gift from King François I of France; and payments to her apothecarist, her silk woman, her ironmonger, her shoemaker, and for two pieces of ribbon for her long hair that she had worn up to her beheading.[55]

CHAPTER 4

THE MAIDENS' CHAMBER

The whole peace, unity, rest, and quietness of this realm
and of the subjects of the same standeth and dependeth on
the certainty and surety of the succession in the Imperial
Crown of this Realm.

—An Act of Parliament (1536)

Anne Boleyn had been dead for sixteen months. Hampton Court resembled, once again, a building site when Katharine Bassett and her younger sister Anne crossed its new stone entry bridge over the moat and under the gatehouse.[1] It was the autumn of 1537, and the grounds were damaged from the kilns, which had burned seven hundred thousand of the required bricks. An additional one and a half million bricks were imported by river to the site where 450 workmen, all often paid overtime, swarmed about the estate to implement the legion changes Henry VIII had decided upon in the aftermath of his second wife's execution. Throughout the construction work, Hampton Court remained active as a royal residence. Gardeners and guardsmen worked outside the palace while priests, nobles, page boys, and ladies-in-waiting lived within. Katharine and Anne Bassett passed through the gatehouse and into the Base Court, where they might have heard or smelled seaweed-wrapped fish rolled in barrels to the nearby kitchens, where stews were made, pies baked, and fires tended. Officers of the palace spicery, in charge of the supply of fruit and herbs, and

73

of guarding the hugely expensive imported spices, jangled as they moved, for the palace larders, located next to the Base Court, were locked at night to make sure courtiers or their servants did not go on successful midnight snacking raids.

The Bassett sisters were, at least theoretically, to join the ranks of the ladies-in-waiting, fulfilling their mother's dreams for them. They each arrived with two new gowns, one in silk and another in damask, so that they could uphold their family's reputation by looking the part. Born into an old family of the Devonshire gentry, Katharine and Anne might have enjoyed the relatively quiet life of their elder half sisters Jane and Thomasina, who had avoided both court and wedlock in favor of a lifetime's grant of rooms at their ancestral home, the manor of Umberleigh. There, Jane Bassett busied herself with looking after her cow and horse, spoiling her greyhounds, who "liveth upon one of the beds day and night," and feuding with the local priest whom she repeatedly accused of stealing fish from the estate's lake.[2]

Jane and Thomasina had remained in Devon after their father's death and their stepmother's remarriage, whereas Katharine and Anne had gone with their mother Honor and their five full siblings across the English Channel to join her new household in Calais. As it had been in the 1st Lord Daubeney's lifetime, the French port city remained under English control. It was increasingly beleaguered both by the possibility of a French attack and by bitter sectarian divisions among its residents, which tormented the town's lord deputy and the girls' stepfather, Arthur Plantagenet, Viscount Lisle, an uncle of Henry VIII. He was so mentally exhausted by the port's difficulties that he battled with what we would now recognize as depression; as one of the viscount's correspondents put it, "[I]t grieveth me not a little that you are weary of life."[3] Arthur, referred to as "My Lord the Bastard" since his birth out of wedlock to one of Edward IV's mistresses, had given Katharine and Anne access to a wider network of privileged contacts than had their natal family.[4] His unambiguous bastardy had rendered him safely irrelevant during the Wars of the Roses, and his genial nature kept him safe subsequently, serving first in the household of his half sister Elizabeth of York and then at the court of her son Henry VIII, who described his uncle as a man with "the gentlest heart living."[5] By contemporary standards, he had been a good stepfather to Katharine, Anne, and their siblings.

Like many in the Calais elite, the Bassetts' mores were caught somewhere between the cultures of their English birth and France, which surrounded their home on all sides. Anne Bassett, for instance, was bilingual, yet she could read and write only in French, cemented when their mother sent her daughters to a French convent to continue their schooling. The youngest of the Bassett sisters was referred to as Mary by her compatriots but always signed her letters with the French form, Marie. After the convent, Katharine had been brought back to Calais, where she lived with her mother, stepfather, and elder sister Philippa. Meanwhile, Anne and Marie were sent to complete their education in the households of French aristocrats, as were their brothers George and James. Honor's prioritizing of her younger daughters over the eldest was an indicator of her social ruthlessness— Anne and Marie were more beautiful than Philippa and Katharine, so their mother decided to focus on getting the younger pair to court.[6] Here, too, she looked to both sides of the Channel; Marie Bassett's guardian had recently presented her to Queen Eleanor of France, which had delighted Honor.[7] During her time in France, Marie had remained in regular contact with her family in Calais, writing often to Philippa and sending Katharine gifts she thought she would appreciate, including a copy of the Gospels.[8] Anne Bassett had no such intellectual interests—their mother despaired at Anne's preference for gambling at cards over the music or dancing lessons she would need to excel as a courtier.[9] Nevertheless, Anne's education in etiquette and social graces under her French guardian, a "good lady, who is of noble descent and of a very great house," had included accompanying her patroness on a 246-mile journey across France to look after the woman's daughter during the final stages of a pregnancy.[10] Although Anne was less intelligent than Katharine, she was better educated, by contemporary standards, more beautiful, and certainly more widely travelled, and Honor wanted to launch her into life at the English court. However, in June 1536 the matriarch's plans ran into an obstacle when Henry VIII's new queen, Jane Seymour, vetoed Lady Lisle's petition on the grounds that Anne, at fourteen, was too young to join the Queen's household as a maid of honor.[11] Lady Lisle shifted her focus to the overlooked Katharine, whom the Queen judged to be "of sufficient age," only to receive the upsetting news less than a week later that Queen Jane had changed her mind again and awarded the position to Katharine's cousin Mary Arundell.[12]

All this had happened within a few weeks of Jane Seymour's marriage to Henry VIII in May 1536, and it struck Lady Lisle as a worrying harbinger of what lay ahead for her relatives. The unexpected and meteoric rise of the Seymour family that spring had spelled potential disaster for the Lisles and the Bassetts. First, one of their main previous allies at court had been Henry Norris, executed for alleged adultery with Queen Anne, whose favor had also been assiduously courted by Lady Lisle with gifts of monkeys and songbirds. The latter had been a triumph, "which doth not cease at no time to give her Grace rejoicing with her pleasant song"; it helped to atone for the self-inflicted disaster of the monkey, since "her Grace loveth no such beasts nor can scant abide the sight of them."[13] Secondly, after years of network building with Norris and Boleyn, the family's allies had been replaced by former enemies: three years earlier, Lord Lisle had been involved in a fractious dispute over contested land in Somerset and Devon with a minor courtier named Edward Seymour, Jane's eldest brother. Now he was Viscount Beauchamp.* Nothing if not resilient, Lady Lisle found another songbird, which she gifted to Lord Beauchamp; it was received not quite so poorly as Anne Boleyn's monkey, since Beauchamp loved the warbling bird—until a peckish feline evidently preferred a meal to a melody and ate the viscount's new pet, a loss which Beauchamp "took right grievously."[14]

An intentional avian appetizer did, however, serve Lady Lisle well with the Seymours. During Queen Jane's pregnancy, she and the King had asked the Lisles to send quails from Calais, which they specified should leave Calais in good health before they were killed on arrival in England to ensure that they were fresh when served at the royal table.[15] Once more, a feathered faux pas nearly grounded Lady Lisle's ambitions,

---

* Pronounced "Beecham."

since both the King and the Queen thought the first batch of birds had been too thin, ordering "that your ladyship shall hereafter send them [that] be very fat, or else they are not worth the thanks."[16] The next tribute of cross-Channel quails was more satisfyingly plump and, in what seems unlikely to have been a coincidence, were served to Queen Jane when her table was waited on by Lady Lisle's niece, the Countess of Sussex, and family friend the Countess of Rutland. Lady Sussex was the former Mary Arundell, whom Queen Jane had chosen a year earlier instead of Katharine Bassett. The Countess's wedding had left a vacancy in the Queen's household, where the maids of honor were always unmarried girls from noble backgrounds, sent to court so that the Queen could act as both their chaperone and matchmaker. Over the roasted quails, the two countesses suggested that Katharine Bassett fill Lady Sussex's place among the maidens, and, pushing their luck, tried also to win an extra place for her younger sister. Anne had been too young the previous June, but she was sixteen by 1537. There were limits to the Queen's post-quail bonhomie, however, and she refused to be flattered into expanding her household's size beyond its set limits. As the letter to Lady Lisle in Calais relayed, "the matter is thus concluded that your ladyship shall send them both over, for her Grace will first see them and know their manners, fashion, and conditions, and take which one of them shall like her Grace best, and they must be sent over about vi [six] weeks hence."[17]

Katharine and Anne Bassett thus entered Hampton Court in a spirit of unwilling competition, to be directly compared with each other to see which of them would, in the course of one short meeting, win Queen Jane's favor. The sisters were escorted under the Anne Boleyn Gate and into the Clock Court, bypassing the nearby chapel in whose windows a stained glass rendering of the Virgin Mary's mother, Saint Anne, had recently been replaced by one of Saint John the Evangelist, the new Queen's patron saint.[18] In the palace gardens, the Boleyns' heraldic leopard had been given a fresh coat of paint and a spate of stonemasons' orthodontics to become the Seymours' panther—a sight familiar to the Bassetts, since the same animal was part of their stepfather's coat of arms. They were brought upstairs to see the Queen, who was in residence in the rooms Anne Boleyn had occupied while she waited for her apartments to be finished. Those had been completed on schedule; however, new stained glass and some reconfigured anthropomorphic heraldry could not apparently exorcise the spirit of the apartments' original owner. Even though Anne Boleyn had died only a few weeks after the new Queen's Apartments were completed, the entire wing was soon under construction again, gutting much of Anne's designs.[19]

Physically, Queen Jane, whom Parliament loyally described as "chaste, pure, and fertile," was pale and of medium height.[20] The girls' stepfather was told by a friend at court that the new Queen was gentle and kind; some courtiers dissented, though, thinking her "proud and haughty"—a tactic that they cynically suspected she had adopted to hide her inferior intellect.[21] Others suggested the opposite: namely, that Jane had prioritized her safety over an advertisement of her natural intelligence, a conclusion tellingly reached by the Emperor's ambassador to England, Eustace Chapuys, who seemingly revised his previously contemptuous assessment of Jane's intellect after several conversations with her.[22] Other observers noticed, too, that Jane was "firm" when it came to dealing with her servants, and applauded her dignity and circumspection.[23]

Since marrying into the royal family, Jane Seymour had always been magnificently dressed. Even the dolls that Queen Jane liked to collect were clothed expensively, one in a "gown of white cloth of silver and a kirtle of green velvet . . . [and] two little [doll] babies, one in crimson satin and one in white velvet."[24] But when Katharine and Anne Bassett curtsied before her in September 1537, the Queen had made a concession to her comfort and her health, with her dress unlaced as she entered the final month of pregnancy. On the subject of clothes, at the sisters' first audience with her, Queen Jane made clear her disapproval at the Gallic cut of French-educated Anne's gown.[25] The remark was subsequently exaggerated into a claim that, as queen, Jane Seymour waged a sartorial campaign against the French fashions favored by her predecessor who, like Anne Bassett, had been educated in France. Specifically, Jane allegedly banned the French hood—a round headdress that curved around the back of the head with a veil flowing down behind it—which an unverifiable tradition holds was popularized in England by Anne Boleyn. According to the traditional story, Jane pettily insisted that the ladies of the court favor the more conservative English gable hood, the style of headdress worn by Queen Jane in all her known portraits. Henry VIII's surviving inventories, however, list French hoods owned by Queen Jane, including one decorated with emeralds.[26] Therefore, it seems unlikely that Queen Jane ever banned the French hood at court, but some other unspecified element of Anne Bassett's outfit seemed inappropriate to the Queen. On such a detail, Katharine Bassett might have emerged as the Queen's new maid of honor, but it was not to be. Once again, the younger Bassett proved the favorite. Jane wanted the younger Bassett to serve her. Katharine would have to be found a place elsewhere or go home. Conscious of how expensive new clothes were, the Queen said that Anne could wear out her current dresses—only afterward should her mother commission clothes for her in the English style.[27]

Their family's friends escorted the sisters to another part of the palace to digest the news that Anne would join the Queen's household and to decide what to do about Katharine. Their cousin Lady Sussex gave Katharine a taffeta gown to try to lift her spirits, and the Lisles' agent in London, John Husee, was touched by the Countess's kindness, telling Lady Lisle that Sussex was "very good and loving" to the sisters.[28] Katharine still hoped that she might be able to stay at court, perhaps in service to the King's eldest daughter.[29] In the interim, the Countess of Rutland took Katharine in as one of her attendants, and another relative, Lady Jane Dudley, "highly feasted your ladyship's said daughters, with right good dishes and great cheer."[30] Then the Queen changed her mind about a specific element of her offer. Regardless of the expense to the Lisles in replacing them, Jane did not want to see Anne wearing French clothes in her presence again. Lady Sussex gave her cousin outfits to wear in the meantime, despite general agreement that the English headdresses did not flatter Anne as much as those she had brought with her. As Husee told her mother with somewhat remarkable honesty, "I saw her yesterday in her velvet bonnet that my Lady Sussex had [at]tired her in, and methought it became her nothing so well as the French hood; but the Queen's pleasure must needs be fulfilled."[31] Katharine Bassett's lack of education in courtly manners was also a concern. Even though Katharine remained in the entourage of Lady Rutland rather than the Queen, Lady Lisle was asked to send over an etiquette guide for her along with the new clothes for Anne.[32]

As one of the Queen's maids of honor, Anne was provided accommodation in the Maidens' Chamber, which, at Hampton Court, was likely located in a ground floor room on the east-facing side of the Anne Boleyn Gate. All six of the maids shared a bedroom, with three beds for the six. They were watched over by "the Mother of the Maids," the grim Mrs. Stonor, whose previous assignment had been to serve and spy on Anne Boleyn during her imprisonment, and who had a vaguely similar role as informant and guardian to the maids; it was partly Mrs. Stonor's responsibility that the young women's reputations remain intact until the Queen, as their chaperone and patron, helped find them a husband at court who met with their parents' approval. At some point in the next week or two, Anne was given the privilege of a small bedroom of her own, for which her mother sent over new bedding.[33]

On Saturday, September 9, Anne placed her hands on the Bible to swear loyalty and obedience as a member of the Queen's household.[34] The next Sunday, she performed her first public duty when she accompanied Queen Jane to the rooms prepared for her confinement, the "taking to her chamber," through which the Queen removed herself from public and male company in the final stages of her pregnancy. With the other ladies of the household, Anne Bassett accompanied her queen through the palace to the doors where Jane formally took leave of everyday life. Every window bar one had been covered with fabric, blocking out light into rooms decorated with plain tapestries, lest allegorical figures induce delirium during childbirth; even the hangings of her bed were of a single pattern. The doors closed on Queen Jane, her midwives, and her women, while the court waited the next few weeks in nervous expectation of a prince. As a newcomer and an un-married virgin, Anne Bassett does not seem to have been on duty regularly during the Queen's isolation, known as her confinement.

Naturally, there were concerns about the Queen's well-being. Made-leine, Queen of Scots, had died earlier that summer, leaving King James without an heir. Anne Bassett was aware of the complexities of pregnancy, since they had recently affected her own family. Only a few months before, their mother had been about to order a cradle for a new child when, some-time after the middle of March, Lady Lisle realized it had been a phantom pregnancy.[35] Like many early modern women, Henry VIII's mother had died in childbed, and there was sympathy for the dangers faced in bearing children. That concern went only so far when it came to royal women, how-ever, and the pressure on all queens consort to give birth to a healthy male heir was never exactly subtle.[36] It was considered a duty.

Even in this context, the pressure on Jane Seymour was exceptional. In part, this was because of the tragedies endured by her two immediate pre-decessors, who, if not specifically brought down by their lack of sons, had certainly been left vulnerable by it. Jane's womb was also expected to fix the chaos created by her husband's whims. He had disinherited his daughter by Katherine of Aragon in 1533 and his daughter by Anne Boleyn in 1536, removing both ex-princesses from the line of succession, although they were still received at court intermittently depending on their father's fluctuat-ing affection toward them. Crucially, he never questioned their paternity. Henry's only acknowledged bastard, the Duke of Richmond, had died ei-ther from the plague, tuberculosis, or a combination of both in 1536, the same year that the King's senior legitimate niece had been imprisoned in the Tower of London for eloping with one of Anne Boleyn's uncles. This meant that between Anne Boleyn's execution—or, more specifically, her daughter Elizabeth's disinheritance—and Jane Seymour's giving birth, there was no clear heir to the English throne. While none was confirmed, all could contest. If Henry VIII suffered a stroke or heart attack, or fell off his horse, who came next? His legitimate, royal, but foreign nephew King

James V of Scots? A strong body of opinion in England argued that the throne could never pass to a foreigner, although this was contested by those citing as precedent the country's conquest by William of Normandy in 1066 and the subsequent reigns of kings William II, Stephen, and Henry II. All of whom had been born in territory that was neither part of, nor held by, the English Crown.[37] If not James of Scotland, then, would the throne pass to Henry's disgraced niece from the senior royal line or the obedient, married niece in the junior? Propriety favored the latter, primogeniture* the former. What about his daughters: the elder ex-princess conceived before the break with Rome or the younger one born after it? Or why not some prominent noble born in England and in wedlock, with a Y chromosome and royal ancestry, such as Richard III's great-nephew Lord Montagu? Not all these claims were equally credible, yet thanks to the King's erratic private life and his refusal to craft a contingency for the succession, none was impossible. That the period between May 1536 and October 1537 did not result in civil war, with the probable supplement of an invasion by Scotland, is due solely to the biographical quirk that Henry VIII did not die during that period and the biological quirk that Queen Jane gave birth to a boy at the end of it.

The three and a half weeks of Queen Jane's confinement at Hampton Court gave Anne Bassett time to acclimatize herself not only to the palace at which she was a newcomer but also to the homeland she had last seen as a child. The Catholic England of her childhood was, if not quite dead and buried, in extremely poor health. The theological nature of the new Church of England was becoming increasingly receptive to Protestant ideas and seemingly impervious to opposition, of which there was much initially, especially at the closure of the country's larger monasteries and pilgrimage centers. Rumor had it that Queen Jane's sympathies lay with the conservatives. Some even thought, though this seems a stretch, that she hoped for

---

* Inheritance passing to the firstborn or first son of the previous incumbent. Failing that, to the next in line in the same family.

her country's reconciliation with the Vatican.[38] Realizing that such opinions risked alienating her husband's affections, she either changed her mind or muzzled her thoughts. Anne Bassett's parents were, like the Queen, silent conservatives, who watched the terrible fates doled out to those who shared their sympathies but not their silence. The north of England had risen in rebellion against the Reformation the year before, attracting enough support that the 1536–37 insurrection known as the Pilgrimage of Grace was the closest the Tudor dynasty ever came to being overthrown by its own subjects. Neutralized by the King's tactical mendacity—promises of pardons and parlay—the rebels dispersed long enough for soldiers to arrive and brutalize the North, executing thousands of those who had been promised mercy if they laid down their arms. One of the rebellion's leaders was hanged in chains outside the gates of York to rot toward death.[39] Ireland, too, had erupted into the first of its many religiously motivated troubles. This had likewise proved serious for the government, as most of the Irish eastern seaboard, bar the port city of Waterford, sided with the rebellion.[40] The leader of that uprising was the dashing, harp-playing "Silken" Thomas FitzGerald, Earl of Kildare.* Neither the guile employed nor the grief engendered by the government were too different from those used against the North. In both cases, Henry had dispatched unprecedented orders to his deputies that it was acceptable for them to kill women and children in order to punish the rebellions.[41] The results were later boasted of in letters to and from.[42] In return for surrendering, Lord Kildare was promised safe conduct to London, which, to his cost, he trusted.[43] He was executed alongside five of his uncles in 1537.

With the north of England and the east of Ireland cowed back into obedience, the monasteries in England and Wales continued to close, as did the shrines and pilgrimage centers. The vast amounts of land confiscated from the abbeys were bought by or gifted to supporters of the Reformation or, as was the case with the Church lands near Hampton Court, absorbed by the Crown, which turned them into one of the largest hunting demesnes in Eu-

---

* Formerly Lord Offaly, he had succeeded his father as earl in December 1534.

rope. Hampton Court Chase was a ten-thousand-acre royal estate sprawling to include not just the palace but several other hunting lodges and smaller residences. It gave the King an opportunity to ride out on the days when he was not needed in council. Like all the monastic orders, Hampton Court's former owner, the Order of the Knights Hospitaller, ceased to have a presence in England, with the Brothers either renouncing their vows under the government's amnesty to end monasticism or choosing to become religious refugees in Scotland or Europe.

The King frequently spent the night at one of his homes that lay within the Chase, many of them also former assets of the Catholic Church. We do know that he was back at Hampton Court itself during the first week of October, when he noticed Anne Bassett for the first time. He remarked on her beauty to some of his attendants, including a friend of the Bassetts, a courtier named Peter Mewtas, who replied that Anne's sister Marie was even more beautiful—a comment for which he later apologized to Lord Lisle in a letter, with the explanation that he made the joke before he realized it might seem an insult to Anne.[44] Henry VIII had commented on his wife's ladies-in-waiting before. A week after his wedding to Queen Jane, he had pointed to two of the prettiest and told his gentlemen that he regretted not spotting them before he proposed to Jane.[45]

No other woman mattered to Henry when, on Friday, October 12, Hampton Court awoke in the small hours to the news that the Queen had been safely delivered of a son, after an agonizing three-day labor. It was the eve of the Feast of Saint Edward the Confessor, the eleventh-century English king whose cult had, thus far, escaped the Reformation's attentions. The date decided the baby's name. Hampton Court stood as the epicenter of a rejoicing that spread outward through a divided country, desperate for certainty after the instability of the past decade. The Bishop of Worcester earnestly compared the baby's arrival to the nativity of Saint John the Baptist, Christ's prophetic kinsman who had been born to saints Elisabeth and Zechariah after their many painful years of infertility.[46] One of the King's nieces from the favored junior branch of the family, Frances Grey, Marchioness of Dorset, told her uncle that it was "the most joyful news, and glad tidings, that came to England these many years."[47] Admittedly, Lady Dorset was unlikely to express a different opinion from Edward's parent, especially not when said parent was Henry VIII, but her reaction was mirrored or magnified by most of her compatriots. On receiving the news that the Queen was pregnant, the town of Dover had lit celebratory bonfires; the response when the pregnancy produced a son was euphoric.[48] Colleges at Cambridge gave handsome rewards to the messengers who brought them the news from Hampton Court. The southern and western ports organized parades. Pageants were held in the towns and cities in the east part of the kingdom, with apples, bread, nuts, and wine provided for the revellers. In the capital, the mayor rode through the streets "thanking the people and praying them to give laud and praise to God for our prince" as a two-thousand-gun salute thundered from the parapets of the Tower. St. Paul's Cathedral led the city churches with the ringing of bells that pealed over the sounds of the musicians who took to the streets to play for the people. The rest of London's church bells tolled from the moment the news was announced in the morning until ten o'clock that night; services of thanksgiving were offered within.[49] Celebratory bonfires lit up the afternoon and evening, while wine and beer were distributed to the crowds at the city's expense.[50]

Patriotism mingled with a touch of xenophobia in those rejoicing that Queen Jane's English ancestry meant that no "strange blood" flowed in Prince Edward's veins, and, because of his gender, there was no possibility of marrying a foreign king or prince who might subjugate England to his homeland.[51] Whatever ballads might have been sung mocking her at the time of her elevation to the throne, Queen Jane was now widely celebrated as mother of the heir.[52]

Anne Bassett needed more new clothes. This time the royal household would settle the bill. Chamberlains doled out yards upon yards of precious fabric to the Queen's ladies-in-waiting with instructions to make dresses for themselves to wear to the christening that Monday. Anne Bassett was one of three hundred courtiers handed tapers of virgin wax to light the baby's way to Hampton Court's chapel as he was carried in the arms of his godmother and half sister, Mary Tudor. Held by another courtier, Anne Boleyn's four-year-old child, Elizabeth, clutched a processional candle on the first occasion she had seen her father since he ordered her mother's execution. The Archbishop of Canterbury and the Duke of Norfolk were asked to stand as the Prince's godfathers around the solid silver octagonal font commissioned for the occasion, while the Garter King of Arms called out the titles of Edward, Duke of Cornwall and Earl of Chester.[53] The Queen's eldest brother, elevated from Viscount Beauchamp to Earl of Hertford, helped escort his infant nephew back through the palace to his mother's rooms, since, following a custom laid down in the sixth century, biological parents did not attend their children's christenings.

The day after her son's baptism, the Queen hosted a party for four hundred guests. Afterward, Anne Bassett and the other women were allowed down to the courtyards, where the palace fountains were still pumping red wine.[54] A few days later, Queen Jane developed diarrhea due to a postnatal infection, and she began to hemorrhage.[55] Her frightened servants were blamed for giving Jane to eat "such things that her fantasy in sickness called for" although, in reality, nothing they gave the Queen could have hastened or prevented her end.[56] Ironically, Jane may have been damned to this agony by her exalted position, for doctors in the royal household, all of them more familiar with academic texts than practical experience of childbed, had shunted the midwives to one side in order to claim a share of the glory for the birth of a prince.[57] Debate continues among historians about the precise nature of Jane's illness—some unextracted placenta that produced septicemia is the most popular modern theory—but all agree that something terrible occurred during Prince Edward's birth, the results of which did not become clear until a week later.[58]

The celebrations at Hampton Court shuddered to a halt. Eight days after the christening, a rumor shot through the palace that the Queen was dead.[59] At sunrise the next day, the story was dispelled or, rather, delayed as the Bishop of Carlisle, the Queen's "ghostly father"—a contemporary colloquialism for her confessor—was brought to her apartments to administer the sacrament of Extreme Unction, more commonly known as the Last Rites. The King seemed either unwilling to accept reality or staggeringly callous. He wanted to leave for another hunting trip. This may have reflected a more complicated attitude toward death and bereavement: following the Bishop's visit to the Queen, Henry told courtier Sir John Russell that if his wife did not improve, "he could not find it in his heart to stay."[60] Henry's chief minister, Thomas Cromwell, had gone into London during the celebrations, and the Duke of Norfolk, who stayed at Hampton Court, sent a messenger by river with a letter for Cromwell that advised him to return to the palace at once.[61] In Norfolk's estimation, there was a good chance that the Queen would be dead even by the time his message reached Cromwell.

He was right. The Queen died at Hampton Court shortly before midnight on October 24, twelve days after her son's birth. No surviving source mentions Henry VIII being at her bedside during her final hours.[62] The fountains stopped, the church bells tolled for the departure of a soul, and the chamberlains returned with fabric for mourning. Shortly after the morticians arrived, every window in the Queen's rooms had been removed to air the fumes that accompanied the embalming process. When that was finished, the corpse was taken to the palace chapel, where ladies from Jane's entourage, including Anne Bassett, kept vigil in shifts for the next week. At nightfall on November 8, the body was brought to the courtyard. A lifelike wax effigy of the late Queen, garbed in her royal robes and wearing a crown, topped the coffin. Among the forest of torches lighting the way, there were twenty-nine unnamed maidens—Anne Bassett was almost certainly one of them—clutching a taper, one for each year of Jane Seymour's earthly life. As they had lit the Prince's way to his christening, the flames illuminated the path as the Queen's cortege moved off from Hampton Court for her funeral at Windsor.

CHAPTER 5

THE GREAT
WATCHING CHAMBER

Yet must you give men leave to look, for they will look upon you.

—Jane Boleyn, the Dowager Viscountess Rochford (1541)

Various colorful and often contradictory stories exist to explain the origins of most colloquialisms. According to one, defecating acquired the euphemism of "doing your business" thanks to places such as the House of Common Easement at Hampton Court, also known as the Great House of Ease. It contained two rows, each with fourteen toilets, none of which was separated from each other into a self-contained cubicle.* As people sat next to one another in the Great Ease, they discussed the business of court, and hence—allegedly—the phrase "doing your business" was coined. Christmas was an especially fruitful time for topics of conversation in the Great House. Over the twelve days, which ran from Christmas Day on December 25 to the Feast of the Epiphany on January 6, also known as Twelfth Night or Kings' Day, hundreds of aristocrats, as well as members of the gentry, the clergy, and their servants, descended on whichever palace the royal household had chosen for Yuletide.

---

* Their excrement fell into water below, which was walled off to then be released into the adjacent river at high tide; it was prevented from floating back into the palace moat by a sluice.

Courtiers were, almost without exception, members of the landed classes, which meant that they derived much of their income from their estates. Thus, many were allowed to leave the court during late summer and early autumn to oversee their properties in the countdown to harvest at Michaelmas, the Feast of Saints Michael, Gabriel, and Raphael, the Archangels. During those months, the King reduced his entourage as he went hunting at his smaller rural residences.[1] Some courtiers rejoined the court after Michaelmas in October or Martinmas (Feast of Saint Martin) in mid-November, when estates that depended on livestock typically selected which animals to cull before winter and which to move into barns.[2] More returned in time for the Christmas round of merrymaking, gift giving, and networking, particularly for the raucous parties on Twelfth Night.

Among those returning for the Christmas of 1540–41 was Lord William Howard, who arrived at Hampton Court for the Tenth Day. Trim and athletic, he rode on horseback, accompanied by the few servants who he was entitled by court rules to bring with him, passing the Great Ease on his right just before he rode through the entrance gate. William Howard's exact date of birth is unknown, although the year was probably 1510. He was the 3rd Duke of Norfolk's much younger brother, a Cambridge graduate, a veteran of both diplomatic and military campaigns, "a very valiant person," father to two children, and, at the age of about thirty, married for the second time after losing his first wife in childbirth.[3] His second wife, Margaret, the daughter of a Welsh landowner, was in residence at Hampton Court as one of the Queen's ladies-in-waiting.[4] The queen in question was William's niece, Catherine Howard. He seems to have been her favorite uncle, and they had last been in each other's company only a few weeks earlier, when Lord William came to court at Halloween.*[5]

William was accompanied that Christmas by Anne of Cleves, the twenty-five-year-old German princess who had married Henry VIII twelve

---

* The two days after Halloween—All Hallows, or All Saints, and All Souls—were days of spiritual significance in the Church calendar and All Saints was marked at court with a High Mass publicly attended by the King and Queen.

months earlier and been divorced by him six months after that.* Nineteen days after their annulment, Henry had married Lord William's niece, one of Anne's maids of honor. A journey to Hampton Court with the woman supplanted by his niece was not a prospect that Lord William relished. But, a fellow diplomat explained later, William had encountered the former queen on the road and felt he "could not well, for courtesy's sake, refuse to accompany her to the gates."[6] Anne of Cleves was travelling from Richmond Palace, the largest of several magnificent properties gifted to her by her former husband in alleged gratitude for her cooperation with his annulment suit.[7]

A queen for six months, Anne of Cleves had never been given the opportunity to visit Hampton Court before she lost her crown. Tall, pale, with a long nose and no longer considered too thin, she had once been mocked by English courtiers for her atrocious dress sense—specifically, the clothes she had brought with her from her German home city of Düsseldorf, which they cruelly described behind her back as "monstrous . . . apparel."[8] In the months since the end of her farcically short marriage, Anne had become fluent in English, recovered her appetite, discovered a love of wine, and bought a new wardrobe of expensive gowns in French and English styles. When she and her entourage dismounted from their horses in the palace courtyard, she was greeted by a delegation headed by the Duchess of Suffolk, another of her former ladies-in-waiting. The Duchess escorted Anne into Hampton Court, which was, a decade after it had come into royal possession, finished at last to Henry VIII's specifications, with his £62,000 worth of investment catalogued in 6,500 pages of expenses.[9]

Lord William headed inside separately, where the story of his accidental rendezvous with the former queen was good for a giggle with many of his fellow revellers. Charles V's ambassador, Eustace Chapuys, could not yet

---

* In modern terms, Henry VIII was technically never divorced. His marriages ended with annulments, retrospectively declaring them to never have been legally valid; in contrast, a divorce implies the ending of a marriage that was legal until its dissolution. In early modern sources, the terms *divorce* and *annulment* are often used interchangeably, as the modern concept of a divorce was then unavailable under canon law.

afford to see the humor in the situation. He had served as his emperor's representative in England for a decade from 1529, returning briefly to his home on the Continent in 1539 until Charles V decided that he could not do without Chapuys's expertise and politely yet firmly coaxed him out of retirement and back across the Channel.[10] In London, Chapuys returned to his old life of writing in ciphers, missing his son, paying informants, guessing which of his dinner guests were spies, keeping the Hapsburgs abreast of developments at the English court, and paying exorbitant sums for his favorite Swiss cheese and French wine to be imported from the Continent. His master was worried by the implications of Henry VIII's Christmas invitation to Anne of Cleves, whose brother Duke Wilhelm of Cleves proved a constant headache to Hapsburg rule in Germany with his alliances to other prominent anti-Hapsburg families.[11] Was it possible that Henry was planning to set aside Catherine Howard and restore Anne of Cleves? Publicly, Anne appeared content with her demoted situation; privately, when she had discovered that Henry wanted to end their marriage, a friend observed, "Good Lord, she made such tears and bitter cries, it would break a heart of stone."[12] Chapuys, whose understanding of Henry VIII was shrewder than most, thought that those spreading rumors that the Hampton Court Christmas summons was a prologue to Anne's restoration as queen were betraying their ignorance of Henry's personality, since Henry never returned to those he had abandoned.[13] If, however, he was wrong about a possible Clevian triumph, Chapuys promised his masters, "I will seize every opportunity of indirectly thwarting it."[14] If necessary, he intended to torpedo Anne's reputation to ensure that an anti-Hapsburg rebel did not have a queen of England for a sister. Yet he was not initially much impressed by Catherine Howard, whom he first met at a formal audience at Hampton Court on December 6.[15]

Chapuys, like everybody else at Hampton Court that Christmas, wondered how Queen Catherine would, or even could, handle the manners minefield of hosting her predecessor. Described as a "great beauty" by a palace servant, the new Queen was about eighteen or nineteen years old in 1541.[16] Glittering in the treasure trove of jewelry gifted to her by her husband, she presided over the Christmas court with a mastery of etiquette that eventually impressed even the cynical Chapuys.[17] Catherine's manners were flawless, as she proved when she deftly handled the reunion with Anne of Cleves by showering her with gifts and attention. The two queens danced together on Twelfth Night, possibly in the Great Watching Chamber: a long room at the end of the Great Hall with stained glass windows three times a man's height, an enormous fireplace casting out light and warmth into a room decorated with tapestries, and capped by a gold and white ceiling interspersed with Henry's coat of arms and that of the late Jane Seymour.[18] The room was used far more often for festivities during Henry VIII's reign than the cavernous adjacent Great Hall itself. Different doors led off from the Watching Chamber to the King's private apartments, back into the Great Hall, to a servants' corridor leading down to the kitchens, and to a gallery leading to the east and south sections of the palace. A final door led to a toilet for members of the court who found themselves too far from the House of Easement. Palace rules stipulated: "Being all alone, [you may] let it go, otherwise you must disguise the sound by coughing." The musicians perhaps drowned out any suspicious coughing sounds from the far end of the room as the Queen danced with Anne of Cleves.

Although the new calendar year did not start until March 25, the secular and European New Year date of January 1 was sometimes used by the English court as an excuse for another round of presents. If the Queen and King wished, etiquette permitted them to receive their new year's gifts in their private chambers—even from their enormous beds.[19] The royals traditionally gave back more in gifts than they received, and the reciprocity of dazzling presents punctuated a Christmas court that tried as much as possible to avoid dangerous topics of conversation. The French ambassador had noticed a few months earlier that ever since Queen Catherine's marriage into the royal family, "Nothing [is] spoken of here but the chase [hunting] and the banquets to the new Queen."[20]

It was safer to talk about one another than about God or the King and so gossip thrived. Sir William Parr's wife had run off to have an illegitimate child with a defrocked priest, and Lord Cobham's sister Elizabeth was living apart from her husband, Thomas Wyatt, after he had allegedly caught her in bed with another man. While claiming heartbreak, Wyatt had since had at least two affairs of his own.[21]

The new Queen's relatives were out in force that Christmas—although there were so many Howards that as much is true of nearly any given moment at the English court for most of the sixteenth and seventeenth centuries. Her cousin Henry Howard, Earl of Surrey, was a poet and equestrian, "witty and learned to a high degree." Her brother Charles, a skilled swordsman, had recently been appointed to the King's staff as a gentleman of the Privy Chamber, the elite band of gentlemen-in-waiting who attended to Henry VIII in his private rooms and often became closer to the monarch than his chief advisers.[22] Henry preferred to surround himself with youth and vitality, so Charles Howard joined a Privy Chamber dominated by young men such as Thomas Culpepper and Thomas Paston, whose jobs as the King's closest attendants required them to be well spoken, familiar with palace etiquette, dancing, and sports.[23] That Christmas, some Privy Chamber gentlemen were among those invited to dance with Queen Catherine and the former Queen Anne.

Also present was well-meaning and unremarkable Gregory Cromwell, judged "so weak, that he was almost thought a fool," facing his first Christmas without his father, Thomas, the King's former chief minister who had been executed for treason, corruption, and heresy in July.[24] The axe had fallen on the same day that the King and Catherine were married. Seven days before Christmas, Gregory was ennobled at Hampton Court in his own right as Baron Cromwell, a partial rehabilitation probably secured by or for his wife, Elizabeth—Jane Seymour's younger sister.[25] In the three years since Jane's death, the Seymours had remained one of the great families at court, their position secured by the survival of Jane's son as heir to the throne. Elizabeth Cromwell was a lady-in-waiting to Queen Catherine; her brother Edward, Earl of Hertford, was one of the King's most influential councillors; and a younger brother, the promiscuous Sir Thomas, enjoyed court life. There had been talk of a marriage between Thomas Seymour and Queen Catherine's cousin Mary, Dowager Duchess of Richmond, who was unenthusiastic at the suggestion, and with good reason.[26] Scandal seemed to follow Thomas Seymour; for instance, that summer, the King had reprimanded him for challenging another courtier to a brawl. Meanwhile, a woman arrested for theft included in her testimony details of how Thomas had "first of all debauched her."[27]

The question of religion dominated life at Hampton Court, as it did the rest of the country. The King had lurched in a more conservative direction theologically, a point that he underscored to the country by burning several radically Protestant preachers in public. The Seymours favored the Protestant—sometimes known as the reformist—cause, unlike their late sister Queen Jane. Queen Catherine, however, set the tone for the majority of courtiers with her conspicuous neutrality on matters of religion, walking the tightrope of the Catholic–Protestant hybrid established by Henry VIII. She attended Mass and kept feast days as required of her, without ever seeming so sympathetic to religious traditionalism that she could be accused of papism. She owned a copy of the New Testament in English, yet she did not personally interpret the Scriptures in any way that might lead to an accusation of heresy. Giles Daubeney's son was another pious pragmatist. The man who had transferred Hampton Court's lease to Cardinal Wolsey a quarter of a century earlier had so far survived the lethal progression of Henry VIII's reign, during which he had even been elevated through two rungs of the nobility to become Earl of Bridgewater. He was miserably married to Queen Catherine's aunt and namesake, Lady Katherine Howard. Neither Lord nor Lady Bridgewater felt compelled to hide how much they detested each other, and they had since separated.[28] We do not know what Lord Bridgewater made of his former home's transformation into one of Europe's most splendid palaces, but he was there that Christmas to make the New Year's gift of a solid silver spoon to King Henry.[29]

Eleven days after the Christmas festivities ended—with the former queen returning to Richmond and the new one still in residence at Hampton Court—Sir Thomas Wyatt, superb poet, subpar diplomat, and Elizabeth Cobham's estranged husband, was arrested at the palace on suspicion of treason and taken to the Tower of London. Wyatt's sudden loss of liberty was attributed to his reformist sympathies. To remind both factions that it was the King who remained in control of Church and government, Wyatt was joined in custody by Sir John Wallop, who was recalled as English ambassador to France to be arrested for his alleged loyalty to the Pope.[30] Wallop wept in tear-sodden apology for anything he had ever said or intimated that might have caused distress to his king.[31] The Queen's uncle William replaced him and prepared to depart for life in Paris. The ambassadors at Hampton Court noticed the terror beneath the courtiers' smiles, as they feared who might be next to be arrested.[32] The "fair and beloved" Queen Catherine, meanwhile, carried on with preparations for the forthcoming visit to Hampton Court of a Scottish diplomat, Sir James Campbell.[33] If she felt any twinge of unease at her husband's rapid turning of Fortune's wheel, she hid it brilliantly.

CHAPTER 6

THE HAUNTED GALLERY

You have heard of King Henry's amours, always
dissolute—sometimes fatal?

—Alexandre Dumas, *Catherine Howard* (1834)

For thirteen days in the autumn of 1541, a single corridor at Hampton Court was the nexus of a crisis. Now referred to as the Haunted Gallery, it originally ran from the King's and Queen's private apartments past their holy day closets—halfway down the gallery and on the right—to the Privy Council Chamber at the far end of the corridor. Although the apartments were demolished during renovations in the next century, the latter two rooms survive and can still be visited, as can the gallery connecting them. Many believers in the supernatural identify the gallery as the site of a screaming ghost or an oppressive feeling of dread, lingering from the misery of 1541.[1]

For Lady Margaret Douglas, Henry VIII's elegant twenty-six-year-old Anglo-Scottish niece, the fortnight of the crisis began with loss but without drama. She had been at a hunting lodge in Bedfordshire with her uncle's court when she received the news that her mother, the Dowager Queen Margaret of Scots, had died at her castle outside Edinburgh after a series of strokes.[2] No mourning seems to have been ordered in England for the late queen, and, if it was, its duration was short enough to have passed by the time the royal household returned to Hampton Court ten days after her death. Henry VIII was not close to his eldest sister. At one of her last public audiences, the Dowager Queen had told Henry's representative, "though I be forgot in England, shall I never forget England."[3] Henry had frequently rebuffed his sister's pleas for financial assistance and mocked her for disrespecting the sacrament with her numerous marriages, in which he ironically outnumbered her by a ratio of two to one.

Margaret Douglas was the only surviving child from the second of Queen Margaret's three marriages, which had ended when her Scottish father, Archibald Douglas, the 6th Earl of Angus, abducted her from her mother's care while she was still an infant. Angus took the child to England, where she eventually joined her uncle's court as a lady-in-waiting to Anne Boleyn.[4] Interested in the arts, especially literature, Lady Margaret had been an amanuensis to the poet Sir Thomas Wyatt, Cardinal Wolsey's goddaughter, and one of Anne Boleyn's favorites. She weathered Wyatt's imprisonment, Wolsey's disgrace, and Boleyn's execution only to end up first in the Tower of London and then rusticated to a convent in punishment for her secret betrothal to Boleyn's uncle, Lord Thomas Howard the younger.* He was also imprisoned, in what many privately thought to be an overreaction by Henry VIII, who claimed the romance proved that Howard had plotted either to seize the throne or to corrupt the line of succession.[5] Unlike Lady Margaret, Thomas did not live long enough to chance a pardon—he died of a fever in the Tower, aged twenty-five, and his body was only returned to his mother, the Dowager Duchess of Norfolk, on the condition that she bury him without pomp as a sign to the world that he had died in disgrace.[6] While the authorship of the poems attributed to Margaret Douglas is contested, there are credible grounds for believing that she composed, rather than simply transcribed, one which ends with a heart-tugging memory: "Of him that I have caused to die."[7]

Lady Margaret was received back at court and into the Queen's house-

---

* This was not Thomas Howard, 3rd Duke of Norfolk (1472–1554), but his much younger half brother (1511–37) with, confusingly, the same Christian name. In an era with a smaller pool of available names and large families, it was not uncommon for families to have two children with the same name. The Thomases Howard had two sisters named Elizabeth.

hold as one of the "Great Ladies": the blue-blooded half dozen who usually accompanied the Queen on state occasions. In practice, queens were closer to the eight women of their Privy Chamber or their nine Ladies Attendant, all of whom were in more regular contact with her than the higher-ranking Great Ladies. As the King's niece, Lady Margaret was one of the most comfortable residents at Hampton Court: her rooms, called a double lodging, included a private bedroom and garderobe, as well as a servant's room, and were located on the ground floor at the courtyard. Queen Catherine presented Margaret with a pair of earrings, so we can assume a friendly or at least polite relationship, but there is no evidence that they were particularly close.[8] In 1541 Margaret accompanied the Queen and the court on a June-to-October tour of the northern counties.

Around that time, Lady Margaret embarked upon a second romance with a member of the Howard family—this time with Queen Catherine's brother Charles, the King's attendant and the nephew of Margaret's dead fiancé.[9] Although it does not seem as if the relationship went as far as Margaret's liaison with Charles's late uncle Thomas, the behavior of the King's niece and the Queen's brother were nonetheless bound to attract attention, which in its turn gave rise to gossip.

The first day of November was the Feast of All Saints, a holy day of obligation in the liturgical calendar when the Queen, wearing her crown, walked in procession from her private apartments to her closet above the palace's public chapel to hear Mass with her ladies-in-waiting. For Queen Catherine, the All Saints' Mass turned into a triumph thanks to her husband's instructions to the officiating Bishop of Lincoln that he offer up prayers of thanksgiving for the King's happiness at "the good life he led" with the Queen.[10] The next day, the Feast of All Souls, or the Day of the Dead, was quieter; the day after that was enlivened by a rumor that one of the Queen's servants had been arrested at Hampton Court on a suspicion of piracy.[11] The man, Francis Dereham, had joined her household that summer. He had lived previously in Ireland, where he had allegedly committed his crime, and, before that, had been a ward of Queen Catherine's grandmother the Dowager Duchess of Norfolk. He served the Queen as a gentleman-usher, so it is entirely possible that Margaret Douglas had never taken notice of him. People like him opened doors for people like her. What need had she to pay any of them much attention until gossip rendered one of them unexpectedly interesting? Talk in the palace was that Francis Dereham "hath been noted before with that offence" of piracy.[12] None of the other servants liked Dereham very much—his braggadocio had already alienated some of his immediate superiors in the household—yet it still seemed excessive for him to have been sent to the Tower of London.[13] Cases of piracy in Ireland often simply entailed unregistered trade, in light of which Dereham's alleged crimes did not seemingly merit a cell in the Tower.[14]

Two more members of the Queen's household were then asked to answer questions by the Privy Council. The first, Katherine Tilney, was a relatively low-ranking chamberer—one of the maidservants who carried out basic housekeeping tasks such as tending the Queen's fires, tidying the apartments in the morning, and delivering messages. The second, far more unusually, was Queen Catherine's Welsh aunt, Lady Margaret Howard.[15] The entourage of the Queen's uncle the Duke of Norfolk was seen returning on horseback to the palace courtyards, even though the Duke was supposed to be in quarantine following the death of one of his servants from the plague. Norfolk was joined by the ailing and elderly Duke of Suffolk, who had recently received the King's permission to stay on his Lincolnshire estates until after Christmas and was not therefore expected back at court until the spring. Norfolk emerged agitated from a meeting in the Privy Council Chamber, which was noticed by those waiting in the gallery, as was the fact that the council was keeping odd, long hours, with many members going to and from the capital on unexplained errands.[16] Norfolk had recently been put in charge of inspecting fortifications along the northern border, which prompted speculation in the palace that there was about to be a declaration of war against Scotland. From Lady Margaret Douglas's perspective, that would be a headache, even though she would unquestionably have sided with England, as she did in most things.

There was also a rumor that there had been a rebellion in Ireland, yet the questioning of the Queen's aunt and one of her chamberers, as well as the detention of her gentleman-usher for alleged piracy, kept speculation focused on Catherine's entourage.[17] The French ambassador told his spies to watch Catherine's ladies-in-waiting, confident that their behavior would confirm for him what was happening. Andrew Pewson, a servant of the Queen's grandmother, arrived at Hampton Court on a specious errand that everybody could tell was an unconvincing cover for his attempt to truffle out information for his anxious employer back in London. The arrival at the palace of theologians corroborated the theory that Queen Catherine was in trouble, since biblical experts were usually the advance party for one of Henry VIII's matrimonial reconfigurations. Any doubt that something terrible was bearing down on the Queen's household was dispelled when Catherine herself was ordered to stay in her apartments and "whereas, before, she did nothing but dance and rejoice . . . now when the musicians come, they are told that it is no more the time to dance."[18]

Sounds of music gave way to screams of terror, if one of Hampton Court's most enduring legends is to be believed. On Sunday, November 6, the Archbishop of Canterbury, the two recalled dukes, and the Bishop of Winchester headed a delegation that was escorted up the stairs to the Queen's apartments. They told Catherine that they had uncovered evidence that, before she first came to court, she had been betrothed to Francis Dereham, the erstwhile pirate, and that she had lost her virginity to him—a combination of action with promise which, under contemporary canon law, meant the pair had entered into a binding precontract that made it legally questionable for either of them to marry anybody else. Previous rumors of Dereham's involvement with piracy in Ireland had given the Privy Council a convincing pretext to bring him in for questioning without arousing Queen Catherine's suspicions. As Lord Herbert of Cherbury put it later, the councillors deliberately set about "making these pretences to the intent [that] no spark of suspicion should rise of these Examinations" until they had enough evidence to confront Catherine.[19]

The Queen initially dismissed the councillors' claims as nonsense. At some point, not very long after, she descended into panic and gambled that the only way to save her position as queen was to reach her husband. She made a mad dash past the guards stationed outside her apartments and reached the gallery that led to where her husband was hearing Sunday Mass in his Holy Day Closet, overlooking the chapel. She very nearly made it. The guards caught up with her and dragged her, sobbing for mercy, back to her rooms. A story at Hampton Court holds that it is the sounds of Catherine Howard's screams that can be heard on occasion in the Haunted Gallery.

It is difficult to trace the origin of this horrible anecdote, as it does not seem to have any firm contemporary backing in the sources. Everything up to her dash can be corroborated. It fits with what we know of Catherine's mental well-being at that time, although the layout of her apartments and the route she would have taken from them to the gallery suggest that the way would have been difficult, if not quite impossible.[20] If it did happen, the only possible day was Sunday, November 6, 1541, in the narrow window of time between when Catherine was first told of the investigation into her private life and Henry's decision to go hunting in the Chase, after which he did not return to Hampton Court but spent the night at the Palace of Whitehall in the city. Eustace Chapuys was right. Henry did not return to those he had abandoned. Perhaps Queen Catherine knew that as well.

In the week that followed the King's departure, the Queen tottered on the edge of a nervous breakdown. The Archbishop of Canterbury called regularly to her rooms to quiz her about the accusations, which were growing so precise in detail and from so many eyewitnesses that it was logically impossible to disbelieve them in their entirety. Realizing that she was unlikely to survive the scandal as queen, some of Catherine's own staff turned against her by offering their services as spies for the Archbishop.[21] Chief among the turncoats was the Queen's thoroughly unpleasant brother-in-law and vice chamberlain, Sir Edward Baynton, who told him that when the Archbishop left her rooms, Catherine would try to withdraw certain details of her testimonies. She made three confessions to Archbishop Cranmer, one of which—by far the longest and the most detailed—she fatally tried to cancel.[22] The Archbishop let the Queen retract as and when she asked to do so, only for him to then cite the multiple inconsistencies in her testimonies as proof that she was hiding even greater secrets.[23] He left Hampton Court to give a full report to the King in London, and the palace was put under guard.

Sealed within, the remaining courtiers tried to make sense of what was happening. There still had been no official announcement. It does not seem from the surviving evidence that Lady Margaret Douglas was asked to testify against her mistress. Her lack of intimacy with Catherine saved her, while the opposite damned the Queen's favorite lady-in-waiting, Jane Boleyn, Dowager Viscountess Rochford, to interrogation, during which she suffered a mental collapse so severe that she was declared temporarily insane. Servants whispered that the Queen had committed bigamy— that she had secretly married Francis Dereham, or somebody else, before first coming to court in 1539. Scandal's magnetic attraction to exaggeration was on full display with the rumor that Queen Catherine had once had eight or nine lovers. She was barren, some concluded, and Anne of Cleves would soon be restored to the consort's throne; Catherine would be stripped of her title and sent to some rural backwater to rot into irrelevance. A delighted Anne seemed to believe this particular twist in the tale and moved her household back to Richmond to be conveniently close should her ex-husband send for her.[24]

The chance that Lady Margaret would be damaged by the terminal fragments of Catherine Howard's career heightened when her lover Charles was first barred from visiting his royal sister and then banished from court.[25] Catherine was escorted from her rooms and down a private staircase, through the gardens, and to a waiting boat. It bore her, with a reduced household of four ladies-in-waiting, to Syon Abbey, the disused riverside convent where Margaret Douglas had been detained after her disgrace five years earlier. Margaret was not one of the four selected to go with her. Queen Catherine almost certainly did not know as her barge rowed away that the Archbishop's suspicions had prompted a search of the room at Hampton Court occupied by Thomas Culpepper, one of her husband's favorite attendants, which unearthed a letter written to him by Queen Catherine. It contained phrases such as "I never longed for a thing so much as to see you" and "[I]t makes my heart to die to think what fortune I have that I cannot always be in your company."[26] It had been written after Catherine's marriage.

Lady Margaret may have been similarly unaware that Culpepper was also facing ruin and that the case against the Queen had changed focus from pre- to post-marital matters. On the day of Catherine's departure from Hampton Court, Lady Margaret joined the remaining staff as they gathered to hear that their jobs had been terminated. The royal household would pay a quarter of their annual wages, and those who had nowhere to go would be allowed to temporarily join the household of the King's daughter Mary, who was leaving Hampton Court for propriety's sake to go to the countryside, where she would lodge with her four-year-old half brother, Prince Edward. Lady Margaret, as the most senior member of the Tudor family left at Hampton Court after her cousin Mary, was told to go with Queen Catherine's widowed cousin, twenty-two-year-old Mary Fitzroy, Dowager Duchess of Richmond, who was retreating to Kenninghall, her father's country estate 125 miles away in Norfolk.[27]

Just after the declaration disbanding the Queen's household had been made, the Archbishop of Canterbury asked if he might have a word with Margaret. Her affair with Charles Howard had been noticed by her uncle, the King, or perhaps reported to him by the sycophantic or frightened, and Henry had sent explicit instructions for the Archbishop to put the fear of God, as it were, into Margaret. Henry ordered Archbishop Cranmer to "call a part unto you my Lady Margaret Douglas; and first declare unto her, how indiscreetly she hath demeaned herself toward the King's Majesty, first with the Lord Thomas, and now secondly with Charles Howard; in which part ye shall, by discretion, charge her with overmuch lightness, and finally give her advice to beware the third time."[28] With those "exhortations and good advice" ringing in her ears, Margaret Douglas went to Norfolk with the Dowager Duchess of Richmond, where the latter's father, the Duke of Norfolk, apparently treated her as an honored guest.

Twenty months later, on July 12, 1543, Margaret walked through the Haunted Gallery with fellow guests to her uncle's sixth and final marriage. It took place in the Queen's Holy Day Closet, next to the room to which, allegedly, Catherine Howard had been running to entreat Henry for a pardon. Since then, Catherine had been beheaded at the Tower of London on February 13, 1542, and her brother Charles had wisely fled all the way to Venice, where he set up home in a house manned by five armed servants.[29] Even if Charles Howard had remained in England and somehow clawed his way back into royal favor, it is unlikely that Margaret would have had any interest in a personal reconciliation. The Archbishop's chilling warning to "beware the third time" seems to have entered into her soul. Given what had happened to Queen Catherine, she can have been under no illusions about just how dangerous a romantic mésalliance could be for royal women.

The small wedding service at Hampton Court was presided over by the conservative Stephen Gardiner, Bishop of Winchester, with Margaret and her cousin Mary in attendance as the highest-ranking guests. Henry's sixth wife was a model of propriety. A dowager baroness twice over at the age of thirty-one, with no children, she is better known to history by her natal name of Katherine Parr. With long ginger hair and pale skin, she had "a lively and pleasing appearance, and is praised as a virtuous woman."[30] She was intelligent and dignified, with a love of luxury and fashion. The man who embroidered many of her gowns was French, her hatmaker was Italian, her jeweler was Dutch.[31] Her spaniel, Rig, wore a crimson velvet collar with gold thread detail, and her pet parrots were fed on hempseed. She preserved her complexion with milk baths for which her bath oils, almond oil, perfumes, and rose water accompanied her from palace to palace.[32] She understood French and Italian, though she was wobbly on Latin; she was an excellent dancer, interested in philosophy, and a keen collector of coins. As lady of the manor at Snape Hall in the northern county of Yorkshire during her second marriage, she had been in residence when the estate was occupied by the rebels of the Pilgrimage of Grace in their quest to overturn the Reformation. Katherine and her stepchildren had been held hostage, after which she developed a strong antipathy to the north of England.

It is unclear if that experience also played a role in Katherine's alien-
ation from religious traditionalism, nor is it certain when she, to all intents and purposes, became a Protestant. She was the first English queen
to write a published book, and her writings suggest a spiritual catharsis,
similar to something modern evangelical Christians might recognize as
the experience of being "born again," sometime around 1545. In her words,
Queen Katherine called it a moment when "I feel myself to come, as it
were, in a new garment before God."[33] Her first book, released in 1544, was
her translation from Latin into English of *Psalmi seu Precationes*, a biblical
commentary attributed to the Catholic theologian and martyr Cardinal
John Fisher. The next two—*Prayers or Meditations* (1545) and *The Lamentations of a Sinner* (1547)—were mostly Katherine's own words. Without
being too reductive, *Prayers or Meditations* is more Protestant than *Psalmi
seu Precationes*, and the evangelical evolution continues with *The Lamentation of a Sinner*, which articulates an unambiguously Protestant view of
salvation.

The fracture lines over the religious issue were drawn much more
clearly by the mid-1540s. The blurring in the 1520s and 1530s between con-
servativism and reformism, or evangelicalism and traditionalism—which
leaves as debatable the religious ideologies of Anne Boleyn, Jane Seymour,
and Anne of Cleves—crystallized in the 1540s and 1550s with the far less
ambiguous confessional divide of Protestantism and Catholicism. There
were still many, such as the late Catherine Howard, who were prepared to
toe the line set by the government, but an increasing number, like Katherine Parr, picked a side. Margaret Douglas nailed her colors to the mast,
too, with her allegiance to traditional Catholicism. While resubmission to
the Vatican remained anathema while Henry VIII lived, to conservatives at
court, it seemed possible that they might nonetheless secure certain victories
for their cause.

Margaret Douglas remained in Katherine Parr's service despite their
diverging views on religion, and Queen Katherine was a guest at Margaret's wedding when, in 1544, she submitted to a marriage arranged for
her by the King to a fellow Scottish émigré named Matthew Stewart, Earl

of Lennox.[34] "Young and good-looking," according to Chapuys,* Lennox was Catholic, wealthy, ambitious, yet pathologically lazy—even his friends lamented his "great sloth."[35] Educated in France, he had returned to Scotland to make the most of the political vacuum created by King James V's death in 1542, which had left the crown to his six-day-old daughter, Mary, Queen of Scots. However, Lennox had been outmaneuvered in Scotland by his political enemies; abandoning his Francophile loyalties, he fled south to England, "where he was honourably received by the king, who, besides treating him munificently in other respects, gave him Margaret Douglas, to wife. She was the sister of James, late king of Scots, and daughter of the Earl of Angus, by the sister of Henry, king of England; a princess in the flower of her age, celebrated for exquisite loveliness of shape, and elegance of form."[36]

Henry VIII saw enormous potential in his infant great-niece across the border, specifically with his plan to force the Scottish government to send its child-queen south to England, where she would be betrothed to his son, Edward. Lennox, whose ancestry as a great-grandson of King James II made him one of the highest-ranking Scottish subjects, would serve as a useful pawn in Henry VIII's scheme to bring Scotland under English rule. He promised to serve as Henry's "Governor" of Scotland once submission was achieved and the Queen of Scots had been sent to complete her education in the south of England. As English armies, delegated to Edward Seymour's command, swarmed across the border on Henry's orders, the Scottish Earl of Huntly joked with gallows humor that the southerners had a very odd version of wooing as they set out to "win" Queen Mary's hand for Prince Edward.

Margaret's marriage to Lennox grew into a great love match, as their surviving letters to each other attest. She was pregnant with their first son, the future Lord Darnley, whom they christened in honor of King Henry in 1545, and so it is unlikely that she attended on Queen Katherine at Hampton

---

* A less impressed diplomat was Sir James Melville, Lennox's fellow Scot, who described him as "very lusty, beardless, and lady-faced."

Court during the latter's regency. The King was leading his armies in a ruinously expensive invasion of France, with the Queen in charge of domestic policy until his return. As expected, Katherine performed her duties as temporary head of government superbly. With an ailing king whose heir turned nine that year, many at court saw Katherine Parr's regency as a dress rehearsal for the inevitable protectorate that would have to be established if, as by then seemed very likely, Henry VIII died before his son reached adulthood. Whether that future regency would be dominated by a Catholic or Protestant agenda intensified the stakes in the final years of Henry's reign. As those tensions mounted, so did the internecine viciousness of the court.

CHAPTER 7

THE TILTYARD

Woe to thee, O land, when thy king is a child.

—Ecclesiastes 10:16

In October 1549, armed men stood in the Base Court staring at their eleven-year-old king, Edward VI, as he delivered a speech written for him by his frightened uncle. Twelve years earlier in the same place, drunken revellers had celebrated Edward's birth. The only time he had ever spent with his mother, Jane Seymour, although he could not remember her, had been at Hampton Court. He looked like her, with the same grey or pale-blue eyes and a similar complexion, coloring, and mouth. Jane's relatives took the reins of power in the weeks after Edward's accession, when he had been nine years old and, like the realm itself, in need of a protector. Katherine Parr's regency in 1544 had been a rehearsal, but not for her. She found herself excluded from power after her third husband's death, as the King's uncle and Katherine's fellow Protestant Edward Seymour elbowed the competition out of the way, secured a victory for the reformist cause, and once again scaled the aristocratic pecking order to become Duke of Somerset.*

His regime lasted until 1549, when it faced two of the largest rebellions in English history. The Western Rebellion, which swept through most of Devon

---

* Katherine married for a fourth time to another of Edward VI's uncles, Sir Thomas Seymour, in 1547 and died of postnatal complications in 1548.

and Cornwall, was motivated by opposition to the aggressive pace of religious reform. The eastern uprising, beginning in Norfolk and subsequently called Kett's Rebellion after one of its leaders, took place largely in response to the economic problems bequeathed by Henry VIII and the greed of the land-owning classes in the region. To the south, the Duke of Somerset had to surrender various French towns conquered by Henry VIII in 1544 because there was not enough money left to defend them. Northward, he ordered the withdrawal of the English army from Scotland. As failures engulfed his regime, Somerset received warnings at the start of October 1549 of a "certain conspiracy" to remove him from power.[1] It frightened him enough to sum-mon supporters to Hampton Court, where he raided the palace armory to equip them.[2] Then he paraded his charge, nephew, and king to address them with the plea that they would "be good to him and his uncle."[3]

It was not enough to soothe Somerset's fears of the "rage of the people."[4] After Edward VI ended his short speech and returned to his rooms, the decision was taken to move him elsewhere. Hampton Court had been built as a house of entertainment, not to withstand a siege. The Duke ordered the Captain of the Guard, Sir John Gates, to get his men ready to escort him and the boy king under cover of darkness to fortified Windsor Castle, where Somerset planned to barricade himself with the child who was the source of his authority.[5] Their journey ended with their arrival in an unfur-nished, unprepared, and freezing castle, where Edward soon fell ill with a terrible cold.

The October 1549 flight from Hampton Court was a desperate act that, instead of saving the Duke of Somerset's career, effectively ended it. He was ousted from power and later condemned to death for treason. Edward VI was still young enough to require a Protector, a position secured by the Lord High Admiral John Dudley, Earl of Warwick, who mimicked Som-erset by helping himself to a dukedom—in his case, that of Northumber-land.[6] Dudley eschewed Somerset's mistake of speaking to the King as if he were a child. The new Protector, who had seven sons of his own, suspected that if he infantilized Edward VI, he would be cast off in resentment once Edward became a legal adult.

The royal household returned to Hampton Court for the summer of 1551 to hide from another outbreak of plague. Somerset's downfall had not magically fixed the myriad problems the country faced—on July 18 the government issued a proclamation from Hampton Court denouncing those who "slanderously whisper and spread abroad false rumours of the further abasing of the coinage," a policy that had carried over from the later years of Henry VIII's reign and was widely blamed for the kingdom's economic problems.[7] Concerns about the coinage and economy continued to preoccupy the council throughout the summer.[8] Nonetheless, there was a sense that things had changed; like the Duke of Northumberland, everybody at court knew that Edward's majority was not far off. Courtiers watched for signs of how a monarchy led by him might look. The young monarch insisted on a rigid adherence to etiquette, which required even his sister Elizabeth to curtsy to him five times before she sat in his presence.[9] Gentlemen avoided wearing hats in Edward's favorite colors of red, white, or violet, since nobody wanted to look as if he were competing with him.[10] Observers also kept a close eye on the dynamic between the King's former schoolmates who had stayed with him for companionship after he succeeded to the throne—and who, by 1551, looked set to form the nucleus of his Privy Chamber as he entered adulthood.

In particular, they watched Barnaby Fitzpatrick, the sixteen- or seventeen-year-old heir to the Irish barony of Upper Ossory. On August 15, 1551, Edward's childhood playmate became his adult confidant by taking his oath to join Edward's Privy Chamber. Barnaby was outgoing and charismatic, if temperamental, and, for those at court, everything indicated that he would become the King's right-hand man once the young monarch assumed control of the government. Edward shared many of his late father's interests, particularly in military architecture, which, along with defense and foreign policy, he discussed often and privately with Barnaby.[11]

On his mother's side, Barnaby—christened Brian Mac Giollapadraig in the Irish county of Laois* where he was born—was a nephew of James Butler, who had unwillingly lived at Hampton Court in Cardinal Wolsey's

---

* Pronounced "Leash."

household thirty years earlier. Barnaby had a dash of royal blood in his veins, too, being the heir to the defunct Irish kingdom of Osraige, which, four hundred years earlier, his family had lost when their lands fell to Anglo-Norman invaders.[12] The deposed royals were pushed back to the Slieve Bloom Mountains, where, in the early thirteenth century, they settled as noblemen over the northernmost part of what had once been their kingdom. It was almost certainly there, on or in sight of the slopes of the Slieve Bloom, that Brian was born to his father, also named Brian, head of one of the oldest Gaelic noble families, and his wife, Lady Margaret Butler. Their estates abutted the Pale, the area of Crown loyalty that ringed Dublin and her sister towns on the eastern Irish seaboard. The Pale, fragile since the Wars of the Roses, was once more on the ascendant in the later years of Henry VIII, and for those families, like Brian's, whose estates lay on its borders, the choice was assimilation or evisceration. Brian bent the knee to Dublin—and, through it, London—relinquishing his ancient claims to long-vanished kingdoms in return for an anglicized aristocratic title—Osraige became the barony of Upper Ossory, and the family acquired an Anglo-Irish surname: Fitzpatrick.[13]

When he was about five years old, little Brian was sent to live in the Pale, where his mother's relatives, with their ties to the royal court, scored a social coup in winning for him a place in the Prince of Wales's schoolroom. Brian set sail from Ireland; "Barnaby" landed in England. He joined Prince Edward's household and shared in his studies, where he has gone down in history as the Prince's whipping boy. By this account, Edward, as Henry VIII's only son, was such an exalted person that his tutors did not dare beat the Prince if he misbehaved; so, every time Edward disappointed them, they whipped Barnaby in lieu. There is, however, no contemporary evidence that this was the case and the role of a whipping boy likely never existed; Barnaby's status as Edward's "proxy for correction" is first mentioned in a book written 102 years after Edward died.[14] The widespread legend of Barnaby Fitzpatrick the Whipping Boy, still repeated, did not gather real momentum in popular culture until the nineteenth century, when, in the context of the first sustained effort to gain full Irish political independence from Britain, the story of an Irish boy beaten for the mistakes of an English prince acquired a potent political utility. In fact, Barnaby became Prince Edward's closest friend and, on the cusp of adolescence, was invited to carry "a banner of ancient arms" at Henry VIII's funeral procession in the opening months of 1547.[15]

By 1551, Barnaby was a physically healthy teenager and, with no extant references to ill health, he wanted to enjoy the life he led at Edward's side. Edward VI enjoyed plays so much that he sometimes directed his own productions, and he loved to watch the tumblers, tightrope walkers, and jugglers invited to entertain him.[16] The King and his friends played tennis in the palace's indoor court, where spectators placed bets on the outcome. An indoor bowling house was built for the King's coterie to provide a poor-weather alternative to the palace's three existing outdoor alleys. As he grew, King Edward inherited Henry VIII's strength; martial activities, particularly archery, hunting, and jousting, became favorite activities for Edward, Barnaby, and their circle, which included the Protector's son, Lord Robert Dudley, and Henry Sidney, heir to Penshurst Place in Kent.

This group of friends had recently lost two of their number to that year's outbreak of the plague. Sometimes referred to simply as "the Sweat," it was a disease that appeared, mutated, then vanished in the sixteenth century; it was noted for the ease of its transmission and the speed of its kills. It was said that the Sweat meant a man could be merry at dinner and dead by supper. One of Edward's and Barnaby's companions, Henry Brandon, who had succeeded his father as Duke of Suffolk in 1545, had been studying under supervision at St. John's College, Cambridge, when he fell ill. The news reached the King at Hampton Court that the teenage Duke had died from the epidemic and the dukedom had passed to his younger brother, Charles. The Sweat carried the new duke into the grave one hour after his brother.[17] Even in an era accustomed to sudden deaths, particularly in consequence of plague, the double death of the Suffolk brothers shocked many and there was widespread sympathy for their mother, the Dowager Duchess. Edward VI's clique had always been close, and it seemed particularly cruel that the brothers had been snatched away on the brink of what was then regarded as adulthood.

Entertainments were organized at Hampton Court to distract the household from fear of the plague and sorrow at the death of the Suffolks.

One afternoon, Henry VIII's former jester, Will Somers, came out of retirement to caper up and down when he skipped onto the one-thousand-foot jousting arena, the tiltyard, with a broom clamped between his legs, dressed in a parody of a knight's armor. The King and the court watched and laughed from the encircling tiered platforms as Somers mocked the pretensions of jousters. After his performance to cheer up the King, Somers returned to the small set of rooms at Hampton Court that he had been granted to live in during his retirement.

Court could never be solely about pleasure, however, and Barnaby was expected to continue his father's work in advancing their family. The elder Brian had been the first Gaelic lord to take an Anglo-Irish title; now Barnaby was among the first of their class to convert to Protestantism. Anything else in Edward VI's presence was ill-advised, for his reign proved one of the most intensely Protestant in British history. The King had already quarrelled several times with his eldest half sister and heiress apparent, Mary, a Catholic. In their feud, he was encouraged by several of his advisers who believed that Edward had been sent by God to fulfill for the English Reformation the kind of sacral kingship practiced in the Bible by Jehoshaphat and Josiah, kings of Judah. Of the two, Josiah was the preferred comparison, both for the parallels he shared already with young Edward and those that English Protestants hoped to encourage as Edward matured. According to the Bible's second book of Chronicles, Josiah had inherited the throne as a child of eight to Edward's nine.[18] Josiah "did that which was right in the sight of the Lord"; crucial to the ensuing glories of his thirty-one-year rule was the destruction of idolatry that he embarked upon early in his reign. The Bible records of Josiah that

> *while he was yet young, he began to seek after the God of David his father: and in the twelfth year, he began to purge Judah and Jerusalem from the high places, and the groves, and the carved images, and the molten images. And they brake down the altars of Baalim* in [Josiah's]*

---

* A pagan deity, more commonly referred to as Ba'al.

presence; and the images, that were on high above them, he cut down; and the groves, and the carved images, and the molten images, he brake in pieces, and made dust of them. . . . And he burnt the bones of the priests upon their altars, and cleansed Judah and Jerusalem. And so did he in the cities of Manasseh, and Ephraim, and Simeon, even unto Naphtali. . . . And when he had broken down the altars and the groves, and had beaten the graven images into powder, and cut down all the idols throughout all the land of Israel, he returned to Jerusalem.[19]

The carved images that needed to be "made dust of" in Edward's England and Wales were not statues of ancient pagan deities such as Ba'al or Astarte but those of the Virgin Mary, the saints, the angels, and even of the crucified Christ. The problem for sixteenth-century reformers was not the subject of the religious art; rather it was the very existence of carved images, which they feared might be venerated by the Christian faithful, who would then be accidentally led into the sin of idol worship by believing a human-made statue to be the source of divine grace. Catholics claimed that the Old Testament prohibition on carved religious images pertained only to false gods; Protestants contended that it applied universally. Convinced by the latter's arguments, Edward's government ordered a purging of English churches, from cathedrals down to parish level, of any art that might smack of "papistry"—Catholicism or Christianity before the Reformation. The chapel at Hampton Court, where Edward had been baptized, was no exception, although its stained glass windows, including the ones depicting his mother's patron saint, were spared.

An evangelical experience of Christianity, then as now, rested on three things. The first, beyond Edward VI's power to grant his people but certainly experienced by him, was the sense of a personal relationship through prayer with Christ, whereby the penitent accepted, via a private emotional interaction, Christ's redemption of his or her sins. The second was frequent personal study of the Bible as a pathway to the relationship with Christ necessary for that salvation, while the third was a preaching, well-educated ministry to encourage better understanding of the Bible. The latter two—access to the Bible and to good preachers—were major goals for the Church of England under Edward VI's leadership, and, as with the campaign against Catholicism, the example was set by his court. The new Book of Common Prayer, with its banishing of Latin from church services, its establishment of an unambiguously Protestant definition of Holy Communion, and its removal of any mention of Purgatory, prayers for the dead, or prayers to the saints, was published with Edward's blessing. On his personal order, the royal library was gutted of "all superstitious books, as Mass books, legends and such like."[20] Some of the more fervently Protestant preachers were invited to Hampton Court, where the court was routinely expected to listen to sermons lasting three or four hours, with kings Josiah and Jehoshaphat providing not infrequent topics of inspiration. One of these orators, Thomas Lever, soon had Barnaby Fitzpatrick in his sights as a potential risk to Edward VI's soul and rule.[21]

As children, Barnaby and Edward had bonded over their love of the Bible, but, as with many friendships founded on faith in childhood, puberty proved an awkward milestone as sexuality and spirituality came into competition with each other. Barnaby was three or four years older than Edward, and if, at about seventeen, he had either become sexually active or simply begun expressing more open interest in women, pious Edward was distressed on his behalf. Whether rumors about Barnaby's flirtations had reached Lever's ears and spurred his campaign against him we do not know, but Edward VI's letters make it clear that he took it upon himself to safeguard his friend's moral health—and that the question of Barnaby's interest in the opposite sex was the first point of concern. The King advised Barnaby, "For women, as aforth you may, avoid their company." If Barnaby could not suppress thoughts of temptation, "apply yourself to riding, shooting, or tennis, with such honest games—not forgetting, sometimes, when you have leisure, your learning; chiefly reading the Scripture."[22] The advice does not seem to have worked, and Lever encouraged Edward to distance himself from his favorite.[23]

Thomas Lever was not an enemy to be taken lightly. He was not intimidated by court figures—as he had recently proved with a letter to Edward's councillors reminding them that they were deluding themselves if they believed they owed their influence to "your own powers and policy" rather than "the might and Wisdom of God," who could cast them down as easily as he had raised them.[24] The previous spring, Lever had been among those who persuaded a tearful King Edward to sign the first death warrant of his reign that condemned a fellow Protestant to burn for heresy. A Londoner named Joan Bocher had been arrested and put on trial for preaching in public that Christ could not physically have been born of the Virgin Mary but must have been only a spiritual entity. Lever had been among the preachers sent to debate with her in prison in the hope of securing a recantation that would spare her life. When he failed to convince her, he lobbied for her execution. Edward resisted initially, fretting that by burning Bocher before she had a chance to repent, he ran the risk of complicity in sending her soul to hell. As guardian of his people's spiritual welfare, surely it was Edward's job to keep Joan alive in the "hope of conversion," as he put it, rather than kill her before she had the opportunity?[25] He gave in after sustained pressure that, in allowing Joan—"the devil's daughter" according to one of her former fellow evangelicals—to live, Edward was endangering the souls of others who might be led astray by her preaching.[26]

While Barnaby never drifted into similarly lethal controversies, the incident had demonstrated the tenacity of Lever and his allies in pursuing what they perceived as the righteousness of their cause. It also highlighted the extent of their influence with the King. Many English Protestants believed that the Reformation under Henry VIII had been a missed opportunity—having stalled, changed direction, and been mired in corruption thanks to the avarice of Henry's favorites. They were determined that his son would not be similarly distracted. Edward's marriage negotiations seem to have provided the perfect opportunity to remove Barnaby from court.

One of the men who visited Hampton Court in 1551 was the Marquis de Fronsac, a diplomat who arrived to discuss King Edward's possible marriage to a French princess, Elisabeth of Valois. Negotiations seemed set to founder on the question of religion, since the French royal family had made it absolutely clear that it would never permit Elisabeth's conversion to Protestantism. Given Edward's religious views, very few expected him to accept marriage with a Catholic. Yet Edward VI had no intention of mimicking his father by marrying a subject. Nor were there any suitable Protestant princesses of marriageable age or, by Edward's standards, possessed of a sufficiently grand lineage.[27] As both Edward's representative and spy, Barnaby Fitzpatrick left Hampton Court that autumn as part of a delegation sent to the French court to pursue the possibilities of arranging a royal marriage. Edward's parting advice to his friend was to "behave himself honestly [cleanly or virtuously]" in France by "more following the company of gentlemen, than pressing into the company of ladies."[28]

On the surface, Barnaby was an odd choice for the mission. There were others in the royal entourage, less likely to be missed but equally trustworthy, who could just as easily have gone to France.[29] But then, none of them had been identified by the chaplains as gateways to spiritual backsliding. Was Barnaby's trip to France an example of being "kicked upstairs"—a seeming promotion designed to politely get rid of a troublesome influence? If that was what men like Lever hoped, they underestimated the depth of Edward's affection for Barnaby. The King's early letters during Barnaby's stint in France were the usual devout didactics: he was not allowed to attend Mass or accompany the French royal family on the Catholic custom of pilgrimage, even if expressly invited to do so by King Henri II, since both were papist superstitions and "with safe conscience, you can not do any such thing being brought up with me and bounden to obey my laws."[30] Soon, however, the unmistakable tone of missing his friend creeps into their correspondence: "I am gladder the oftener I hear from you," Edward wrote in one.[31] King Henri had taken a shine to Barnaby, too, and appointed him as a gentleman in his chamber, prolonging Barnaby's stay in France. Edward was worried, and peeved, when Barnaby, in joining Henri II's campaign against the Hapsburgs, became the first of them to serve as a soldier. Edward wrote: "For, whereas you will all have been occupied in killing of your enemies, in long marchings, and painful journeys, in extreme heat, in sore skirmishings, in divers assaults; we have been occupied in killing of wild beasts, in pleasant journeys, in good fare, in viewing of fair counties, and rather have sought to fortify our own than to spoil another man's."[32] Within a few months, it was clear that Edward's main objection to the war lay not in its violence but in the fact that it kept his friend from him. In September 1552 he begged Barnaby, "Take some occasion to ask leave for this winter to come home." In the same letter, he mentioned that the Sweat had broken out again.

The two friends never improved on their summer at Hampton Court in 1551. Edward fell ill, and, whatever his disease, it laid waste his health and left him fatally vulnerable.[33] In the spring of 1553 he likely developed the bronchopneumonia that killed him shortly before his sixteenth birthday. Barnaby was back in England by the time of Edward's agonized death at Greenwich Palace. With Edward's last breath, Barnaby became yesterday's symbol, out of favor with the ensuing Catholic restoration, although he was permitted to attend Edward one last time for his funeral at Westminster Abbey. The jester Will Somers was also invited.[34]

Barnaby tried to win back royal patronage by volunteering to help suppress a rebellion against the new Queen in Kent. He was allowed to fight, but Mary I had no interest in reviving Barnaby's career at court. Stumbling out of a tavern one night in an ugly, drunken mood, he started a brawl with a Catholic priest. He was taken in front of the local sheriffs, the worse for wear, the next morning and reprimanded. After that, Barnaby returned to Ireland, "his father's country," whose language he did not speak and whose people he barely remembered.[35] His mother had died during his long absence in England and his father remarried to a neighbor whom Barnaby called "the most naughty and malicious creature alive."[36] He went to war in the Crown's service in the north of Ireland, became Baron of Upper Ossory, married a fellow Irish aristocrat with whom he had a daughter, held together his family's estates, rescued his wife and daughter after they were kidnapped by his enemies, accused his stepmother and her family of witchcraft, and served as one of Elizabeth I's lieutenants in the counties of Laois and neighboring Offaly.[37] But when he died in 1581, Barnaby Fitzpatrick had never come as close to truly great power as he did, aged seventeen, at Hampton Court.[38]

CHAPTER 8

THE PRIVY GARDENS

At about the ninth hour, she went down to the garden to
walk. And she saw a laurel, and sat under it, and prayed
to the Lord, saying, "O God of our fathers, bless me and
hear my prayer, as You blessed the womb of Sarah, and
gave her a son Isaac."

—The Protoevangelium of Saint James the Just, 2:7

Both the weather and the reception were cold when Edward VI's youngest surviving sister, Elizabeth, arrived at Hampton Court to see their eldest in April 1555.[1] Mary, England's first crowned queen regnant*, had been on the throne for nearly two years, with Elizabeth as her heiress presumptive. Elizabeth had every reason to expect that this visit to Hampton Court would end with her again losing her place in the succession, as she had for nine terrifying days two years earlier.

Then, their dying brother Edward had feared that the new religion would be buried alongside him if Mary acceded. Since his older sister's faith was not considered a disqualifying factor by most of her compatriots, Edward cited as justification for excluding her their father's dissolution of his

---

* A female monarch who inherited the crown in her own right, rather than acquiring it through marriage, in contrast to queens consort. Queens regnant exercised political power and authority as a monarch, in further contrast to queens consort who had no official power over legislation unless they served as regent.

marriage to her mother, Katherine of Aragon, Henry VIII's first wife. The same had happened to Anne Boleyn, which meant disinheriting Elizabeth, too—collateral damage that Edward felt was justified if it kept Mary off the throne. He declared that the crown should pass instead to their cousin once removed, Lady Jane Grey.[2] As zealous a Protestant as King Edward—she had once referred to Catholicism as "the stinking kennel of Satan"—Lady Jane famously lasted about nine days as queen before the country rallied behind Mary.[3] Seventeen-year-old Jane went from monarch to prisoner in the Tower of London.

Elizabeth had entered London in triumph at Mary's side when she deposed Jane, but within months, the sisters' relationship had become strained when the links between Protestantism and sedition were made even more explicit—at least in Mary I's eyes—by the Wyatt Rebellion, which erupted against her in the southern county of Kent in early 1554. Mary believed the rebels had aimed to depose her and replace her either with Elizabeth or their imprisoned cousin, Jane. The rebels insisted that they only wished to prevent their queen's forthcoming wedding to her cousin once removed Prince Philip of Spain, fearing that England might be swallowed up by the Hapsburg Empire. As she had when she rallied an army to oust "the Nine Days' Queen," Mary Tudor showed great bravery in the face of the rebellion. She delivered rousing speeches to her soldiers, who went on to crush the uprising—or, in Mary's words, the act of treason that had failed thanks to "the assistance of Almighty God and the help of our good and loving subjects."[4] Jane was executed, Elizabeth imprisoned, and the wedding to Philip went ahead, along with the abolition of the Church of England, as Mary led her kingdom's resubmission to communion with the Vatican. Bonfires had been lit for the street parties that celebrated England's reunion with the papacy, a testament to the popularity of Catholicism in some parts of the country even after six years of persecution under Edward VI and fourteen under Henry VIII.[5]

Meanwhile, Elizabeth spent some months in the Tower of London, wondering if she would soon be buried alongside her mother in the fortress's chapel of St. Peter ad Vincula.[6] Mary and most of her advisers believed that, before the uprising, its leaders had secretly informed Elizabeth of what they planned to do and, rather than alert her sister to the plot against her, Elizabeth had waited to see which way the political wind blew. Knowledge of, and failure to prevent, a rebellion was an act of treason. Elizabeth refused to confess, and, when no evidence against her could be found, she was transferred from the Tower to eleven months of rustication in the Oxfordshire countryside. There, Elizabeth had used a diamond ring to scratch onto a windowpane, "Much suspected of me. Nothing proved can be, Quoth, Elizabeth, the Prisoner." Her critics felt this was tellingly ambiguous, suggesting a lack of evidence rather than an absence of guilt.

After winning the throne, dismantling a church she detested, undoing much of her father's and brother's work, and marrying the man she had chosen in the face of a rebellion she had defeated, Queen Mary believed that God had blessed her with a pregnancy conceived during her Hampton Court honeymoon with Philip, which was perhaps why the royal couple decided to return there for the birth. It was also to Hampton Court that Mary summoned Elizabeth at the tail end of an unseasonably overcast April, so that she could be present for the birth of the child who would replace her in the line of succession.

From the moment her feet alighted on the Hampton Court cobblestones, it must be said that Elizabeth delivered a virtuoso performance in pretending to be delighted at her sister's pregnancy. She even made sure to be spotted sewing baby clothes for the prince-on-his-way. It was a particularly impressive pretense in light of Mary's refusal to see her, which signalled to everybody that Elizabeth remained under suspicion and out of favor. Other high-ranking courtiers at Hampton Court took the opportunity to advertise their dislike of Elizabeth. Her distant kinsman, Cardinal Reginald Pole, the Pope's representative to England and new Archbishop of Canterbury, avoided speaking to her, despite occupying apartments near to hers. Remembering that Elizabeth suffered terribly from migraines and also had an aversion to strong smells and noises, her cousin Margaret Douglas had a new kitchen installed directly above Elizabeth's bedroom.

After three or so weeks of this, Elizabeth received a summons to Mary's apartments. She was fetched after sunset and escorted through the Privy

Gardens. The twenty-one-year-old Elizabeth was terrified that an assassin might be lurking behind the manicured hedges and that she was being lured into a trap by her enemies, perhaps with the Queen's connivance. To her relief, she was accompanied by Sir Henry Bedingfeld, a scrupulously honest courtier who had helped run her exiled household for the last eleven months and would later be appointed captain of Queen Mary's guard. The Privy Gardens, which were for the royal family's private use to walk, converse with their friends or favorites, and relax away from prying eyes, were located on the south side of Hampton Court. Encircled by a wall, which on one side bordered the rest of the palace gardens and, on the other the river, the gardens were accessible from the royal apartments by a private staircase. They also had the Water Gate, a covered wharf and walkway that the King and Queen used with their attendants.[7] At the foot of the Privy Stairs, Bedingfeld left Elizabeth in the care of the Queen's Mistress of the Robes, who had been sent down to meet them on Queen Mary's orders. In her midforties, the lady-in-waiting's real name was Susan Tonge, although she was better known, then and later, as Susan Clarencieux or Susan Clarencius due to her husband's appointment as Clarencieux (now Clarenceux) King of Arms, one of the men in charge of verifying heraldic claims from those who wished to join the gentry or the aristocracy. Susan Clarencieux did not think highly of Elizabeth Tudor and probably never had. She had detested Elizabeth's mother, for whose sake she had been dismissed briefly from serving Mary in retaliation for the latter's refusal to acknowledge Anne as the rightful queen of England. Susan escorted Elizabeth up the stairs to the Queen's Apartments, where the heiress sank to her knees in a curtsy as she entered her sister's presence.

Queen Mary I was thirty-nine years old, but thanks to her excellent complexion, she was always judged to look younger than her age.[8] She had the red Tudor hair, a small mouth like her father's, and a low-pitched voice.[9] She was shortsighted, a problem exacerbated by her tremendous work ethic as queen. She was known to often keep reading and writing until midnight to ensure that she stayed on top of government business, and the candlelight cannot have helped her eyesight. She was a keen horsewoman and hunter, an excellent musician and dancer, and a competent linguist.[10] She was also courageous. Mary had endured much uncertainty in the twenty years between her parents' divorce and her half brother's death and from those years she had emerged as a woman of principle if, like most of her contemporaries, unimpressed by anyone, however brave, who held principles contrary to her own.

The meeting between Mary and Elizabeth in May 1555 was recorded in a sixteenth-century source that is notoriously hostile to Mary. John Foxe's *Acts and Monuments*, popularly referred to as *Foxe's Book of Martyrs*, details Elizabeth's journey through the Privy Gardens, the escorting roles played by Henry Bedingfeld and Susan Clarencieux, and the sisters' subsequent reunion in the Queen's Apartments. With those details, Foxe was most likely telling the truth; he wrote during Elizabeth's lifetime, when the sisters' meeting was still well known by many at the English court. Where Foxe cannot, unfortunately, be trusted is in the words that his account gives to Mary and Elizabeth. They are implausibly precise and numerous, and it is hard to imagine how Foxe came by eyewitness testimonies for them.[11] Similarly dubious is Foxe's claim that Mary's husband spied on the entire conversation, hidden behind an elaborate wall hanging.

The interview ended in a stalemate and in Elizabeth's return to her rooms without confessing—much to Mary's frustration. To the Queen's credit, it is very hard to imagine her father letting anybody return to their rooms if they were suspected of disloyalty, no matter how fervent their denials or how close their relationship to him. Like the rest of the court, Elizabeth's focus henceforth waited to see what would happen with Mary's pregnancy and if it would end with a niece or nephew for Elizabeth, who would safeguard the Catholic counterrevolution into the next generation.

During the rest of their time at Hampton Court in 1555, Queen Mary and Prince Philip wrote affectionate letters to his father and her ex-fiancé, Emperor Charles V, who, three decades earlier, had visited the palace as Cardinal Wolsey's guest when they discussed a marriage between Charles and a young Mary. As suspected at the time, the Emperor had no intention of going through with the arrangement, and, shortly after he left, he had married Philip's future mother, Isabella of Portugal. However, thereafter Charles had taken a protective interest in his English cousin; his help and his power had proved useful to her when she came under sustained pressure from her brother King Edward VI to relinquish her Catholicism. It was only the threat of tensions with the Hapsburg Empire that had forced Edward to leave Mary in something approaching peace. When she took the throne in 1553 and announced her intention to marry, Charles offered his son. Eleven years Mary's junior, Philip was dapper and elegant without necessarily being considered handsome, beautifully mannered, of average intelligence, and, like Mary, industrious when it came to his royal and political duties. Philip had lost his first wife, Princess Maria-Manuela, during the birth of their son, Don Carlos. That Philip already had an heir from a previous marriage soothed English concerns about a permanent loss of independence—Don Carlos would inherit his father's Hapsburg dominions, while any child that Philip fathered with Mary would be heir to the Tudor thrones. Philip, too, awaited the birth of his second child, albeit in far better spirits than his sister-in-law Elizabeth, whom he treated with great courtesy.

Mary, Philip, and Elizabeth were seen in public together for Mass in Hampton Court's Chapel Royal to mark the room's reconsecration to Roman Catholicism. In court and country, there were rumors that Elizabeth remained in her heart a Protestant, suspicions that were not assuaged by the catalogue of stomach complaints and migraines that fortuitously forced Elizabeth to take to her bed every time she was due to take Holy Communion by the Roman Rite. For the Queen, Elizabeth's theological theatrics were almost as dangerous as her suspected sympathy for the Wyatt Rebellion. Until Elizabeth publicly buckled and took Communion from a Catholic priest in the palace chapel before a large congregation, she would remain a figurehead for disaffected English Protestants.

Mary I's restoration of Catholicism had claimed its first victim on February 4 that year, when the Protestant clergyman John Rogers was burned to death before a crowd in London. Among the spectators was his grieving wife, Adriana, breastfeeding their child. Rogers recited Psalm 51 on his walk from prison to stake, and he kept praying until the fire reached his face. At the moment the flames consumed him, a flock of doves, a traditional symbol in Christian iconography of the Holy Spirit, flew over the site of execution.[12] To many in the crowd, this was a sign from God that Rogers's soul had been received into Heaven.[13] He went down in English Protestant lore as the "Proto-Martyr"—some Catholics mocked the nickname by calling him the "Pseudo-Martyr"—the first of 283 who would die in the same manner and for the same cause over the next three and a half years.[14]

Those burnings earned the Queen the damning sobriquet of "Bloody Mary," although the nickname first appeared in anti-Catholic polemics written decades after her death.[15] Recently, Mary I's reputation as the archetypal bigoted tyrant has been challenged by several excellent studies and biographies that emphasize her tenacity, her courage, and her many personal acts of kindness to her staff, as well as her intelligence and her commitment to making her reign a success.[16] However, it is not true that Mary I's executions paled in comparison with those being inflicted in Europe. Even in the context of the sixteenth century, Mary's was an extensive policy. What is perhaps even less palatable to modern readers is the strong evidence from the 1550s that the burnings, far from weakening popular support in England for Catholicism, increased it in some parts of the country.[17] Many of those executed by Mary I's government were hard-liners who were resented for the destruction of Catholic churches and culture during Edward VI's reign, as well as for their own deafening indifference to those who had faced similar horrors under previous reigns. John Rogers the Proto-Martyr had supported death by burning for other people, including the radical Protestant preacher Joan Bocher. In contrast, Queen Mary's restoration of saints' days and veneration of the Virgin Mary was generally applauded, as was her investment in the future education of a revived English Catholic clergy.

Mary's religious policy nonetheless remains notorious, and contemporary criticism of it cannot fairly be dismissed out of hand.[18] She embarked upon a brutal crackdown on heresy after a generation when, thanks to her father's and brother's policies, the numbers of heretics had, in her eyes, mushroomed. With English and Welsh Protestantism failing but not yet fatally so, Elizabeth remained a problem, her Protestantism proving as distressing to Mary as her own Catholicism had once been to Edward. If Mary died without an heir, the next queen would almost certainly rule as a Protestant, undoing Mary's life's work. Philip's chamberlain, the future Prince of Éboli, wrote back to Spain, "May it please God to grant [the Queen] the issue that is so sorely needed to set affairs here to rights and make everything smooth. . . . this pregnancy will put a stop to every difficulty."[19] As they had been with Jane Seymour eighteen years earlier, the kingdom's eyes were fixed on Hampton Court. Prayers were offered for "our most gracious Queen Mary, so help her that in due season she may bring forth a child, in body beautiful and comely, in mind noble and valiant."[20]

Mary withdrew from male company. From her windows, she watched a procession of the Eucharist through the Hampton Court grounds. An embroidered canopy, held by deacons and altar boys, fluttered over the sacrament as censers cast incense into the summer air, and the Latin prayers rang out as faithfully at Hampton Court as they had in the days of the Knights Hospitaller. In the Queen's rooms, all but one of her attendants prayed for, and with, the Queen for a safe delivery. The dissenting voice was that of a lady-in-waiting named Frideswide Strelley, a Member of Parliament's widow.[21] Frideswide had never been convinced that her mistress was pregnant. However, her attempts to caution the Queen were ignored, even at the end of May, when the baby was three weeks late. Mary's other attendants drowned out Frideswide's concerns by assuring their Queen that the physicians must have made a mistake about the dates. It is unclear why Strelley was ignored, unless the fact that she never had a child was used to discredit her advice. Like her late husband, Robert, who had passed away a year earlier after a long illness, Frideswide had been in Mary's service for years, serving her loyally before she became queen, and she was allegedly one of Mary's favorite ladies-in-waiting. Quite possibly, she was ignored because she was saying something that the Queen did not want to hear, and nobody else wanted to take responsibility for telling her.

As the court's residency at the palace dragged into June, Hampton Court became a cesspit. The sewers were filling up, the local merchants were almost out of food to sell, and the moat was nearly dry—its fish consumed and its water was used to supplement the palace's struggling plumbing. Mary went for a walk in the Privy Gardens, unusual for a woman in seclusion, but, as queen regnant, she had every right to circumvent etiquette. Her husband's chamberlain noticed that she was "walking all about the garden on foot, and she steps so well that it seems to me that there is no hope at all for this month."[22] The limits of privacy in the Tudor context are shown by just how many people heard about the Queen's "secluded" stroll. Gossip tore through the palace about why the delivery was so delayed.

The mystery of Mary's pregnancy has been incorporated into a modern depiction of her as someone driven by an emotional desire to recover from her parents' divorce by building a happy family of her own, even if achieving it meant sacrificing her political effectiveness. To present Mary in that light requires forgetting the wealth, privilege, and happiness that she enjoyed as one of England's major landowners during her brother's reign, as well as the speed and determination with which she crushed her enemies, in the space of a fortnight, when they tried to prevent her from becoming queen in 1553. Mary was an astute, sometimes brilliant politician. She did not express a strong desire to have children until she became queen, at which point she regarded providing an heir as one of her duties as a monarch.[23] In preparation for her marriage to Philip, she had put a great deal of energy into ensuring that he did not encroach on her power as sovereign. As his wife, Mary gave Philip the use of the King's Apartments at Hampton Court, and she permitted various features of Hapsburg court etiquette to be adopted at Hampton Court, including closing doors between various rooms and further limiting access to the royal family—to the displeasure of many of her staff, who thought the new Spanish customs "strange."[24] However, as monarch, Mary did not yield her authority to her husband.

In the King's Apartments, Philip had started to worry about their situation by early June. Mary was still in seclusion when Philip wrote to his brother-in-law, the Archduke Maximilian, "The Queen's pregnancy turns out not to have been as certain as we thought. Your Highness and my sister manage it better than the Queen and I do." The latter sentence was a reference to Philip's sister Maria being eight months pregnant with her sixth child. Aside from personal concern about his wife, Philip was also on a political deadline. He had planned to stay at Hampton Court until their child was born, after which he needed to get back to Europe. His father was preparing to relinquish the throne, as the empire that had already seemed unwieldy when Charles dined at Hampton Court with Cardinal Wolsey thirty-three years earlier was no longer fit for purpose. Charles had decided not to inflict it on future generations. The Hapsburg Empire would split along Spanish and Austrian lines, with the Emperor abdicating at the end of 1555 in a series of ceremonies through which the Spanish territories (Spain, Naples, Sardinia, Sicily, the Netherlands, and the empire in the Americas) would go to Prince Philip, making Mary queen consort of Spain, Naples, Sicily, and Sardinia.[25] The Austrian heartlands of the dynasty, along with the German claim and the kingdoms of Bohemia, Croatia, and Hungary would pass to Ferdinand, Philip's uncle and Charles's younger brother. Prince Philip thus needed to leave England before the end of summer to be at his father's side for the abdication, and his correspondence reveals that he did not know how to broach the subject without humiliating his wife. If Philip left Hampton Court, it would be tantamount to a public announcement that the Queen had either lost a pregnancy or never conceived. To his chamberlain, Philip fretted, "Let me know what line I am to take with the Queen about leaving her. . . . I see I must say something, but God help me!"[26]

June bled into July, Hampton Court stank, and the Queen, sequestered in her apartments, could not bring herself to confront the fact that she was not pregnant. When pressed for information by Parliament, where doubts were also multiplying, a courtier could report only that "the Queen has withdrawn, and no one else enters her apartments except the women who serve her." Mary had not been seen in public for nearly four months, three months after the baby was due. Then her womb seemed to deflate. Servants, again spying on Mary when she walked in the Privy Gardens, reported back to any nobles and ambassadors willing to pay for information that the Queen was no longer visibly pregnant. Not long after that, in her bedchamber one evening, the Queen gave voice at last to the painful reality. Weeping, she took Frideswide Strelley's hand in her own and whispered, "Ah, Strelley, Strelley, I see they be flatterers, and none true to me but thou."[27]

What happened with the Hampton Court pregnancy of 1555 divided both contemporaries and historians. Someone at the Venetian embassy in London, as the representative of an anti-Hapsburg government, spread a malicious rumor that the Queen had covered up a miscarriage because what she lost was a shapeless deformed mass, a common charge in contemporary propaganda to suggest that one or both parents were being denied offspring by heaven.[28] A phantom pregnancy has plausibly been suggested, perhaps similar to the one her mother allegedly endured in the first year of her marriage.[29] Mary I might have been pregnant at some point toward the end of 1554, when her doctors and ladies confirmed that she was expecting, but lost the fetus at a fairly early stage—perhaps in the first trimester—without realizing it. Another suggestion—that the pregnancy was a misdiagnosis of a uterine tumor that later contributed to Mary's death—is the most popular. However, it does not explain why the Queen's womb deflated noticeably, nor is it now universally accepted by Mary's biographers that she ever had cancer.[30] Frideswide Strelley's doubts that the Queen was ever pregnant, as well as the other evidence mentioned here—especially Philip's comment to his brother-in-law that the "pregnancy turns out not to have been as certain as we thought"—suggest that a phantom or misdiagnosed pregnancy is the likely theory to explain the events at Hampton Court in 1555. In early modern medicine, mistakes regarding pregnancies were made all the time.

In July, the Queen returned to her public duties for a brief audience with the French ambassador and his brother, whom she upbraided for Henri II's alliance with Süleyman the Magnificent, Sultan of the expanding Ottoman Empire, since Mary "had felt the inroads of the Turks in[to] Christendom as if it had been her own kingdom."[31] Mary and Philip later discussed her meeting with the ambassador and the issue of the Franco-Ottoman alliance with Cardinal Pole, in which she reiterated that as "a Christian and Catholic princess all her life," she could not understand how the French monarchy could morally bring itself to forge an alliance with a non-Christian power.[32] She then dictated a letter to one of her ambassadors, Sir John Mason, whom she instructed to privately inform Mary's cousin the Dowager Queen of Hungary that she was not pregnant. Nothing more was said publicly about the Hampton Court pregnancy.

Thus Elizabeth remained heir. Her servants packed her things as she accompanied Mary and Philip on the short distance through Hampton Court Chase to the relative seclusion of Oatlands Palace, a smaller home built for Henry VIII, where the royal family kept the Feast of the Assumption that year. Two weeks later, Philip left for the Netherlands. The cleaning crews had been sent into Hampton Court to shovel away the excrement, offal, and animal bones; the rushes from the floors were burned; the windows, opened; and the place was scrubbed to make it ready for the Christmas that had been planned there. Mary then changed her mind about keeping Yuletide 1555 at Hampton Court. She decided instead on her palace at Greenwich.

CHAPTER 9

THE PARADISE

What thing more wretched can be imagined, than men serving a woman? That is, free men, who are born to rule, serving slaves, who are born to obey? Therefore rightly, miserable England, we can weep for your situation, who serve such a perverse and impious woman, a Jezebel, and, subject to her, endure the harshest tyranny.

—Annibale Scoto, *In P. Cornelii Taciti Annales et Historias Commentarii* (1589)

Under the later Tudors, audiences at Hampton Court were often granted in the Paradise Room. It is a pity that it, too, was a casualty of renovations in the late seventeenth century, for sources from the sixteenth frequently identify the Paradise as the wonder of the palace. "Everything glitters so with silver, gold, and jewels, as to dazzle one's eyes," wrote a German visitor. One of his compatriots and contemporaries, the Duke of Württemberg, thought the Paradise was the finest room at Hampton Court, which was itself "the most splendid and most magnificent royal palace of any that may be found in England, or, indeed, in any other kingdom." The Paradise's walls were decorated with Persian tapestries, and there was a table made from Brazilian wood and inlaid with silver, a gift from the King of Portugal. There was also a backgammon board with dice of solid silver, and nearby a number of fine musical instruments, some of them made from glass.[1] The former kept petitioners occupied while they waited for the sovereign's arrival and the latter afforded said sovereign the opportunity to advertise her exceptional musical ability, apparently by accident, when she was "caught" playing exquisitely as ambassadors were ushered into her presence.

The musical monarch at the center of the Paradise in October 1562 was Henry VIII's youngest daughter, Elizabeth I, twenty-nine years old, intellectually brilliant, and, now that the anxiety of living in her sister's shadow had lifted, vibrantly healthy. She had the high cheekbones of her mother, Anne Boleyn, her father's coloring, and her Tudor grandfather's distinguished nose. She was more like her mother in her build, with a small appetite, as well as having Boleyn's sense of humor. She shared her father's enjoyment of bearbaiting, cards, and chess. Like both her parents, she was a superb dancer and equestrian. She was keenly interested in mathematics and astrology—her coronation date had been selected after lengthy consultations with the astrologer and alchemist Dr. John Dee. Elizabeth was fluent in French, Italian, and Latin—she relaxed by translating works of Roman philosophy into English and then back into Latin—she spoke excellent but not fluent Greek and Spanish, and she had varying degrees of competence in Welsh, Cornish, German, Hebrew, and Irish.[2]

Yet these capabilities were negated in the eyes of many of her contemporaries by Elizabeth's gender, in a generation increasingly neurotic about a perceived social, or political, rebalancing between the sexes. Given monarchy's historical tendency to weight everything in favor of a male heir, the first six decades of the sixteenth century had produced more than their fair share of female rulers. By the time Elizabeth succeeded Mary I in November 1558 to her own Anglo-Irish thrones, those of Scotland and Spain had also had female sovereigns, while female regents had led the governments in Scotland, England, Wales, Denmark, Norway, Sweden, the Netherlands, France, Portugal, Austria, Spain, Hungary, and Florence. Until Elizabeth, all Europe's female heads of state had been Catholics; inspired to apoplexy by this state of affairs, John Knox, founder of the new Scottish Protestant denomination of Presbyterianism, had penned a polemic against female monarchy, titled *The First Blast of the Trumpet Against the Monstrous Regi-*

ment of Women. Published with astonishingly bad timing from the Protestant perspective—just as Catholic Mary I died and Protestant Elizabeth I became queen in England—Knox had tried to walk back, a little, of his book's argument that a government headed by a woman was a demonic inversion of the natural order established by God. He had, he explained, been referring to Catholic princesses and queens. Elizabeth remained unmollified and regarded his attack on female rulers as an attack on her. Nor did she like his implication that a subject had the right to reject his sovereign if he did not like her religion. As a devout but not fanatical Protestant, Elizabeth nurtured an antipathy toward the more hard-line denominations such as Presbyterianism and its English cousin, Puritanism, that grew rather than waned for the rest of her life.

Possibly claustrophobic, prone to migraines, and sometimes exhausted by the pressure of ruling, there was no doubt of Elizabeth's courage if it is judged as the quality of overcoming fear rather than its absence. In 1562 even a rumor that she was to be poisoned at a banquet did not dent Elizabeth's bravery, although suspicions that the alleged murder attempt had been orchestrated by supporters of her half-Scottish, half-French cousin Mary, Queen of Scots, resulted in Elizabeth pointedly favoring the Spanish ambassador at the expense of the French and Scottish representatives.* As the ambassador, Álvaro de la Quadra, Bishop of Aquila, informed his master, Elizabeth's former brother-in-law, King Philip II, "They cannot make too much of me here at Hampton Court. It is curious how things change."[3] It certainly was. Despite their felicitous politeness to each other every time they met, Elizabeth was paying Quadra's servants to spy on him for her, while he found her so insufferable that he told his masters that negotiating with Elizabeth was akin to dealing with someone who was demoniacally possessed.[4]

Four years earlier, when Elizabeth first came to the throne, she had made a very public point of rejecting the Spanish alliance symbolized by

---

* Technically, Mary, Queen of Scots, was Elizabeth I's cousin once removed. As with most of their contemporaries, the two monarchs used the word *cousin* to cover a wide set of relationships.

her sister's marriage to Philip. She insisted that she owed her throne to the laws of God and Parliament, with a heavy emphasis on the former. However, French animosity and English fears about the Franco-Scottish alliance had raised Spanish credit in English eyes, and Elizabeth correspondingly lavished favor on de la Quadra, inviting him to hear her play in the Paradise. At the same audience, they discussed King Philip's suggestion that Elizabeth consider a marriage proposal from his Austrian cousin the Archduke Karl, who was attractive, healthy, seven years Elizabeth's junior, and, as the Emperor Ferdinand's third surviving son, far enough down the line of succession that he could spend most of his life living in England as her husband without too many commitments in central Europe.[5] Karl was, however, a Hapsburg and a deeply devout Roman Catholic, both of which counted against him to many of Elizabeth's subjects, particularly those still resentful of the foreign policy complications caused by her sister's union with Philip II. That alliance was blamed by some for involving England in a Hapsburg war against France, which had retaliated by conquering Calais.[6] The bishop-ambassador hoped that a prince from the Austrian side of the family might serve Hapsburg interests without riling too intensely those with memories of Calais. To de la Quadra's suggestion that she invite the Archduke Karl to England as her prospective bridegroom, Elizabeth deployed her usual complimentary noncommittals before asking the ambassador to dine with her the next week. Flattery-laced delays were a favorite tool of Elizabeth I's diplomacy.

As had been the case with her sister and predecessor, the pressure on Elizabeth to marry and produce an heir to the throne was immediate and unambiguous. This was not a burden solely inflicted on female royalty; as mentioned, Emperor Charles V and other male monarchs were also often petitioned or badgered by their subjects on the issue. However, early modern medicine and politics both meant that marriage posed far greater risk to female royalty than to male. Beyond the biological possibility that a pregnancy might kill them, there was the near certainty that marriage would diminish their power, as everything in sixteenth-century law favored the rights of men over women.

For instance, when it came to English jurisprudence, all a woman's earthly possessions became her husband's the moment they wed. Mary I had worked hard with her councillors to prevent that from happening with Philip in 1554, yet there were many who wondered how sustainable that solution would be if the couple were to produce a child. A wife was supposed to be subject to her husband; a monarch was subject to nobody. If Elizabeth married a foreign royal, would England be sucked into another war? Or would her husband become regent, de facto king, if she died in childbed giving birth either to a child who did not live or a baby who needed his foreign relatives to hold the reins of government until he reached maturity? The marriage question dominated Elizabeth's early years as monarch. As ruler of a wealthy nation, she did not lack for prospective husbands: along with Archduke Karl of Austria, Elizabeth had thus far been courted by a trio of Scandinavian suitors in the persons of King Erik XIV of Sweden, King Frederick II of Denmark, and Johan, Duke of Finland. Shortly after her succession, she had received, rejected, and been faintly repulsed by a halfhearted proposal from her sister's widower, Philip II, who eventually remarried to a French princess.[7] Elizabeth could have avoided these potential overseas entanglements by marrying one of her own subjects, as her father had her mother, although that hardly seemed the most encouraging precedent. However, if she wed her second cousin the Duke of Norfolk, or the Earl of Arundel (head of one of the oldest aristocratic families in England), both of whom were recently widowed and had been suggested as possible husbands at various points since her accession, their elevation might have roused the jealousy of other great noble families and turned them against her.[8] With the sole if hardly insignificant issue of the succession, the safest policy for Elizabeth, by far, was to remain unmarried. This seemed to be her personal inclination. In 1559 she told an ambassador that she found "the celibate life so agreeable and was so accustomed to it" that she had no desire to take a husband.[9]

Many wondered if Elizabeth would have married her childhood friend Lord Robert Dudley had it been possible. A former gentleman in Edward VI's household, Dudley was either confident or arrogant, depending on how much one liked him. He had been loyal to Elizabeth even when she was out of favor during Mary I's reign. Elizabeth's and Robert's passion for each other was obvious, and, after she appointed him to the court post of Master of the Horse, Lord Robert was frequently in the company of the young and energetic queen. She loved to ride to the hunt, which was the Master of the Horse's duty to organize. The liaison between the Queen and Lord Robert had already caused several scandals, with gossip about the English queen's "loose morals" spreading gleefully in Catholic courts abroad. Interestingly, several Catholic ambassadors to England wrote to their masters rebutting claims that Elizabeth had slept with Robert. They insisted that she was a woman of virtue by contemporary standards, although the sooner she found a husband to end her emotional attachment to Dudley, the better.[10] Some of Elizabeth's councillors who had previously squirmed at the prospect of another European consort had since warmed to the idea if it meant unseating Dudley's position as her favorite. This faction had strongly encouraged Ambassador de la Quadra to promote Karl of Austria.

With the Karl-praising audience at an end, the Queen retired to her apartments. It had been a difficult afternoon, not simply because of the ambassador's wearying tenacity in pushing the Archduke's suit, but also because Elizabeth had started to feel nauseated during it. Whereas her late sister had taken the Queen's rooms and allocated their father's former suite to her husband, Elizabeth occupied the King's Apartments to advertise her position as reigning sovereign. She had reason to feel grateful for her parents' demand for excellent plumbing in the royal apartments; she ordered her women to draw her a hot bath after the interview with de la Quadra. The water was heated in the unseen furnace by servants and then poured through taps into the Queen's bath, after which she took a long walk in the autumnal chill settling over the palace gardens.[11] Such contrasting temperatures were supposed to shock her body into feeling better; instead, Elizabeth went to bed that night complaining of a high temperature, fatigue, and a general ache. The next day, she tried to resume the business of governing until she felt too sick to finish a letter to Mary, Queen of Scots, discussing the weakness of the French government and the plight of French Protestants. She admitted as much to Queen Mary with the words "My hot fever prevents me writing more."[12]

Doctor Burchard Kranich, a respected German physician, was summoned from London. The Catholic Kranich had emigrated to England during Mary I's reign in order to flee the violence many eastern German Protestants were inflicting on their Catholic neighbors, then decided to stay after Elizabeth's accession. Dr. Kranich's surname is given with a bewildering number of variants, even by sixteenth-century standards, when standardized spelling was never a priority. They include Burcot (a bastardization of his first name) and anglicized forms such as Craneigh, Craunighe, and Cranye. As had been made clear by Mary I's pregnancy seven years earlier and the chorus of well-meaning sycophants who surrounded her, the powerful and important do not benefit from being advised only by those who are afraid to tell them the truth. Brutal honesty was a large ingredient in Dr. Kranich's success, as he demonstrated when he informed Elizabeth that she had smallpox. An outbreak that summer had killed Margaret Russell, Countess of Bedford, whose husband served as one of Elizabeth's advisers. As with all plagues, smallpox was regarded as more of a threat during the warmer months, and so, by October, many assumed they were safe. The Queen's temper, never too far from the surface, snapped at the mention of smallpox, and she belittled Kranich's expertise, rebutted his diagnosis, and sent him back to London. Elizabeth tried to will her health into reality, losing a little more of the battle with each passing day. By October 16, the Queen could not speak; by the end of the day, she was unconscious.

Elizabeth's chief minister, Sir William Cecil, arrived at Hampton Court for an emergency session of the council. The news was brought to him and his colleagues in the Council Chamber, at the end of the Haunted Gallery, that Elizabeth remained unconscious in her rooms at the other end of the corridor. Inside the Council Chamber, her advisers had to decide what to do if the Queen died. Her reign was four years old; the restoration of an independent Church of England and its second repudiation of the Pope was only three. Elizabeth was childless and unmarried, and had refused to nominate a successor lest it encourage plots to make that successor her replacement. In consequence, as Cecil put it, the "state of this crown depends only on the breath of one person, our sovereign lady."[13] To describe the councillors at Hampton Court as worried would be an understatement. As a contemporary noted, "Great lamentation are made. No one knoweth the certainty for the succession; every man asketh what part shall we take."[14]

Elizabeth always claimed that the right to succeed was defined by primogeniture, but her father's matrimonial misadventures and the contested state of his will had created too many candidates, with external authorities, such as Parliament or the council, assuming that they would need to interfere to secure a peaceful transition of power. This was what shaped the discussions in 1562. There was unanimous agreement among the privy councillors not to offer the English and Irish crowns to Mary, Queen of Scots, since she was a Catholic and a foreigner. Margaret Douglas, with a Scottish husband and Catholic faith, does not seem to have been given much consideration either, despite her royal ancestry and two healthy sons.[15] Some suggested bringing Elizabeth's Protestant cousin once removed, Lady Katherine Grey, to Hampton Court in preparation for naming her as queen should Elizabeth die. A few, keen to see the throne return to male leadership, put forward the candidacy of Henry Hastings, 3rd Earl of Huntingdon, a major landowner in the North, a Protestant in his late twenties, and a distant descendant of the House of York.[16] The consideration of Huntingdon as a potential King Henry IX shows how desperate some of the councillors were, since even a generous-spirited observer could not claim that Huntingdon possessed a close blood claim to the crown—on his mother's side, he was Edward IV's three-times great-nephew, while his closest direct ancestor on the throne was his six-times great-grandfather King Edward III, who had died in 1377. Other councillors—this was the most radical suggestion yet—proffered the idea that a panel of judges and learned men be summoned to decide upon who was the most fitting heir, as had been done in the days of the Old Testament.[17]

While the palace planned for the worst, it continued to hope for the best, and Dr. Kranich was fetched back from London with the order to resume treating the Queen. The anecdote that he refused at first, only to yield when Elizabeth's Boleyn cousin Lord Hunsdon threatened him with a dagger, is likely apocryphal.[18] Ushered back into her rooms, Kranich ordered Elizabeth's ladies-in-waiting to wrap her body—everything except her head—in red flannel. It was an old technique pioneered by Arab doctors, although it struck a superstitious frisson, as it felt like wrapping Elizabeth in her shroud. She was then laid on a pallet, or small daybed, next to one of the largest fireplaces, where a fire was lit and kept burning while the Queen sweated in her cocoon next to it. Dr. Kranich mixed her a poultice, which he fed to her himself before leaving her women specific instructions on taking care of her. After two hours by the fireside, Elizabeth began to talk, to the initial relief of her servants. Some of them, like Kranich, remained concerned that the dreaded pustules associated with smallpox still had not appeared on the Queen's skin.[19] Contemporary wisdom held that the longer they stayed beneath the surface, the deadlier the strain of smallpox was likely to be.

The collective mood in the Council Chamber was soothed only briefly by their Queen's recovery of the power of speech. Upon regaining consciousness, Elizabeth clearly believed that she was about to die and acted accordingly. Her chaplains were sent for, and, when she was sufficiently lucid, she tried several times to pray with them. Her short time as monarch had been overshadowed by the scandal concerning her romance with Lord Robert Dudley; now, apparently convinced that she was about to meet her maker, Elizabeth summoned the entire council to hear her final wishes: that, upon her death, Lord Robert should be appointed Protector of the Realm until an heir was proclaimed. Then, grabbing the hand of one of her servants, "The Queen protested at the time that although she loved and had always loved Lord Robert dearly, as God was her witness, nothing improper had ever passed between them."[20]

She nevertheless left £500 to a man named Tamworth, Dudley's favorite servant, which many later interpreted as hush money, since Tamworth may have stood watch outside any chambers where Elizabeth and Robert had met to be intimate. However, it is difficult to explain why the Queen, who evidently believed she was about to die and kept trying to focus on God with her chaplains, would make a point of focusing on details of the Dudley affair if her claims of no sexual contact between them were a lie. She could have discussed many other matters while addressing her councillors, without the risk of endangering her immortal soul with a deception on what she believed to be her deathbed. Whether the relationship between Elizabeth and Robert was consummated at a later date is beyond the purview of this book, but there seems no good reason beyond arched eyebrows to doubt that she was telling the truth about their relationship during her brush with death in 1562.

Unlike historians, her advisers were largely indifferent to the Queen's protestations about her love life. They were more concerned with, and horrified by, Elizabeth's political orders. Only a fever or the blindness caused by love could explain the Queen's decision to entrust the government to Lord Robert after her death. Robert had no royal blood, and, in the eyes of his enemies, he came from a family tainted for three consecutive generations by treason. His father, the late John Dudley, the "Bad Duke" of Northumberland, had been executed for treason in 1553 after his tenure as Edward VI's protector ended with him trying to seize the throne for his daughter-in-law at the Tudor sisters' expense. Robert's late brother Guildford had met a similar fate, while their grandfather Edmund had been one of the first men executed under Henry VIII, again on a charge of treason. Moreover, Robert had no political experience—certainly none that could equip him to hold the realm together during the uncertainty of an interregnum before a new monarch was chosen. To most of the public and to Europe, Robert was also indelibly tainted by the mystery of his wife's death two years earlier. Amy Dudley, suffering from advanced breast cancer, had been found dead at the bottom of a staircase. Whether Amy Dudley was pushed, jumped, or fell remains one of the great mysteries of British history.

An inquest had exonerated Lord Robert of complicity in Amy's death, yet the scandal, as well as his family background and lack of experience, made him a disastrous choice as regent. But the councillors, reluctant to disagree with Elizabeth when she was already under such physical and emotional distress, said nothing of this at the time. Instead, they lied with a promise to do everything she had asked should she die. As de la Quadra put it, "Everything she asked was promised but will not be fulfilled."[21]

When the pustules appeared on her hands and face at last, Elizabeth began to scream and sob. Dr. Kranich snapped at her, "God's pestilence! Which is better? To have pox in the hand, or in the face, or in the heart and kill the whole body?" The physician was relieved, knowing that the sores marked the end of the most dangerous phase of the disease. At that news, several of Elizabeth's advisers burst into tears of relief, or joy, and fell to their knees to give thanks to God for her recovery. Coins were minted to celebrate the Queen's deliverance. The brush with death had frightened sovereign and subjects alike; Elizabeth later summarized those two weeks at Hampton Court by writing, "Death possessed almost every joint of me."[22]

She returned to her public duties on October 25, fifteen days after first falling ill.[23] Remorseful of her previous rudeness to Dr. Kranich, she rewarded him for facing down her temper. By telling her things she did not wish to hear, he had arguably saved her life, in acknowledgment of which she made him a personal gift of golden spurs that had once belonged to her paternal grandfather, King Henry VII, and the grant of a countryside estate.[24] The celebratory mood did not permanently exorcise the councillors' memory of the terror they had felt when Elizabeth seemed close to death with no clear heir. Still paranoid about being overshadowed by a designated successor, as her sister had once been by her, Elizabeth's reluctance to be pressured into marrying or naming an heir intensified after 1562; the councillors' deliberations about the succession during her illness increased her already lively distrust of Lady Katherine Grey and even briefly turned her against the Earl of Huntingdon, of whom she had previously seemed quite fond.[25]

Those of Elizabeth's ladies-in-waiting who had stayed by her side during those fifteen days were as heroic as they were loyal. Each knew the risks of staying so close to a patient infected with smallpox, and two paid a heavy price. Sybil Penne, who had first joined the household as a nurse to Elizabeth's brother Edward VI, attended the Queen devotedly, as did Robert Dudley's sister and Elizabeth's close friend, Lady Mary Sidney. Both contracted smallpox, presumably from Elizabeth. Sybil died, and Lady Mary was so horribly disfigured that she suffered a nervous breakdown and retired from life at court. Her husband, the diplomat and soldier Sir Henry Sidney, was on a mission to Le Havre, France, when his wife fell ill; he wrote later, "I left her a full, fair Lady, in mine eyes at least the fairest, and when I returned, I found her as foul a lady as the small pox could make her, which she did take by continual attendance on Her Majesty's most precious person sick of the same disease, the scars of which, to her resolute discomfort ever since, hath done and doth remain in her face."[26] The Sidneys' marriage remained a happy one, although, tragically, their seven-year-old son caught the disease from his mother, likewise surviving with severe scarring. Sybil Penne—whose death occurred at the palace on November 6, 1562—allegedly joined Catherine Howard as one of Hampton Court's ghosts. Referred to as the "Grey Lady," her specter was first identified in 1829, when her tomb was moved during the renovation of a local church, and it is, to date, the ghost reported most frequently by believers in hauntings at Hampton Court.[27]

Elizabeth I, too, was haunted by the legacy of 1562—choosing not to live again at Hampton Court until 1567.[28] In the years to come, an alliance between Parliament and council to convince her to pick a husband amounted sometimes to bullying that lasted until Elizabeth went through menopause. In regards to her long-term reputation, Elizabeth is still described as bald and severely deformed from having contracted smallpox, although such a description is not borne out by any eyewitness testimony. Even hostile accounts from nearly forty years later, describing her as having grey hair underneath her iconic red wigs, do not mention weeping facial sores, nor the use of the infamous white makeup.[29]

The question why Elizabeth I continues to be presented by so many modern writers with a ghoulish focus on her appearance has been posed sensitively by some of those studying her recent depictions in popular culture.[30] This pockmarked woman with soot-colored teeth and bad breath seems to function as the comedically grotesque aspect of a legend that was gathering momentum in Elizabeth's own lifetime—namely that, given her success as a ruler, she could not possibly be a biologically or socially "typical" woman. There had to be something else that explained her extraordinary career. Some claimed that she must have been promiscuous and attributed the successes of the Elizabethan era to the men she bedded or allowed to dominate her. Others presented Elizabeth as a hatchet-faced grotesque, a gargoyle of monarchy. And, of course, there are also the spiritedly stupid conspiracy theories that she was either a hermaphrodite or a changeling—a male who was somehow smuggled in by her terrified servants to pass as Elizabeth when the real one died of an illness as a child, with all those involved somehow managing to pull off the deception for the next half century.[31]

It does not matter to supporters of this cocktail of the improbable that the real Elizabeth underwent a semipublic gynecological examination in the 1570s to prove her ability to bear children in the event of a proposed marriage with the French Duke of Anjou, nor that dozens, if not hundreds, of servants over the course of her life saw her in a state of undress. The implicit point is that Elizabeth I could have held power for forty-five years only if she either were a man or depended on one. Such conspiracy theories may be understandable in the febrile context of the sixteenth century; modern writers who continue to peddle such bunkum have far less excuse.

CHAPTER 10

EMPTY ROOMS

"At Westminster,"
Said I, "The man that keeps the Abbey tombs,
And for his price doth with who ever comes,
Of all our Harrys, and our Edwards talk,
From King to King and all their kin can walk:
Your ears shall hear nought, but Kings; your eyes meet
Kings only."

—John Donne, "Satire IV" (c. 1597)

Thomas Platter the Younger was about twenty-five when he visited England in the autumn of 1599. He was born in the Swiss city of Basel and his brother Felix was a famous physician. Their father had been the scholar Thomas Platter the Elder, in more ways than one, since he was about seventy-five when his youngest son was born. Not yet ten years old when his father died, Thomas had later followed Felix in the study of medicine at Montpellier in France, before, in his early twenties, embarking on four years' travel through western Europe. He loved England but was puzzled by its customs. He was surprised by both the number of pubs and that of witches. "I have never seen more taverns and ale-houses in my whole life than in London," he wrote, "and it is the custom in the latter to erect partitions between the tables so that one table cannot overlook the next. . . .

Numerous witches are found in England, for report goes that they do not punish them with death there."[1]

Thomas concluded that England had "many fine robust men," because in ancient times giants had lived there. A Protestant, he admired Queen Elizabeth, "who has ruled the country well," and he was struck not just by her power but also by the lives of English women, who, he felt, "have far more liberty than in other lands, and know just how to make good use of it, for they often stroll out or drive by coach in very gorgeous clothes, and the men just put up with such ways, and may not punish them for it." Platter enjoyed his time in "large and splendidly built" London, "the capital of England and so superior to other English towns that London is not said to be in England, but England to be in London, for England's most resplendent objects may be seen in and around London." He saw sturgeon and salmon being fished by locals from the Thames, and he went to the theater to see one of the first performances of William Shakespeare's new play *Julius Caesar*. He attended cockfighting and bearbaiting, noticing at the latter that a lot of the bears' teeth had been deliberately broken short so that they could not fight back against the dogs sent in to attack them. The baiting ended when "lastly they brought in an old blind bear which the boys hit with canes and sticks" for the crowd's entertainment, until the creature broke free and lumbered, whimpering and cowering, back into its stall.

With a letter of introduction, Platter left the capital and went to Nonsuch, a hunting lodge built for Henry VIII. There he was granted an audience with Lord Cobham, Lord Warden of the Cinque Ports, whose post tasked him with authority over five ancient English ports in the southeast: Dover (where Platter had disembarked), Hastings, Hythe, New Romney, and Sandwich. Platter asked Lord Cobham's permission for him and his friends to tour some of England's palaces—when the Queen was not in residence, of course. The dim yet amiable Cobham went one better, not only permitting them to visit a few of the royal residences but also asking if they would like to see the Queen in person, since she, too, was at Nonsuch. Platter and his friends leaped at the opportunity and were ushered into the Presence Chamber in time to see the sixty-six-year-old Elizabeth enter:

very straight and erect still, who sat down in the presence chamber upon a seat covered with red damask and cushions embroidered in gold thread . . . and there was a canopy above, fixed very ornately to the ceiling. She was most lavishly attired in a gown of pure white satin, gold-embroidered, with a whole bird of paradise for panache, set forward on her head studded with costly jewels, wore a string of huge round pearls about her neck and elegant gloves over which were drawn costly rings. In short, she was most gorgeously apparelled . . . She had a dignified and regal bearing, and, as noted above, rules her kingdom with great wisdom and in peace and prosperity and the fear of God, [she] has up till now successfully confronted her opponents with God's help and support. . . . God has preserved her wonderfully at all times. As soon as the queen had seated herself, her lady-in-waiting, very splendidly arrayed, also entered the room, while her secretary stood on her right.

As it was a Sunday, there were prayers and a short sermon, after which the Queen retired to her private apartments.

Lord Cobham advised that they visit Hampton Court first, because Elizabeth had left it only recently to come to Nonsuch. Cobham would give them letters under his seal so that the palace's caretakers would show them around. Elizabeth had travelled with "some three hundred carts of bag and baggage as is her custom"; however, as Nonsuch was so much smaller, the majority of the palace's decorations had not gone with her and remained at Hampton Court. Platter and a few friends departed by coach, since Nonsuch was one of the few royal homes without access to a river. They broke their journey of about six miles by spending the night at an inn in the town of Kingston upon Thames from where, on the next morning, Monday, September 27, 1599, they went to Hampton Court. Platter was in awe: "Hampton Court is the finest and most magnificent royal edifice to be found in England, or for that matter in other countries."

These tourists were lucrative for the skeleton staff left behind in every large Tudor home when the residents moved. Usually under the command of a governor, who lived there with his family throughout the year, the housekeeper, caretakers, guards, and gardeners could rake in a tidy supplemental income by charging the curious who wanted to be shown around the near-empty palace. We do not know who Thomas Platter's first guide was, although we know he had three that day—the first presumably being a servant attached to Hampton Court's housekeeping staff. Whoever it was, their guide led them through the gatehouse to the Base Court, which was then mostly covered by a lawn, and under the Anne Boleyn Gate, where Platter saw the "beautiful clock, cleverly devised from which one can tell the time by the sun, and also observe the movements of the moon."[2] In the palace's third courtyard, they were shown a large fountain, which looked to be made of white marble, and their guide told them that a favorite prank among servants and courtiers was to spray bystanders with the fountain's water; if done right, it would "wet them well."

Escorted inside, they saw the Great Hall—or "a banqueting hall," as Platter described it. He does not seem to have been impressed by it. He spent less than a sentence on it in his subsequent account of his English travels. He was much more interested in the galleries decorated with "such elegant tapestr[ies] of good gold, silver, and pure silk that the like is nowhere to be found in such quantity in one place." He loved the Chapel Royal, where he asked to play the organ. After a few impromptu tunes from Platter, the guide then took the party up to the Haunted Gallery to show them the balcony where the monarch sat during the chapel's religious services. Platter gazed at the ceiling decorations, noticing the proliferation of heraldic roses and portcullises, a device he recognized from some of the English coinage.[3] The chapel's ceiling was also decorated with multiple carvings of the royal family's French and Latin mottoes: *Dieu et mon droit* ("God and my Right") and *Dominus mihi adiutor* ("The Lord is my help").

Platter and his friends were taken outside to be introduced to one of the palace gardeners, who agreed to be their next guide "after we had offered a gratuity." The gardener, also nameless in Platter's account, showed them hedges, bushes, and flower beds of hawthorn, ivy, roses, lilies, juniper, rosemary, and holly, and topiary in the shapes of mythical heroes and centaurs.

The palace's maze was "similarly decorated with plants and flowering trees, and two marble fountains," Platter would recall, "so that time shall not drag in this place; for should one miss one's way, not only are taste, vision, and smell delighted, but the gladsome birdsongs and [s]plashing fountains please the ear, indeed it is like an earthly paradise."

The remunerated gardener handed them over to the palace's governor, to whom they presented Lord Cobham's letters of permission and introduction. Etiquette required that the guests then be introduced to the governor's wife and their daughters, whose first act was to bring Platter to see a curiosity: "a lively and lifelike portrait," as he put it later. It had once belonged to the English privateer Sir Martin Frobisher, who, five years earlier, had died in consequence of a wound he received while fighting the Spanish off the northwestern coast of France. The portraits depicted an Inuit family—father, mother, and child—whom Frobisher had kidnapped from what is now Baffin Island in northeastern Canada. He forcibly brought them to England, where the father, Kalicho, died from brain damage perhaps inflicted when he was captured or, more probably, when he attempted to fight off his tormentors, either on the transatlantic voyage or after they reached Bristol. Inspecting this "portrait of a wild man," Platter noticed that the father's face looked "much waled" (whipped or beaten). Kalicho had spent the last few days of his life propped up in public and in his kayak, from which, despite also having had a rib broken by his captors, he was ordered to throw darts at ducks to entertain customers. Kalicho's widow, Arnaq, standing next to him in the portrait, died in Bristol within days of her husband, having succumbed to the measles. A few days after her parents' funerals, their infant daughter, Nutaaq—depicted in the portrait nestled in her mother's hood—was taken to London to be displayed in front of paying crowds at a local inn. She survived for a week before she too died, almost certainly from the disease that had killed her mother. The family were the second, third, and fourth Inuit kidnapped by Martin Frobisher. He had done the same only a few months earlier to an Inuk man, who had also died in the explorer's custody, in this case, after two weeks after being taken to England.* It is possible that this man died from a wound after he badly bit his tongue in rage or fear while trying to resist or remonstrate against his kidnappers. The injury went untreated and may have become lethally infected. We do not know the victim's name. It was left to later scholars to find out possible names for the family depicted in the Hampton Court painting. Platter either was not told by his guides or did not consider it worthy of record. He concluded that the family "looked like savages."

"Then," according to Platter's discordant next paragraph, "we saw a picture of Love." After turning away from the Inuit painting, the tour group were delighted to see an allegorical portrait of "the Image of True Love," depicted as a woman with romantic mottoes painted across her body. "We then entered a room containing many fine royal beds," Platter continued, "also numerous canopies and royal chairs, all very lavish and ornate; and the walls everywhere were hung with extremely costly tapestries worked in gold, silver, and silk." Some of the tapestries depicted the assassination of Julius Caesar, others were inspired by the life of the biblical figure Lot, and the palace still had the series based on the life of the ancient Roman general Pompey the Great, kept in the rooms once occupied by Elizabeth's mother and possibly where her first stepmother, Queen Jane Seymour, had died sixty-two years earlier. Platter noticed quite a few decorations inspired by the travels of the biblical hero Tobias, whose journey, under the protection of the Archangel Raphael, to perform an exorcism in the city of Ecbatana was memorialized in many of the palace's tapestries and pictures.[4] Henry VIII's tapestries depicting various scenes from the life of the patriarch Abraham—which, at the time of writing, are still displayed in the Great Hall—were, even then, "the finest and most artistic in England; indeed the representations are immense in size."

Treasures littered the palace, including relics of Elizabeth I's parents.

---

* Both the first and last of the four victims—the Inuk gentleman whose name is not recorded and the child, Nutaaq—are buried at St. Olave's Church on Hart Street in the City of London. There was some debate later over whether or not Kalicho was the husband and father of Arnaq and Nutaaq, or whether he was kidnapped separately to mother and child.

The tourists saw a hunting cap, horn, and silken dog leashes that had belonged to Henry VIII and "a very costly bed" embroidered exquisitely by Anne Boleyn and her ladies-in-waiting. There were Elizabeth's virginals, unusually and expensively made of glass, inscribed with the words *Cantabis moneo quisquis cantare rogans* ("Whomsoever one bids sing, let him not refuse"). They walked around the Paradise and Elizabeth's private library, where Platter was impressed by an antique Bible in Latin and the Queen's collection of working clocks. Unlike the gardener, the governor and his family were too polite to ask for a tip. It was unspoken yet expected. The tourists had come with gifts for the family, which were presented over a farewell drink before the guests left by river to travel to Windsor Castle. Many of the things Thomas Platter saw that day—the bed embroidered by Anne Boleyn, Henry VIII's treasures, half the palace itself, and the portrait of the Inuit family kidnapped together and dead within days of one another—would not survive the century to come.

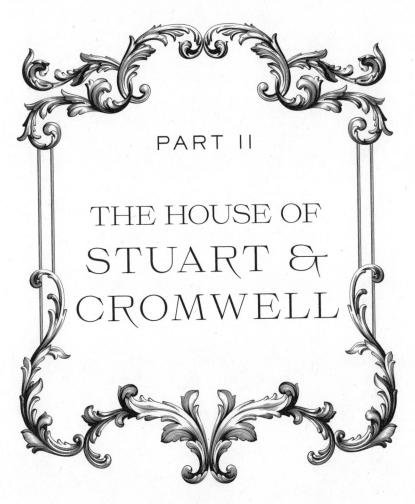

PART II

THE HOUSE OF STUART & CROMWELL

Great people lived and died in this house;
Magistrates, colonels, Members of Parliament.
Captains and Governors, and long ago
Men that had fought at Aughrim and the Boyne.

—W. B. Yeats, *Purgatory* (1938)

CHAPTER II

THE PAGES' CHAMBER

Shall we their fond pageant see?
Lord, what fools these mortals be!

—William Shakespeare,
A Midsummer Night's Dream (c. 1596)

Preserved and restored today, a Pages' Chamber lies off the corridor that links the Great Watching Chamber to the Haunted Gallery. In good weather, light streams in through its windows onto a long table between a door and the fireplace. The court's page boys, who were usually in their teens, once slept on its floor. Little had changed in servants' accommodation since Lord Daubeney's day, and the Pages' Chamber was their bedroom, their dining room, and their jealously guarded common room. Every morning, they woke to roll away the sleeping bags and pillows that constituted their beds, washed themselves with cold water and sponges, dressed in their livery, ate breakfast, and began their day of errands. With its whitewashed walls and spartan furnishings, at the time of writing the room looks much as it might have as December 1603 turned to January 1604, when Hampton Court was wrapped in fogs and mists so heavy that people could barely see a few feet in front of them. The page boys had to take extra torches down to the wharf and courtyards to light the way of those arriving to celebrate the busiest Christmas anybody at the English court could remember. It was not even, really, the English court anymore, but, as some of the English murmured unhappily, a British one.

Elizabeth I was gone. Nine months earlier, she had died in her bed at the nearby Palace of Richmond, "mildly like a lamb, easily like a ripe apple from the tree," according to an eyewitness, after a reign of forty-five years.[1] The passing of a queen who had been on the throne longer than most of her subjects had been alive felt like the end of an era; as a London pamphleteer reflected later, they were a people "almost begotten and born under her; that never shouted any other *Ave* but for her name, never saw the face of any Prince but herself." That sense of the "strange outlandish word 'change'" was augmented by Elizabeth's death in the small hours of March 24, the day before the start of England's new calendar year.[2] Her death brought quietly to a close the rule of the Tudor dynasty, with the crowns of England and Ireland passing to her Scottish kinsman, King James VI, head of the House of Stewart.*

He was the only son of Elizabeth's dead rival Mary, Queen of Scots, and, through her, a great-great-grandson of Elizabeth of York and Henry VII. Through his late father, Lord Darnley, he was a grandson of Lady Margaret Douglas.[3] The Stewart dynasty had ruled Scotland since 1371; from there, on several occasions, it had launched major invasions of English territory, the penultimate of which, led by James's great-grandfather, remains to date the largest foreign invasion of England.[4] Some in England thus characterized James VI's accession to their throne as the stealthy culmination of a Stewart conquest, and even those who did not frame it in quite such strong terms objected to being ruled by a foreign-born king. In particular, there was resentment in the towns and in Parliament at King James's proposal to replace the name of England with a resurrection of the ancient Roman name of Britannia as "Britain," to celebrate the unification of a greater British polity under a single royal house.

There had been other contenders for the crown during the twilight of

---

* Stewart was typically the spelling used for the dynastic name in Scotland; in Ireland, England, and Wales, it was generally spelled Stuart, which was also used by both of James VI's parents.

the Tudors, some of whom had hoped to turn anti-Scottish xenophobia to their advantage, but King James's cause crucially won the support of many members of the aristocracy, who fawned over him with diligent shamelessness as he progressed south in the weeks after Queen Elizabeth's death. He benefited, too, from the Virgin Queen's dwindling popularity in her later years, during which enthusiasm for the sovereign was eroded by the heavy rainfall of six consecutive terrible summers with correspondingly dire harvests and rising food prices.[5] While millions were still devoted to Elizabeth, whom they felt had "lived and reigned and died in peace and full of glory" until "she laid down her head in the grave as the most resplendent sun setteth at last in a western cloud," many others were eager to see a new reign—unknowingly confirming Elizabeth's shrewd assessment of her own subjects when she wrote, "I know the inconstancy of the people of England, how they ever mislike the present government and have their eyes fixed upon that person that is next to succeed. More men love the rising sun than the one that sets."[6] Remaining James VI in his native Scotland, the "rising sun" became James I in England, Ireland, and Wales.

For palace servants, the new Jacobean[*] regime offered a wealth of possibilities, primarily through the possibility of wealth. Elizabeth I had neither husband nor children, which meant no respective household staffs had been required for individual members of a royal family. This had meant fewer corresponding opportunities for jobs, advancement, and competition. In all the time it had been a Crown property, Hampton Court had never yet hosted a monarch with a spouse and more than one legitimate child; King James, in contrast, was married with a daughter and two sons. The youngest of the princes, three-year-old Charles, Duke of Albany, had stayed temporarily in Scotland in the care of servants until he was judged strong enough to make the long journey to southern England. It was a sensible precaution. Two other children in the Scottish royal nursery, Princess Margaret and Robert, Duke of Kintyre, had died as infants—in Margaret's case, after her first birthday and in Robert's, eight months before. King

---

[*] From the Latin *Jacobus* for James.

James's Danish wife, Queen Anna, had also suffered a miscarriage shortly before leaving Edinburgh, and she travelled into England accompanied by an infant's coffin carrying "the body of the male child of which she had been delivered in Scotland." She felt forced to do so to rebut her critics, who cruelly accused the Queen of fabricating her miscarriage to manipulate the public's sympathy.[7] New subdivisions of the household were formed to care for this royal family, with the two elder royal children being set up with their entourages at Oatlands Palace in Hampton Court Chase.

The mood at Hampton Court as the Stuarts' first Christmas in England approached was a celebratory one. The season had already included parties for the wedding in the chapel of nineteen-year-old Sir Philip Herbert, the Earl of Pembroke's younger brother, and sixteen-year-old Lady Susan de Vere, the Earl of Oxford's daughter.[8] The groom's handsomeness was frequently commented upon at the time, as was his love of the arts, an interest he shared with his well-educated bride, who had joined Queen Anna's household as a lady-in-waiting. Her uncle, Robert Cecil, was the King's chief minister and the King himself had helped arrange Philip and Susan's marriage, which meant that the banquets following their wedding were particularly splendid. It is doubtful that any of the palace staff felt well rested, as the wedding set the tone for the manic magnificence of the 1603–04 Christmas. There were even more gifts than usual, as those hoping to forge connections with the new regime expressed their goodwill, from the mulberry satin gown gifted to Queen Anna by Queen Margaret of Spain, to the traditional gold from different bishops, or the perfumed gloves for the King from several gentry families, all of which had to be delivered, sorted, and catalogued by the servants.[9] The staff benefited, undoubtedly, from the largesse of the season—among them Queen Anna's jester, Thomas Drury, who had recently received a new green velvet jacket from his employer.[10]

The page boys could not go to sleep until the court retired. Even if some were tempted to sneak a quick nap, they may have been kept awake by the voices and music from the Great Watching Chamber next door, where refreshment tables were laid out with snacks and drinks for the revellers. Some of those who had been out of favor under Queen Elizabeth were present to celebrate a revival in their fortunes, noticeably the Howard earls of Northampton and Suffolk. Despite their kinship with the late queen, the Howards had lost their dukedom of Norfolk when the last incumbent, Thomas, was beheaded for treason in 1572, and in 1595 his eldest son, Philip, had died in prison after refusing to abjure his Catholic faith.[11] Lord Northampton was rumored by court gossips to have had both female and male lovers, as was his fellow patron of the arts Henry Wriothesley, Earl of Southampton, who had narrowly escaped execution after participating in a rebellion against Elizabeth I. Southampton had been pardoned by her but not forgiven, and he was not welcomed back to court until his long-rumored sympathy for King James secured his return upon Elizabeth's death.*

Alongside those of the English nobles, the page boys heard a broader variety of accents in the Great Watching Chamber than they had at previous Christmases. Lord Kinloss's Scottish accent was, perhaps, not entirely unfamiliar to them, since, before the post was rendered redundant, he had visited Queen Elizabeth at Hampton Court as Scotland's ambassador to England. That Christmas, he was joined by more of the King's Scottish favorites who had moved to England with their sovereign; they included Sir George Home and Sir Thomas Erskine, the latter of whom was the newly appointed Captain of the Guard, replacing Elizabeth I's appointee, the explorer Sir Walter Raleigh, who was out of favor and in the Tower for his alleged complicity in a plot to replace King James with one of his English cousins.[12]

Along with the Scottish accents, servants at Hampton Court also heard the Danish of the Queen's visiting younger brother Duke Johan of Holstein and the north Irish of Hugh O'Neill, Earl of Tyrone, who was short in height with "a strong body . . . valiant, affable, and [with a] profound wit."[13] A year earlier, Tyrone had been another persona non grata with the English government, called "so horrible a traitor" for his leadership of the

---

* During the rebellion, Southampton had put his influence in the theater world to dangerous use by commissioning a revival of Shakespeare's play *Richard II*, in which an out-of-touch autocrat is overthrown in favor of his cousin. The point, about as subtle as a brick through a window, did not go unnoticed either by the audience or by Elizabeth.

Irish uprising, the greatest and longest of the rebellions against Elizabeth I. Tyrone had, however, so much respect for his enemy that he had wept when he heard of the Queen's death, and he accepted her successor's offer of pardon.[14] Peace was very much one of King James's priorities, and so, along with extending an olive branch to former rebels and outcasts, he had also opened up diplomatic negotiations with the Spaniards, which had been firmly shut down by Elizabeth ever since her defeat of the Spanish Armada fifteen years earlier in 1588.

At the height of his rebellion against Elizabeth, Lord Tyrone had been in secret communication with the Spanish government. We do not know if he discussed old plans, no longer necessary, with the Spanish ambassador, Don Pedro de Zúñiga, Marquis of Flores Dávila; both men were present at Hampton Court that Christmas, as were the ambassadors for the kings of France and Poland-Lithuania, the Grand Duke of Tuscany, and the Duke of Savoy and the Republic of Venice, the last of whom praised Hampton Court for its "furnishings of the royal apartments [which] are the richest that the crown possesses."[15] These ambassadors were constantly jockeying for prominence over one another. Servants and courtiers had been amused by the contretemps between the French and Spanish envoys, who, during a ball, "hold hard for the greatest honor" of dancing with the nine-year-old heir to the throne, Prince Henry-Frederick, in what seems to have ended up as an undignified, musically accompanied scramble. Dignity took a back seat to fun that Christmas, with drunken aristocrats creating more work for the staff when they fell over and took one of the refreshment tables down with them.

Their jobs in the palace gave the page boys a front row seat not only to historical developments and irritating cleanups, but also to the splendid entertainments launched that Christmas, which would soon become a staple of life in the Stuart court. Queen Anna had a passion for the arts—plays, in particular—and so one had been performed every night since the Twelve Days of Christmas began. William Shakespeare, a forty-year-old poet-playwright from Stratford-upon-Avon, with receding dark hair and a well-trimmed beard, was basking in royal favor after a successful performance in the Great Hall of his off-season comedy *A Midsummer Night's Dream*, as well as the much more seasonally appropriate *Twelfth Night*.[16] *Troilus and Cressida* had been presented, as had both parts of his *Henry IV*, and *Henry V*. Moralists had long denounced the London theater scene for the degeneracy and corruption they claimed it spread. From their censorious perspective, it is worth remembering that it was illegal for women to appear on the London stage as actresses, and so, while homosexual intercourse was still technically a capital offense thanks to legislation introduced by Henry VIII, the era's most popular plays pushed those brutal boundaries on same-sex intimacy to their limit. To take, by way of example, two of the shows performed at Hampton Court that Christmas, when Shakespeare's King Henry V wooed Princess Catherine of France, the court was watching two men. In *Twelfth Night*, a male actor plays a female character named Viola, who disguises herself as a man named Cesario, who finds employment serving Orsino, Duke of Illyria, with whom she falls secretly in love while still pretending to be Cesario. In that guise, she has attracted the romantic attention of a female palace servant named Olivia, also played by a man, who falls in love with "Cesario" without realizing that Cesario is actually Viola. By the middle of the play, an allegedly accidental lesbian love story was being performed in Hampton Court's Great Hall by two men, one in traditional female attire and the other in male attire, donned within the play by a woman impersonating a man. At the culmination of *Twelfth Night*, Olivia transfers her affections to Viola's brother Sebastian, with whom she lives the proverbial happily ever after; as does Viola, who, once she casts off her male clothes to reveal she was never a man named Cesario, confesses her love to Duke Orsino, who returns her affections and proposes. What the audience saw at Hampton Court was four men, two of them still playing women, kissing in the center of the Great Hall, before the court applauded the performance. Small wonder that the growing number of English Puritans characterized the theater-loving world of the Stuart court as Sodom and Gomorrah with a props department.

If the theory is correct that Shakespeare debuted a newly edited version of *Hamlet* at Hampton Court that Christmas, then "the man from

Stratford" clearly had an eye to the main chance with the play's inclusion of Helsingør—which he anglicized as Elsinore—the Danish town where King James and Queen Anna had spent their honeymoon.[17] Shakespeare was determined to do better under the Stuarts than he had under Elizabeth, who was at best an inconsistent enthusiast of his work, and he predicted correctly that Queen Anna would prove a more supportive patron.[18] Anna, who was already being praised by her husband's new subjects for her "fashion and courteous behaviour to the people," was so delighted with many of the Christmas shows that she broke with protocol by inviting the actors back to her rooms, where feasting and dancing continued into the small hours.[19] The servants went to bed late and woke up early to prepare the palace for that day's entertainments.

For the secular New Year of January 1, Shakespeare's plays were replaced by a masque, a phantasmagoria that merged dance and the spoken word with elaborate costumes, fantastical sets, and corresponding budgets. Page boys and nobles entered a Great Hall transformed for *The Masque of the Chinese Magician*, with a set resembling the heavens installed at the far end of the room; from this, the magician character appeared to deliver a long monologue to King James, while artificial clouds were maneuvered into position. In the course of the entertainment, the clouds were conjured by the magician to serve as transport for "certain Indian and Chinese Knights to see the magnificency of this court; and thereupon a traverse was drawn and the maskers seen sitting in a vaulty place with torchbearers and other lights which was no unpleasing spectacle." The music began as maskers entered, playing the fictional foreign knights who had travelled to see Hampton Court's legendary splendor. The "warriors" included the recent bridegroom Sir Philip Herbert, who was struggling to dance elegantly under the weight of his jewel-encrusted costume; he picked out his wife from the spectators and invited her to join him in the dance, which ended when one of the knights publicly presented King James with a jewel he had bought recently for himself, worth £40,000.[20]

A week later, it was Queen Anna's turn when she took the role of Athena, mythical goddess of Wisdom, in *The Vision of the Twelve Goddesses*, a masque commissioned by her from playwright Samuel Daniels. The Countess of Bedford, who had recommended Daniels to the Queen, was cast as Vesta, goddess of the Home, while the ten other roles were parcelled out to other high-ranking women of the court—including Venus, goddess of Beauty, which went to the famously beautiful Penelope Devereux, Lady Rich, and Flora, goddess of Spring, who was played by the newlywed Lady Susan.[21] The Great Hall was again transformed for the evening. An artificial mountain had been constructed for the set near the screen at the lower end of the room; several other pieces representing Sleep's Cave and a Temple of Peace were positioned across the hall. Servants, courtiers, councillors, and guests watched from the upper end, near the entrance to the Great Watching Chamber. The page boys were on duty for this performance. Kitted out in costumes of white satin embroidered with golden stars, they were positioned around the hall, each holding a flickering candle of virgin wax, to light the way as the Queen glittered into view of the audience wearing "a helmet full of jewels, and her whole attire embossed with jewels of several fashions." Anna-Athena was joined by the eleven other goddesses, leading to her husband, where they all curtsied to him. The Queen's costume was daringly cut just below her knees; the future Lord Dorchester, watching in the Great Hall, joked that it meant he "might see a woman had both feet and legs, which I never knew before."[22]

The King's cousin Lady Arbella Stuart recognized the mutilated dress, as did many others.[23] All twelve goddesses wore recycled state gowns that had once belonged to the late Queen Elizabeth; Arbella heard that, in preparation for *The Vision of the Twelve Goddesses*, Anna had sent two of her ladies-in-waiting—the Countess of Suffolk (Juno, queen of Olympus) and Lady Audrey Walsingham (Astraea, goddess of Justice)—with "warrants to take of the late Queen's best apparel out of the Tower at their discretion."[24] The pieces were brought to Hampton Court, where Anna's seamstresses slashed, sewed, and styled them for use in the masque. Elizabeth I's dresses were, admittedly, hopelessly out of fashion by the younger generation's standards and would have needed substantial alterations before Queen Anna wore them in any capacity, but some of the more traditionalist courtiers were dismayed at seeing Gloriana's gowns reduced to props; opponents of a political union between Scotland and England bristled at the masque's mention of "uniting strange nations with affection" and a land called Britain.[25]

For Puritans, the affront to tradition went far deeper than politics or Anna's sartorial recycling. Given that actresses were prohibited from performing in London, it struck Puritans as grotesque for their King's wife to appear in a production alongside her intelligent ladies-in-waiting. Many of the Puritans were discomfited, even disgusted, by the storylines of popular plays, and especially by the previously mentioned moral implications of male actors pretending to be female characters, those female characters passing successfully as men, or male actors kissing each other as their characters fell in love. Although they could not decide if it was preferable to see two men embracing in front of large crowds rather than women appearing on stage, the sense grew among the English evangelical community that the Stuart royal household was out of step with the godly, and that God would, in time, make clear His displeasure.

Some of the faithful thought that God had already sent a warning that summer. As proof, they could cite the bodies of the recently dead victims of the plague. It was not true that the virus had appeared after James's accession, as some of his mounting number of critics claimed. The King had arrived in England at a time when the epidemic was already gathering momentum, as that year's strain of the plague mutated into the most lethal in decades. Even in the village of Hampton, which was far enough outside London to usually prove safe during the annual outbreaks, the plague of 1603 had killed more than a fifth of the residents.[26] Within the palace boundaries, two or three victims were lost daily to the plague while preparations for the coronation continued. Eventually, reality had to be acknowledged, as hundreds perished every day, and the disease defied expectations by growing stronger rather than weaker. More than a thousand Londoners died during the week of the coronation alone. As the plague began to infest the countryside, the royal children were no longer considered safe in their bucolic bubble and had been evacuated from Oatlands.

The mood in the cities swung between terror and merriment, with many people refusing to miss the festivities surrounding James and Anna's arrival from Scotland. When the danger was judged, at last, to have cooled with the arrival of the winter frosts, the relief helped fuel the defiant hedonism of the Christmas of 1603—for it was not only the dawn of a new age for the monarchy but also a celebration, filled with alcohol, food, music, and jokes, by people who felt they had escaped death. They danced and feasted because they still could. Nonetheless, alongside the relief, there remained an undercurrent of unease—proof of a fear that they hoped could be drowned out by noise of balls, banquets, and musicians. The thick mist still lay over the passing river at Hampton Court, and servants continued running back and forth with more torches to light the way from wharf to palace, as a courtier reflected, "[W]e fear we shall now stumble into the sickness which till now we have miraculously [e]scaped."[27]

CHAPTER 12

THE HAMPTON COURT
CONFERENCE

There should be one more exact Translation of the
Holy Scriptures into the English tongue.

—The King James Bible, Preface (1611)

The palace itself seemed to be nursing a hangover after Christmas. The damage inflicted by the celebrations necessitated hiring workmen to replaster the floors in the Great Hall and the Watching Chamber.[1] Entering the latter from the former and turning right, one faced guarded doors leading to the King's private rooms. Privacy, in the context of early modern monarchy, was a relative term, and on Thursday, January 10, 1604, a large group of men was granted the honor of meeting their King.

They were ushered in to kneel before a thirty-seven-year-old man with ginger hair and matching beard. He was tall and broad shouldered, but with thin legs and a tongue slightly too large for his mouth. At the time, people mocked King James I's appearance, wondering how someone they considered so unattractive could have been born from a father described as among "the lustiest and best proportioned" noblemen of his generation and a royal mother praised for possessing "beauty . . . beyond compare."[2] They mocked, too—behind his back, of course—James's terse, tactless way of speaking and his constant fidgeting.[3] However, even the most caustic critic could not deny the King's intelligence. James I was not simply well read but also the author of several books, including *Basilikon Doron*, a self-help manual on the Divine Right of Kings for the admittedly rather niche market of absolute monarchs; he had also written a book attacking the new craze for smoking tobacco imported from the Americas, and *Daemonologie*, a textbook for witch hunters. All three—divine right, diabolical arts, and smoldering tobacco—were points of passion for James. He had symbols to ward off witchcraft carved into his bed frames and doorways, and had inaugurated the North Berwick witch trials seven years earlier in Scotland, when he sanctioned the use of torture after having become convinced that terrible storms that had engulfed Queen Anna's ship as she attempted to sail to Edinburgh from her native Denmark had been conjured by necromancers. He also believed that his exiled mother's execution on Elizabeth I's orders in 1587 had been foreseen by soothsayers in Scotland, who warned James ahead of the event that they had beheld visions of her blood-soaked head. In pursuit of his vendetta against witches and sorcerers, James had collected books on divination, spell casting, and black magic. He guarded these contraband texts diligently, claiming that, since kings were morally stronger than their subjects, it would be unwise to let something so corrupting be seen by ordinary men.

Many of the bishops, deans, privy councillors, and evangelicals escorted into the King's Apartments struggled to read King James, too, for he was far more complex than his reputation as a bibliophile might suggest. With his caustic sense of humor, James had punctured the pretensions of many of his aristocratic hosts on the journey south after Elizabeth I's death, mocking the absurd family trees that traced their ancestry back to Adam and Eve. He seemed contemptuous, too, of the ordinary people who had lined the roadsides to cheer his arrival, joking to his entourage that he would "pull down my breeches, and they shall also see my arse!"[4] During an earlier audience in the King's Apartments, the courtier Sir John Harington had been caught in one of James's impromptu lectures on witchcraft. James asked Harington if he knew why the Devil "so often worked in old women."

Knowing that the King's sense of humor leaned toward the scatological, misogynist and erotic, Harington responded with "a scurvy jest" that "we were taught thereof in Scripture where it is told, that the Devil walketh in dry places."[5] For this, Harington was rewarded with a laugh, although it did not put James off for long from warning him about the ever-present threat of sorcery. James thought his new Welsh and English subjects were far too lax when it came to the dangers posed by witchcraft. Sixteenth-century Scotland had one of the highest levels of witchhunting in Europe, and James encouraged more vigorous persecutions to be introduced in England and Wales. He also thought the English were rather too fond of tobacco, the smoking of which he banned in Hampton Court's Great Hall.

James was passionate about religion, and he took seriously the other role he had inherited from Elizabeth I, as Supreme Governor of the Church of England. Elizabeth had established that title at the same time she had restored the Church's independence from the Vatican—softening it from her father's and brother's title of Supreme Head—as well as passing several pieces of legislation in the immediate aftermath of her Catholic sister's death. Elizabeth's ensuing policy of via media ("middle road") on religion was intended to win over the support of the majority for the Church of England, and, having devoted so much of her energy to establishing it in the first two years after becoming queen, Elizabeth had seen no good reason to return to the subject in the forty-three years that followed. A hard line had been taken against her in retaliation by the papacy, with the result that fines, imprisonments, and, later, even executions were handed down by Elizabeth's government against those English and Welsh Catholics who felt her church—moderate as it might be—was simply too far removed from the teachings and practices of Catholicism for them to support it. At the same time, the availability of the Bible in English saw many new interpretations of the Scriptures; these in their turn led to the growth of many different denominations of Protestantism, some of which, chiefly the Puritans and Calvinists, felt that the Church of England remained too much like Catholicism, particularly in the decoration of its churches, its use of music in services, and, above all, its preserving a hierarchy of bishops. The latter was decried as a particularly dangerous hangover from Catholicism. As the Puritans put it in their writings, "Archbishop[s], Bishop[s], Deans, Archdeacons, Deacons, Chancellors, Commissaries, Officials, and all such as be rather [are] members and parts of the whore and strumpet of Rome."[6] By the time Elizabeth I died in 1603, the Church of England was thus under considerable internal strain, and just over a thousand Puritan preachers had signed the Millenary Petition with the specific request that the King reform the Church he now commanded, which they submitted to James on his arrival in England. James had initially intended to convene a synod of experts in November, but this was pushed back to January on account of the tenacity of that year's plague.

Much as James's personality remained something of an enigma during this early stage of his rule in England, so did his religious views. For those gathered at Hampton Court in 1604, the King could be all things to all people. Catholics hoping for an end to the Elizabethan discrimination remembered that James was the son of the late Mary, Queen of Scots, whose execution at the height of anti-Catholic paranoia in the 1580s, as well as her considerable bravery in the face of death, inspired many of her English coreligionists to regard her as a martyr. In contrast, the Puritans focused on the fact that James had not seen his Catholic mother since she had been overthrown and fled into exile while he was still in the cradle, whereafter he had been raised by his guardians as a Presbyterian. Surely a lifelong Presbyterian would share Puritanism's antipathy toward bishops and thus abolish the office in the Church of England?

Perhaps both sides should have researched King James more diligently. First, he had done very little to stop his mother's execution and absolutely nothing to rescue her from de facto house arrest in England during the two preceding decades. Second, he had done even less to alleviate the position of Scottish Catholics and had, at one point, privately told an Irish delegation that "he would rather fight in blood to the knee" than grant full legal toleration of Catholicism.[7] When it came to his track record with Presbyterianism, this was a king who once snapped in a debate with its ministers, "I give not a steaming turd for thy preaching!" and who had quarrelled relentlessly with the Presbyterian Kirk* in Scotland, most passionately over his support for maintaining bishoprics, whose continued existence, James believed, was part of the same divinely ordained hierarchy that blessed the monarchy's mandate. If the bishops fell, kings would not be far behind them. In his nine months since becoming king of England and Ireland, however, James had played his cards close to his chest; thus, every shade of religious opinion gathered in the Hampton Court Presence Chamber had reason to hope that he was on their side.

Those illusions were rapidly shaken when James began speaking. He announced that he intended, by and large, to preserve Elizabeth's via media, since, to his mind, there "appeareth no cause why the form of the Service of God wherein they have been nourished so many years should be changed."[8] He flattered, then disappointed, the Catholic lobby by referring to Rome as the Mother Church. His choice of words here deliberately advertised the nimbleness of James's grasp on theology. Mother-church imagery had been, for centuries, redolent of devotion to the Virgin Mary, something which would appeal to the Catholic lobby in 1604, however its citation in his speech simultaneously enabled the King to evoke a New Testament verse by Saint Paul about spiritual "children" and to thereby patronizingly characterize Catholics as those who had not yet reached theological maturity in the form of a church that took the best bits of what he saw as Christianity's Catholic "childhood" while jettisoning those teachings and trinkets that were no longer helpful.[9] There was no such oscillation from compliments to criticism for the Puritans, whose stauncher members the King dismissed as an infestation in "the bowels of the nation" for their politicized sermons and biblical literalism.[10] He outright rejected their pleas for stricter enforcement of observing the Sabbath on Sundays, although he lifted Queen Elizabeth's ban on home Bible study groups, which were and have remained a staple of evangelical spirituality and community.

The conference unfolded at Hampton Court over several days, with

---

* The Presbyterian governing body, from the Scottish word for *church*.

the King using etiquette to underscore his words to these "grave, learned, and reverend men," as he politely called them. The bishops were granted a separate audience in the King's private drawing room on Saturday the twelfth, during which James sat among them—a gesture that, if not quite denoting equality between king and bishops, certainly suggested royal respect. The most senior of this group was John Whitgift, the loquacious and fine-living Archbishop of Canterbury, who had prayed with Queen Elizabeth on her deathbed and crowned King James in Westminster Abbey the previous summer. Despite his occasional gestures of sympathy toward their movement, the Puritans had targeted Whitgift as a symbol of everything they disliked in Elizabeth's Church, accusing him in their propaganda of a long-running homosexual liaison with the vice chancellor of Cambridge University. James liked Archbishop Whitgift and treated him especially well at the bishops' audience. In contrast, during the main Puritan meeting on Monday the fourteenth, the delegates were required to kneel before the King and his eldest son, Prince Henry-Frederick, nine years old and included in the ceremony as a symbol of monarchical continuity. Father and son sat beneath a velvet canopy—James on a throne, Henry-Frederick on a stool—in the intentionally intimidating splendor of the Presence Chamber.[11] James was unimpressed by the representatives' inarticulacy. He did not seem to realize—or care—that inviting a group of people into the heart of one of the largest royal residences in the world, then requiring them to kneel while they faced the two most senior members of their royal family, might have left some of the Puritans feeling understandably discombobulated. James refused to even contemplate negotiating on the issue of bishoprics; when one of the few Puritans confident enough to speak pressed the point, James snapped famously, "No bishop, no king!" and stormed out of the room.[12]

In terms of reforming and reinvigorating the Church of England, the Hampton Court Conference of 1604 ultimately has to be judged a spectacular failure, with the significant exception of its increasing investment in the education of future clergymen. Its consequences radicalized some disappointed Catholics to the extent that, eighteen months later, they launched the foiled Gunpowder Plot that aimed to blow up King James and Prince

Henry-Frederick as they attended the opening of Parliament. Had the plan succeeded, almost the entire ruling class of Protestant England would have been obliterated. Some equally frustrated Puritans concluded that England was beyond redemption, and so, in the same year, they boarded a ship called the *Mayflower* to start life across the ocean in a community they could knead into being without being legally required to attend weekly Anglican services.

There had, however, been several remarkable thinkers representing the Puritan cause. They were determined not to leave Hampton Court empty-handed, and, although they failed in many of their objectives, they nonetheless had one towering achievement that they were turning into a reality even as the *Mayflower* was loaded with supplies and the plotters' barrels were loaded with gunpowder. Among the most prominent and impressive of the Puritan delegates was Dr. John Knewstubs, a Fellow of St. John's College at the University of Cambridge. Knewstubs did not secure his desired outlawing of clerical vestments, despite his impassioned arguments that they looked like the robes of ancient pagan priesthoods for the Roman cults or the Egyptian goddess Isis. Knewstubs's colleague Dr. Laurence Chaderton was another Cambridge man as Master of Emmanuel College, where he had instituted a strict regime under which Holy Communion would be administered only to those students he deemed spiritually worthy of receiving it. Chaderton was also a former wrestler, a keen herbalist, and a convert to Puritanism from Catholicism. At sixty-eight, he was already elderly by early modern standards; incredibly, he was to live a lot longer, dying aged 104 in 1640.

They were joined at the palace by Dr. John Rainolds, President of Corpus Christi College at the University of Oxford, de facto leader of the Puritan delegation and a man who refused to let the agony he endured from gout prevent him from serving the cause in which he believed. Like Chaderton, Rainolds had the convert's zeal in having left his childhood Catholicism to become a Puritan. He had paid a heavy price for this leap of faith, particularly through a permanent estrangement from his brother William, a Catholic theologian and priest, who died in exile in the Hapsburg Netherlands rather than accept Protestantism in England. Rainolds's rejection of his youthful tastes also included embarrassment over his student days as an amateur actor—his greatest role had come as a young undergraduate at Oxford, aged about seventeen, when he was cast as the Amazonian queen Hippolyta in a play performed to welcome Elizabeth I on a royal visit to the university. Rainolds had since evolved to become one of the harshest critics of cross-dressing roles as a corrupting influence on public morality.

Ironically or appropriately, depending on one's view, it was Dr. Rainolds, in those fraught days at Hampton Court, who is traditionally given credit for suggesting the one work in the history of the English language that, to date, has outsold William Shakespeare: the King James Bible. Rainolds asked the King to commission "one only translation of the Bible to be authentical and read in church." For the preceding four decades, there had been two Bibles at work, often against each other, among English Protestants. Puritans preferred the Geneva Bible, so called because it had largely been produced in Geneva by English Protestants living in Switzerland during the persecutions under Queen Mary I; after she died, they brought their work with them back to England. Traditionalists—or High Anglicans, as they might be known in modern parlance—typically used the Bishops' Bible, a translation approved by Elizabeth I and first published in England in 1568. Added to this mix was the Douay-Rheims version, an English-language edition of the New Testament released by Catholic scholars who had fled the Elizabethan persecutions and established a seminary in France; by the time of the Hampton Court Conference, the Douay scholars were working on translating the books known in Christianity as the Old Testament. Given that there are today dozens of translations used as a matter of individual preference by Christians, Dr. Rainolds's concerns over, at most, three (and in practice, two) "competing" Bibles might seem like tears over an empty grave. However, in 1604 Rainolds was correct in identifying that this tension regarding translation stood at the heart of the divisions within Protestantism. Many Protestants believed that the Bible was the infallible, directly revealed Word of God. How, then, could it be that while also existing in multiple, varying versions?

For James, the petition to authorize a new edition of the Bible spoke to many of his deepest, most cherished beliefs. The delighted King was able to cast himself as the modern equivalent of Constantine the Great, the Roman emperor who had presided over the Council of Nicea in 325, at which many of the early Church's major internal disputes had been, more or less, ironed out, unity had been successfully prioritized, and debates over certain contested books in the Bible resolved. This great enterprise of a new English-language translation of the Holy Scriptures, commissioned, authorized, and propagated by the Crown, was the Divine Right of Kings in action. It is hard to imagine, at least from James's perspective, a clearer example of a monarchy acting as Heaven's deputy—God's lieutenants, as James himself called kings in his book *Basilikon Doron.* James would give to his people God's Word, thereby serving as a conduit of God's Will.

The commission granted at Hampton Court in 1604 took seven years to complete. There was something resolutely practical about its division of labors, first to committees based in three centers of excellence: the Church's epicenter at Westminster and the universities of Cambridge and Oxford. All were subdivided into two committees per location, which were in turn allocated different sections of the Bible to translate, with relevant experts appointed to each committee based on their skills and previous fields of research. There were seventy-nine books within the Bible—although, later in the seventeenth century, this would be generally reduced in Protestant versions to sixty-six—contained in three broad sections that Christians referred to as the Old Testament, the Deuterocanonical Apocrypha,* and

---

* This Apocrypha is part of a collection of thirteen works of Jewish religious writings respected in Catholicism and Orthodoxy but eventually ignored by most Protestant denominations. Composed between the third century BC and the early first century AD, they were never regarded as being as sacred as the Old or New Testaments. They are distinct from the other Apocrypha—those more famous today for containing alternative narratives on the youth and life of Christ—which have never been part of the Christian canon. Protestantism's definitive rejection of the so-called Deuterocanonical Apocrypha came in 1646 with the Calvinist publication of the Westminster Confession of Faith, which ruled that, since the thirteen books were historical records rather than spiritual instructions, "The books commonly called Apocrypha, not being of divine inspiration, are no part of the Canon of Scripture; and therefore are of no authority in the Church of God, nor to be any otherwise approved, or made use of, than other human writings."

the New Testament. The First Westminster Company of translators was allocated the first twelve books of the Old Testament, while the Second Westminster committee was tasked with translating the Epistles, a series of letters between the early Christian communities, written in Greek and subsequently catalogued as the twenty-one books at the middle of the New Testament. At Oxford, Dr. Rainolds sat on the First Company of experts who dealt with the texts at the middle of the Old Testament, from the First Book of Chronicles through to the Song of Solomon. Elsewhere at Oxford, its Second Company of translators was entrusted with the four Gospels, dealing with the earthly life of Christ, the Acts of the Apostles, and the Book of Revelation, the latter generally regarded then and now as one of the most difficult books in the Bible thanks to its series of prophetic allegorical visions pertaining to the Apocalypse, or End of Days.* Elderly Dr. Chaderton sat as a member of the First Cambridge Company to work on the final seventeen books in the Old Testament, while the second set of Cambridge gentlemen were handed the thirteen books of the Apocrypha. For seven years, these scholars worked with diligence and integrity to produce a translation of the Bible that would, they believed earnestly, offer their fellow Christians "a whole armoury of weapons, both offensive and defensive; whereby we may save our selves and put the enemy to flight"— the enemy being Satan.[13] Some of the scholars did not live to see the fruits of their labors. Dr. Rainolds was among them, contracting and dying of tuberculosis three years into the seven. He had continued hosting thrice-weekly meetings of his translation committee in his college rooms even as illness consumed his frame to the point of emaciation. In order to reinforce their own consciences and religious zeal, King James kept up pressure on the committees throughout. He was invested not just politically but also

---

* Revelation's topic and title both derive from the Greek *Apokalupto* ("I, reveal" or "I, unveil"). The book is thus sometimes listed in older editions as "The Book of the Apocalypse to Saint John the Divine." The Apocalypse was, originally, the revelation to Saint John of how the world would end, but, in time, the word *Apocalypse* in English came to be used to describe the event itself.

spiritually, as well as being intellectually fascinated by how the translators reached their conclusions.

The ghosts of 1604 can still be seen in some of the words chosen for the King James Bible. For instance, when it came to the first verse in the Epistle to the Philippians, the translation chosen by the Second Westminster Company was, "Paul and Timotheus, the servants of Jesus Christ, to all the saints in Christ Jesus which are at Philippi, with the bishops and deacons."[14] Their decision to translate the Greek *episkopois* (literally, "overseer") to "bishop" was a clear victory for the High Anglican wing of the Church of England, which argued that maintaining its hierarchy of bishops was supported by the Bible and the earliest Christian congregations.[15] The translators had to wrestle with older debates, too. No one, for instance, envied the Second Westminster Company, whose mandate saddled them with the so-called Johannine Comma—*comma*, in this case, meaning an alleged insertion rather than a point of punctuation. Located in the First Epistle of Saint John's fifth chapter, in its seventh and eighth verses, some believed that the original text had been mutilated by a half sentence inserted into the Bible to justify explicitly the doctrine of Trinitarianism—the interconnected deity of God the Father, Son, and Holy Ghost.* The Johannine Comma is nowhere to be found in the oldest Latin translations of the New Testament, nor in any of the surviving Greek originals, and so there was a strong suspicion among biblical scholars that part of the verse had been interpolated by a pious forger in the fourth century. In 1522 the philosopher Erasmus of Rotterdam had omitted it from his acclaimed *Paraphrases on the New Testament*, only to yield to public outcry and reinsert it in future editions. Like Erasmus before it, the Second Westminster committee ultimately chose to keep the Comma in its final version.

Beyond long-running controversies, the potential pitfalls of translation

---

* The Comma reads, "For there are three that bear record in heaven, the Father, the Word, and the Holy Ghost: and these three are one. And there are three that bear witness in earth, the spirit, and the water, and the blood: and these three agree in one." The originals seem to read, "For there are three that bear record, the spirit, and the water, and the blood: and these three agree in one."

tormented the scholars, with debates over the proper way to translate Greek for the New Testament, Hebrew for the Old, and to discuss any risks inherent in the fact that Christ had almost certainly spoken Aramaic, but those words were recorded in Greek. They consulted both the original documents, or as close as one could get, and the writings of saints and scholars who had gone before them, particularly the sixteenth-century evangelist William Tyndale, whose work on translating Hebrew into English proved invaluable. The companies of theologians knew that an error on their part would take the millions reading this Bible, and living by its words, one step further away from God. The entire structure of the Church could be changed or weakened. A mistranslated pronoun or an overzealous pluralization could, for instance, imply either that there clearly had been women in positions of spiritual leadership in the early Church or, in contrast, that because of their gender, no woman had ever been judged so much as worthy of address by Saint Paul. Entire lives have been lived, justified, ended, brutalized, inspired, or uplifted based on how a single sentence in the Bible was interpreted by the people reading it. Correct translation could not have mattered more.

One contested word in particular had special relevance to King James himself: *sodomy*. The biblical story of Sodom and its sister city of Gomorrah was that angels had taken human form to visit a holy man named Lot, who had settled in Sodom with his family. The angels specifically took on the appearance of males, and, according to the Bible, on the night of their arrival, "the men of Sodom, compassed the house round, both old and young, all the people from every quarter: And they called unto Lot, and said unto him, 'Where are the men which came in to thee this night? Bring them out unto us, that we may know them.'"[16] (*Know*, in the proverbial biblical sense of the word, meaning sexually.) Lot begged the men of Sodom not to do "this evil thing," and when he refused to hand the angels over to the men for sexual assault, the crowd threatened violence against his home. In retaliation, Sodom and Gomorrah were destroyed by the wrath of God, with only Lot and his daughters ultimately spared from destruction. Gomorrah's specific sin is not mentioned, but the term *sodomy* entered Christian morality. Today the standard definition of sodomy is that it is a pejorative term for homosexuality, the latter being a term invented in the 1860s but that some modern evangelical translators of the Bible feel comfortable using as a direct stand-in for older translations' use of *sodomy*. Many in James I's lifetime felt the same and believed that the sin of sodomy was that of sexual intercourse between two men. Others argued that the story of Sodom did not in any way pertain to consensual sex; rather it seemed to point to the horrors of gang rape. Nor were the targets of this intended assault even human, let alone men.[17] They only had that appearance; the Bible is very clear that they were angels. In consequence, some theologians argued that *sodomy* meant *blasphemy*, an attempted assault on the Divine.[18] Other Christian philosophers had said that *sodomy* meant any form of sexual contact, even within heterosexual intercourse, through which there was no possibility of a pregnancy, including masturbation and oral sex. Some believed that Christ, when referencing the sin of Sodom later, seemed to be describing it as cruelty to refugees and visitors, or, specifically, a violation of the laws of hospitality.[19] *Sodomy* was thus, by the early 1600s, a potent but imprecise condemnation among Christians. In *Basilikon Doron*, King James called it a sin which "ye are bound in conscience never to forgive."[20] When he wrote this, James was either reflecting on the myriad interpretations of *sodomy* or serving as a stunning example of religious hypocrisy.

Many readers of history despair of the tendency to force the long dead out of the historical closet, arguing that too much modern interpretation is brought to bear in analyzing the languages and attitudes of long ago. Given King James's role in the most cherished translation of the Bible in English, this is a particularly tense debate, and certainly there are myriad examples of historians and readers interpreting early modern sexual dynamics in a misleadingly solipsistic way. However, one could respectfully argue that the platonic argument is quite difficult to sustain in light of letters between James and the Duke of Buckingham, whose "thoughts are only bent on having [your] legs soon in my arms."[21] It is untrue, as has been stated by some modern scholars, that James I was never suspected of homosexual romances in his lifetime, or that it is only modern readers who reached this conclusion.[22] When James was a teenager, his Presbyterian guardians and ambassadors to Scotland had suspected that he had successive romantic or sexual relationships with at least two courtiers.[23] Rumors about James's affairs even reached Elizabeth I in England, and when James succeeded her, shrewd courtiers realized that they could turn the mutterings to their advantage. Catherine Howard, Countess of Suffolk, a glamorous and ruthless noblewoman who served as Queen Anna's Keeper of the Jewels, advanced her family's position in royal favor through handsome gentlemen she found to catch the King's eye. She passed on this information to Robert Cecil, James's chief minister, who stated that attractive men were "an excellent good instrument to conserve his Majesty's good opinions."[24] It should be noted that James was also responsible for at least nine pregnancies with his wife Queen Anna, and he may at some point have visited a brothel in south London with some of his male favorites.[25] Two of his courtiers, Sir Edward Wotton and Sir John Harington, praised James's chastity, although, tellingly, they both specified chastity with women.[26] Observing how openly and affectionately James kissed his male favorites in public, his courtiers were in little doubt about what went on in private.[27] Secret passageways were constructed to link James's bedrooms with those of his favorite male courtiers.

Halfway through the seven years of his great Bible commission, King James fell in love with twenty-three-year-old "straight-limbed, well-favoured, strong-shouldered" Robert Carr, youngest brother of a Scottish lord, after he saw Carr break his leg from being thrown off his horse during a joust.[28] James already had reason to be well disposed toward the Carr* family: Robert's late father had been one of the few Scottish nobles to support James's first favorite, the Duke of Lennox. Ordering his personal physicians to nurse Carr back to health, James visited the young man's sickbed for hours at a time; during these visits, he taught the patient his beloved

---

* As with the royal family's name of Stuart/Stewart, Carr's name had been anglicized from Kerr, both by the era's fluid attitude to spelling, emphasizing phonetics over consistency, and by Robert's move south after 1603.

Latin. The King later knighted Carr and, in the year that the Bible was finished, ennobled him as Viscount Rochester. In the public rooms at Hampton Court, just as at Whitehall, Richmond, Greenwich, or the royal hunting lodges littered throughout the country, the King smoothed wrinkles in his favorite's clothes and gazed at him with such undisguised adoration that, in the eyes of a fellow Scottish aristocrat, Carr was "exceeding great with his Majesty, and if I should say truly, greater than any that ever I did see."[29] Thanks to James's patronage, Carr became one of the wealthiest men in the country. He married a member of the Howard family and was elevated through another rung of the noble hierarchy to become Earl of Somerset. A courtier joked in a letter, "If any mischance be to be wished, 'tis breaking a leg in the King's presence."[30]

In 1611 the version of the Bible commissioned at Hampton Court seven years earlier was finished at last. It is still referred to by the name a delighted James bestowed on it that year—the Authorized Version—and it bears, too, his name, by which it is more commonly known. Many editions continue to carry the preface composed by the committees when they dedicated the final product to King James's patronage. Even allowing for the florid flattery of the period, the preface captures a sense of James's interest in the project that, more than anything else, has enshrined his name for posterity:

> To the most high and mighty Prince, James by the Grace of God, King
> of Great Britain . . . and Ireland, Defender of the Faith, &c.,
>   The translators of The Bible, wish Grace, Mercy, and Peace, through
> Jesus Christ our Lord.
>   Great and manifold were the blessings (most dread Sovereign) which
> Almighty GOD, the Father of all Mercies, bestowed upon us the people
> of England, when first he sent your Majesty's Royal person to rule and
> reign over us. For whereas it was the expectation of many, who wished
> not well unto our Zion, that upon the setting of that bright Occidental
> Star Queen Elizabeth of most happy memory, some thick and palpa-

ble clouds of darkness would so have overshadowed this land, that men should have been in doubt which way they were to walk . . . the appearance of your Majesty, as of the Sun in his strength, instantly dispelled those supposed and surmised mists. . . .

But amongst all our Joys, there was no one that more filled our hearts, then the blessed continuance of the Preaching of GOD's sacred word amongst us, which is that inestimable treasure, which excelleth all the riches of the earth, because the fruit thereof extendeth itself, not only to the time spent in this transitory world, but . . . unto that Eternal happiness which is above in Heaven. . . .

There are infinite arguments of this right Christian and Religious affection in your Majesty: but none is more forcible to declare it to others, then the vehement and perpetuated desire of the accomplishing and publishing of this Work, which now with all humility we present unto your Majesty. For when your Highness had once out of deep judgment apprehended, how convenient it was, that out of the Original sacred tongues, together with comparing of the labours, both in our own and other foreign Languages, of many worthy men who went before us, there should be one more exact Translation of the holy Scriptures into the English tongue; your Majesty did never desist, to urge and to excite those to whom it was commended, that the work might be hastened, and that the business might be expedited.

At this point, the translators could not resist a moment of academic pique in taking a swipe at both their Catholic and Puritan critics:

If on the one side we shall be traduced by Popish persons at home or abroad, who therefore will malign us, because we are poor Instruments to make GOD'S holy Truth to be yet more and more known unto the people, whom they desire still to keep in ignorance and darkness: or if on the other side, we shall be maligned by self-conceited brethren, who run their own ways, and give liking unto nothing but what is framed by themselves, and hammered on their Anvil; we may rest secure, supported

within by . . . having walked the ways of simplicity and integrity, as
before the Lord; And sustained without, by the powerful Protection of
your Majesty's grace and favour.[31]

In many ways, it would be easy to dismiss the preface, and even the translated text itself, as a product of the political and religious tensions of the
early seventeenth century. There are moments, as mentioned, in which that
unquestionably happened. A few of its controversies rumble on. Although
most modern editions of the Bible have cut it, some Protestant fundamen-
talists cite the Authorized Version's inclusion of the Johannine Comma
as proof of the verse's validity.[32] Likewise, the difficulties threatening any
translation, let alone one on the scale and importance of the entire Bible,
cannot be dismissed lightly.

The King James Bible is a work of somber yet soaring beauty. It is still
seen by many English-speaking Christians as *the* Bible, to the extent that
some modern biblical scholars have despaired over its influence, arguing
that too many Christians will weigh every subsequent edition not against
the original Greek or Hebrew but by gauging how close it is to the King
James Version.[33] A quarter million copies of the King James translation are
still sold every year by the Oxford University Press alone.[34] Even strident
critics of organized religion have praised the text for the splendor of its vo-
cabulary and the role it played in shaping English literature and culture.[35]
From a king sitting among a group of bishops in a drawing room at Hampton Court, and from evangelicals kneeling in that same palace a few days
later, flowed a translation of an ancient text that has shaped millions of lives
in the centuries since.

CHAPTER 13

THE QUEEN'S
BEDCHAMBER

She loved pomp and grandeur, tumult and intrigue.

—Maximilien de Béthune, Duke of Sully (1560–1641)

Fifteen years after she had first danced the role of Athena in its Great Hall, Anna of Denmark kept a more muted Christmas at Hampton Court. "All grace and fairness, of fine height" was how a Venetian visitor had described Anna in the year she played Athena; sadly, by the winter of 1618, the Queen was struggling to hide how terrible she felt.[1] The birth in 1607 of her final child, Princess Sophia, who died on the same day, had left Anna with unspecified gynecological issues. It is perhaps telling that one of the personal prayer books she commissioned at that time focused on the biblical miracle known then as "Christ healing the woman with the bloody issue."[2] Five years after that, Anna's doctor Sir Theodore de Mayerne informed her that she had gout. A leg ulcer followed, prompting longer and longer trips to the southwestern English spa town of Bath, which brought the Queen some relief but never a cure. In the spring of 1615 a diagnosis of dropsy was delivered. Dropsy—a since-retired medical term—covered several ailments, most commonly congestive heart failure, along with bloating through malnutrition, as well as liver or kidney failure.[3]

An impetus to live and to do so boldly was one of Anna's most marked characteristics. Even as her legs tormented her, her joints ached, and her heart struggled, she appeared in public with her towering blonde coiffure intact, wearing farthingale hoops four feet in width, shimmering with jewels inserted into her hair and roped around her neck. She was festooned in pearls worth more than a county's annual income. Precious stones shone on her fingers, bracelets glittered in the light, and, when she ran out of space, more jewelry was pinned onto her ruff.

Anna planned to use her winter at Hampton Court to recuperate, during which time she turned forty-four. She was frequently visited at the palace by her second son, eighteen-year-old Charles, Prince of Wales, whose thank-you letters to his mother revealed how much he enjoyed their time together and how grateful he was for the excellent quality of the food, or "good dinners," he ate when he visited her.[4] If the Prince noticed how little his mother ate at those meals, he was apparently too polite, or too anxious, to say. Courtiers had no such qualms, however, with one writing to a friend: "The Queen is somewhat crazy again, though they say it is but the gout. She is generally well wished, and the care of her welfare makes the world more fearful."[5] The word *crazy*, at that time, indicated a state of physical distress rather than its later negative association with mental illness or anger.

When she felt strong enough, the Queen and Prince Charles took the air together in the Hampton Court gardens or discussed pieces in her famous art collection. Charles often spent the night, sleeping in a small room next to his mother's bedchamber in case her health suffered a further deterioration.[6] Anna hoped to live long enough to arrange Charles's marriage and to avoid the humiliation, as she saw it, heaped upon her daughter, Elizabeth, who, to assuage another surge of anti-Catholicism in London, had been married off to a minor German prince, Frederick V of the Palatinate and the Rhine, whose Protestant faith was unassailable but whose family tree, from Queen Anna's perspective, was risible. She wanted Charles to marry either a Spanish princess or an Austrian archduchess yet, for this plan to work, Anna would have to wait at least four to five years, quite probably longer, depending on who emerged as her future daughter-in-law.[7] The only princesses she considered worthy of her son's hand were too young:

Maria-Anna of Spain was only twelve, while the Austrian possibilities, the archduchesses Cecilia-Renata and another Maria-Anna, were younger still. If she wanted to achieve her goal, Anna would have to be patient. Yet time was ever more obviously against her.

The Queen's Bedchamber was on the second floor of a tower, with windows facing east toward the hunting grounds. It had doors accessing two long galleries. A third door led toward Anna's Presence Chamber, where she could receive honored guests who entered from an adjoining reception room called the Watching Chamber to differentiate it from the Great Watching Chamber off the Great Hall. It was in these rooms that Anna had entertained the actors she admired during her first Christmas in England. On Twelfth Night 1619, she was in such agony that her team of physicians were summoned, and, on their recommendation, the household's return to London was postponed indefinitely. In her current state, the Queen could not be moved. In the depth of winter, the long journey from Hampton Court to the capital would expose her to icy roads or the freezing air blowing off the river. Until she felt strong enough to travel, Anna and her entourage would continue to relax in the warmth and luxury of Hampton Court.

The palace fires were stoked, as kindling was added to palace gossip that the Queen was at death's door. Determined to counteract this speculation, Anna made a point of walking from her apartments through a palace gallery. As intended, she was observed by servants and nobles who were so convinced by her performance that the rumor mill reversed to churn out the story that Anna would soon recover. Behind closed doors, however, the ladies-in-waiting watched as the Queen's appetite evaporated and she needed their help more frequently while walking. In the last week of February, the Queen's fit of coughing ended with her hacking up blood; her doctors were fetched and arrived at her rooms just after midnight. She had tuberculosis, or consumption as it was called then. Some ladies-in-waiting tried to stay awake in the room next to her bedchamber, in case the Queen needed them in the small hours, but she told them to go to their own rooms to get some sleep. Only her maid, also named Anna, who had accompanied her from Denmark decades earlier was allowed to stay at her bedside.

When so ordered, the maid brought her a glass of red Rhinelander wine; after she drank it, the Queen rallied and said defiantly, "Now have I deceived [disproved] the physicians."[8] Anna may not have been ready to accept death, but to her attendants it seemed obvious by then that she would become the second queen to die at Hampton Court.

Her life had begun in palaces as splendid. Thanks in part to the shrewd economic policies of her father, King Frederick II, Denmark was one of the wealthiest countries in Europe by the time Anna was born there in 1574.[9] Educated in a world of art, affluence, and elegance, Anna had learned from childhood how to use a palace as a stage and, in adulthood, Hampton Court had been the site of some of her most memorable performances as queen, including the triumphs of her first Christmas masque. Maybe she recalled a more raucous evening a few years later in the same hall with the same playwright when Anna's visiting, hard-drinking brother King Christian IV became so inebriated that he collapsed midway through one of the very first performances of *Macbeth*?[10] With its witches tormenting a Scottish monarchy, *Macbeth* exhibited another shrewd set of topic choices by Shakespeare in his quest to keep James I's favor. It was a shame that the Danish king had to be carried from the hall in a drunken stupor from Shakespeare's shortest Tragedy.

Wild parties and corresponding spending had proliferated throughout Anna's queenship, yet while parliamentary criticism of her extravagance was justified, her detractors often regretted dismissing her as a frivolous lightweight. When she first became Queen of England, the Spanish diplomat the Count of Gondomar had privately told his king, Philip III, that Anna's "chief pleasure is dancing and music," and that she had no discernible political interests.[11]

One man who rued underestimating Anna was her husband, who arrived at Hampton Court to dine with her after he learned just how ill she was. As James's continued residence in a nearby hunting lodge showed, the royal marriage had become a business arrangement—a largely respectful one, in which both the affection and the arguments of earlier years had long since faded. They had been through much together. Of their seven children, they had buried five. Margaret, Robert, Mary, and Sophia had died as infants, but it was from the death of their eldest that the King and Queen's marriage never really recovered. Seven years before Anna's quiet winter at Hampton Court, her husband had collapsed sobbing and screaming when servants told him that typhoid had suddenly killed his eighteen-year-old heir, Prince Henry-Frederick. At this news of her eldest's death, Queen Anna had locked herself in a darkened room, crying and refusing to speak to anyone. Their grief, however, had ultimately driven the couple further apart. James no longer called her "my Annie," as he had when they were first wed; she no longer seemed to worry about his increasingly heavy drinking or his declining health. He was so sick by the opening months of 1619 that courtiers made coldhearted bets that the King would be in his grave before the Queen was in hers.

Anna had been fifteen years old when James, then twenty-one, presented her to the people of Scotland as their new queen and ordered the witch hunts to punish the sorcerers who had conjured the storm that had nearly wrecked her ship from Denmark. She had sought refuge from that tempest in Norway, also ruled by her father, to which James gallantly sailed to "rescue" her. On the surface, the episode looked like a scene from a medieval chivalric romance—Anna, the willowy, blonde princess, trapped by storms and dark forces—and that, coupled with her youth, deluded both James and his advisers into thinking they could mold her into the kind of consort they wanted. Anna realized very quickly that the choice for her was between living with difficulty or dimming silently. Had she followed what the Presbyterian Kirk and their supporters in Scotland wanted of her, she would have ossified while still breathing, mute even in her prayers, silent except for the screams of childbirth—a demure, "godly," safely irrelevant queen. Instead, to their astonishment, the teenage Anna transformed herself into one of the most formidable forces in Scottish politics. She hired Catholics to her household staff and hosted balls, despite the Kirk's abhorrence of both. She hired Protestants, too, and refused to abandon her friends when they became political liabilities. From pulpits across Edinburgh and the Lowlands, sermons thundered against the woman whom the preachers mockingly nicknamed the "dancing queen" for her constant "night-walking and balling."[12] To persuade her that she must reform her lifestyle, representatives of the clergy went to Edinburgh Castle to deliver a sermon in person to Anna, who replied through a messenger that she did not want to meet them that night because she was having too much fun "at the dancing."[13]

She quarrelled openly with her husband when he favored another family's interests over hers, and she had marked those members of the Scottish elite who were against her, who mocked her, belittled her, or tried to diminish her influence. When Elizabeth I's death made Anna queen consort of England and Ireland, fourteen years after she became Queen of Scots, the wise would have acted on the observation of an ambassador who summarized Anna as "full of kindness for those who support her, but, on the other hand, she is terrible, proud, unendurable to those she dislikes."[14]

Yet still she was underestimated—though no longer by King James, who had come to begrudgingly admire his wife's refusal to back down in a feud. In a court that festered more than most with intrigue and double-dealing, Anna of Denmark became a consummate schemer. She had no firm political agenda, at least not in comparison to her husband's devotion to the Divine Right of Kings. What she demanded was to be treated with respect and to be allowed to enjoy her life. She negotiated the latter with James, who settled Anna's substantial bills for her balls, masques, art acquisitions, stables full of the most expensive hunting horses, vast numbers of servants, hundreds of dresses, and mountains of jewelry. When it came to the issue of respect, she often took matters into her own hands. The faction at the English court led by the Howard family began to irritate her, especially after their power increased through the marriage of a Howard to the King's favorite, Robert Carr. The death of several of James's older advisers left a vacancy at the heart of government that was filled increasingly by Carr or—more accurately, given his less than dazzling intellect—his Howard in-laws. After another disagreement, Henry Howard, 1st Earl of Northampton, lost his temper and referred to the Queen as "only the best subject, yet no less a subject than I."[15]

Perhaps these courtiers thought they could be contemptuous of their "dancing queen" because of her husband's marked preference for handsome men such as Robert Carr. The latest favorite by 1619 was George Villiers, offspring of a minor family in the Leicestershire gentry. Fresh from a gentlemen's finishing school in France, he had been brought to court by a family friend and immediately captured the King's attention, reminding him of religious art that depicted beautiful Saint Stephen, the first Christian martyr. James said openly that "he loved the Earl of Buckingham more than any other man." From penury, Villiers, or "Steenie," as the King called him, after Saint Stephen, had risen to become an earl with a commensurate income, also awarded to him by James. By the time King James visited his dying wife at Hampton Court, Steenie had been elevated again—to Marquess of Buckingham—and he would soon become a duke, the highest rank possible in the English nobility. He and the King wrote letters in which James called Steenie his wife and Steenie called the King "Dad" or "Husband." Sometimes Buckingham called himself James's "dog," which, interestingly, was what Anna called Steenie in her letters to him. Perhaps she did so to remind Steenie what very few at court realized: she had helped pick him for her husband.

Anna of Denmark was a sniper from the sides. It is often very difficult to say with certainty how far she was involved in many of the Jacobean court's intrigues; however, there are often strong clues that leave as the logical conclusion—or at least something far more than a guess—that she was the brains behind a plot. We know that she, along with nearly everybody else, was struck by Steenie's handsomeness at his court debut. His astonishing good looks were nearly always the first thing eyewitnesses commented upon in testimonies of him—"beautiful" is used on many occasions, and William Laud, the future Archbishop of Canterbury, confided in his diary to have had recurring erotic dreams about him: "in my sleep, it seemed to me that the duke of Buckingham came into bed with me; where he behaved himself with great kindness towards me, after that rest, wherewith wearied persons are wont to solace themselves."[16] Added to Villiers's exceptional looks was the blessing of his mediocre ability, which made him an even more attractive pawn for Anna. Robert Carr, in contrast, had become too arrogant, thereby making many powerful enemies. They included George Abbot, the current Archbishop of Canterbury, who allied with the Queen to promote Steenie at Carr's expense.

While his patrons made sure to invite Steenie to every court event at which James might grow more infatuated, tensions between the two factions heightened. Carr's long-term friend, and possibly his former lover, Sir Thomas Overbury, burst into "sudden and contemptible laughing at" the Queen when he saw her during a stroll through the gardens; this was a breach of etiquette so embarrassing that Anna "went to the king with tears in her eyes and complained." She did not cry for long.[17] Rumors soon started that Overbury was the real brains behind the Howard faction, nominally headed by Carr, who was allegedly Overbury's puppet. The gossip fuelled King James's resentment; he was already jealous of Overbury's closeness with Carr. Overbury was an ambitious man; maybe he would like an embassy abroad. Moscow, perhaps. A brutal civil war had recently ended with a national Russian council electing a new royal family, the House of Romanov. The Russian fur trade was lucrative to the English economy, and with peace restored under the young Tsar, Overbury could serve king, country, and merchants as ambassador.

Anna and her supporters could not possibly lose. Either the irksome Overbury would accept the post and vanish on a diplomatic mission to a country a thousand miles away; or, given that his temper seemed to be his career's worst enemy, he would refuse. The latter won out. This angered James, who overreacted by ordering Overbury's detention in the Tower of London for disobedience. Panicking, Overbury tried to blackmail Carr into saving him and perhaps signed his own death warrant with the phrase, "Whether I die or live, your shame shall never die."[18] It seemed that Overbury was going to tell everyone about the true nature of Carr's relationship with the King, until somebody poisoned Sir Thomas, and he died in prison.

Everyone assumed that the murder had been ordered by either Carr or his wife, Lady Frances Howard, both of whom were ruined by the ensuing scandal. James refused to execute the Carrs, although due to the public outcry, he had no choice but to banish them from court; the couple spent years in admittedly comfortable confinement at the Tower. Frances pleaded guilty at her trial, so it is difficult to doubt that she, and likely her husband, were involved in the poisoning. An overlooked participant, accused initially of aiding the Carrs in their plot to poison Overbury, was a Scottish courtier named Sir David Wood, a long-standing servant to the Queen; Wood was acquitted despite the damning revelation that Frances had confided in him about plans to murder Overbury.[19] Had the Queen's faction received intelligence from Wood, or somebody else, that Robert Carr's Howard wife intended to kill Thomas Overbury and, rather than report what they had heard, they stood back to allow her to do it, knowing that it would get rid of Overbury and his killers in one fell swoop? Whatever the truth, the scandal ended with Overbury dead, Carr ruined, James frightened, the Howards neutered, and Queen Anna once again supreme at court with a reliable new favorite who owed his place in her husband's bed, and his resulting fortune, to her good graces.

While nobody would ever claim they were a love match, few could deny as they dined together at Hampton Court in early 1619 that Anna and James had weathered a series of political storms and scandals that would have destroyed more gentle personalities. Unlike both of James's parents—one beheaded, the other found half naked and strangled by his enemies in the rubble-strewn gardens of a detonated Edinburgh mansion—they had survived to face a natural death, sitting across from each other, enjoying "good dinners" at a riverside palace. James, too, understood that Anna did not have long left. In her time as queen, she had lived among a "world of brave jewels."[20] Cash-strapped James hoped to persuade his wife to leave most of it to him. Prince Charles suspected that avarice rather than affection was behind his father's revived displays of uxorious goodwill. Anna was not fooled, either. Her will bequeathed most of her finest possessions either to Charles or to his sister Elizabeth, who was by then living in the German city of Heidelberg with her husband. Anna evaded discussing her will with James, while also never admitting that her condition was terminal.

The Queen's refusal to concede just how sick she was may have had something to do with her religious faith, an issue she knew would come to a boil at her deathbed. Born a Lutheran in Denmark and badgered into nominal Presbyterianism in Scotland, Anna had, quite possibly, converted to Catholicism at some point in the 1590s after studying the religion with two of her Catholic ladies-in-waiting, both of whom were subsequently dismissed from royal service by King James. The Queen's conversion had, of necessity, been surrounded by such secrecy that even the Vatican was uncertain of its authenticity; Pope Paul V wrote with a telling double qualifier that "it might be true that she might be a Catholic."[21] After her move to England in 1603, the rumors of conversion were fuelled further by Anna's lackluster attendance at Anglican services and by her obvious, if ultimately futile, preference for her children to marry into Catholic European royal houses.[22] In the aftermath of the Gunpowder Plot of 1605, her husband's government had intensified its attacks on British Catholics. The Pope wrote with alarm of the "cruelty and pitilessness of that King, increasingly, against the poor Catholics," while, in contrast, thousands of English Protestants felt their government was not doing enough to stamp out the threat of papism—"that enemy, that serpent, within our own realm."[23] In this context, the rumors about Queen Anna's alleged Catholicism had acquired a toxic importance.[24] She would likely face pressure to settle the issue on her deathbed.

On the first day of March 1619, lords and ladies of the county came to Hampton Court to pay their respects to Queen Anna. Admission to the royal presence underscored the landed classes' place in the social hierarchy, as well as advertising certain families' seniority in relation to their neighbors and rivals. In her sixteen years as Queen of England, Anna had usually been punctilious in her observation of etiquette, in contrast to her husband, who thought most of it an absurd waste of time.* On March 1 she was in so much pain that she ordered her Danish maid to close the apartment doors before the well-heeled mob arrived. This offended Elizabeth Stanley,

---

* Not always. She had enjoyed getting rip-roaring drunk while bowling with her ladies-in-waiting.

Countess of Derby, who barged into the royal apartments, determined to curtsy to the Queen as was her right and to be formally acknowledged by her. Exhausted after so many recent nights in which sleep had been either interrupted or prevented entirely by her poor health, Anna told the irate Countess to leave her alone and go to supper. A concerned Prince Charles had moved to Hampton Court that day to be with his mother. When Anna urged him not to worry and to go back to his own estates, Charles said, "No, I will wait upon your Majesty."

"I am a pretty piece to wait upon," she replied wryly.[25]

Hoping for some rest, she told Charles to go to supper and ordered her maid, "Now lay by me to sleep, for in seeing you repose, I shall feel disposed to sleep." Maid and queen fell asleep on Anna's canopied bed for a few hours until the Queen woke, disoriented and distressed, having nearly choked on her own blood while asleep. The Prince of Wales was fetched from his room. When he knelt by her bed, the Queen reached out her hand and touched "his head and gave him her blessing."[26]

Mother and son were not left in peace for long. Someone had tipped off the Archbishop of Canterbury and the Bishop of London, who nudged Anna's doctors out of the way to quiz the dying queen on her religious beliefs. From the Protestant perspective, their account of what happened next rings almost too good to be true. The Bishop claimed he had urged Anna, "Your soul, Madam. Make a sign that Your Majesty is one with God and longs to be with Him." To which the Queen is supposed to have replied, "I renounce the mediation of all saints and my own merits." That was an oddly specific Protestant statement in its rejection of the Catholic doctrine of intercession of the saints. The news was nonetheless disseminated to the people that their queen had died unambiguously Protestant. Whether that was true or not, we do not know. We can be certain, however, of the personal detail that Prince Charles took his mother's hand as he asked her if she wanted him to settle any debts she had and to provide for her servants until they found new jobs. Anna answered, "Yea," and lost consciousness. She died in her bedchamber just before dawn on March 2, 1619. Courtiers who had taken the bet that James would predecease Anna were wrong by six years.

CHAPTER 14

THE WHARF

No glimpse of the Sun was seen, as if darkness, confusion, and deformity had possessed the world and driven light to Heaven.

—Sir William Davenant, *Salmacida Spolia* (1640)

Charles Stuart arrived at Hampton Court under the cover of darkness twenty-three years after he had travelled there for his mother's final days. He had stayed in the palace many times since, although never in circumstances as secretive or shambolic as in 1642. He had been Charles I, King of England, Scotland, and Ireland for seventeen years, and his journey—or flight—to Hampton Court had been made with Scotland convulsed by rebellion, Ireland in the middle of a civil war, and England on the brink of one. A few days before they escaped London, Charles's wife confided to a Dutch envoy, "Everything is preparing for rebellion."[1] The period would later be referred to as the English Civil Wars or the Civil War era; given that it convulsed the entirety of the British Isles, its alternative name—the Wars of the Three Kingdoms—seems more accurate.

The royals arrived by barge on a Thames so swollen by heavy rain that it had burst its bank at several points along the way.[2] A supporter standing on the palace wharf to receive them thought that King Charles looked "most disconsolate [and] perplexed."[3] There were very few courtiers brave enough to accompany the King out of London. Even the Queen's onetime favorite lady-in-waiting had betrayed some of the royals' plans to their ene-

mies, and Charles was left embittered by the treachery of those who "having eaten our bread and being enriched with our bounty have scornfully
lift[ed] themselves up against us."[4] Despite the fact that the Captain of the
Guard had also abandoned Charles, many of the soldiers had not followed
the officer's lead, and, while the royal family lacked in noble attendants,
they reached Hampton Court with an unusual number of armed followers.

King Charles I, forty-one years old, short in stature with brown hair to
his shoulders and a neat beard, was usually a model of dignity, to the extent
that many considered him cold, secretive, and aloof. He had been underfed
as a child, possibly as a consequence of his ankyloglossia; colloquially, he
was "tongue-tied."[5] He had worked hard to overcome his stammer, as well
as his weak legs, choosing, at the age of fourteen, to start exercising by daily
running a long race until he could complete it without stopping and then
until he regularly won the race.[6] He had likewise forced himself to attend
extra horse-riding lessons until he became an excellent equestrian. Charles
had learned from infancy to overcome certain physical obstacles, where it
was possible and safe to do so, as well as to hide his perceived emotional
vulnerabilities. For someone to have noticed that he was "disconsolate, perplexed, [and] in need of comfort" on the Hampton Court wharf speaks to
how unusual the circumstances of 1642 were.

His wife, Queen Henrietta Maria, disembarked after him. The youngest sister of the King of France, she was shorter than her husband, with
dark brown hair and eyes. She had spent her honeymoon with Charles at
Hampton Court. Charles had never taken a mistress, the couple were together almost constantly, and after the loss of their first child, a short-lived
son named Charles-James, they had seven children together. Three of them
were with their parents that night, helped off the barge after their mother*:

---

* The title of Princess Royal was introduced to Britain at Henrietta Maria's suggestion, inspired by Madame Royale, which was traditionally given to the eldest daughter of French
kings. It has subsequently been held by the eldest daughters of George II, George III, Victoria,
Edward VII, George V, and Elizabeth II. She also introduced the title of Queen Mother from
the French monarchy, becoming the first woman in British history to officially use it to denote
a widowed queen consort who was also mother of the new monarch.

eleven-year-old Charles, Prince of Wales; ten-year-old Mary, the first British royal to use the title Princess Royal, as the sovereign's eldest daughter; and eight-year-old James, Duke of York.

Much of the furniture in palaces of the early modern period was re-assembled to move with the court from residence to residence. Hampton Court's caretakers had not expected the royal family's arrival, and so they entered a palace that was empty, dark, and almost colder than the January weather outside. The Stuarts had left London in such haste that even the King's and Queen's Apartments were practically bare. Eventually a bed was found for them in a room typically allocated to a lady-in-waiting. Charles, Henrietta Maria, and the three children spent the night there huddled to-gether for warmth. When morning arrived, they planned their next move.[7]

The safety of the youngest royal children was not a priority. Princess Elizabeth and Prince Henry seemed safe in one of the junior palaces, with a large and loyal household surrounding them.[8] Mary the Princess Royal was also the Princess of Orange, thanks to her wedding, at the age of nine, to the thirteen-year-old Dutch Prince Willem. The marriage treaty had stipulated that the child-spouses would live separately until they were older, but, in the panic at Hampton Court the King's advisers suggested bringing forward the Princess Royal's move to the Netherlands. They could tell the public that, upon reflection, it would be easier for a future Princess of Or-ange to complete her education in her adopted land and that, as her mother, the Queen wished to go with her to help her settle in. Then, under the guise of chaperone, Henrietta Maria could stay safely in the Netherlands until the situation in England calmed. Another mooted possibility was for the Queen to return to her native France, where her brother King Louis XIII would certainly grant her asylum and possibly financial assistance. Henri-etta Maria had vehemently opposed previous suggestions that she leave her husband, even temporarily, telling him, "I wish to share all your fortune, and participate in your troubles as I have done in your happiness. . . . [T]here is nothing in the world, no trouble, which shall hinder me from serving you and loving you above everything in the world."[9] The Queen remained defi-ant about the threats facing her, also telling her husband, "As to the rebels, neither their writings nor their threats shall ever make me do anything. Much less shall they frighten me."[10] At Hampton Court, as she took stock of what had happened over the past few days, Henrietta Maria finally accepted that she had become such a liability for the monarchy that to save her life, and quite possibly her husband's throne, she would have to go abroad.

How had it come to this? It is reductive, although not by much, to say that Charles I was dealt a bad hand and then played it poorly. The long-term forces that had helped shape his parents' lives—sectarian tensions and the promulgation of divine right monarchy—defined his own. Charles had inherited his mother's love of the arts, but none of her cunning or political flexibility; he had completely accepted his father's politics, and he was even more religious. Charles's belief in absolute monarchy had led him to disband Parliament in 1629 and refuse to summon it again for the next eleven years—a period known as the Eleven Years Personal Rule to its supporters and the Eleven Years Tyranny to its opponents. As far as it was possible within the English political system, Charles had made a relative success of those eleven years, despite public grumbling at his refusal to recall Parliament, which traditionally had the right to vote funds to the Crown. To keep absolutism afloat, Charles had resorted to an increasingly dubious series of fiscal policies that galvanized opposition against him. Without additional costs or strains—namely, war—the Personal Rule could just about function, until it was capsized by Charles's catastrophic attempt to impose Anglicanism on Scottish Presbyterianism.

There had already been frustration among English Puritans about Charles's promotion of High Anglicanism within the Church of England. To try to do the same with Presbyterianism seemed lunatic. Even King James had never attempted to push a union of the churches. When a Presbyterian reverend loyally tried to read from the new prayer book mandated by the King, an enraged Edinburgh market-trader threw a chair at him and called on the rest of the congregation to join her in walking out of the church in protest. This led to riots and then rebellion throughout Scotland, which Charles did not have the money to suppress. He summoned Parliament, in the naïve hope that it would vote him the revenue needed to deal

Oxburgh Hall gives us some idea of how Hampton Court appeared at the dawn of the Tudor era.

The tomb of "prudent, just, honest, and loved" Lord Daubeney, who rented Hampton Court for a country estate where he hosted King Henry VII and Queen Elizabeth of York.

Henry VIII's brilliant chief minister, Cardinal Thomas Wolsey, who transformed Hampton Court into a palace.

The Anne Boleyn Gate (*left*), with its famous clock, and the Great Hall (*right*). The space beneath the hall was once cellars to store the court's vast amount of beer.

Anne Boleyn, the first queen to reside at Hampton Court when it was a Crown property. She encouraged an extensive series of expansions and beautifications.

Still on display at Hampton Court, this painting is a piece of dynastic propaganda for Henry VIII's plans for the succession. The King sits at the center, with his son—the future Edward VI—on his right hand. They are joined by Queen Jane Seymour, seven years after she died at Hampton Court, who is painted here because she was the mother of the heir. To Edward's right is the second in line, his eldest sister, Mary, and to Queen Jane's left, Elizabeth. The two figures in the doorways are court jesters, also known as Fools, to tell viewers that only fools would question Henry's succession laws. The figure on the portrait's far right is Henry's jester and favorite, Will Somers, who later lived at Hampton Court after his retirement.

Hampton Court's first royal wedding was between Henry VIII and his sixth wife, Katherine Parr.

A later painting of the three-to four-hour Protestant sermons which the boy king Edward VI made mandatory for his entire court.

Mary I and her Spanish husband, King Philip II. The mystery of what happened with Queen Mary's pregnancy at Hampton Court continues to divide historians.

Elizabeth I, whose reign nearly ended after four years when she almost died at Hampton Court in 1562.

A sketch from the lost original that was on display at Hampton Court in 1599. The mother and child (nestled in her mother's hood) were Inuit, who were kidnapped and brought to England.

The Oxford theologian Dr. John Rainolds, one of the early champions of the King James Bible.

A never-knowingly underdressed Anna of Denmark, who, in 1619, became the second queen to die at Hampton Court.

This portrait of Charles I on horseback was one of the three portraits he chose to decorate his rooms when he was a prisoner at Hampton Court in 1647.

Charles I also chose this portrait of his five eldest children to decorate his rooms at Hampton Court—the baby on the right, Princess Anne, had died in infancy. From right to left after her are Princess Elizabeth; the future Charles II; the future James II; and Mary, Princess of Orange. As was customary with upper-class boys, Prince James is dressed in feminine clothes. This ended on a boy's seventh birthday.

Britain's "republican princess" Elizabeth, Lady Claypole, Oliver Cromwell's favorite daughter.

with the Scottish insurrection; instead, Parliament's members refused to give Charles anything until they had a chance to voice a decade's worth of complaints. Many in Parliament sympathized with the Scottish Presbyterians, and London was overwhelmingly on the side of Parliament. When Charles violated parliamentary privilege by attempting to arrest five of his most critical MPs, the city erupted.

It had, however, been the third of Charles's three kingdoms that specifically put Queen Henrietta Maria's life at risk. Politics and religion are seldom entirely separate, certainly not in a seventeenth-century context; however, one could just about say that England exploded over politics, Scotland over religion, and Ireland over both. In 1641 there had been a series of massacres in Ireland in which thousands of Protestants were killed during a Catholic uprising. The long-term impact of 1641 in defining an Irish Protestant identity, particularly in the north, where most of the massacres occurred, is beyond the remit of this narrative, but while it is true that some of the more graphic accounts* and the casualty figures were exaggerated in subsequent anti-Catholic propaganda, there is no doubt that what was done was horrific.[11] The digitization of the survivors' testimonies by Trinity College, Dublin, is one of the most exciting developments in public access to Irish history in the twenty-first century and they can make for bone-chilling reading. Entire villages were wiped out—Protestant women were subjected to rape, many of them were then beaten, and some had their noses sliced, after which they were denied clothes and driven into the hills or mountains to die from exposure. One of the rebels, a convert from Protestantism named Jane Hampson, was begged by ten victims to at least kill them with a quick blow to the head rather than force them back into their cottage to be burned alive. She refused. Children were not spared; some were thrown off bridges in their mothers' arms. Communities were "driven like hogs" from the church where they sought shelter and forced at gun-

---

* Particular controversy continues to surround the claims made by eyewitnesses about the rebels' treatment of pregnant women, such as the claim made by Mulrony Carroll, a survivor of a massacre of civilians at Kilmacrenan in County Donegal, that he saw three women murdered "one of whose bellies they ripped up, she being great with child, so the child sprang out of her belly."

and pike-point into a local river, where they drowned. Survivors who swam back to shore were shot.[12] Others were immolated along with the churches in which they hid. Soldiers who had been serving elsewhere returned to find "their houses burned, their wives and children murdered."[13]

When the news about what had happened in Ireland reached England, the reaction was a cocktail of fear and fury—and a scapegoat was needed. The monarchy's critics were not slow in finding one. The Queen, they reminded the public, was a Roman Catholic, like the rebels. As a foreigner and a Catholic, Henrietta Maria had never been popular in England. Every detail of her life that could be presented to imply complicity in the Irish deaths was utilized. Her godfather was the Pope. For years, she had lobbied on behalf of Irish Catholics and had succeeded in repealing anti-Catholic initiatives in Ireland, most memorably when she persuaded her husband to restore the ancient right to make pilgrimage to a famous shrine to Saint Patrick.[14] Was it really credible that she knew nothing about the rebellion before it happened? She was by birth a member of the French monarchy, which, six decades earlier, had done nothing to save thousands of its Protestant subjects when they, too, were butchered by armed Catholics, in the Reformation's worst sectarian massacre. Four of her mother's relatives had been elected popes in years gone by. Her sister Elisabeth was Queen of Spain through marriage to a man who still protected and implemented the Inquisition. Henrietta Maria was also widely blamed in England for encouraging her husband's absolutism, so that he could rule in a fashion similar to her French brother and Spanish brother-in-law, and—so her enemies insisted until their lie acquired credibility by repetition—she must be working in secret to restore Catholicism, by bloodletting if necessary, starting with the massacres in Ireland. England would be next. When *The Tears of Ireland*, a book vividly detailing the slaughter of Irish Protestants and indicting all Catholics as complicit, circulated in London, the Queen became the star in every conspiracy theory. Her detractors claimed that having been a friend to Irish Catholicism for years she must have known of plans for a rebellion and, furthermore, they blamed her for the King's poor relations with Parliament.

This criticism of the Queen was unfair and inaccurate. Far from encouraging her husband, Henrietta Maria had unsuccessfully begged him not to push Anglicanism on the Presbyterian Kirk. Nor did she sympathize with those who had orchestrated the violence in Ireland. The Puritan lobby in Parliament was strong, however, and, according to the Venetian ambassador, "[T]hey persuaded themselves that the king's action and his resentment were due to the advice of the queen. Accordingly, they decided to accuse her in parliament of conspiring against the public liberty and [of] secret intelligence in the rebellion in Ireland."[15] To impeach the Queen was unheard of, yet Parliament pressed ahead to bring her before them as "a subject like any other." Rioters in Westminster and Whitehall openly expressed a desire to lynch Henrietta Maria if they could. The few Catholic churches allowed in London thanks to the Queen's patronage shuttered themselves in fear; two of her Catholic advisers, Walter Montagu and Kenelm Digby, fled at her urging, while the Pope's envoy in London, Carlo Rossetti, hid at the Venetian embassy, from where he was spirited out of England in disguise. With hatred of the Queen reaching a fever pitch after the King's failed arrest of the five MPs, the royal family had evacuated to Hampton Court amid a winter downpour.

On their second day at Hampton Court, during which plans were also discussed about making Oxford the interim royalist capital in defiance of parliamentarian London, a servant arrived in a panic with a warning that parliamentarian troops were on their way to apprehend the King and bring both him and his family back to London under de facto house arrest. The royals bolted again, fleeing this time—as the Duke of Somerset had with Edward VI long before—to Windsor Castle and leaving Hampton Court all but empty behind them.

By the time Charles I returned to Hampton Court five years later, the civil war had left eighty-four thousand of his subjects dead on various battlefields across England, Ireland, Scotland, and Wales. He had not seen his wife in more than a year. After a brief initial exile in France, she had returned to his side, during which time they had another child, Henrietta-Anne. Nick-named "Minette," she had been disguised as a boy and smuggled out of the country by her governess to join her eldest brother and mother, who had already returned to France. This second separation would, Charles suspected, prove longer than their first.

The royalists had lost the war and with it the chance for Charles to return to his personal rule. It was as a prisoner from Hampton Court that the King would have to negotiate with his enemies about what kind of political settlement should emerge from the civil wars. His captivity was not onerous. It was the height of summer when Charles I returned, and he was allowed to exercise in the palace's tennis court, which he had ordered rebuilt during happier times. He was permitted to decorate his rooms with whatever paintings he wanted from his collection, one of the largest in the world. He asked for a picture of himself on horseback, a half-length of his wife, and a group portrait called *The Five Eldest Children of King Charles I*. The entire family was thus reunited on his walls, and partly in his rooms, when two of the latter's sitters were brought to spend afternoons with their father.

As the monarchy's fortunes declined, Charles had seen his children less frequently until they fell into parliamentarian custody. They were first reunited at a roadside tavern en route to Hampton Court after he, too, was taken prisoner. Even the famous Parliamentarian general Oliver Cromwell had been moved, calling the royals' reunion "the tenderest sight that ever his eyes beheld."[16] The two elder children in the group, James, then fourteen, and Elizabeth, who was eleven, wept when six-year-old Prince Henry did not initially recognize their father, who knelt down to him and said, "I am your father, child, and it is not one of the least of my misfortunes that I have brought you and your brothers and sisters into this world to share my miseries."[17] Subsequently, the royal siblings, like their father, had been well treated. They were entrusted to the care of Algernon Percy, 10th Earl of Northumberland, an aristocrat who had supported the Parliamentarian cause during the war but who took the princess and her two brothers into his home at Syon House, which was conveniently close to Hampton Court.[18] Lord Northumberland regularly brought James, Elizabeth, and Henry to visit the King at the palace, where something resembling a full royal household had been reconvened to take care of the prisoner-monarch. Charles was "loving to all the children," but he was especially proud of Elizabeth, who was fluent in French with a working knowledge of Greek, Hebrew, Italian, and Latin. Her experiences of being cared for, however respectfully, by her family's enemies had made the eleven-year-old princess watchful and reserved. The King had similar personality traits, and he hugged Elizabeth often, particularly when he seemed overcome by the fact that three of his children were prisoners.

Northumberland, perhaps keen to cultivate an appearance of normality, suggested that the King and Prince James might have a portrait painted to commemorate their reunion. The King agreed, as he did to Northumberland's suggestion of Peter Lely as the artist. The resulting work would subsequently become one of Lely's most admired pieces; the poet Richard Lovelace was so moved by it that he dedicated his poem *Lucasta*, "To my worthy friend Mr. Peter Lely: on that excellent picture of his Majesty, and [Prince James] the duke of York, drawn by him at Hampton-Court." On the surface, Lely was painting royals who headed a monarchy that was clipped but in no real danger of destruction. Apart from the new guards with their Parliamentarian military uniforms, Hampton Court looked and functioned much as it had in the years before the wars, with a king whose children joined him from their smaller home nearby, while an artist came to paint a royal portrait, and servants milled about, performing their chores. Although the children resided with Northumberland, and Charles's household was watched over by another Parliamentarian, Oliver Cromwell's cousin Colonel Edward Whalley, some Royalists, such as the Earl of Southampton, were allowed to take up residence so that they could attend on Charles. On Thursday evenings, to catch the foreign post, Charles kept to his bedchamber to write letters to his wife and friends in Europe. The King was also permitted visitors, the most prominent of whom were the Parliamentarian generals Henry Ireton and Oliver Cromwell, or their representatives, who were sent to negotiate a peace deal in person with him.

The King had met the two generals before, in the immediate aftermath of the Royalist defeat, when both had removed their hats and bowed to him. Ireton and Cromwell were united by their politics, by their Puritan faith, and by family—Ireton had recently married Cromwell's daughter Bridget. Of the two men, Ireton was the negotiator more inclined to compromise, as he had shown with his tact in persuading one of the Royalist commanders, Lord Hopton, to disband the defeated yet sizeable regiments under his command. Described by a contemporary as a man "of a melancholic, reserved, dark nature, who communicated his thoughts to very few," and by another as "a very grave, serious, religious person," Ireton had already moderated several key points in *The Heads of Proposals*, Parliament's suggestions for securing peace, since he knew some of them would be unacceptable to King Charles.[19] In pursuing this path of moderation, Ireton risked his popularity with the army, which had risen during the civil war to become as powerful a force as the Parliament it defended; many of his men thought Ireton far too generous to the defeated Royalists. The adjusted proposals brought to Charles at Hampton Court included clauses that Parliament would control the army and all major chief offices of state, as well as judicial appointments, but only for the next decade. The bishoprics would not be abolished, but they would lose some of their power, and the Church of England would cease to be maintained by a mandatory tax—known as the tithe—on the entire population. As his deference to Charles was reported back in London, Ireton was mocked in pamphlets for going to Hampton Court to "kneel, and kiss, and fawn upon" a king whom many Parliamentarians had already nicknamed "the Man of Blood."

With so many dead in consequence of the war, there were plenty on the Parliamentarian side who did not want a compromise with the King. They wanted an unambiguous victory, and, for the first time in British history, there was a significant minority calling for an abolition of the monarchy. Men like Ireton knew that a future without the monarchy might create more problems than it solved—most Parliamentarians had fought with the goal of creating a monarchy limited by Parliament, not a republic. The question of what should replace the Crown would open a political Pandora's box. There was also the fact that although his court was British—in that he was attended by English, Irish, Welsh, and Scottish grandees—Charles I was not technically a British monarch, and there was no such thing yet, legally, as the British monarchy. He was, separately, King of England, King of Scots, and King of Ireland, and if the London Parliament pressed ahead with deposing him as their king, there was no legal requirement for the parliaments in Dublin and Edinburgh to do the same.

As the summer of 1647 turned to autumn, it was becoming clear not only that those parliaments would refuse to depose Charles in tandem with London but also that they resented the presumption that they should. If Charles was deposed, what, therefore, should be done with him? Should he be imprisoned in England, despite legally remaining the king of two sovereign nations that might declare war to free him? Or should he be allowed to go to his subjects in Ireland or Scotland, from where he might launch another war to regain his throne in England? The millions of remaining English and Welsh royalists would accept only a postwar settlement approved of by their king. Peace within the British Isles could only feasibly be secured if Charles I signed off on it. Despite the cost to his own popularity with the radicals, Ireton therefore had good reason for being flexible during the Hampton Court negotiations.

Another of those allowed to visit Charles at Hampton Court was James Butler, 1st Marquess of Ormond, whose family was no less influential than it had been in the days when another James Butler came to Hampton Court just over a century earlier.* The thirty-seven-year-old Marquess arrived at the palace to resign in person as Charles's Lord Lieutenant of Ireland after formally surrendering Dublin to a Parliamentarian force led by Colonel Michael Jones. Charles had enhanced the Butler title from an earldom to a marquessate in recognition of Ormond's devotion to the monarchy, first during the rebellions of 1641 and then through the civil wars.[20] Although the Marquess was a Protestant, he had many Catholic relatives, including his brother-in-law Lord Muskerry, a prominent member of the Irish Catholic Confederation formed by the Catholic elite of Ireland in the aftermath of

---

* See chapter 2.

the 1641 uprising. The confederation shared many of the rebels' goals with regard to ending the favoritism shown to Protestants in Ireland; however, it was keen to realize those objectives with less horror than 1641. Through his brother-in-law and others, the Marquess of Ormond knew that many of the Catholic confederates were, by 1647, willing or even eager to pledge their support to the royalists. Faced with the prospect of a Puritan-dominated government emerging in London, the Irish Catholic Confederation and Irish royalists were prepared to ally under the mantra that my enemy's enemy is my friend. The fact that Charles I was married to a Catholic princess who was safely in Paris, from where she could lead negotiations in his name, was also agreeable to the confederation.

The Marquess of Ormond's debrief of the situation in Ireland reminded Charles I that there was also a sizeable section of royalists—old, new, and returned—who did not want a compromise, either. The King knew already that some of those who had led the Presbyterian rebellion against him in Scotland were likewise unenthused about being told what to do with their monarchy by an English parliament, and from Scotland the royalist Duke of Hamilton was feeding Charles the same kind of encouraging information as Ormond was about Ireland. Just as this news increased his confidence, Charles was also receiving information that fed his fears. The negotiations between King and Parliament had dragged into late autumn when Colonel Whalley received a letter from his cousin Oliver Cromwell, warning him of a plot to commit the "most horrid act" of murdering Charles while he was in custody at Hampton Court. Whalley showed this letter to the King.

Thanks to surviving inventories, we know that, among the older portraits still decorating the walls at Hampton Court in 1647, there was one of Richard II, King of England from 1377 until he was overthrown in 1399.[21] Richard had survived his deposition by just over a year until being murdered while in custody. Charles had already begun to fear that he might soon share the same fate as Richard—or, indeed, Edward II, Henry VI, and Edward V, all of whom had vanished within a year of losing power. He also resented the fact that as a prisoner, no matter how comfortable, he had limited room for maneuvering in his negotiations with Parliament. He knew how hated he was by radicals, and Oliver Cromwell's unexpected warning of a murder plot heightened his paranoia. In the privacy of his apartments, Charles warned his three children to never allow themselves to become pawns of his enemies. He suspected, correctly, that there were some in Parliament who thought the answer to the problem was to depose—or murder—him, skip over the adult Prince of Wales, who had chosen exile at his Catholic mother's side, and replace them either with Prince James or Prince Henry, as a child-monarch they could mold into an obedient Puritan who cooperated with Parliament. Oliver Cromwell was briefly among those who favored the proposal to make Prince Henry their next king. Charles told all three of his children to never willingly go along with such a plan, and, if anything happened to him, to be guided by their eldest brother and their mother.

On Thursday, November 11, the King went to his bedchamber to write letters for the foreign post. Colonel Whalley arrived at five o'clock to escort him to prayers in the chapel, as usual. The servants explained that the King had not yet finished his correspondence for that week and asked if Colonel Whalley would mind returning an hour later. Charles was still not ready at six. By seven o'clock, Whalley had started to worry. He even hunkered down at the keyhole to the King's bedchamber. At eight o'clock, respect for etiquette had to be abandoned. Whalley ordered one of the servants to open the door to the King's Apartments, which revealed that the doors had been bolted from the other side. Whalley dashed down through the palace to the Privy Gardens, from where he accessed the Privy Stairs and raced up the stairs toward the King's bedchamber. There was still the possibility that Charles had collapsed from sudden ill-health, until Whalley saw the King's cloak lying on the floor of the dressing room with no sign of Charles. They searched the remaining rooms, in which they found Charles's two dogs—his greyhound, Gypsy, and his spaniel, Rogue—and three letters. In the first, Charles thanked his jailers for their kindness to him during his imprisonment and asked that they look after his dogs. In the second, he left specific instructions for the care of his famous art collection. His third was to Parliament, in which Charles wrote that he was leaving so that he could negotiate with them more freely.[22]

Charles had most likely fled, with one or two attendants, earlier that evening, through the Privy Gardens to a waiting boat prearranged by his supporters. After disembarking, they rode to an inn at Sutton, just south of London, where Charles, in disguise, arrived shortly after dawn on Friday, November 12. Fresh horses were waiting for them, and by the afternoon, they were being hidden at the country house of the Dowager Countess of Southampton, whose son was one of the royalist nobles who had been allowed to join Charles's incarceration at Hampton Court. On Saturday the thirteenth, the King sailed to the Isle of Wight. By February, a second civil war had started.

Charles I lied prolifically to his captors about his willingness to negotiate; instead, he chose to reignite a hideously bloody conflict rather than compromise. While it is true that Charles was in a difficult political position in 1647, and equally true that he had many fine qualities—not the least of which was his courage and his view that "None but cowards are cruel"—it is hard to accept his claim that he was escaping solely to improve his negotiating position. The Marquess of Ormond's visit, the revival of the royalist cause in Scotland and Ireland, and its continuing strength in England and Wales all indicate that Charles knew, even hoped, that he would be able to recommence—and this time win—a war that had already cost tens of thousands of lives. The King cannot be exonerated from the consequences of his escape from Hampton Court.

Nevertheless, there are several unanswerable questions about Oliver Cromwell's complicity. Cromwell was far less interested in compromise than Ireton, yet he knew that harsh action against the monarchy could be justified only if Charles broke his oath and abandoned negotiations. It does not say much for the effectiveness of security at Hampton Court that King Charles was able to make it through the Privy Gardens and to the wharf without being apprehended. Why were there no guards at the Privy Stairs or anywhere along the route he would have had to take to flee? Cromwell's letter to his cousin Colonel Whalley, making dire if unspecific insinuations that Charles's life was imperilled so long as he remained at Hampton Court, was shown to Charles, who fled within thirty-six hours of reading it. If Cromwell really believed that the King's life was at risk from a radical assassin, the lackluster security at the palace appears even more baffling. Whalley was not only Cromwell's kinsman but also one of the first who answered his call to enlist in a Parliamentarian regiment when the war began. His loyalty to his cousin was absolute. It is certainly possible that Cromwell was sufficiently averse to the prospect of negotiation with the Royalists that he allowed Charles I ample opportunity to flee and even helped manipulate him into doing so. A former ally of Cromwell's wrote that, by fleeing Hampton Court, the King had fallen "into Cromwell's mouse trap."[23] The evidence that Cromwell played this game is by no means conclusive, but neither can it be dismissed entirely. Unlike the undeniable fact that it was Charles I who took the final, fateful decision of fleeing Hampton Court to restart the civil wars.

CHAPTER 15

THE TEMPORARY
PALISADE

*For these things that have lately come to pass have been
the wonderful works of God, breaking the rod of the
oppressor as in the days of Midian, not with garments
much rolled in blood but by the terror of the Lord; who
will yet save His people and confound His enemies.*

—Oliver Cromwell, future Lord Protector
of England, Scotland, and Ireland (1648)

On the January morning in 1649 when Charles I's decapitated head
thumped into the sawdust of a scaffold erected outside his former
Banqueting House at Whitehall, Hampton Court was full of squatters.
The English monarchy had died with Charles; the purpose of its surviving
palaces was unclear. In the chaos that had followed Charles I's escape from
Hampton Court, farmers, villagers, travellers known then as gypsies, and
tradesmen had set up shop and home in the palace's abandoned galleries,
halls, apartments, stables, and kitchens. The palace at Greenwich had fared
even worse. Having been used as a detention center for Royalist prisoners
during the war and then leased to a biscuit manufacturer, it was past the
point of redemption.[1] A parliamentary commission recommended levelling
Henry VII's palace at Richmond to auction off its materials. At Hamp-

ton Court, large tracts of the estate were sold to private citizens; Oatlands Palace, for instance, the sixteenth-century hunting residence in the Chase, went to a wealthy parliamentarian who demolished it and sold its bricks to the Weston family. Hampton Court proper was expected to go the same way, until it was saved by Oliver Cromwell, who, "for the maintenance of his state and dignity," designated Hampton Court as his weekend house when he became England's first republican head of state in 1653.[2]

Having quashed the quixotic and ineffective parliamentary republicanism that had initially replaced the monarchy, Cromwell became Lord Protector of the Commonwealth,* head of a regime held together largely by his military genius and his iron will. Throughout, there were fears that the Stuarts would return—Charles I's widow and her five children were living safely in Europe. To prevent their return to power, some of Cromwell's supporters urged him to create an alternative monarchy by crowning himself king. He rejected that idea, but he and his wife adopted the honorific Your Highness.[3] Commissioners arrived at Hampton Court to make the palace fit for the new Lord Protector, his wife, children, and grandchildren. They evicted the civil war squatters and returned the palace to its former splendor. Although much of the royal art collection amassed by Charles I and his predecessors was auctioned off to ameliorate government debts from the war, more than enough was kept to decorate Hampton Court.[4] The tennis courts and bowling greens were restored, the palace was thoroughly cleaned, and the plumbing improvements ordered by Charles I and Henrietta Maria made it one of the most comfortable homes in the British Isles. Cromwell decided that he and his wife, Elizabeth, would live together in the former Queen's Apartments, eschewing the rooms from which Charles I had fled—those were turned into offices for Cromwell's advisers and bedrooms for his servants.[5] An outdoor pulpit was erected in one of the courtyards. Charles I's private Oratory was renovated into a bedroom for a Puritan preacher, and, in the chapel, some of the art commissioned by Wolsey, which had survived even Edward VI, was destroyed in a burst of

---

* This period is also known as the Protectorate or the Interregnum.

iconoclastic zeal. "The pulling down of the popish and superstitious pictures at Hampton Court" was applauded by a London newspaper that informed its readers, "there was pulled down the picture of Christ nailed to the Cross, which was placed right above the high altar, and the pictures of Mary Magdalen and others weeping by the foot of the cross and some other such idolatrous pictures." All the chapel's remaining images of the Virgin Mary were also destroyed, as was one of Saint John the Evangelist. The stained glass windows went, too, as "order [was] given for the new glazing of them with plain glass."[6]

With these changes in place, Hampton Court was judged ready for its new residents. For the next five years, every Friday, almost without fail, Cromwell and his family arrived from London by river or road, always with a large number of guards. The Cromwells loved Hampton Court.[7] The Great Hall hosted the celebrations after their daughter Mary's wedding in the palace's chapel to Lord Fauconberg, who had fought for Parliament during the wars. The festivities included a "spoken masque"—devoid of music or set—during which Cromwell read aloud Latin verses in praise of godly government. One of the bride's sisters offended the guests when she observed snobbishly that the generals' wives looked as if they belonged at home "washing dishes."[8] Said joke was, unsurprisingly, "extremely ill-taken" by those who found themselves as its punchline, including Lucy Hutchinson, a Calvinist poet and memoirist, who described all the Cromwell sisters bar Bridget, the eldest, as "insolent fools."[9]

As Mary Cromwell's wedding to Lord Fauconberg showed, aristocratic titles were not abolished with the monarchy. In fact, Cromwell created several new peerages, including the barony of Claypole for a young Member of Parliament "very dear to me" after he married Cromwell's second and favorite daughter, Elizabeth, known in the family as Betty. She was described by one of Cromwell's earliest biographers as "the joy of his heart."[10] It was Betty who cracked the mean-spirited joke at Mary Cromwell's wedding, and their father worried that she had been corrupted by the temptations of secular society, telling his wife that their daughter had been too "cozened with worldly vanities and worldly company."[11] He may have underestimated his favorite child as much as he loved her; her insult to the wedding guests was perhaps a moment of uncharacteristic or youthful cruelty, since many other sources from the time indicate that Betty Claypole became respected for her attempts to intercede for petitioners with her father.[12] She was particularly admired for her unsuccessful attempts to persuade her father to halt the execution of Charles I's former chaplain-turned-royalist-spy, Reverend John Hewett. Some monarchists were ungrateful for Betty's intercessions on their behalf; one memoirist described her as only one small step above "the fishwives of Billingsgate," thereby lobbing back at her the same unappealing snobbery she had once flung at the generals' wives.[13]

In the summer of 1658 Betty came to Hampton Court in a fragile state, emotionally and physically. She arrived with her husband, John Claypole, and their three surviving children: ten-year-old Cromwell, Henry, who was five or six, and the toddler, Martha. Betty's youngest son, Oliver, had died of an unknown illness that June while still a toddler. Betty's recent pregnancy, possibly her fifth, had left her grappling with physical complaints in conjunction with depression at her son's death.[14] Throughout July, she weakened further as she lay in the garden-facing apartments that she and her family had been given on her father's orders.[15] From there, she wrote to a relative, "I have been so extremely sick of late that it has made me unfit for anything."[16] One of her brothers-in-law wrote in frustration that "the physicians do not understand thoroughly her case." It was perhaps uterine cancer. The same brother-in-law observed that throughout the summer, Betty "hath been troubled with great pains in her bowels, and vapours in the head," and her father's personal doctor recorded "an inward imposthume [an abscess] of her loins."[17] She may have had several illnesses concurrently, as not all her symptoms were consistent with cancer. As the household prayed for her, Betty took to her bed, with her husband and parents keeping vigil. Not wanting to distress them further, she stifled any outward sign of pain. Apothecarists administered many potions and medicines, with their emphasis increasingly on what we might now categorize as palliative care.

Refusing to leave his daughter's side, Cromwell dispatched a deputy to represent him back in London for an audience with the incoming Dutch ambassador, who understood tactfully that the Protector was distracted with "great sadness for the mortal distemper of Lady Claypole."[18] When Cromwell did go to the capital briefly for government business, he returned immediately to Hampton Court. Betty died there in the small hours of August 6, 1658, at the age of twenty-nine. Her body was taken to the wharf to be transported back to London. The barge carrying her coffin was respectfully accompanied throughout its evening journey by boats bearing flaming torches and filled with her family's advisers and staff. Her father was so distraught that not only was he unable to attend Betty's funeral at Westminster Abbey but also his wife and their daughter, Lady Fauconberg, were sufficiently worried about him that they too missed the ceremony in order to watch over him. The chief mourner at the nighttime interment was Cromwell's widowed sister, Robina, who was joined by hundreds of guests, including Betty's widower, her brothers, Richard and Henry, and her other sisters, Bridget, Lady Fleetwood, and Lady Frances Rich.[19]

In the weeks that followed, Cromwell kept to Hampton Court, where he wrestled with the worst in a long series of depressive episodes that had affected him for most of his adulthood. In his late twenties, he may have sought medical help for what his doctor referred to as Cromwell's "valde melancolius" ("extreme unhappiness"), which was accompanied by prolonged stomach pains.[20] Cromwell credited that period in his life with bringing him to a fuller relationship with Christ; he was born again after realizing that, in his own words, he was "chief of sinners" by failing personally to accept Jesus as his Lord and Savior. From that point on, Cromwell felt that God had not only redeemed him but also had marked him for greatness like his biblical hero Gideon. He progressed from life as a minor landowner to become a member of Parliament and, from there, despite having no formal military education, one of the greatest generals of the seventeenth century. In later speeches, Cromwell said that when confronted by a dilemma, he thought on God with the question, "What would He do?"

Cromwell had remained throughout his life a devoted family man—he abandoned his university education at Sidney Sussex College, Cambridge, a year before graduating, instead returning home to look after his mother and sisters when his father's sudden death left him head of the family. He had a similar sense of loving duty after marrying Elizabeth Bourchier, a fur trader's daughter with whom he had nine children and who, decades into their marriage, he still wrote to from campaign to tell her, "Thou art dearer to me than any creature." Yet his depression had returned on many occasions. Their eldest son Robert had fallen ill and died while away at boarding school; his second, Oliver, volunteered for the Parliamentarian armies where he lost his life thanks to smallpox; his youngest, James, died in the year of his birth. Nothing, however, had prepared anyone around Cromwell for his reaction to Betty's death in the summer of 1658. He was heartbroken. As has happened many times before and since, the loss of a loved one accelerated another's march into the grave. He was already suffering from gout, his stomach was in agony again, he was often constipated, he struggled to urinate.

Sometimes he went riding in the Hampton Court grounds, which were diminished in size by the parliamentary auctions yet still substantial. A mounted bodyguard accompanied Cromwell during these excursions, protecting him from any enterprising royalist assassins; the wooden ramparts installed around the palace itself were intended to shield him from similar threats. The defenses had hidden much of Hampton Court from view for the first time in its history, ringing it behind a guarded wooden palisade—a fort to protect the Protector, who had many enemies, nearly all of whom were unmoved by his grief at his daughter's death.

A royalist assassination plot had been foiled only a few months earlier. The King's supporters could not forgive Cromwell either for Charles I's execution or for rendering viable "the maintenance of this republic" in a country that most thought could not function—perhaps not even exist—without its monarchy.[21] Many Europeans had initially gazed in horror at England's execution of its king, and yet, through his determination and strength, Cromwell had turned a pariah republic into one of the most respected states in the world. He had maintained, funded, and expanded its army and navy in an increasingly militarized century, while in his domestic policy, he had restored peace and order to England and Wales after a civil war whose victims, as a percentage of the population, made it the bloodiest in English history.[22] In 1656 Cromwell embarked upon a policy that some of his people described as "the great dishonour of Christianity and public scandal of the Protestant religion," when he retired the 366-year ban on Jews living in England.[23] By licensing a group of immigrants to establish a synagogue on London's Creechurch Lane, Cromwell was effectively rescinding King Edward I's edicts that had expelled, at terrible human cost, the entire Anglo-Jewish community in 1290. It has been argued that Cromwell's Jewish policy was less about righting a historic wrong and more a consequence of his belief that Christ would not return to Earth until all Jews had willingly converted to Christianity. This idea was widespread in contemporary evangelical-millenarianism, as was the theory that the Jews' conversion would be achieved more by kindness than persecution.[24] Cromwell's role in the re-legalization of Judaism in Britain thus perhaps boils down to the age-old moral quandary of whether an action should be judged more by motivation or result.

Cromwell is traditionally associated with introducing the phrase "warts and all" into the English language, when he insisted that the portraitist Samuel Cooper not flatter him by leaving out the large wart beneath his bottom lip, nor the smaller one above his right eyebrow, but rather include "all these roughness, pimples, warts, and everything as you see me. Otherwise I never will pay a farthing for it."[25] There were many warts on Cromwell's career, none greater than his actions in Ireland, which have, unfortunately, been downplayed in some histories of his extraordinary career.

The Marquess of Ormond was correct when he told Charles I at Hampton Court in 1647 that the alliance between the royalists and the Irish Catholic Confederation would become one of the greatest bulwarks of monarchism in the British Isles. The Marquess had left Hampton Court and made straight for the southern ports; from there, he crossed to France to liaise with Queen Henrietta Maria, who was able to use the situation to her advantage.[26] Not only could her conference with Lord Ormond provide her husband with an Irish army that might destroy his English enemies, but as part of those negotiations, the Queen hoped to achieve one of her own major long-term goals: to end all existing discriminations against her fellow Catholics in Ireland. To entice even more Catholics to the royalist cause, Henrietta Maria promised that the repeal of anti-Catholic laws would be achieved if the Irish Crown survived. The Queen's policy inspired the Pope to offer a huge sum of money to the royalists.[27] Pleased with how negotiations had gone with the Queen, Ormond returned to Ireland, where he became de facto leader of the royalist-confederate alliance, which attracted widespread support. The Irish Catholic Confederation also sent a delegation to Paris, where, conditional on the Pope's approval, they offered to entrust the government of Ireland to Henrietta Maria and the Prince of Wales.[28] If the monarchy fell in Wales and England, Ireland had made it abundantly clear that it did not intend to obediently follow suit.

Cromwell had led his army into Scotland to crush royalism just before Charles I's execution; he crossed the sea to Ireland to do the same after it. Appointed by Parliament as the new Lord Lieutenant of Ireland, Cromwell and his twelve thousand "Ironside" soldiers, veterans of the English civil war, successfully took twenty-five fortified towns in his forty weeks there, thereby ending the royalist threat. Nothing he ever did became more notorious than his siege of Drogheda,* a fortified port thirty miles north of Dublin. Cromwell wrote on September 16, 1649, five days after it was taken, of how determinedly the royalists had defended the town, even after a bombardment by cannon. When the Governor of Drogheda refused to surrender, Cromwell warned him, "If this be refused, you will have no cause to blame me."[29] The walls were breached during the second attack. According to an eyewitness, Cromwell's men spilled so much "blood of our noblest citizens . . . that it inundated the streets. There was hardly a house that was not defiled with carnage and filled with wailing."[30] The one-legged royalist Governor of Drogheda, Sir Arthur Aston, was dragged from the battlements and beaten to death in front of jeering soldiers. Cromwell's letters reveal that as regards the military

---

* Pronounced "Drocka-duh."

defenders, "Our men getting up to them, were ordered by me to put them all to the sword," and, far more unusually, with respect to noncombatants, "I forbade them to spare any that were in the town."[31] Cromwell is clear that, at a bare minimum, he ordered his men to slaughter one thousand unarmed civilians who ran for sanctuary in St. Peter's, the town's Catholic church, confirming that "in this very place, near one thousand of them were put to sword, fleeing thither for safety."[32] A Protestant royalist clergyman recalled how thirty Protestants were sheltering in a private residence in Drogheda when Cromwell's soldiers kicked in the door and began firing their pistols at them. An Irish poet, Éamonn an Dúna, who survived the massacre, joked darkly a decade later that the only English words he knew were those he had heard frequently at Drogheda: "shoot him, kill him, strip him, tear him, a Tory,* hack him, a rebel, a rogue, a thief, a priest, a papist."[33] The thirty survivors of the soldiers' garrison were deported to slavery in Barbados.† Even days after the town had fallen, when, by all conventional military protocol, it should have been spared as a surrendered site, any Catholic clergy caught in the vicinity were publicly executed. Heber MacMahon, Catholic Bishop of Clogher, was captured, hanged, and posthumously decapitated, and his head sent to be displayed on a pike at the gates to the northern city of Derry.[34]

Cromwell's supporters claimed the oddly specific, and low, casualty figure of 3,552 for Drogheda. "Not a man more or less," jibed a disbelieving royalist journalist. Given the chaos, it is unlikely that we will ever have a precise figure but, at the most conservative estimate, it was a lot more than that. At least three thousand royalist and Catholic Confederation soldiers were killed when the walls were breached, in addition to the thousand or more civilians murdered in the massacre at St. Peter's Church. More were killed in the days that followed. The Marquess of Ormond told King Charles's

---

* Then a pejorative term for a royalist.

† As with some Protestant stories of the earlier massacres mentioned in the preceding chapter of this book, some of the anecdotes told about the fall of Drogheda—such as babies being torn from the arms of their Catholic mothers to be nailed, while still alive, to the doors of Catholic churches—are mercifully untrue.

nephew Prince Rupert that his scouts had confirmed to him Cromwell's "bloody execution of almost all that were within" the town when it fell.[35]

Irish historian Dr. Micheál Ó Siochrú has persuasively argued that Cromwell's correspondence "strongly suggests a man ill at ease with his conscience. As always, Cromwell found solace and comfort in his religious convictions, the unshakeable belief that he was doing God's will."[36] Those qualms reappear in Cromwell's subsequent and disingenuous attempts to justify what was done, not just at Drogheda but also at his subsequent siege of the coastal city of Wexford. Wexford perhaps deserves to be even more notorious than Drogheda: it surrendered to Cromwell's army, which then, again on his orders, butchered hundreds of civilians. Parliamentarian propaganda tried to blame what had happened at Drogheda on the Marquess of Ormond's message to the garrison not to negotiate with Cromwell. Yet Wexford's willingness to surrender did not save it from burning and bleeding like Drogheda, which had refused to do so.

Along with blaming royalist obstinacy for the siege, Cromwell insisted later that the killings in 1649 were retaliation for the murder of Irish Protestants by Catholics during the massacres of 1641. He called it "the righteous judgement of God upon those barbarous wretches, who have imbrued their hands in so much innocent blood." His supporters, like the poet Thomas Cobbes, believed him, refusing to pity the Drogheda dead on the grounds that, during the anti-Protestant massacres, "Many of their fellow subjects have they slain, / Crying for quarter, though too much in vain."[37] There is a mountain of evidence to show that this was not true: the majority of the 1641 massacres were perpetrated in the nine counties of Ulster, the most northern of Ireland's four provinces. Drogheda, like Wexford, is in the eastern province of Leinster. If Cromwell really was intent on exacting vengeance in kind for 1641, it is odd, to say the least, that he never set foot in Ulster. Nor did he spare Irish Protestants who sided with the monarchy.

The fiction that 1649 was retribution for 1641 was maintained in the next stage of Cromwell's plan. He commissioned an Oxford-educated cartographer, William Petty, to draw up some of the most accurate maps seen yet. The results—in the Down Survey, or *Hiberniae Dilenatio*—are beautiful and sinister. They enabled the English republic to know exactly what land existed in Ireland, who owned it, and who they could take it from. By the end of Cromwell's career, two-thirds of all the land in Ireland had undergone a forcible change of ownership. A contemporary priest wrote that any Catholic landowning families were "deprived by Cromwell of all their immovable property, and are all compelled to abandon their native estates and retire into the province of Connaught."[38] Connaught, or Connacht in Irish, is the westernmost of Ireland's four provinces—also the smallest, and the one with the most extreme weather and the least fertile soil. Whether or not Oliver Cromwell ever actually said "to Hell or to Connaught" to describe the only two places he would ever willingly send Irish Catholics, it has become one of the most notorious phrases from the seventeenth century as well as being the name given to his enforced resettlement policy.[39]

There was, however, a third Cromwellian option between Hell and Connacht: the Caribbean. Over the course of the 1650s, it is estimated that somewhere between ten and twelve thousand Irishmen were seized and deported to work as indentured servants on the sugar and tobacco plantations in Barbados.[40] Forty thousand more, nicknamed "the Wild Geese," fled from Ireland to Europe, the vast majority of them granted asylum by the French and Spanish monarchies.[41] Poverty and depopulation were so extensive that the government had to incentivize organized wolf hunts, with rewards for how many were killed from the packs that confidently roamed the streets of Dublin, where they were observed attacking "poor children who lost their parents" during the wars or the ensuing breakdown in food supplies.[42] By 1658, after two decades of civil war, sectarian massacres, deportations, transportations, and emigration, the Irish population had fallen by a third since the 1630s, and its Catholic landowning elite had, as a class, ceased to exist, either dying in exile or in penury in Connacht.[43] Cromwell bears more responsibility for this than any other individual in his generation, but in his attitudes, Cromwell marched firmly in step with his Parliamentarian colleagues, who, two years into the civil wars, had decided to punish Ireland for its support for King Charles by decreeing that "no quarter shall henceforth be given to any Irishman or papist born in Ireland captured on land or at sea."[44] Irish women had been tied back-to-back then thrown overboard when a Royalist ship was captured by the Parliamentarian navy; Irish soldiers who surrendered with Royalist garrisons were executed, while their English comrades were spared.

It was the desire for revenge on the part of those who blamed Cromwell for what had been done to Charles I or to Ireland that had necessitated the construction of the wooden palisades that ringed Hampton Court. Scotland, too, which Cromwell invaded a second time after the Irish campaign of 1649–50, remained a hotbed of unrest. To maintain order, Cromwell's regime had on its permanent payroll forty thousand soldiers, creating in effect a military state in both Scotland and Ireland—as well as a hole in the national budget that turned into debilitating debt. The auctioning of palaces and art, including the melting down of most of the original crown jewels, could not keep pace with this military expenditure. To sustain the unsustainable, Cromwell had resorted to raising taxes without parliamentary approval; royalist eyebrows arched to the ceiling, as a similar fiscal overstep had been a major motivation for the initial rebellion against King Charles.

Along with personal grief over his daughter's death, the Lord Protector was thus also weighed down by political challenges. While he mourned and worried in the former Queen's Apartments at Hampton Court, he took comfort from having the Bible read aloud to him, especially the fourth chapter of the Epistle to the Philippians, to which he had turned after his son Robert's death at school years earlier and whose words he credited with helping bring about his own moment of being born again in Christ.[45] It contains the verses:

> *Brethren, whatsoever things are true, whatsoever things are honest, whatsoever things are just, whatsoever things are pure, whatsoever things are worthy love, whatsoever things are of good report, if there be any virtue, or if there be any praise, think on these things. Which ye have*

both learned and received, and heard, and seen in me: those things do,
and the God of peace shall be with you.[46]

Eleven days after Betty's death, Cromwell felt well enough to go for a ride on the Hampton Court estate. Surrounded by his mounted guard, he was approached by George Fox, the thirty-four-year-old son of a basket weaver who had come at his prearranged time to discuss the question of religious toleration. Cromwell had extended toleration to every significant religious group in Britain with the exception of Roman Catholics and Quakers, a then derogatory name for the Religious Society of Friends, of which Fox was a cofounder. Cromwell admired Fox for his honesty and his skills as an orator; he was grateful, too, for the kind letters of spiritual comfort that Fox had sent Betty during her final illness at Hampton Court.[47] However, he strongly opposed the Quakers' promotion of pacifism, particularly after Fox's public refusal to promise that he would take up arms to prevent a restoration of the monarchy. He also rejected their theology that personal revelation in spirituality was as important, if not more so, than the words of the Bible. Fox intended once again to tell the Lord Protector in no uncertain terms how unjust was the lack of toleration for the Quakers, until his words were stayed by the sight of Cromwell. Fox wrote, "I saw and felt a waft of death so forth against and around him that he looked like a dead man already." Fox was intercepted by one of Cromwell's attendants, who told him that "the doctors were not willing I [should] speak with him."[48]

The meeting was to be rescheduled, but it never took place. In the middle of the night, Cromwell collapsed from the pain in his bowels. He then took the decision to return to Whitehall, where he died on the third of September. When the news reached an Irish royalist, he wrote, "[I]nto his life he fitted about sixty years' worth of age, but a millennium's worth of evil . . . so damn his dead ashes to Hell, traveller, and then be on your way."[49] In England, Cromwell was mourned and eulogized by his supporters, who felt "we have lost a Captain, a Shield, the Head, an Heir of Restraint, the Breath of our Nostrils, a Healer, a Shepherd, a Father and a Nursing Father, a Cornerstone, a Builder, a Watchman, an Eye, a Saviour, a Steersman and a Rector, a Pilot" to the ship of state.[50]

Within two years, the republic that Cromwell had helped mold had unravelled, and the monarchy was restored. Another set of government-appointed commissioners arrived at Hampton Court to expel all traces of a man they had regarded as the greatest squatter of them all. Of all those who held court at the palace over the centuries, the tenure of the extraordinary and controversial Oliver Cromwell—simultaneously one of the most admired and reviled political figures in British history—remains the hardest to discern during visits to Hampton Court today.

CHAPTER 16

THE COUNTESS
OF CASTLEMAINE'S
QUARTERS

Restless he rolls from whore to whore,
A merry monarch, scandalous and poor.

—John Wilmot, 2nd Earl of Rochester,
"A Satire on Charles II" (c. 1673)

Having once painted Cromwell's portraits, Peter Lely achieved his goal of becoming a court artist after the restoration of the monarchy in 1660. Charles I's son, Charles II, later knighted Lely for his services, and ten of his works hang today in the Communications Gallery at Hampton Court. Originally commissioned for display at Windsor Castle and known as the "Windsor Beauties" series, they depict prominent women of the Restoration-era court, including Frances Stewart, Duchess of Richmond and Lennox, who, of all the faces on Hampton Court's walls, is the one whose image has been replicated the most since. Her father was Queen Henrietta Maria's physician, and she served the Queen Mother as a maid of honor in the 1660s.[1] Frances's beauty attracted the attention of King Charles II, whose advances she rejected by eloping with his distant kinsman, the Duke of Richmond. However, a lifelong friendship developed

229

afterward between Charles and Frances, who was chosen in 1667 as the model for Britannia when the allegorical figure was minted onto British coins. Along with appearing on these coins in her own lifetime, Frances's face then appeared on every penny struck by the Bank of England from 1797 until the decimalization of the currency in 1970. Frances-as-Britannia remained in circulation on the fifty-pence piece until 2008, when a new design was announced.

A prominent courtly figure missing from the Windsor Beauties series is Charles II's wife, Catherine of Braganza, who arrived at Hampton Court on May 29, 1662, at about nine o'clock in the evening. It was the middle of a heatwave, and, even after sunset, makeup ran down the parboiled faces of the court ladies. The twenty-four-year-old Portuguese princess had reached England two weeks earlier, and this was her first extended stay in one of her new husband's palaces. Hampton Court's use by the Cromwells had saved it from falling into ruin like so many of the other royal estates, and some improvements had been carried out already since the Restoration of the monarchy, including the revival of the Chapel as an Anglican place of worship, the revamping of Charles I's tennis court and the stables, and the creation of the Long Water, Hampton Court's new canal, upon which boats shaped like swans punted up and down, carrying courtiers. Even so, there was "whitewashing and matting, putting up ledges for hangings, painting, and gilding a balcony" in order to have it ready to receive the new Queen; during the works, a young chorister was killed tragically when he was hit by a workman's cart.[2] The court's sojourn at Hampton Court, which still had several leaking roofs despite the refurbishments, bought time for the workmen while a similar revitalization was carried out at Whitehall, the largest palace in Europe at the time and the royals' main residence in the capital. On Catherine's arrival at Hampton Court, the Lord Chancellor, the privy councillors, the ambassadors, and "all the nobility, gentry, and ladies of the court were formally presented to her, classed, according to their degrees, in different rooms, through which her Majesty passed" before she reached her bedchamber, with its new crimson, velvet-upholstered bed and expensive mirrors; the latter were wedding gifts from Catherine's mother-in-law.[3]

Shy,* kind, and religious, "short of stature, prettily shaped, [with] languishing and excellent eyes," according to the contemporary writer John Evelyn, Catherine of Braganza's twenty-three ensuing years as queen are credited with popularizing the drinking of tea in the British Isles.[4] She also inspired a fad for forks by using one when she dined in public; they had existed for centuries, but, as late as the reign of James I, their use was tellingly mocked in English plays as an affectation of comedically pretentious characters.[5] Catherine's first stay at Hampton Court also set the tone for a queenship in England that was to be beset by humiliations brought about by her husband's thoughtlessness. During her honeymoon, Queen Catherine nearly fainted when she realized that Charles II's mistress had been appointed as one of her ladies-in-waiting; she subsequently became so upset that she suffered a nosebleed when Charles refused to dismiss the woman because he had already promised her the honor of joining the Queen's household.[6] Having once criticized his cousin King Louis XIV for pressuring *his* wife, Marie-Thérèse of Spain, to formally receive his mistress at court, Charles II swiftly abandoned any such principles when it came to his own queen. A kind or gentle nature is often mistaken for a weak one; Charles II made that error with his wife, who, although she could not overrule her husband even within her own household, refused to make her humiliation easy for him. The newlyweds quarrelled so loudly that their shouting could be heard beyond the closed doors of their rooms. According to the Chancellor, Lord Clarendon:

> *The passion and noise of the night reached too many ears to be a secret the next day: the whole court was full of that, which ought to have been*

---

* Catherine of Braganza is described as shy by several sources recording her arrival in 1662, however, given that she did not speak English yet, it is questionable if this was a character trait rather than an understandable reaction to circumstance.

known to nobody. And the mutual carriage and behaviour [the next day] between their Majesties confirmed all that they had heard or could imagine: they spake not, hardly looked on one another. Everybody was glad they were so far from the town (for they were still at Hampton Court), and that there were so few witnesses of all that passed. The Queen sat melancholic in her chamber in tears, except when she drove them away by a more violent passion in choleric discourse; and the King sought his divertissements in that company [his mistress] that said and did all things to please him; and there he spent all the nights.[7]

When Catherine's mother-in-law, Henrietta Maria, joined her at Hampton Court, it was the Queen Mother's first visit to the palace since January twenty years earlier when she had arrived and left as a fugitive. She returned by carriage—her household had four for her use, each drawn by six horses—and she was met in the courtyard by her eldest son, who escorted her to the top of the stairs to the Great Hall, where Queen Catherine waited to greet her.[8] In the years since Henrietta Maria had last seen Hampton Court, her husband had been executed, their daughter Elizabeth had died a few months later in parliamentarian captivity, aged fourteen—possibly from tuberculosis exacerbated by a fever caught while playing in the rain— and in 1660 a smallpox epidemic had killed Mary, Princess of Orange, and her younger brother Prince Henry, Duke of Gloucester. Of Charles I and Henrietta Maria's nine children, only three were still alive by 1662. Small wonder that in her native France, Henrietta Maria was nicknamed *La Reine Malheureuse* ("the Queen of Sorrow").[9] She was delighted that her new daughter-in-law was a Catholic and a princess, writing in a letter to her own sister, the Dowager Duchess of Savoy, that "my daughter-in-law is the best creature in the world who shows me the greatest goodwill. . . . [S]he is a saint."[10] Charles agreed eventually, describing Catherine in a letter to his chief minister "as good a woman as ever was born."[11]

The Windsor Beauties portraits stand as a reminder that perhaps no court in British history, including Henry VIII's, has been so defined by its monarch's sex life. It was a source of obsession in Charles II's lifetime, when it was both mocked and celebrated in the burgeoning pamphlets and press with language that makes today's most vicious media attacks seem tame. During Charles's long-lasting affair with the French noblewoman Louise de Kéroualle, an anonymous critic pinned a note to her doors that read:

Within this place a bed's appointed,
For a French bitch and God's anointed.[12]

When sex workers in London were attacked by gangs of armed Puritans in 1668, they pointed out the contrast between the violence, lack of safety, and public punishments—such as the ducking stool—that they faced, and the privileged security accorded to the King's lovers. Why were the brothels, known as "bawdy houses," being torn down in a morality drive by young Londoners "who did not go and pull down the great bawdy-house" at Hampton Court and the Palace of Whitehall?[13] The Bawdy House Riots of 1668 attracted not only the furious sex workers but also thousands of their clients, who clashed with their attackers. Two of the city's most famous madams were the alleged authors of a satirical entreaty, the Poor Whores' Petition, which they tauntingly addressed to Charles's mistress, "the most Splendid, Eminent, and Serene Lady of Pleasure" in the kingdom, asking her why she did not intervene to help her colleagues in the sex industry.[14] They were all plying the same trade, but they were at risk and she was not. As others mocked later, "The reason why she is not duck'd, / Because by Caesar she is fuck'd." There was also a fear that the King's mistresses were able to wield undue, and often secret, influence over his policies. The poet Lord Rochester complimented the King on his physical attributes while simultaneously mocking him for his alleged weakness of character:

His sceptre and his prick are of length,
And she may sway the one who plays with th'other.[15]

The King's adulteries mattered financially, for the extravagance of his court stood in unedifying contrast to the monarchy's straitened finances.

Charles II was the first English king in a half millennium to both acknowledge the majority of his illegitimate children and endow many of them
with aristocratic titles.[16] This, understandably, produced an abundance of
criticism from moralists on one side and pragmatists on the other, who
could not understand why Charles II saw no contradiction in repeatedly
crying poverty to Parliament while presiding over a court full of his lovers
and bastards, upon nearly all of whom he settled fortunes.

Louise de Kéroualle, born into well-bred poverty in Brittany, first came
to England in the entourage of Charles's sister Minette, Duchess of Orléans.*
She stayed after Minette returned to France, and Charles became besotted
with the woman he nicknamed "Fubbs" because of her weight—thinness
was not considered fashionable or particularly attractive in Restoration high
society. He named one of the early royal yachts *Fubbs* in Louise's honor,
made her Duchess of Portsmouth and their bastard son a duke. King
Louis XIV also made Louise a duchess—of Aubigny—an accolade that
heightened the suspicion in England that she was a French spy. Tensions
between the King's lovers saw passive, and sometimes open, aggression at
the palace. Louise, in particular, did not warm to Nell Gwyn, who, of all
Charles's mistresses, was by far the most popular with the public. Born
into abject poverty—far more real and brutal than the kind endured by
the young Louise—Nell had made a name for herself as a comedic actress
after Charles II repealed the laws prohibiting women from appearing on
stage. Her rags-to-riches story had great public appeal (she was nicknamed
"Cinder-Nell" as a pun on Cinderella), as did her sense of humor and lack of
pretension. During a visit to Oxford in 1681, her carriage was mistaken for
that of Catholic Louise de Kéroualle, the alleged spy. The Oxonian crowd
began shouting "Catholic whore!" at the coach, whereupon Nell popped
her head out the window to cheerfully reply, "Pray be silent, good people,
you are mistaken—I am the *Protestant* whore!"[17] When a rival actress, Moll

---

* Henrietta-Anne (1644–70), "Minette" in the family, Charles I's and Henrietta Maria's youngest
child and a French princess by marriage to Louis XIV's younger brother, Philippe, Duke of
Orléans (1640–1701).

Davis, was due to spend a night with the King, Nell sent her a box of sweet-meats to convey a lack of hard feelings. Alas, she sent the sweetmeats after they had been vigorously laced with a strong laxative, which kept Moll out of the "Merry Monarch's" bed for the time being.

Nell had two sons with Charles, one of whom lived to adulthood to be made the 1st Duke of St. Albans by his father. That dukedom was not won without a struggle on Nell's part, since Charles proved reluctant to bestow such a high title on a child born to a common actress. He relented eventually through shame when Nell insisted on referring to their son as "little bastard" until his father gave him a more respectable title. She faced worse snobbery—some of it intensely vicious—from Charles's courtiers, who savaged her background in poems like the one probably authored by Rochester, "A Panegyric upon Nelly":

> *Even while she Cinders rak'd, her swelling*
> *Breast With thoughts of glorious*
> *Whoredom was possess'd*
> *Still did she dream (nor did her Birth withstand)*
> *Of dangling sceptres in her dirty Hand.*[18]

Another of Charles's mistresses who resided for a time at Hampton Court was Hortense Mancini, the chic Italian niece of France's late chief minister, Cardinal Jules Mazarin. An intelligent and charismatic person who dressed in male or female attire, Hortense bolted from a French nunnery to which she had been banished by her abusive, obsessively religious husband. Before escaping the convent, she had an affair with another of its unwilling guests, Marie, Marquise de Courcelles. The couple enraged the Reverend Mother by swapping the chapel's holy water with ink, as well as running through the nuns' dormitory with their hunting dogs in the middle of the night, shout-ing, "Tally-ho!" Hortense fled in disguise as a pistol-toting highwayman and made it to the Channel ports before her possessive husband got word that she was missing. Furious that the fortune left to her by her uncle had been co-opted by her husband, Hortense came to England, ostensibly to visit relatives but also to rekindle her friendship with King Charles, whom she had first met when he was living in Paris as an exile following his father's execution. On reuniting, they became lovers, and Charles granted Hortense a sizeable annual pension in her own name. She lost Charles's affection, however, when she began an affair with his illegitimate daughter the Countess of Sussex, who had spent most of her early years and adolescence living at Hampton Court in the suite of rooms granted to her mother by the King.

Of all Charles II's many lovers, Lady Sussex's mother spent the most time at Hampton Court, and as much Nell Gwyn was loved by the public, Barbara Villiers was hated. Another of the Windsor Beauties, it was she whose service as a lady-in-waiting was foisted on Catherine of Braganza in 1662. Barbara's father, Lord Grandison, had fought for the Royalists during the civil wars, which meant the family endured comparative financial hardship throughout the republican 1650s. During those years in London, Barbara and other young royalists had enjoyed living in defiance of the Puritan morality promoted by a government they despised. In the late 1650s Barbara wrote what has plausibly been identified as the first English-language letter unambiguously organizing a threesome. The recipient was her lover Philip Stanhope, 2nd Earl of Chesterfield, another down-on-his-luck royalist, and the referenced friend was the Duke of Hamilton's daughter, Lady Anne Hamilton: "My friend and I are just now abed together contriving how to have your company this afternoon. If you deserve this favour, you will come and seek us at Ludgate Hill, about three o'clock, at Butler's shop."[19] Barbara later married the royalist Roger Palmer, and at the balls held to celebrate the return of the monarchy, she was identified in a courtier's diary as "a pretty woman that they [say] have a fancy to make her husband a cuckold." When Barbara's first child, Anne Palmer, was born a year later, her husband and the King both thought they were the biological father, and Lord Chesterfield was also suggested; it was the King, however, who was generally considered the most probable candidate.[20]

Barbara's confidence, determination, and beauty won her many admirers in the early years of her career at court. When Peter Lely first painted her, he complained that Barbara was one of those who possessed a charm that did not translate well to canvas and that it was "beyond the compass of art" to capture her "exquisite beauty." Samuel Pepys, a Protestant, a naval official, and a courtier, was unsettlingly obsessed with her. He confided in his diary that, when he went to a Catholic chapel to watch Barbara as she accompanied Queen Catherine to Mass for Christmas Eve 1667, he had been so overcome by his fantasies that he had an orgasm—"I did make myself do *la cosa* ["the thing," used in bawdy poetry at the time as a euphemism for male ejaculation] by mere imagination, *mirando a jolie mosa** and with my eyes open, which I never did before—and God forgive me for it, it being in the Chapel."[21] This guilt did not stop Pepys, in the same diary entry, from giving his assessment of the Catholic Mass, at which "their music [is] very good indeed, but their service I confess to [find] frivolous"—a curiously confident judgment on solemnity from a man who had just orgasmed in the middle of a church. Then he shared a coach ride home with friends, the company amusing themselves with "mighty mirth in their talk of the folly of this religion."[22] Another point raised and agreed upon in the Christmas carriage ride home was how striking Barbara had looked in her evening wear, or "night clothes," as Pepys called them.

As King Charles's mistress, Barbara traded being Mrs. Palmer for the title of Countess of Castlemaine when her husband Roger was granted an earldom. He rejected the offer initially, feeling too humiliated to accept it, until the King made it clear that the earldom, like the breakdown of his marriage, was not something about which he had a choice. Riches and influence followed. The new Countess became a patron of Peter Lely, who painted her in the guise of a Roman goddess and—duly mocked by the court wits—as three Christian saints. Posing in one portrait as the Virgin Mary with the King's bastard son Charles Fitzroy dressed as the Christ Child shocked Barbara's growing number of critics, to whose displeasure she was defiantly indifferent. In the first four years of their relationship, she bore

---

* To prevent it being easily understood if found by somebody else, Pepys wrote his famous diaries in shorthand, including bastardized French, Spanish, and Italian terms to further obfuscate his meaning. This phrase seems to mean "by looking at a pretty/beautiful maid/maiden."

three sons to Charles—Charles, Henry, and George—all of whom were made dukes, and a daughter Charlotte, who married the Earl of Lichfield. The five children, including their eldest sister, Lady Anne, whose paternity was questioned but who was assumed by most to be the King's daughter, were eventually given a section of Hampton Court to use, where they were joined by their mother's sizeable household of servants and sycophants.

The Countess's ground-floor quarters faced the river and were situated directly below the King's Gallery, which meant that he could access them easily and discreetly. Their location also meant that her rooms had doors leading to the fountains in the Queen's Courtyard behind and into the Privy Gardens, in front and to the left. The remit of what constituted Lady Castlemaine's rooms expanded as the years passed. The fashion for aristocratic ladies to have a dairy or small farm as a retreat is associated more commonly with the eighteenth century, but the fad originated with noblewomen at the French court in the seventeenth. Rustic farms had been built on country estates belonging to Louis XIV's mistress Athénaïs, Marquise de Montespan, and to Hortense Mancini's sister Anne-Marie, Princesse de Conti. Barbara had a dairy installed near a water gallery at Hampton Court. The water gallery, built on the riverside some time between Wolsey's surrender of the palace to Henry VIII in 1529 and Anne Boleyn's downfall in 1536, had been used by several royals in the intervening century as a belvedere for private dinner parties or gatherings, and Barbara followed in their footsteps after it was redecorated to her taste. When Charles extended Barbara's remit to the palace's grounds by appointing her Keeper of the Hampton Court Parks, she had the orchard, planted during Cardinal Wolsey's lifetime, torn down.[23] At least Hampton Court was spared the fate of Henry VIII's dilapidated palace of Nonsuch, which was also given to Barbara; she had it demolished and sold for parts.

Hampton Court with Barbara as chatelaine was not always a happy place. The King frequently visited to tuck the children in at night, but Barbara did not have a warm relationship with them.[24] She was allegedly a harsh disciplinarian, even by the standards of the seventeenth century, which would likely mean she beat her children frequently or had servants do it for her. Allegations of her cruelty as a mother seem to have surfaced later. Even allowing for possible exaggeration, however, Barbara's bond with her children later in life was not strong. It has been suggested that seventeen-year-old Anne embarked upon her affair with thirty-one-year-old Hortense Mancini in part because Hortense was Barbara's rival, and an emotionally damaged Anne nursed profound resentment against her mother. The second son, Henry, future Duke of Grafton, went abroad to serve in the army at the first available opportunity; he was killed, aged twenty-seven, fighting at the siege of Cork. His younger brother George grew up to become a spy for his father's government and was sent on espionage missions to Italy at the age of seventeen. In his early twenties, he enraged his ambitious mother by eloping with a chicken farmer's daughter named Katherine. Mother and son's relationship had reached a nadir shortly before George's elopement when Barbara's then lover, an actor named Cardell Goodman, was convicted of plotting to poison both George and his brother Henry. Whether he meant to weaken them or to remove them as the two main beneficiaries of their mother's will is unclear, unlike the fact that even after Goodman's conviction, Barbara continued her relationship with him.

The sordid pain of their family dynamic was some years off as the five siblings grew up at Hampton Court, yet it seems that the rot set in early with Barbara's indifference, and even potentially cruelty, to her children. Few contemporaries, however, criticized Barbara for her parenting, as opposed to her extravagance, promiscuity, and politics. Her spending, especially the incomes she won for her cousins and children, made her particularly disliked. Politically, Barbara was credited, or blamed, for helping to end the career of Charles's chief minister, Lord Clarendon.

Loathed as she was as "the curse of the nation," Barbara's behavior seemed tame when compared with those who paraded around Hampton Court at the same time. They included the Earl of Rochester, who wrote plays such as *The Farce of Sodom*, with characters named Queen Cuntgratia and Fuckadilla, the courtier in charge of Cuntgratia's dildo.[25] The court witnessed cruelty like that of the Duke of Buckingham: when faced with his wife's distressed plea that she could not live under the same roof as his

mistress, whom he had brought to reside in their family home, Buckingham replied, "Why, Madam, I did think so, and therefore have ordered
your coach to be ready, to carry you to your father's."[26]

An alternative to Barbara's confrontational behavior was for her to quietly endure a life full of humiliations, like those of young ladies-in-waiting
who, the moment they arrived at the palace, were the subject of bets between male courtiers competing among themselves to take the newcomers' virginity.[27] The Countess faced threats of violence, too, from her fellow
aristocrats. One night, while strolling through a London park, she was am-
bushed by three mask-wearing noblemen (she never figured out their identities) who surrounded her as they delivered insults, including their hope
that they lived long enough to see her corpse dumped on a dunghill, as legend claimed had happened to Edward IV's mistress Jane Shore. After this
fright, Barbara managed to walk back to the Palace of Whitehall, where
she fainted. Barbara was often unpleasant, cruel, and vindictive, as was the
environment in which she lived. She was damned to be judged far more
harshly than any of her male contemporaries, and, while the intensity of
the public's hatred for her was, to a very large degree, explicable because
of her actions, it is also worth noting that very few of the male courtiers to
Charles II attracted comparable ire for similar behavior.

Barbara's relationship with the King began to unravel amid an increasing number of quarrels. As her position slipped, she desperately tried to
mend bridges with Queen Catherine by sending her gifts of cheese and
cream for her table.[28] But no amount of dairy products would move the
Queen to speak on her rival's behalf, and Barbara's star continued to dim.
One evening, Charles visited her, but she kept him waiting on the other
side of a locked door shouting unconvincing excuses while, in a panic, she
hid her naked cousin and lover John Churchill, Winston's ancestor and,
later in his own life, a celebrated British general and Duke of Marlborough.
Barbara's last child, named in her honor,* was acknowledged by the King as

---

* Lady Barbara Fitzroy is referred to in histories more often as Benedicta, the name she chose
for herself when she took the veil as a Benedictine nun at a French convent in 1691.

his daughter even though he suspected Churchill was the biological father. Barbara had taken other lovers during her relationship with the King, including a circus acrobat named Jacob Hall, actor Charles Hart, and courtier Harry Jermyn. The latter was Master of the Horse to King Charles's brother Prince James and had, in his numerous seductions, shamelessly exploited the perceived glamor of having survived a near-mortal wound from a 1662 duel with one of the Howards and the future Earl of Roscommon, after they all quarrelled over their competing affections for the Countess of Shrewsbury.[29]

Apart from Lady Shrewsbury, Harry Jermyn's rumored past lovers at court included Fanny Jennings, who was married unhappily to an officer of the Household Cavalry; his employer Prince James's future wife Anne Hyde, subsequently Duchess of York; and King Charles's widowed sister Mary, Princess of Orange.[30] Although the latter two liaisons almost certainly existed solely as figments of court gossip, Charles II had never forgiven Jermyn, since he felt that Jermyn's behavior around Princess Mary had inspired the rumors in the first place and that Jermyn had failed to deny the speculation with sufficient vigor, even after Mary's death. Already resentful over the rumored intimacy with his beloved sister, Charles had previously banished Jermyn from court for six months for flirting with Barbara; the King's realization in 1668 that Jermyn was sleeping with her, coupled with his suspicion that John Churchill's child was being passed off as the King's, helped end Barbara's ascendancy. She was dismissed from court; shortly beforehand, Charles made her Duchess of Cleveland in recompense. Her downfall was unlamented, partly because of her spending and her vindictiveness toward her political opponents. No doubt there was also a large element of jealousy behind this hatred from those who wished they had access to the riches Barbara had secured for herself, while many others had never forgiven her for her unnecessary humiliation of Queen Catherine at Hampton Court in 1662—even Barbara's former lover Lord Chesterfield subsequently transferred his allegiance from the mistress to the Queen.

After Barbara's eclipse, she was permitted to keep her suite of rooms at Hampton Court, a fact that irritated the palace's housekeeping staff, who found her insufferable. Charles kept his distance, with consequences for the palace's upkeep. His last prolonged stay at Hampton Court was of two weeks in 1669, when he and Queen Catherine retreated in mourning for Charles's mother. Henrietta Maria had died in France from an accidental opium overdose administered by her doctors as she tried to cure the chronic insomnia that she suffered from in her later years.[31] Following his mourning for the Queen Mother, Charles spent only a total of five nights at Hampton Court in the last sixteen years of his reign, and he clearly disliked the palace. Whether Charles held painful memories of his escape first to and then from it with his parents in 1642 seems unduly sentimental in explaining his relative lack of interest in Hampton Court, particularly in comparison to his love of Whitehall, which one would expect to have provoked a stronger adverse reaction as the site of his father's beheading. His dislike was partly aesthetic and partly a result of his aversion to awkward scenes. James I and Charles I had modernized Whitehall, while Hampton Court, which still looked much as it had when Henry VIII died more than a century earlier, had begun to feel rather dated. Throughout the 1670s, staying there also meant spending time with his former mistress. He limited himself to flying visits to tuck in his often unhappy children.

Queen Catherine visited the estate more often than did her husband, yet still infrequently, staying in the apartments on a separate floor of the palace to Barbara's. She was accompanied by her own retinue, which included her household priests and almoners, Portuguese attendants such as her favorite, the Countess of Penalva, and Catholic ladies-in-waiting such as Lady Frances Bellings and Barbara Howard, Countess of Suffolk. Hampton Court's distance from London made it more appealing for the Queen's household, since the 1670s proved a difficult decade for her.

Charles II's fertility, with almost a dozen illegitimate children acknowledged during his reign, seemed almost obscene as his wife suffered a series of stillbirths. The final one very nearly killed her, and, after it became clear that there would be no more pregnancies, Parliament submitted a petition to the King asking him to divorce the Queen. The more rabid of the divorce lobby, chief among them the Duke of Buckingham, even hatched a scheme to kidnap Queen Catherine and send her to America.[32] Those lobbying for a new queen wanted Charles to marry a Protestant princess or noblewoman to produce a legitimate heir. Belatedly coming to his wife's defense, Charles II angrily rejected the divorce proposals.

Tension over the royal marriage escalated into the Exclusion Crisis of 1679–81 after Charles's younger brother and heir, Prince James, Duke of York, converted to Catholicism. Faced with the prospect of a Catholic king following Charles's death, Protestant hatred of the "barren" Queen Catherine intensified, alongside similar feelings for Prince James and his new Italian wife. All three Catholic members of the royal family found themselves unwillingly cast in a lethal conspiracy theory called the Popish Plot, fabricated by Titus Oates. A charismatic but failed preacher, Oates claimed that a vast network of Catholic terrorists at the heart of the British elite were planning, with Queen Catherine's support, to assassinate the King, put Catholic Prince James on the throne, and start the wholesale persecution of Protestants.

The Popish Plot remains one of the most frightening scandals in British history because of its widespread impact without a scintilla of corroborating evidence. Reading of it with the benefit of hindsight, its atmosphere reads like a nightmarish fusion of the Salem witch trials and the McCarthy hearings. It reached such a fever pitch that twenty-two Catholics were executed on the basis of Oates's fraudulent denunciations, including three laborers whose employer was tortured into committing perjury against them; a bank clerk named William Staley; William Howard, Viscount Stafford; and Oliver Plunkett, Archbishop of Armagh.[33] Prince James and his wife, Mary-Beatrice of Modena, had to relocate to Europe temporarily because their lives were at risk from Oates's supporters; they were not allowed to take their six-year-old daughter, Princess Isabel, out of the country with them because she stood so high in the line of succession. They had been allowed back to Scotland but not England when Isabel fell ill and died, without either of her parents at her side. The tragedy pushed her mother into a nervous breakdown so intense that her doctors temporarily feared for her sanity. Oates's accusations against Queen Catherine were debated in Parliament, in a painful echo for King Charles of the ways in which his mother had been unjustly accused of complicity with the Irish rebellion a generation earlier. Until the judiciary finally pushed back by refusing to be intimidated into finding Oates's newest victims guilty on insufficient evidence, the Queen, as well as the Duke and Duchess of York, were frustrated hostages to a fantastic lie. Catherine of Braganza's visits to Hampton Court in the 1670s thus offered a chance for her to hunt and relax in the Chase with her friends, as the increasingly unfashionable palace became a temporary retreat for her—even if it did necessitate once more being under the same roof as Lady Castlemaine, who had helped inflict the first of many humiliations Catherine had survived.

CHAPTER 17

THE ORANGERY

On the banks of that beautiful river
There the bones of our forefathers lie,
Awaiting the sound of the trumpet
To call them to glory on high,
In our hearts, we will cherish their memories,
And we all like true brethren will join
And praise God for sending us King William
To the green grassy slopes of the Boyne.

—Anonymous, "The Green Grassy Slopes of
the Boyne" (Irish song, eighteenth century)

The monarchy and Hampton Court were both transformed in the late 1680s. William III, like Anne Boleyn long before him, made for an unlikely royal revolutionary. He lacked her charisma, and her tragedy; he lacked, too, the spectacular scale of her failure. The Dutch Prince of Orange who became King William III was, in many ways, undertaker to the political process that had begun—or at the very least gathered pace—during Boleyn's lifetime. William buried the Divine Right of Kings in the British Isles, and he did so definitively, without regret or sentiment. He did the same to half of Hampton Court and, had funds not dried up, he would have carried on until, with the exception of the Great Hall, he had seen the whole palace reduced to rubble and rebuilt. Money proved to am-

245

bitious Stuart kings what biology had been to brilliant Tudor queens: an ever-present, impersonal force lacerating reigns, careers, and lives.

In February 1685 Charles II died without legitimate children, and the throne passed to his younger brother as King James VII in Scotland and James II in England, Ireland, and Wales. Many English politicians had spent a decade trying to prevent James from ever taking the throne, in retaliation for his abandonment of Protestantism. They argued that, given that an English monarch was also Supreme Governor of the Church of England, it was not unreasonable to expect that monarch to be a member of the religion he or she was going to lead. However, between 1685 and 1688, a Catholic king was reluctantly accepted by the majority as an interim measure because Mary, James II's Protestant daughter from his first marriage, was heir to his throne. It was a question of patience for Protestants until, in 1688, James's second wife, the Italian and Catholic Queen Mary-Beatrice, gave birth to a son who, unlike his male siblings, lived. On the basis of gender, he outranked his Protestant half sister in the succession. During her three years as queen, Mary-Beatrice of Modena had shown herself to be far more flexible in her public interactions with Protestantism than either of the previous two consorts. Unlike them, she had wrestled her own conscience into accepting coronation by a Protestant archbishop. Her ecumenical pragmatism stopped at the nursery door. When it came to their son's spiritual welfare, neither Queen Mary-Beatrice nor King James could in good conscience allow the child to be raised as a Protestant. Seeing a line of Catholic kings stretching at least into the next century, James II's enemies spread the rumor that the new heir, Prince James Francis Edward, was a changeling.

From the rooms granted to her by her father at Hampton Court for use as her country residence, Princess Anne—James's youngest daughter, also from his first marriage—had been preparing the ground for this lie from the moment she heard of her stepmother's pregnancy. She had made constant malicious insinuations that the Queen's "bump" did not look real, that her "great belly is a little suspicious." A Tuscan diplomat stationed in England felt that "no words can express the rage of the Princess . . . at the Queen's condition; she can dissimulate it to no one."[1] Code-naming her stepmother "Mrs. Mansell" in her correspondence, Princess Anne told anybody who would listen that there was "so much just cause for suspicion" that the Queen's pregnancy was a fiction. She also felt that "it really is enough to turn one's stomach to hear" praise for Mary-Beatrice's dignity or beauty.[2] Princess Anne did not cease her attacks even after tragically suffering a phantom pregnancy at the same time that she was spreading rumors about her stepmother. Anne insisted that she would never believe the child was really a Stuart, unless it was a girl or "except I see the child and she parted"—meaning if she personally witnessed the labor.[3]

When she was invited by the Queen to attend the birth, Anne faked an illness to provide herself with plausible deniability about her half brother's legitimacy. Right on cue, rumor then claimed that one of Mary-Beatrice's household priests had kidnapped a healthy baby boy and—when hers was allegedly either born sleeping or had never existed—a substitution was made, with the changeling smuggled into the Queen's bedchamber at St. James's Palace inside a warming pan to be passed off as a prince. The Warming Pan Scandal gave focus to resentment against James II, his religion, and his policies, which many worried veered toward the absolutism championed by his late father. London was convulsed by riots until, early one morning, Queen Mary-Beatrice, disguised as a laundress, escaped with her baby and a few servants. Parliament invited James's eldest daughter to seize the throne in conjunction with her Dutch husband, Prince William of Orange, at which point King James, too, was forced reluctantly to flee, joining his wife and son as refugees at the court of his French cousin King Louis XIV.

William of Orange and Princess Mary were spouses and first cousins as grandchildren of King Charles I.* William used his considerable skills as a military tactician to ensure that his father-in-law did not return to power.

---

* William's mother, another Mary, had been one of the three children who accompanied her parents in their rout to Hampton Court on the brink of civil war before she was evacuated to the Netherlands under the pretext of joining his father. See chapter 14.

Backed by France, King James made a spirited attempt to do so by landing with a large army in the south of Ireland, while William and his forces arrived in the north. They met in the middle in a battle on the banks of the River Boyne, which James lost, and then in the west at the Battle of Aughrim, which he lost decisively. The defeat and exile of their Catholic king who, after the Boyne, returned to France, where he died eleven years later, allowed Protestants in the Irish Parliament to enact the Penal Laws against their country's Catholic majority. This legislation, which endured for the next century, was known as the era of the Protestant Ascendancy; this was a misnomer, however, since it also lacerated the civil liberties of Irish Presbyterians in order to shore up the position of the kingdom's Anglican landowning classes as chief beneficiaries of Ireland's laws, until a rebellion in 1798 prompted a series of reforms.[4] William of Orange's arrival in the north of Ireland to win the victories that made the ensuing Ascendancy possible is still celebrated by many Protestants there, with annual bonfires lit on the night of every July 11 re-creating those that welcomed William when he disembarked on Irish soil for the first time in 1690. The anniversaries of his major military victories against his father-in-law are commemorated throughout the summer with marches organized by the Loyal Orange Lodges, a Protestant social confraternity that uses William's heraldic color on its banners, along with his image on thousands of them, typically depicting the moment he forded the River Boyne in victory on top of a white horse.

William III thought privately that the Irish Parliament's Penal Laws were an insane policy formulated, as one of his advisers put it, by "a company of mad men," and the King was appalled by their decision to extend the punitive measures to Presbyterians, since he himself had been raised as a Calvinist.[5] Meanwhile, the London Parliament introduced the Bill of Rights, which rolled back several of James II's arbitrary legal policies and codified religion as a requirement for English monarchs. Henceforth, anyone in the line of succession could neither be a Catholic nor marry one. James II was not only barred from returning, but also his Catholic son in France was expelled from the succession in favor of Princess Anne.[6]

The momentousness of these laws was perhaps exaggerated by the Jacobites—loyalists of the disinherited Catholic branch of the Stuarts—who claimed that the new legislation contravened English precedent stretching back to ancient times. In reality, the monarchy in England has never operated purely by birthright. Primogeniture is usually the preferred criterion, but it has frequently operated in conjunction with others. Between 1066 and 1690, there had been more than a dozen occasions on which the English crown changed hands on a basis other than strict primogeniture.[7] Since the Glorious Revolution, as James II's downfall was subsequently called by its supporters, right of birth has remained the monarchy's primary criterion, but it can be overruled if it contradicts other requirements—which, as of 1689–90, have included conforming to the Protestant faith.

The greater significance of this legislation lay in firmly answering the painful questions posed by the Reformation, with which the Crown had been struggling for a century and a half.[8] Parliament emerged as the main beneficiary of the Glorious Revolution. The price for Parliament's role in creating the revolution was a series of bills that settled once and for all, in the latter's favor, the fraught question over who had primacy in daily government: Crown or Parliament. The Crown retained the right to veto laws, as did the House of Lords, the upper chamber of Parliament in which sat the hereditary aristocrats and the Anglican bishops of England and Wales.[9] The laws themselves were to be drafted by the elected House of Commons, from which Catholics were henceforth barred from sitting in or voting for, even if they owned the requisite amount of property then necessary to qualify as a member of the electorate.[10] The long and agonized questions of the divine in monarchy—both its faith and its right to rule—had finally been settled, after so much struggle and loss. A constitutional monarchy, albeit a muscular one compared with its later iterations, had been created in the British Isles, and its first heads of state were also thus far the modern monarchy's only coruling sovereigns.[11] James's daughter Mary was proclaimed queen regnant as Mary II, with her husband made William III as her coruler, in recognition of her role as rightful heir and his in leading the armies that had made the coup possible. English Protestants were mostly grateful to William, but they did not love him. He seemed too cold and awkward in public, and the citizens of London in particular made obvious their preference for Mary II.

William reciprocated the capital's dislike. Badly asthmatic, he quit London for Hampton Court only nine days after taking the throne. Coal was replacing wood as the preferred form of fuel in most fires, blackening many of London's buildings and wreaking havoc with King William's weak respiratory system. For William's grandparents, Hampton Court had been a haven from riots; for him, it was a refuge from smog, and his first extant praise for the palace focused on the cleanliness of its air. Its accommodation, frustratingly, did not match the location. The palace's condition had declined due to Charles II's indifference and during the Countess of Castlemaine's residency there. Barbara could not be called a conscientious chatelaine. When Mary II returned to Hampton Court in 1689 for the first time since her childhood visits, she described it in a letter to a friend as "a place which has been very badly neglected."[12] In comparison to the couple's small, modern, luxurious homes in the Netherlands, King William and Queen Mary thought their British property portfolio was a ramshackle collection of antique monstrosities that were difficult to clean and impossible to heat. The end of the seventeenth century and dawn of the eighteenth was an age of palace building in which most of the European powers were advertising their pretensions to, or realities of, greatness through large armies and large palaces. In this respect, the British states were lacking. Most of the Palace of Whitehall, hitherto the largest royal residence in Europe, burned down in an accidental fire in 1698, by which point most Tudor-era residences had already fallen apart through accidental neglect or deliberate destruction.

To provide themselves with a suitable residence in the capital for official business, the King and Queen purchased the Earl of Nottingham's mansion in what was then the west of the city, transforming it into Kensington Palace. A worse-for-wear Hampton Court with its perfect location for country living could, it was hoped, be transformed similarly into a showcase for British architecture, furniture, and art in the same way the rebuilt Versailles had for that of France. Work began with the private apartments at the east and south of the palace, all of which were torn down. Once that was done, William and Mary intended to do the same with the north and west wings. The gallery where Wolsey had talked with Charles V shortly after his first meeting with Martin Luther was destroyed and its detritus deposited in a makeshift quarry created in the Privy Gardens, which had become unkempt and unfashionable by the 1690s. The King's Apartments, first used by Henry VIII, and the Queen's, by Catherine Howard, went next. Over the course of the decade, the old apartments were replaced by a magnificent Baroque wing with cloisters, fountain courtyards, mullioned windows, higher ceilings, and wider staircases.

The project was entrusted to Sir Christopher Wren, the acclaimed architect who had designed fifty-two of the churches, including the new St. Paul's Cathedral, that replaced those lost in the 1666 Great Fire of London. His designs for the Royal Hospital Chelsea, the Royal Naval College at Greenwich, and the Sheldonian Theatre in Oxford helped secure, in his lifetime, Wren's reputation as one of the greatest architects in European history. Mary II made it obvious to Wren how impatient she was for the work to be finished and, on December 11, 1689, eleven workmen were pulled, alive but injured, from the rubble at Hampton Court after most of the palace's under-construction southern range collapsed. Two of their colleagues lost their lives. The Queen blamed herself. She worried that she had put unhelpful pressure on the architects and workmen, leading to corner cutting that caused the accident. Guilt-ridden, she entrusted a sizeable sum to a courtier with the order that he use it to pay for the two workers' funerals and send subsidies to their families. The King ordered an inquiry into the accident and subsequently dismissed Wren. William Talman, Wren's assistant, then betrayed his master by stealing the plans and putting himself forward to finish the project at a substantially lower fee. King William awarded the commission to Talman, and the work to transform Hampton Court into a modern palace that would rival Versailles continued.

By the time Hampton Court's quarters were ready for William III to spend a night there, in 1699, Mary II had been dead for five years—carried off

in the smallpox epidemic of 1694—and Sir Christopher Wren was back as
project leader. The remaining sixteenth-century section of the palace was
safe because William, who would die even more deeply in debt than his
extravagant uncle Charles II, had run out of money. He had to content himself with the new King's and Queen's Apartments. If the ghost of Catherine
Howard were to remain in the Haunted Gallery, she would recognize only
half of her original journey. At the corridor's end, the Tudor architecture
gives way abruptly through a doorway that leads to a Baroque vestibule and
the top of a new, sweeping Queen's Staircase.

On another new staircase, this one leading to the state apartments in
the Baroque wing, William had himself painted in the guise of Alexander the Great, defeating kings depicted to symbolize the traditional vices
of Catholicism and absolutism. The state apartments—William's public
rooms—covered the second floor of the new wing. The first to be reached
was the Guard Chamber, where the military theme continued with a fantastic array of weaponry mounted on the walls, beneath which guards
checked petitioners and visitors to see if they were dressed properly, sober,
and neither carrying nor hiding any pistols. From there, doors led to the
Presence Chamber, serving as a throne room. Despite his lifelong enmity
with Louis XIV, William III borrowed several etiquette flourishes from
France, including the requirement that his courtiers bow or curtsy to the
throne, even if he was not on it, as they did in the Salon of Apollo at Versailles.* Although both he and his late wife viewed most court etiquette
to be stultifying—and, viewed objectively, quite silly—they were intelligent enough to understand the utility of ritual. No matter how absurd he
found it, William III maintained the tradition that the King should dine
in public, where he was served by nobles while spectators were permitted
to watch. Doing so conveyed a sense of continuity between William III
and his maternal Stuart ancestors, which he felt to be necessary particularly
after the death of his Stuart wife, and the point was underscored further

---

* He seems hardly, if ever, to have used the Presence Chamber, instead conducting audiences
two rooms farther along in the space called the Audience Chamber or Privy Chamber.

by the proliferation of dynastic portraits chosen to decorate the new state apartments. These included William's grandfather Charles I in his robes as King of Scots, his great-grandparents James I and Anna of Denmark, and a portrait of Anna's brother Christian IV, the king who had passed out in the Great Hall while watching *Macbeth*.

A great canopied bed in the King's bedchamber nestled beneath oak and mahogany carvings on the ceiling by Grinling Gibbons, an Anglo-Dutch wood carver and one of the most sought-after decorators of the day, but although William "woke up" and "went to sleep" in his state bed, he seldom slept there.[13] After his nightly ritual of being undressed by members of his Privy Chamber, William slipped through a door to a smaller, private, comfortable bedchamber decorated with paintings of Dutch tulips and of a sleepy Mars, god of war, symbolizing William laying aside his duties to rest. This contrast between the King's Great and Little Bedchambers reflected another development not just in monarchy but in public life in general: there was a greater appreciation of the need to delineate between public and private. The process had been developing at various stages in the Middle Ages, and, as the layout of Hampton Court under the Tudors shows, the concept already existed of limiting access to the royals through the layout of their rooms. However, the idea of privacy was much more clearly defined by the dawn of the eighteenth century. On the first floor of the Baroque side at Hampton Court, William III had an entire suite of private accommodations that was separate from his public rooms. There he could think, work, consult, and relax. He had an oak-lined study and a private dining room, where he hosted dinner parties at which he was served by staff passing plates through from a small alcove that could be shuttered after serving to allow for truly private conversation among the guests.

By 1699 those guests frequently included William's former mistress, the witty and well-read Elizabeth Hamilton, Countess of Orkney. She may initially have known the palace better than had either the King or the late Queen, since her cousin was Charles II's mistress Barbara, Countess of Castlemaine. Elizabeth's affair with a king was far more discreet than Barbara's. The liaison had taken place before Lady Orkney's marriage but during William's—much to Mary II's distress. Elizabeth was one of Mary's ladies-in-waiting, and the two had known each other since childhood, when Elizabeth's mother had been Mary's governess. Tipped off by her servants, Mary had waited outside Elizabeth's door one night until she caught William emerging from her bedroom, close to sunrise and claiming that he and Elizabeth had spent the night there discussing books. After Queen Mary's death, William was so affected by guilt for "the great injury he had done [to] that excellent wife by his adultery" that he belatedly ended his affair with Elizabeth, although they remained friends, and she served as hostess at many of his suppers, in the absence of a living queen.[14]

Speculation ran rampant about what had really transpired between William and Elizabeth. Many assumed, then and later, that it was a sexless friendship born, as William claimed, from their shared love of reading, an interest Mary II did not possess. Even some of Elizabeth's relatives did not believe that the King had slept with her. Attempts to square the circle resulted in a theory, first whispered at court and then committed to paper by the writer Thomas Birch in the next generation, that William III's claim he had never committed adultery with Elizabeth after 1694 was true, thanks solely to the technicality that the couple never progressed past oral sex and mutual masturbation.[15] That might seem obsessively prurient to modern readers, perhaps fairly; however, at the time and since, it was dissected in the debate over William's sexuality, which in turn his opponents used to discredit him politically.

One figure absent from William III's dinner parties, after 1699, was Hans-Willem Bentinck, a Dutch baron who had joined William's household as a child and who, in their midtwenties, at great risk to himself, nursed William through a bout of smallpox that nearly killed him. A brave soldier, Bentinck had been at William's side during his invasion of England and at the Battle of the Boyne. During the early years of his reign, William had made Hans-Willem the Earl of Portland, but their plans to enjoy a rejuvenated Hampton Court together never materialized. Just as the new apartments became ready for occupation, the King and Lord Portland parted company. Their friendship never recovered from a series of arguments, and so Portland did not enjoy the grandeur of the state apartments, nor the intimacy of the Private, with their gorgeous views over the redesigned Privy Gardens, the gravelled pathways of which looped around fountains, under hedge mazes, and past flower beds planted with bulbs imported from the King's Dutch homeland, then a center for horticultural excellence. During the winter, some of the more delicate blooms, including the potted orange trees from William's titular principality, were moved into the new Orangery, a long, tiled corridor that ran the length of the Baroque wing's ground floor, with tall windows and doors opening onto the gardens. A beautiful space in which to talk during either heat or rain, the Orangery led to the rooms of King William's other rumored lover, Arnold van Keppel, a former page whom he had made Earl of Albemarle.* In an odd echo of the affair between his great-grandfather James I and Robert Carr, also promoted to an earldom, William had allegedly first developed romantic feelings for van Keppel after years of knowing each other, while the latter recovered from falling off his horse and breaking his leg in front of the King. There, however, the similarities between the two couples cease. There is far less evidence, even circumstantial, to support the theory that William III had male lovers. In an age when homosexuality was, of necessity, often hidden, it is, of course, possible to argue that many couples would have worked hard to hide the truth of their relationship or that many would have lied not only to others about their feelings but also to themselves. From that, one could conclude that the depth of affection expressed between William III and van Keppel exceeded the plausibly platonic; likewise, the jealousy expressed by William's friend Lord Portland, whose quarrel with the King and subsequent resignation of all his posts at court in 1699 were in protest of van Keppel's promotion—Portland's actions have been interpreted by some historians as far more credibly those of a brokenhearted lover than of a disgruntled general. It has, however, fairly been noted that, after his death, interest in retrospectively "outing" William III did not gather momentum again until it was perceived as a useful political tool: specifically,

---

* A direct ancestor of Camilla, Queen of the United Kingdom.

to undermine the Protestant fundamentalist lobby in Northern Ireland, which promoted the cultural celebration of William at the same time that it organized opposition to every extension of gay rights in Northern Ireland from 1977 to 2020.[16]

William heard these rumors about his private life and responded to them: "It seems to me very extraordinary that it should be impossible to have esteem and regard for a young man without it being criminal." This strikes some as a suspiciously vague rebuttal that contains no unambiguous denial, while to others it rings as the sincere reply of a taciturn man.[17] The evidence that William had strong feelings for both van Keppel and Portland is convincing, yet it is far less so regarding romantic relationships. The conclusion reached by Andrea Zuvich in her recent study of sexual mores in the seventeenth century, that William III was "a heterosexual with a low sex drive due to his chronic ill health," seems to me the most persuasive answer.[18] Either way, Arnold van Keppel and the Countess of Orkney were the two people closest to William III in the three years he spent living in his new accommodation at Hampton Court.

Thanks to his order that the Privy Gardens be dug up again and re-planted five feet lower so that they no longer obstructed the view from the Orangery to the river, major work was ongoing at Hampton Court when William III died, aged fifty-one, at Kensington in March 1702, from complications that arose after he was thrown from his horse. The horse, Sorel, had been confiscated from one of James II's supporters, and the cause of her fall was tripping over a molehill; afterward, Jacobites at their dinners began making a toast to the mole or, as they called it, "the Wee Gentleman in the Black Velvet Waistcoat." Despite being unfinished at the time of William's death, his works at Hampton Court offer us an aperture into the personality of an enigmatic king. The contrast between the state and private apartments reveals the conscientiousness of a man who did not believe in absolutism but who did believe in monarchy, albeit for pragmatic rather than sentimental or philosophical reasons. Walking through his restored private quarters, the visitor gains the sense of a man far more comfortable in private than he ever was in public.

Two hundred years later, Queen Victoria identified William III as the greatest of her predecessors on her throne.*[19] He was certainly one of the shrewdest politician-kings in British history, with all the moral ambiguity that implies; he was above all else a pragmatist rather than an ideologue. His path to power had been paved by James II's choice of principle over pragmatism, with his disastrous series of ham-fisted reforms in the three years preceding William's invasion. To end his father-in-law's regime, William had held his nose and done what he considered necessary. It is hard to believe that William was credulous enough to think that James's son was a warming-pan-smuggled changeling; in that sense, William's Glorious Revolution was based on an inglorious lie that shamelessly harnessed sectarianism, misogyny, xenophobia, and conspiracy politics to push James II off the throne by dragging the names of his wife and child into the gutter. Queen Mary-Beatrice escaped London in disguise, clutching her son, as terrified servants rowed them across the Thames to save their lives from the crowds incited to fury by the lies in which William and his allies had traded.[20]

Yet William might have argued—as have many of his defenders—that Mary-Beatrice and her son were unfortunate and equally unavoidable collateral damage. The attacks on the Queen and the infant Prince of Wales were rendered necessary by James II, not by William III. For the good of the country and its civil liberties, James had to go, and the easiest way to do that was to unfairly, and consistently, attack the legitimacy of his son. Time and time again, William's career was shaped by necessity. He was not, personally, an anti-Catholic bigot. In pursuit of limiting the French power that had threatened the Netherlands for as long as he could remember, William enthusiastically forged the Grand Alliance between himself and the Hapsburg Emperor Leopold I, a Catholic so devout that he attributed his triumphs against an Ottoman army besieging Vienna to the miraculous intercession of the Virgin Mary, subsequently referred to as Our Lady of

---

* Victoria unsuccessfully objected to a naval education for her grandsons because she worried it would lead them to think that their country was superior to others, which she felt was a failing in British kings. She believed firmly that William III's foreign birth and upbringing had afforded him "a freedom from all national prejudices which is very important to Princes."

Victories. James II had allied with France; if he came back to power, France would have a powerful friend as she launched her attacks on the Netherlands. Other partners in William's anti-French alliance included His Most Catholic Majesty King Carlos II of Spain and Vittorio-Amadeo II, who, as Duke of Savoy, was hereditary guardian of the Holy Shroud of Turin, one of Catholicism's most venerated relics. Moreover, and by no means least, Pope Innocent XI applauded William's endeavors against Louis XIV; he preferred Protestant William to Catholic but disobedient Louis, who was aggrandizing his monarchy at the expense of the Vatican's authority over the French branch of the Church. Yet despite his friendliness with the Pope and alliances with every major Catholic western European power bar France—and to keep himself on his new throne—William said nothing as his parliaments enacted anti-Catholic legislation. In the vast State Rooms on the first floor at Hampton Court, we see this William: the king who understood grandeur, who played a part in which he had cast himself reluctantly, who made sacrifices of principle in order to secure what he believed to be long-term benefits.

Hampton Court had been a palace for about 150 years by the time William III transformed it, and in that time, no area of the British Isles had been left untouched by decisions taken in its halls or its council chambers. In the sixteenth century, Hampton Court played host to those responsible for many of the great religious changes that impacted England and Wales; at the start of the seventeenth century, it was the favored venue of the Scottish royal family that became Britain's; while at the middle and end of that century, when it accommodated Oliver Cromwell and William III, it was home to men who made equally seismic changes to Ireland.

The ghosts of those decisions still feel present in the rooms of Hampton Court. In his 2013 paper "Early Modern Violence from Memory to History," American historian Dr. Ethan Shagan reflected:

> *The seventeenth century is alive in Ireland in ways like few other places in the modern world. People, places, and events from that distant past . . . the 1641 massacres, Oliver and Drogheda, William and*

the Boyne—still have meaning in popular culture, still inform public debates and still elicit strong emotional responses. This unique configuration is both a blessing and a curse to the business of professional history. On the one hand, it gives historians of the seventeenth century real relevance. . . . On the other hand, it has made history the handmaid of memory, trapping Irish historiography within a series of problems and paradigms that might better be left behind.[21]

The ambiguities of William III's career faded with time. He became a reputation. In death, William has been presented as the liberator of a country he did not love, a hero for a religious quarrel he did not much care about, and an icon for a sexuality he probably did not possess. The historical William of Orange was not an idealist, yet he did have broad beliefs that he could sublimate to achieve his goals. The two floors of his wing at Hampton Court capture the personal and political complexity of one of the most successful pragmatists in British history.

CHAPTER 18

THE APOTHEOSIS OF
QUEEN ANNE

When as Queen Anne of great Renown
Great Britain's Sceptre sway'd,
Beside the Church, she dearly loved
A Dirty Chamber-Maid.

—Anonymous, "A New Ballad" (1708)

Walking up the magnificent King's Staircase, the viewer can still be overwhelmed by Antonio Verrio's murals on the left. The Neapolitan artist, whose work also decorates the dukes of Devonshire's house at Chatsworth, first came to work in England during the reign of Charles II, for whom he had painted an apotheosis* of Queen Catherine of Braganza on a ceiling at Windsor Castle. In the succeeding decades, Verrio had received commissions from Charles's successors, including William III, who commissioned from Verrio the Hampton Court murals depicting William as Alexander the Great. They were completed in 1702, shortly before William's death. Verrio was then invited to complete his last work for the Stuarts in the Queen's Drawing Room, an east-facing reception room often

---

* The depiction of a political or religious figure in a grand and allegorical manner.

used for socializing or playing cards as gambling became an addiction for the eighteenth-century upper classes.

Upon William's death, the throne passed to his sister-in-law, Anne, Mary II's sister, James II's daughter, and a leading proponent of the Warming Pan scandal. Anne was the first Queen of Great Britain: in 1707 the English and Scottish parliaments merged under the Act of Union, which, a century after he first dreamed it up, realized James I's hope of seeing two of his three kingdoms unite. While the same would not happen with Ireland for another nine decades—at which point the country's name changed to the United Kingdom—the Act of Union of 1707 gave the name Great Britain to England, Wales, and Scotland.*

The two centuries ahead were to witness the emergence of Britain as the world's dominant imperial power. Some early steps toward that imperialism had been taken at Hampton Court: Cardinal Wolsey had hoped, and failed, to stimulate English interest in colonization—some of the earlier tragic consequences of which were attested in the palace's vanished portrait of Kalicho, Arnaq, and Nutaaq; Elizabeth I's Captain of the Guard, Sir Walter Raleigh, had been a colonizer who imported the tobacco that James I banned from the Great Hall. That imperial era in British history would reach its unambiguous maturity after Hampton Court—for a variety of reasons—slipped from relevance in the decades immediately after the Glorious Revolution. However, there is an indicator of Britain's changing direction on the walls of the Queen's Drawing Room, where Antonio Verrio, battling cataracts as he approached seventy and helped by various talented assistants, painted *Britannia Receiving the Homage of the Four Continents*. Europeans did not yet know that Australasia or Antarctica existed,

---

* The prefix of Great was not, as has since been both patriotically and mockingly assumed, intended to be a boast about the greatness of Britain; it was the nomenclature of bureaucracy or geography. As the decades wore on, the banal origins were forgotten while the other meaning of *great* was assumed. The United Kingdom name was maintained after southern Irish independence in 1921, due to the simultaneous creation of Northern Ireland, which remains part of the UK.

so allegorical Britannia sits at the center, surrounded by goddesses representing Africa, America, Asia, and Europe. Its positioning at Hampton Court, directly facing the windows that overlook the palace's Long Water, has been interpreted as an artistic indicator of Britain's increasing reliance on her navy, which may be a bit of a stretch. On the ceiling, Verrio returned to the apotheosis of a Stuart queen: Queen Anne, monarch from 1702 until 1714, flanked by the figures of Britannia and Neptune, crowning her as she is surrounded by symbols of economic and political glory. Britain's growing naval power is intimated with the inclusion of Neptune, traditional personification of the sea. Anne, wearing an ermine-lined purple robe over a golden gown and with her brown hair swept up, gazes down on visitors and clutches a sword and the Scales of Justice.

Why Anne sank so much money into Verrio's last commission remains a mystery, since it was not until four years after becoming queen that she spent a night at Hampton Court; even then, it was only at the request of her husband, who loved the place. Anne's heavy spending on restoring the Chapel Royal, the benefits of which can still be appreciated today, is more explicable, since defending and promoting Anglicanism was a major concern for the devoutly religious Queen. She does not seem to have been fond of Hampton Court. She had known it since childhood and spent much of her early married life there, although finding her a husband to share it with had initially proved difficult.

The Earl of Mulgrave had written her love letters when she was a teenager, until her uncle Charles II put a stop to the correspondence and with it any possibility that one of his subjects might marry a princess so high in the line of succession. Prospective royal bridegrooms in Europe were put off either by Anne's bloodline or her dowry, both of which they judged deficient. On her mother's side, Anne was the granddaughter of a lawyer, and to some European royalty, that "smell of trade" had not been sufficiently deodorized by the lawyer's subsequent elevation to an earldom.[1] The scandalous circumstances surrounding her parents' elopement were also still giggled about in the alcoves of continental palaces, where everybody remembered that *Miss* Anne Hyde had been Prince James's mistress before they eloped in exile during the interregnum.*[2] With a commoner grandfather, a mother who was first a mistress before becoming a duchess, and—one suspects this was a bigger consideration, although everybody was too delicate to say so—a small dowry, few princes wanted to marry Anne Stuart. For Anne, the story ended happily with her marriage to the King of Denmark's younger brother, Prince George, who was unpretentious, good-looking, and equally good-natured, loyal, plodding, and a little bit dull. Courtiers joked that the only reason that Prince George snored so loudly was to help tell the difference between him being asleep or awake. Later in life, he was summarized as "very fat, loves news, his bottle, and the Queen."[3]

There were rumors that Prince George had betrayed his wife with male lovers, which seems highly unlikely.[4] The couple's marriage was strained briefly over his flirtation with his secretary's wife. The success of the Oscar-winning movie *The Favourite* (2018), parts of which were filmed at Hampton Court, has re-popularized the contemporary suspicion that it was Anne who committed adultery, first with her lifelong friend and John Churchill's wife, Sarah, Duchess of Marlborough. Sarah was then pushed out of Anne's bed and favor by the manipulative tactics of Abigail Hill, who married a baron and remained Anne's favorite until the latter's death.[5] As with the first Stuart monarch to reign at Hampton Court, Queen Anne's sexuality had political implications, since, through her relationship with the Queen, Sarah Churchill became a dominant figure in British politics for more than a decade. Abigail promoted a rival agenda to Sarah's, politically as well as personally. The Queen and Abigail were mocked in a number of anonymous doggerels:

---

* Gossip continued for years about her parents' wedding, many claiming that James had gone through with it only because Anne was pregnant, and no princess would take him after the monarchy's downfall. The courtier Samuel Pepys, with his usual sledgehammer turn of phrase, repeated these rumors, characterizing James's marriage as comparable to "he that do get a wench with child and marry her afterwards [it] is as if a man should shit in his hat and then clap it on his head."

[F]or sweet service done
And causes of great weight
Her royal mistress made her, Oh!
A minister of state.

Her Secretary she was not
Because she could not write
But had the conduct and the care
Of some dark deeds at night.[6]

When Sarah showed some of these lampoons to Anne—in the hope of ousting Abigail from royal favor—the Queen was mortified. The evidence remains contradictory about whether her reaction was because the accusations were embarrassing and true or distressing but false, especially when one considers the emerging trend among the aristocracy for female friends to express love for each other in a hyperbolic way, the tone of which reads as distinctly romantic to modern readers.[7]

Those working on the *Apotheosis* at Hampton Court in 1704 would have heard the rumors about Queen Anne's private life, especially since that was the year in which Abigail Hill joined Anne's household, and Sarah Churchill went into eclipse. The men would also have been aware of the many tragedies that the Queen and Prince George had endured in their twenty-one years together. Early in the marriage, they had two daughters, Mary and Anne-Sophia, the younger of whom died six days before the former, who was a few months short of her second birthday. Later, there was another child, also christened Mary, and her brother, George, both of whom lived for less than a day. There were miscarriages in 1687, 1694, two at opposite ends of 1696, and another in 1697, a phantom pregnancy in 1688, and stillbirths in 1684, 1687 (nine months after the miscarriage of the same year), 1693, 1698, and 1700. In sixteen years, between the stillbirths of 1684 and 1700, Anne had five children who lived past birth, only one of whom, William, Duke of Gloucester, born at Hampton Court on July 24, 1689, survived to see his second year. He lived until a few days after his eleventh birthday party, held at Windsor Castle, when he succumbed to an acute bacterial infection that led to pneumonia. His mother, who had lived in fear for her son's health due to his hydrocephalus, stayed at his bedside throughout his last few days of life. She had been a devoted mother, as attested in letters like the one she wrote to her cousin when William was three. In it she expressed her joy in how he "comes out with little things that make one laugh" and her pride in his intelligence, which he exhibited in his quarterly meetings with his uncle and namesake, the King, who liked to quiz the boy to ensure he was one day fit to succeed.[8]

With young William's death in 1700, no Protestant Stuarts remained in the next generation. Anne had suffered so much—too much—in her attempt to continue the dynasty. After her last pregnancy, in the same year as her son's death, it was clear that she probably would not survive another. There was extremely unkind speculation that maliciously blamed Anne for what had happened, by claiming that she was "terribly given to drink and has burnt her insides so badly that she will never be able to have children; consequently, she will probably die soon."[9] Queen Anne's personal tragedy had enormous long-term political consequences. She had never reconciled with her exiled father, James II, whose death in France a year after her son's confronted Anne with the fact that her closest living relative was the younger half brother whom she had spent more than a decade pretending to believe was a changeling.[10] Many thought that Anne must now relent by doing something to restore "the Prince Across the Water" to the succession. Even her estranged stepmother, the Queen-Mother-in-exile Mary-Beatrice, whose reputation had suffered more than anybody's at Anne's hands, expressed that hope when she wrote to her shortly after King James's passing:

I think myself indispensably obliged to defer no longer in acquainting you with a message, which the best of men as well as the best of fathers left with me for you: some few days before his death, he bid me find means to let you know that he forgave you all that is past from the bot-

tom of his heart, and prayed to God to do so too, that he gave you his blessing and prayed to God to convert your heart and confirm you in the resolution of repairing to his son the wrongs done to himself: to which I shall only add, that I join my prayers to his herein, with all my heart, and that I shall make it my business to inspire the young man who is left to my care the sentiments of his Father: for better, no man can have.[11]

There was a rumor that Anne was moved by this letter from her stepmother. If that is true, it was temporary. She had absolutely no intention of climbing down on the question of her brother's legitimacy, nor would she consider leaving her throne to a Catholic. Even if Anne had experienced a change of heart with regard to "the Pretender,"* the legislation enacted after her father's deposition would have made it extremely difficult for her to do anything about it. Under those terms, the next in line was Anne's elderly German cousin once removed, Sophia of the Palatinate and the Rhine, Dowager Electress of Hanover, a granddaughter of King James I on her mother's side. Anne made it clear that she regarded Sophia as her preferred, and rightful, heir.†

Anne saw her Drawing Room *Apotheosis* more frequently in the later years of her reign. After spending two years in mourning for her husband after his death in 1708, the Queen visited Hampton Court often as her health declined. She had allowed Antonio Verrio, who died three years later, to retire with a generous annual pension of £200 after the completion of the *Apotheosis*, which memorialized her at the peak of good health. The Drawing Room Anne did not deal with the fluctuating weight, deteriorating eyesight, a series of strokes, and declining mobility that devastated her well-being between her husband's death and her own six years later in 1714.

In the year after her death, Anne's brother led a failed invasion to re-

---

* Subsequently referred to as "the Old Pretender" to differentiate him from his son Charles, called "the Young Pretender."

† Sophia of Hanover died eight weeks before Queen Anne in 1714, and so the British and Irish crowns passed to Sophia's son.

store the Catholic line of the Stuarts; it was backed by France, where he had grown up and to which he fled after the uprising's defeat. He married a fellow exile, a Polish princess, and in 1745 their son, nicknamed Bonnie Prince Charlie, made the last serious attempt to bring the Stuarts back to power in Britain. His invasion failed even more spectacularly than his father's. Afterward, a decreasingly bonnie Charlie married a minor German princess; they did not have any children together and later separated. Like his father, Charles arrived as a pensioned guest of the Pope in Rome, where, unlike his father, he drank himself to death. His younger brother, Henry, entered the Catholic priesthood and also died in Rome, as a cardinal, in his eighties, ending the direct line of the House of Stuart in 1807. It is Anne—pious, hardworking, tragic, bigoted, self-righteous, vindictive, generous, patriotic, and heartbroken—who remains commemorated as the Stuarts' last monarch on the ceiling of the Queen's Drawing Room at Hampton Court, the palace that played host to many of her dynasty's most romantic, scandalous, controversial, and important moments.

PART III

THE HOUSE OF
HANOVER

The builders did not know how the uses of their work
would descend; they made a new house with the stones of
the old castle; year by year, generation by generation, they
enriched and extended it; year by year the great harvest
of timber grew to ripeness; until, in sudden frost . . . the
place was desolate, and the work all brought to nothing.

—Evelyn Waugh, *Brideshead Revisited* (1945)

CHAPTER 19

THE CHOCOLATE
KITCHENS

They wrote, and rallied, and rhymed, and sung, and said,
and said nothing; they drank, and fought, and slept, and
swore, and took snuff; they went to new plays on the first
night [and] haunted the chocolate-houses.

—Jonathan Swift, *A Tale of a Tub* (1704)

G race Tosier, like many of the celebrities who came after her, had a sig-
nature look: in her case, a wide-brimmed hat and a posy of in-season
flowers pinned to the top and center of her bodice. Beginning in 1714 and
lasting for the rest of the century, the Georgian Era, with its expanding
press, produced recognizably modern celebrities, a cultural trend from
which Grace was among the first to benefit. Her outfits were reported in
publications such as *Tatler* and the *Gentleman's Magazine*, which presented
her to Londoners with descriptions that blended the informational with
the aspirational. Illustrations of her by the engraver John Faber Jr. were sold
to fame enthusiasts in the capital. Faber based his engravings of Grace on
a portrait of her by the artist Bartholomew Dandridge, who had painted
her in a now-lost original that she made available to Faber. Unlike later
eighteenth-century celebrities, such as Lady Emma Hamilton, who brilliantly harnessed the craze to market her own image to pamphleteers, fashion

271

magazines, and artists, Grace did not profit directly from her fame. She did so indirectly by using it to augment footfall to her and her husband's business. Then as now, a connection to royalty proved commercially beneficial, too, and, when not running their drinking house, the Chocolate Box, Grace and her husband, Thomas Tosier, had their own bedroom and workspace at Hampton Court, at the invitation of King George I, who appointed Thomas as his personal chocolatier in 1717.

A private bedroom for a servant was still a rare luxury and thus a mark of status, as was the decision to separate the Tosiers from the rest of the palace kitchens by creating two small rooms from which they could work. Far from the heat and bustle of the main kitchens, the Chocolate Kitchens, whose location was restored in 2013, thanks to the discovery of an eighteenth-century map of Hampton Court, are situated off the cloisters of William III's Fountain Court, where it is easy to imagine Grace, in her floppy hat, walking to and from her workplace.

The chocolate served at Hampton Court in the 1710s and 1720s was drunk rather than eaten. Although it had been known to Europeans for more than two centuries, chocolate's popularity there proved slow burning. Flavored with vanilla or chili, it had been an elite Aztec, Mayan, and Olmec delicacy. The Spanish conquistadors initially mistook it for an aphrodisiac. Some of Charles II's courtiers had regarded it as a hangover cure. The teetotal Quakers promoted it as a social beverage in lieu of alcohol, while the women of the French aristocracy—most famously Louis XIV's glamorous mistress Athénaïs de Montespan—helped turn it into a fashionable drink, a trend mimicked by the British court. Charles's household receipts show that he began spending more on chocolate in 1669–70, around the time of his sister Minette's extended visit. That the culture of drinking chocolate in England was still nascent is indicated by the eventual recruitment from abroad of the European Solomon de la Faya to serve as Charles II's official chocolatier in 1682. Solomon was probably, but not certainly, a member of the Jewish de la Faya family mentioned as living in Amsterdam in the late 1630s, where they are referred to in legal documents as Portuguese merchants. However, their ancestors, like all Jews who refused to convert to Christianity, had been expelled from Portugal in the 1490s.[1]

We know frustratingly little about de la Faya, except to say with some confidence that he must have been very talented, first to be hired by Charles II and then to remain in post throughout the dynastic roulette that followed. He was still serving the Stuarts when Chocolate Kitchens were installed for the first time at Hampton Court, designed by Sir Christopher Wren per the request of William III and Mary II; the latter died before they were completed, while the former was known to enjoy a cup of drinking chocolate at breakfast with the Earl of Portland, another chocolate enthusiast.

From the court, the fashion for hot drinks spread to British cities, towns, and later villages. It was in this environment that Grace and Thomas first started in their profession, at a time when the hot drinks trade was a nascent, lucrative, yet controversial line of work. As the popularity of hot drinks expanded, coffee shops became almost as ubiquitous in late Stuart England as they are in the twenty-first century. These establishments, sometimes called tea parlors or coffee taverns, became social hubs, particularly for supporters of radical politics; many of their meetings were held at coffeehouses, with the result that Charles II and James II both tried unsuccessfully to ban such places from trading.

When politics did not cause tension, health concerns did. Under Charles II, a pamphlet entitled *The Women's Petition Against Coffee* had blamed coffee for causing impotence in London's men, an assertion rebutted by a rival publication claiming that coffee, in fact, had many health benefits, including making "the erection more vigorous."[2] During James II's reign, a physician published *The Manner of Making of Coffee, Tea, and Chocolate*, which reiterated the potential health advantages of these beverages, specifically that of chocolate "in a moderate quantity." Moderation did not win the public's favor, though, and hot drinks continued to be a profitable trade when the Tosiers set up the Chocolate Box on a street called Chocolate Row in Greenwich, from where their fame as chocolatiers grew. Sometime after Solomon de la Faya's death, and three years after Queen Anne's, the post

of King's Chocolatier was awarded to the Tosiers—or, more specifically, to
Thomas. As the chocolatier in the couple, he prepared the King's drinks,
while Grace, who occasionally joined him at Hampton Court, utilized her
considerable business acumen to increase the popularity and profitability of
their shop. The Tosiers' Chocolate Box expanded with an adjoining dance
hall, and business boomed thanks to their association with the royal family.
Grace cleverly emphasized the connections by hosting dances in honor of
King George's birthday, which, by happy coincidence, fell in the same week
in May as Restoration Day, a holiday kept well into the eighteenth century
to celebrate the anniversary of the monarchy's return in 1660 and marked
at court with balls and firework displays. Grace's soirées, hosted by "the
Wife of The King's Chocolate Maker," were aimed at those who wished
to mimic the lifestyle but did not quite make the cut to receive an invitation from the palace.[3] The Tosiers' parties were covered by journalists, who
noted with approval how many "Persons of Quality" attended.[4]

Both in their work at the palace and at the Chocolate Box, Grace and
Thomas had to remain abreast of changing fashions when it came to refresh-
ments. Almond milk, for instance, once mocked as something preferred
by pretentious upper-class women or Catholics, was yielding precedence to
dairy in chocolate and coffee.[5] At various times, there were different fads
for jasmine, mint, long pepper, orange zest, aniseed, chili, brandy, rosewa-
ter, pistachios, cardamom, cinnamon, wine, or port to be added to drinking
chocolate. Sugar was used to counteract the natural bitterness in chocolate, a factor that had contributed to its earlier unpopularity. King George's
late mother and her cousin had corresponded about the new mania for hot
drinks, with the latter writing, "I can drink neither tea, nor chocolate, nor
coffee; all this foreign stuff is repugnant to me: I find chocolate too sweet,
coffee tastes like soot to me, and tea more like a medicine, in short, in this
respect as in many others, I cannot be *à la mode*."[6]

The beans used in the Chocolate Kitchens were mostly imported from
Jamaica, a former Spanish colony conquered by England during Oliver
Cromwell's rule. Chocolate was still being produced in relatively small
quantities, certainly when compared with its mass production in the next

century, or to sugar, some of which was also grown in Jamaica—nearly all of it harvested from plantations or settlements at which the workforce was enslaved. Abolitionist and antislavery sentiment was active in Great Britain during the reign of George I, particularly among the Quaker congregations; it would not be until later in the century, however, that the mass mobilization of British abolitionists began. This would be due to the awareness raised by the best-selling memoir of Olaudah Equiano, a survivor of slavery who subsequently and successfully toured Britain and Ireland to promote his work, and also because the British press began to report more honestly and thoroughly on what was being done, and inflicted, in the colonies. Revealingly, it was sugar that was then targeted by boycotts organized by antislavery activists. The fact that chocolate was not reflects both the economic power of sugar as a foundation of slavery and the small-scale production of chocolate until well into the reign of George III. However, while broad support for abolitionism had not yet developed in Great Britain under George I, serious opposition to enslavement in Jamaica was coming to a boil; the year after George's death, a mass antislavery uprising began, lasting for nearly a dozen years. Known later as the First Maroon War, it saw hundreds mobilize to escape their plantations to establish free communities in the Jamaican mountains. Before that war, conditions in Jamaica were almost completely undiscussed in British periodicals or journals.

Every morning, Thomas began preparing the King's chocolate in the smaller of the two rooms. It was a stuffy place as he roasted the cacao beans over the grate. They were then taken to the table, where Thomas ground and cut the roasted beans until he had enough cacao nibs to take with him to the Chocolate Room, the larger and more comfortable of the two rooms. There he crushed the nibs in a preheated grinder to produce enough chocolate, which was then mixed in a saucepan with whatever additives Thomas or the King had decided on for that day.[7] All of these—the liqueurs and spices—were stored in the Chocolate Room for Thomas's convenience. He would then decant a concoction far thicker than the modern equivalent of hot chocolate into a silver serving pot, which he placed on a tray with delicate porcelain cups. He carried it through the courtyard cloisters and upstairs to the King's Apartments. There he served the drink to his awkward, temperamental sovereign, who spoke German better than he did English—which gave rise to the enduring yet inaccurate claim that King George could neither speak nor understand the language of his British subjects.

The expansion of the relatively free press that had helped make people like Grace Tosier famous also meant—to the shock of many tourists and visitors from elsewhere in Europe, where the presses were still typically tightly controlled by their governments—that even the royal family were not immune from "the lash of these satirical folks."[8] George I, nicknamed "German George," was also privately pilloried by his courtiers for his initial failure to grasp some of the nuances of English dining decorum. These errors were advertised when he continued the old custom of occasionally taking a meal publicly in Hampton Court's Eating Room. The press, meanwhile, publicly guffawed at his difficulties in speaking English and went on subsequently to exaggerate them.

They also had a field day with his unorthodox private life. There was no queen for the journalists to mock or for the Tosiers to serve. Years earlier, George had imprisoned his wife, Sophia-Dorothea of Celle, after discovering her affair with a Swedish nobleman, who disappeared around the time of Sophia-Dorothea's incarceration and whose murdered remains, so rumor claimed, had been vindictively buried beneath her floorboards on her husband's orders. While that seems unlikely, given the stench that would have arisen as the body decomposed, we have absolutely no idea what happened to Count von Königsmarck after he vanished in 1694. Sophia-Dorothea spent the rest of her life under house arrest for adultery, a sin that her husband had been committing throughout their marriage. In the absence of a queen, life at Hampton Court was dominated by King George's tall and very thin mistress, Melusine von der Schulenberg, and his half sister, the Countess of Leinster and Darlington, an illegitimate daughter of the King's late father. Nicknamed "the Maypole and the Elephant"* on account

---

* Melusine, who was made Duchess of Munster and later of Kendall by George I, was also referred to as "the Goose" in Jacobite circles and "the Scarecrow" in Hanover.

of their contrasting weights, the two women vied for dominance over the early Georgian court. The Tosiers were wise enough to keep quiet about the rival socialites, especially since one of their palace colleagues, confectioner Charles Burroughs, was fired after he was overheard repeating the rumor that the Countess of Leinster was not only George I's half sister but also his lover, thanks to her desperate bid to outmaneuver Melusine by seducing the King. Burroughs's claim seems to have arisen from confusion over Lady Leinster's relationship to King George. Legally, she was the daughter of Baron von Platen, her mother's husband, and only people close to the Hanoverian court initially knew who her biological father had been. Since her status as George I's illegitimate half sister was not publicized widely, many were confused about her favor with the King, who made her a countess twice over, prompting the inaccurate conclusion that they were lovers. The two explanations—the truth and the mistake—subsequently merged into the falsehood of an incestuous relationship.

Both women were detested by the Prince of Wales, another George, who had never forgiven his father for the brutal abuse of his mother. It was to be one of the great heartbreaks of the younger George's life that he never fulfilled his dream of liberating his mother from her lifelong detention in the German castle of Ahlden—she died seven months before he became monarch. Like his father the King, Prince George was an adulterer. Throughout the 1710s, he was having an affair with Henrietta Howard, future Countess of Suffolk. Unlike his father, the Prince enjoyed a good relationship with his wife, who knew all about her husband's liaison with one of her ladies-in-waiting. Tall, beautiful, pale, and blonde with blue eyes, Caroline, Princess of Wales, was the cleverest among the new batch of royals—which, given the competition, was not a difficult accolade to secure. In stark contrast to her father-in-law, whose relatives knew and subjects suspected "would have had a better time" living in his homeland at his beloved Herrenhausen Palace and hunting lodges rather than inheriting "all his splendour in England," Caroline emerged as one of the most popular members of the new British royal family.[9]

There was a sense among her contemporaries that Caroline of Ansbach was always meant to wear a crown; as a teenager, she had been betrothed to the future Hapsburg Emperor Charles VI, an engagement that she broke off after months of studying for the requisite conversion to Catholicism. It was almost unheard-of for princesses to jettison a marriage plan, especially one to an emperor, and Caroline was widely applauded for the firm politeness she had shown in rejecting the imperial crown after remaining unconvinced by Catholic theology. She was similarly admired for her intelligence and lack of pretension about her beauty. As the Dowager Duchess of Orléans put it, "Having been ugly all my life, I never enjoyed looking at my bear-cat-monkey face in the mirror, so it is no wonder that I do not do it very often. But to be young and beautiful and yet not enjoy looking into the mirror like the Princess of Ansbach, that is unusual indeed."[10] Even at the French court, which still officially supported the claims of the Catholic Stuarts, Caroline's reputation was sterling. The Dowager Duchess, whose son was regent of France for the young Louis XV, observed, "Everything I hear about the Princess of Wales makes me esteem and like her; she has noble and beautiful sentiments, and I feel much affection for her."[11]

Caroline, her husband, and their children resided at Hampton Court while the King made his return visits to his native German province of Hanover, during which they adhered to traditional court etiquette. The "Prince and Princess dine [publicly] every day at Hampton Court," according to a courtier, "and all sorts of people have free admission to see them, even of the lowest sort of rank."[12] The Tosiers saw less of the Princess of Wales as feuds within the royal family intensified. The King and his son loathed each other, resulting in longer and more frequent spells during which the Waleses were not welcome at court. Thomas Tosier died in 1733, and, the next year, Grace wedded a local brewer named Samuel Vancourt; such was the prestige, and recognizability, of her surname that she kept Tosier rather than take Vancourt. She died a wealthy woman in 1753, in her late eighties, just before drinking chocolate—and Hampton Court itself—fell out of fashion.

CHAPTER 20

QUEEN CAROLINE'S
APARTMENTS

You may strut, dapper George, but 'twill all be in vain,
We all know 'tis Queen Caroline, not you, that reign—
You govern no more than Don Philip of Spain.*
Then, if you would have us fall down and adore you
Lock up your fat spouse, as your dad did before you.

—Anonymous, English poem (c. 1733)

Caroline of Ansbach arrived at Hampton Court in July 1733 to spend the summer, her sixth as Queen of Great Britain and Ireland. She was joined by her husband, King George II, and their seven surviving children, who ranged in age from the unmarried and promiscuous heir to the throne, Frederick, Prince of Wales, then twenty-six, to his nine-year-old sister, Princess Louisa.[1] The Queen had a close bond with her five daughters but a poor and deteriorating relationship with Frederick. Struggling with gout and a hernia, her blonde hair usually either heavily powdered or covered by the wigs that were becoming fashionable for women, Queen

---

* Philip V, French-born King of Spain from 1700 until 1724 and, after a brief abdication, again until his death in 1746. Generally regarded by contemporaries as a weak king who was "dominated" by his Italian wife, Queen Elisabeth Farnese.

Caroline had turned fifty that March, a few weeks before she was burned in effigy by protesters in London. The crisis had passed by July, but the Queen remained worried. She planned to discuss it with the Prime Minister—Britain's first—when he called on her at Hampton Court. Ostensibly, he was coming to finalize details of Parliament's support for the impending marriage of Caroline's eldest daughter, Princess Anne the Princess Royal, to Willem IV, Prince of Orange. Anne, like the elder four of the royal siblings, was a German Hanoverian, born before their grandfather's accession to the British thrones, and some in Parliament had put up hefty resistance to the King's request for an £80,000 dowry for her.[2] Caroline resented having to ask Parliament in the first place—in conversation with her friends, she privately gave vent to her frustration at Britain's curtailed monarchy and blamed the late William III for his reforms, which had turned future British monarchs into "the humble servant of the Parliament, the pensioner of his people, and a puppet of sovereignty, [who is] forced to go to them for every shilling he wanted."[3] Caroline was a pragmatist, however, who knew that there was no point in behaving for the world she wanted rather than how it was. Delusions on that scale were best left to the Stuarts.

Orphaned at thirteen by her mother's death, Wilhelmina-Karolina von Brandenburg-Ansbach—as she had been then—was taken in by a distant relative, Sophia-Charlotte, who was later Prussia's first queen consort. At Sophia-Charlotte's estate on the outskirts of Berlin, young Caroline absorbed her guardian's interest in politics and "philosophical conversations."[4] It was this education that had in no small part given Caroline the confidence to reject the offer of Hapsburg marriage after being unconvinced by the Jesuit priest sent to tutor her into Catholicism. After her marriage to her guardian's nephew George of Hanover and the family's relocation to Britain, Caroline's intelligence enabled her to become the most politically effective member of the new dynasty. At Hampton Court, her favorite home as queen, Caroline was happy when surrounded by bishops and scholars, in whose company she competed as an intellectual equal. When the Bishop of London spoke patronizingly to her at one of her salons by slowly explaining a point of Protestant theology, the Queen felt that he must be "very impertinent to suppose that I, who refused to be Empress for the sake of the Protestant religion, don't understand it."[5] She championed the new cause of inoculation against smallpox, using the prestige of her royal position to counteract fears about the efficacy of the practice. Voltaire, who cannot be accused of privately flattering royalty, praised Caroline as a "philosopher on the throne."[6]

It was not proper protocol for a government minister to meet with a consort rather than with the monarch, and in future generations, such a meeting would have been considered constitutionally inappropriate. However, Caroline was regarded as the power behind George II's throne. The protesters' torching of a proxy for the Queen rather than the King illustrates the public's perception of Caroline's importance, as did the songs and chants that mocked the King as his wife's dim-witted puppet. This was a reductive characterization, especially when it came to foreign policy, in which the King was both more active and interested, but the Queen unquestionably exerted great influence, especially through the royals' relationship with Parliament. When Caroline granted an audience to the Prime Minister at Hampton Court, she could choose to do so in her magnificent public apartments in the Baroque wing or, less probably, in her more comfortable private rooms. She stood as servants ushered in the Prime Minister, who bowed to her and then again over her extended hand. The servants retreated but did not close the doors as they left. Caroline was always conscientious about her reputation, and she never granted an audience to a man unless one or both of the doors were left open.

Fifty-seven-year-old Sir Robert Walpole—tall, heavy-set, with brown eyes, thick dark eyebrows, and a long wig that was still the custom among the older generation—sat at Caroline's invitation and informed her that, as expected, the Tories in Parliament had created difficulties over the Princess's £80,000 dowry. Caroline and her husband had negotiated their daughter's betrothal to Prince Willem because it was popular with the British people; why, therefore, was Parliament standing in its way? The unspoken answer was that many Tories—who, a few decades earlier, had been the faction most likely to vote the royals whatever money they asked for—regarded the House of Hanover as an imported imposition. Many Tories wanted to see the exiled Stuarts, Catholic or not, restored and saw no reason why the British taxpayer should stump up £80,000 for somebody who had been born Anna von Hanover.

Caroline expected the Prime Minister to solve this problem. One of his opponents described Walpole as "the ablest parliamentarian man, and the ablest manager of parliament, that I believe ever lived. An artful rather than an eloquent speaker, he saw as by intuition, the disposition of the House, and pressed on or receded accordingly. So clear in stating the most intricate matters, especially in the finances, that while he was speaking the most ignorant thought that they understood."[7]

Walpole was both beneficiary and manipulator of party politics, which had become an entrenched feature of British government. The Whigs, which Walpole led, and the rival Tories had emerged late in the reign of Charles II, with the split in Parliament caused by the future James II's conversion to Catholicism and the ensuing Exclusion Crisis. Those who backed James's exclusion from the throne formed the nucleus of the Whig movement, while those who opposed them were referred to as Tories—a once pejorative term for royalists during the civil wars. The parties endured beyond the crisis, the Whigs remaining the more liberal of the two; they proved as much with their enthusiastic support for the Glorious Revolution that clipped the monarchy to Parliament's benefit and they were the leading proponents of the Act of Settlement that ultimately disinherited the Catholic Stuarts in favor of their Hanoverian cousins. The Tories were a conservative force, dogged by accusations that many of their supporters were secretly sympathetic to Jacobitism—a charge that, as their sniping at Princess Anne's marriage proved, was not entirely without justification.

In the course of his rise from Member of Parliament to Prime Minister, Walpole had used these divisions to his advantage. He had launched himself into the political arena by cultivating the friendship of influential Whigs in Queen Anne's time, namely the Duke of Marlborough and the Earl of Godolphin, through whose patronage he became Secretary of State for War at a time when there was a great deal of it. He had harnessed the fear of Jacobitism in the years immediately after Queen Anne's death to present himself to the British public—and the new royal family—as a politician who was willing to do whatever was necessary to keep the Protestant Hanovers on the throne. He had helped impeach Jacobite noblemen in the 1710s and used the foiled plots of Stuart sympathizers in the 1720s to further his popularity. Walpole never missed the chance to turn a crisis into an opportunity. He used the economic downturn resulting from the financial crash known as the South Sea Bubble, in which share prices in an overseas trade company imploded, to his advantage. Having exploited anti-taxation riots in Glasgow as the perfect pretext to neutralize his Scottish political opponents, he did the same to rivals in the Irish administration with an opportune scandal over patents.

Although the monarchy's direct authority had been curtailed, it continued to possess significant soft power, through which it could swing the needle to a politician's benefit or detriment. Walpole had thus also made sure to back the right faction at court. As George I's health problems increased in the mid-1720s, Walpole attended the Prince and Princess of Wales's midnight balls at Hampton Court in order to discern what the new reign would look like and whose favor he should curry. Some of his rivals, and allies, had done the same but had instead set out to win the friendship of George II's mistress, Henrietta Howard, which as Walpole crudely put it was backing the wrong "sow."[8] From his observations of the royal family, he realized that George II was far less respectful of, or interested in, his mistress's opinions than in his brilliant wife's, and so Walpole cultivated a friendship with Princess Caroline, who proved an invaluable ally to him after her husband became king in 1727.

However, their alliance had eroded Caroline's popularity, especially in London. She had ignored warnings that it might do so from one of the Prime Minister's opponents, the Earl of Stair, who lost his temper when Caroline refused to listen and shouted at her during their audience. Those who worried that Caroline was "deaf to everything [that] did not come from" Walpole underestimated her. It was a transactional rather than an affectionate relationship. To keep her on his side, Walpole had secured a significant increase in the money voted to the King and Queen by Parliament, for which both George and Caroline were grateful. She understood, too, that her family needed the Whigs to balance the Jacobite threat and was under no illusion as to what kind of man the Prime Minister was. In his pursuit of power in Parliament, he had betrayed his brother-in-law and long-term political ally, Lord Townshend, who, shorn of support in Parliament and receiving none from the court thanks to Walpole's influence with Queen Caroline, resigned; Walpole subsequently became both Chancellor of the Exchequer and First Lord of the Treasury, and thus in effect Great Britain's first Prime Minister.[9] Nor did Caroline delude herself into believing that Walpole's obsequiousness to her in person could be counted as genuine. She knew, for instance, that after she successfully lobbied against him to have her candidate consecrated as the new bishop for the Welsh diocese of Bangor, Walpole had, in a rage, referred to the Queen as a "fat, old bitch."[10] She was seven years his junior.

By the summer of 1733, Caroline had cause to question her support for the Prime Minister. They had both retreated from the capital after the embarrassment and danger of the riots, in which Walpole had burned in effigy alongside Queen Caroline. Like many of those who had backed Walpole on the way up, Caroline worried that his savviness was giving way to hubris, the evolution that had ended, and would end, many a political career. An Excise Bill introduced by Walpole that year was identified by its opponents, rightly or wrongly, as a gateway to higher taxation and an infringement of London's ancient trading liberties: among its provisions, it would have allowed customs officials to enter private homes to search for untaxed goods. Its potential impact on the cost of tobacco was particularly unpopular, and antigovernment cartoons showed the figure of Britannia defiantly smoking a tobacco pipe.

Most of Walpole's allies felt that he should have spotted how unpopular the bill was and backed down before it became a crisis; when it passed in the House of Commons on March 14 by a vote of 265 to 204, the latter ominously included ninety-eight dissident members of Walpole's own party. A subsequent bill dealing specifically with the controversial issue of tobacco passed by a still smaller margin of thirty-six. That should have been the point at which Walpole reconsidered his policy. Instead, he pressed ahead. The ensuing public backlash was swift and intense. Civic representatives of the City of London, headed by the Lord Mayor, submitted a petition to the House of Commons on April 10 asking for the bill to be withdrawn. Two of the legislation's leading parliamentary critics, London MPs Micajah Perry and Sir John Barnard, were celebrated as the city's heroes.[11] Riots had already broken out, at which protesters sang antigovernment ballads with titles such as "Britannia Excisa; Britain Excis'd"—the printed version of which carried a cartoon of Walpole in a carriage drawn by a many-headed dragon, one head of which turned back to vomit money into the Prime Minister's lap, while another tried to devour fleeing citizens caught in the carriage's path.[12] The Tories felt confident enough to start drawing up provisional plans for a new cabinet once Walpole was ousted.[13]

When rumors leaked that the Prime Minister had discussed with the King and Queen plans to order soldiers into London to crush the riots, the politician Thomas Wyndham asked if the government planned to make troops attacking the people one of the "new-fangled trappings of English Majesty." Even one of Walpole's friends called Wyndham's rhetoric "the finest historical rant you ever heard," and it made Queen Caroline and King George nervous.[14] A foreign dynasty that was not yet twenty years on the throne could not afford to be identified by the public as the importer of martial law. With coercion ruled out, Walpole had tried compromise by amending the bill, but it was too late. Realizing that he was losing his majority in Parliament, he withdrew the bill on April 11.

Even before the riots over the Excise Bill, the Queen knew—thanks to a parliamentary investigation into corruption from which the Prime Minister had emerged unscathed but a suspicious number of his allies had not—that Walpole's enemies were circling him. The Prime Minister's critics mockingly castigated the "Robinocracy"—Robin being a popular nickname for Robert—that Walpole had used to stay in office. What he could not manipulate, he bought, and he had created a pork barrel large enough to resemble a buffet of corruption for his allies. When the Prime Minister was not being burned in effigy, he was ridiculed on stage in popular productions such as *The Beggar's Opera* by John Gay, in which everybody knew the character of the thieving highwayman, Macheath, was an allegory for Walpole*— likewise with the revivals of Shakespeare's *Henry VIII*, in which Cardinal Wolsey was frequently costumed in an anachronistic way to draw parallels between him and Walpole.[15]

The question of the Princess Royal's marriage portion was in some ways a test to see if Walpole remained useful to Queen Caroline. He could not afford to lose another vote, about the £80,000 or anything else, if he wanted to remain in office. Before Walpole left Hampton Court in a carriage that took him back to a house he was renting for the summer in nearby Richmond Park, the Queen made it clear to the Prime Minister that she expected the debacle of the Excise Bill to be an unfortunate anomaly rather than a harbinger. She also planned to use money voted to her by Parliament to fund improvements to her quarters at Hampton Court, the public areas of which—particularly the stairs—she felt were spartan in comparison to her husband's. They did not create a sufficient impression of majesty when she met with bishops, philosophers, politicians, earls, theologians, and the Prime Minister. As one of her confidants wrote of Caroline in his memoirs, "the darling pleasure of her soul was power."[16]

---

*In the twentieth century, Macheath inspired the character of Mack the Knife in Bertolt Brecht's *The Threepenny Opera* (1928).

CHAPTER 21

THE QUEEN'S STAIRS

We lounge, & feast, & play, & chatter,
In private Satirise, in Public flatter

—John Hervey, 2nd Baron Hervey, "An Epistle
from a Nobleman to a Doctor of Divinity" (1733)

John Hervey, 2nd Baron Hervey, saw Caroline of Ansbach's improvements as he ascended the Queen's Stairs later that summer. The staircase, with its newly gilded balustrades, was now watched over by *Apollo and Diana*, an enormous painting by the seventeenth-century Dutch artist Gerard van Honthorst. It had been commissioned by Charles I and bought back by his son in 1666, after it had been sold during the post–civil war auctions.[1] Caroline had ordered it taken out of storage and cleaned to be installed above the Queen's Stairs. At the top of those stairs, Lord Hervey passed the empty Haunted Gallery to his left and uniformed guards to his right as he walked through the first-floor apartments toward the candlelit Queen's Drawing Room. An usher announced his arrival, and he sailed into the room wearing even more makeup than most gentlemen in Georgian high society.

In his midthirties, Hervey and his wife, one of Queen Caroline's former maids of honor, had recently celebrated the birth of their sixth child, William; Lady Hervey was at home in the country with the children. Good-looking enough to be nicknamed "Hervey the Handsome" in London pamphlets and always dressed beautifully—one of the Churchills had brought him clothes from Paris for his most recent birthday—Hervey was neurotic, prone to fainting, and thin. (He had just emerged from a diet that required three days a week as a vegetarian, drinking green tea for breakfast, and cutting out alcohol, butter, salt, and sauces.[2]) He was one of the best-connected men in Britain; his days consisted of breakfasts with the Bishop of Salisbury, letters to and from Voltaire, card games with the Duke of Richmond, walks with the Queen, theater with the King and lunch with the Prime Minister, for whom he occasionally wrote pieces of progovernment propaganda under a pseudonym.[3] Fastidious and sensitive, Hervey operated by a series of self-set absolutes governing the trivial—"I hate a pun on any occasion"—and he had a savage turn of phrase.[4] He thought impartiality was a bore; he was camp, with a vicious sense of humor; intelligent; and, if in good spirits, he was great fun to sit next to at a dinner party.

Some of the meals he had endured that summer had stifled Hervey's repartee, such as the three-and-a-half-hour-long dinner with thirty-eight dishes per course held to celebrate the feast day of a German saint who was patron of one of the royals' visiting cousins. It ended with desserts of sugar plum and barley sugar sculpted into pyramids, eagles, and arches. Hervey griped, "[A]ltogether it was one of the most expensive, tawdry, ill-understood, disagreeable German pieces of magnificence that ever was seen."[5] A disagreeable piece of German magnificence might have been the perfect assessment of the British monarchy under George II, who sat at one of the card tables, beneath the *Apotheosis of Queen Anne*, gambling as he did on most evenings at Hampton Court. Also in attendance were the Spanish ambassador—a bore who threw expensive yet dull parties—and the middle-aged Duke of Grafton, gambling-addicted grandson of Barbara Villiers and Charles II. Hervey suspected that something Grafton had taken that evening—possibly an opiate—had made him fall asleep while sitting at a card table between Princess Amelia and Princess Caroline, the King's second and third daughters. On the opposite side of the table was the Princess Royal, whose habit of cracking her knuckles made Hervey feel queasy.[6]

When it did not bore him, Hervey had a keen mind for politics. During the Excise riots, he partied at a masquerade ball until four o'clock in the morning, immediately after which he somehow went home to write a lucid four-point explanation of the legislation for a confused family friend.[7] In London, Hervey's days had been filled with discussions of politics, be it the Prime Minister's narrow avoidance of downfall or fears of an impending war in Europe. The King of Poland-Lithuania had died in February, and, since the Polish monarchy was elective, there was the threat of a war over who should succeed him. A dowager duchess at Hampton Court asked why somebody couldn't just buy the Polish election—after all, that was what they did when things got tricky at Westminster. Russia and Austria backed one candidate, while France—whose king, Louis XV, was married to one of the Polish claimant's daughters—backed another. "I hear of nothing but elections," Hervey complained. "It will be very odd to have all the great Powers engaged in settling a point that naturally should have been of great indifference to them."[8]

At Hampton Court, society gossip was a more popular topic of conversation. While the monarchy had survived the seventeenth century, the court as a center of power had not. By 1733, ambitious men made their careers in Parliament or the armed forces, not in the royal household. Only a favored few at court, those closest to the King or Queen, knew much about government and international diplomacy. Courtiers, Hervey complained, thus fell into one of two categories: "people who can't say anything worth repeating, and the people who won't."[9] Around the gaming tables, they chatted instead about the promiscuous Earl of Lincoln, said to be the most handsome man in England and with a penis so large that the joke in court circles was to wish Lord Lincoln a life as long as his manhood.[10] More politely, the card players could compare notes on what they had recently seen at the theater. Just before coming to Hampton Court, Hervey had attended a new opera by Handel, which left him telling friends that the great composer's "genius seems quite exhausted." He had accompanied the King and Queen to watch a play about Elizabeth I's later years, at which the Duchess of Marlborough proved a particularly irritating audience member, because she used the evening as an opportunity to showcase her emotional sensitivity:

depending on the scene, she either wept audibly or "clapt her hands so loud that we heard her [a]cross the theatre."[11]

The youngest of the five princesses—Mary and Louisa—were still too young to join their sisters at the evening card parties in the drawing room. They remained in the care of a household headed by their governess, the Dowager Countess of Deloraine. Lady Deloraine's husband—yet another grandchild of Charles II via one of his illegitimate sons—had died three years earlier of a heart attack on Christmas Day. The Dowager Countess, only twenty-seven, had gone to court, where she had fallen in love with one of her colleagues, William Windham, deputy governor to the King's youngest son. It was not generally done for the royal children to be cared for by a married governess, and so Lady Deloraine had asked Queen Caroline's permission to accept Windham's proposal. "The Queen told her she had no objection to her marrying," Hervey reported, "though she had an insurmountable one to any married woman being Governess to her daughters. Upon which my Lady has prudently resolved to keep her old employment, and give Mr. Windham no new one."[12] Hervey did not exactly have mixed feelings about the governess: "Don't pity Lady Delo[raine], I beg you," he ordered a friend, "for she is such an idiot that every look tells it, every word makes one sick, and every action makes one peevish."*[13]

He hid his opinion from Lady Deloraine. One time, when she confided in Hervey that people seemed to be avoiding her, she received the gallant reply "that envy kept the women at a distance, and despair the men." In his letters to others, he made fun of her for believing him and for her habit of admiring her reflection in the palace mirrors.[14] Along with Lady Deloraine's reasons for calling off her engagement, Hervey passed on to his friends information about the state of the Prime Minister's marriage. Walpole was living apart from his wife, Catherine, who had taken a lover, and

---

* Queen Caroline later relented and gave her blessing to Lady Deloraine's marriage to Windham, and permission for both of them to keep their jobs at court. She had cause to regret her decision when, a year after the wedding, Lady Deloraine began an affair with the King. An unimpressed Hervey wrote that George II had made "the governess of his two youngest daughters his whore and the guardian-director of his son's youth and morals his cuckold."

the house he had rented in Richmond Park for the summer was his "bower of bliss," as Hervey mockingly put it, with his mistress, Maria Skerrett.[15]

Hervey both laughed at and sympathized with the Prime Minister's situation. He, too, shared a house with the person he loved but to whom he was not married. In Hervey's case, it was a London townhouse on Great Burlington Street with Stephen Fox, Member of Parliament for Shaftesbury and heir to the largest nonaristocratic fortune in Britain.[16] Hervey and Stephen had been introduced by Hervey's friend and Stephen's younger brother, Henry.[17] Friendship turned to flirtation, which, either before or during their shared trip to France and Italy, evolved into love.[18] After they returned to England, Hervey told Stephen, "I can't live without you. . . . I long and pine and fret to see you. What does one live for but to be happy; and what happiness can one have, when one loves one single thing better than all others in the world bundled together, and does not possess it."[19] They met in secret in the brief interludes when Hervey could escape his duties at court. The frequent absences exacerbated Stephen's jealousy, and not without good reason.[20] In March 1730 Hervey decided the couple needed a place of their own, reasoning, "Why should we see one another by Visits, but never have a common home?"[21] Stephen bought the house for them on Great Burlington Street, paying £4,000 for it to the previous owner—Lord Hervey's wife—who seemed to accept the arrangement with equanimity; she later formed a friendship with Stephen.[22]

It was, for both Hervey and Stephen, initially a very happy time, as attested to in Hervey's surviving letters, such as the one dated September 24, 1730, a few weeks after they took the house, in which Hervey reflected on "how warmly, how tenderly, how gratefully, how contentedly and unalterably I am Yours." Or that dated to the next day, in which he admits, "Every Body has some Madness in their Composition, & I freely acknowledge you are mine." "I love you, and love you more than I thought I could love anything," he wrote in another.[23] There is also a letter, written by Hervey immediately after Stephen went about his day's work, that affectionately discusses love-bites that Stephen had left on his thighs.[24] Hervey signed his correspondence to Stephen with farewells to his *caro and carissimo* ("dear and dearest").

In the three years that the pair had shared their home, however, Stephen's insecurities mushroomed until, in the summer of 1733, they threatened to capsize the relationship. A barrage of letters arrived at Hampton Court from Great Burlington Street. Stephen was convinced that, having been brought up in what was disparagingly called the nouveau riche, his "rustic" manners embarrassed Hervey, who he also could not keep pace with intellectually. Hervey sent back reassuring replies—"I should like you better rusty than any other body polish'd"—and begged Stephen not to make good on his threat to quit their home in London to move back to the countryside.

Lord Hervey's flamboyant personality and his bisexuality led to mockery. The Earl of Bath said that Hervey was a Master one minute and a Miss the next. Another contemporary poet, Alexander Pope, called him "an amphibious thing" and joked of Hervey's mannerisms that "now trips a lady, and now struts a Lord." Hervey's "Cherub's Face," Pope continued, should not confuse people into forgetting that he was "a Reptile all the rest; / Beauty that shocks you, Parts that none will trust, / Wit that can creep, and Pride that licks the dust."[25] Criticism was especially strident from those jealous of Hervey's favor with Queen Caroline. She treated him like a son and even referred to him as her "child, her pupil, and her charge."[26] His wit could smooth over any awkwardness, such as the night when he attended a party with the Queen at which he got so spectacularly drunk that he passed out. The next day, to recover from the faux pas, he wrote to Caroline as if he were announcing his death from a hangover:

> [S]ensible of all the gracious distinctions and innumerable favors with which Your Majesty honoured me when I was alive, I thought it my duty to give Your Majesty some notice of my death. On Saturday, the 14th, about 5 minutes after eleven, I died. Some malicious people perhaps may give out that I died drunk, for as I departed this life, just as I took leave of Your Majesty when you retired out of your Gallery, I cannot deny but that I expired with a drop. . . . My resurrection will immediately ensue, and the heaven of your presence again enjoyed.[27]

Lord Hervey understood Queen Caroline better than most at Hampton Court. They walked together in the gardens nearly every day, discussing politics—including their shared support for Walpole as prime minister— and court gossip. Caroline trusted Hervey's command of the latter sufficiently to ask him questions about her eldest son, Prince Frederick. Once the Princess Royal's wedding to the Prince of Orange had taken place, something needed to be done about the Prince of Wales. Twenty-six was far too old for an heir to remain unmarried. Either at one of the card parties or on one of their strolls, Queen Caroline asked Hervey what he thought of rumors at court that the Prince of Wales was impotent.

This was a particularly awkward question to put to Lord Hervey. He had firsthand knowledge that Prince Frederick was *not* impotent, since the two had almost certainly been lovers a few years earlier.[28] During that time, they had referred to each other as Alexander and Hephaestion, after the ancient warrior-king and the general traditionally identified as the love of Great Alexander's life.[29] They had also shared a mistress, in the person of Queen Caroline's maid of honor, Anne Vane.[30] She bore Prince Frederick an illegitimate son, christened Cornwell Fitz-Frederick, whom Hervey suspected might be his own biological child. The Prince, whose list of lovers also included Anne Vane's maid, had fallen out with Hervey, although not over Anne's love or Cornwell's paternity. The precise reason for the disintegration in what was once dubbed coyly their "homoerotic friendship" is uncertain. However, it was suggested at the time that, knowing of Frederick's fraught relationship with his mother the Queen, Hervey deliberately and vindictively set out to win Caroline's favor to cause maximum distress to the Prince.[31] If this was his intention, he succeeded. Prince Frederick was furious at the friendship.

To Hervey's dismissal of the claim that the Prince of Wales was impotent, Caroline confided in her friend that some part of her wished he was, so that the throne might one day pass to his youngest brother and her favorite son, Prince William, for whom a new suite of rooms had just been built at Hampton Court on her orders. Hervey, who described Frederick as "never having the least hesitation in telling any lie that served his present purpose," encouraged Queen Caroline's distrust of her eldest son by pointing out how the Prince seemed to have a contrarian impulse to support anything that he thought might irritate his parents.[32] The King and Queen had already vetoed two of Frederick's suggestions for potential brides—his cousin Princess Wilhelmina of Prussia and Lady Diana Spencer, the Earl of Sunderland's daughter, both of whom had subsequently married elsewhere—and, as much as he annoyed his parents, Caroline knew they would have to arrange a wedding for him.

On the last morning of July, four years later in 1737, Lord Hervey woke up in his rooms at Hampton Court and rang the bell for servants to fetch his breakfast. His relationship with Stephen Fox had fallen apart a few months earlier. Stephen had capitulated to family pressure to enter into an arranged marriage with a Tory heiress who was only thirteen at the time, meaning they lived separately for several years. However, the family pressure to marry also seemingly pushed Stephen away from Hervey, and he left their home on Great Burlington Street.[33] Hervey subsequently had a romance with nobleman Count Francesco Algarotti, a Venetian polymath and art collector who had recently moved to England and arrived to meet Hervey armed with a letter of introduction from Voltaire; Count Algarotti was also flirting with the Herveys' married friend the poet Lady Mary Wortley Montagu.[34] Despite the end of their relationship and the start of new ones for Hervey, he and Stephen still wrote to each other—their most recent letter, from Hervey to Stephen on June 25, included a poem and used his old nickname, "dear Ste"—but they seldom saw each other anymore. Hervey made as much clear when he promised in the same letter "not [to] tell you what day I shall be in town."[35]

Robert Walpole had survived as Prime Minister and was again spending the summer at Richmond Park with his mistress. Hervey's father, the Earl of Bristol, had recovered from an illness whose exact nature is unclear but was serious enough to leave him delirious and bedridden for several days.[36] Lord Bristol was a Roman-philosophy-reading landowner who loved the

Bible, his family, and playing the violin, and hated London, Tories, and the Prime Minister.[37] Hervey had spent hours by his father's bedside during his sickness; of the earl's eight surviving children, he was the eldest and the favorite. Lord Bristol had fathered twenty children in two marriages, Hervey being the second of seventeen born to the second; he had a title of his own because he had used his connections with the Queen and in Parliament to be granted one of his family's older subsidiary titles, the barony of Hervey, to use until such time as he succeeded his father as Earl of Bristol.[38] Thomas and Felton, the brothers nearest and furthest from Hervey in age, were both Members of Parliament for Bury St. Edmunds, a constituency where their father wielded great influence. The three middle Hervey brothers had done what sons with good names and no inheritance were expected to do by choosing between guns and God: William was a captain in the Royal Navy, Henry and Charles were Anglican vicars. They were of less use to Hervey than their brothers in Parliament, who could be recruited to support laws that he, or the Queen, favored.

Apart from his father's recovery, the only other news of interest for Hervey was that Lord Archibald Hamilton, Senior Naval Lord and Member of Parliament for Queensborough, was back at court, accompanied by his wife, Lady Jane. Between them, the Hamiltons represented two of the grandest families in the respective Scottish and Irish nobilities: Lord Archibald's father had been Earl of Selkirk; his mother had been Duchess of Hamilton in her own right; and Lady Jane's father was the Earl of Abercorn. Their pedigree did not impress Hervey, who found Lord Archibald pathetic and Lady Jane insufferable. "Lady Archibald [is] not young, has never been pretty, and [has] lost as least as much as the small share of beauty she once possessed," he wrote. Several years earlier, Lady Jane had an affair with the Prince of Wales; her husband's acceptance, or ignorance, of the liaison increased Hervey's contempt for him. Lord Archibald, he said, "[is] of so quiet, so secure and contented [a] temper, that he seemed cut out to play the passive character that his wife and the Prince graciously allotted him."[39]

Hervey did not usually eat a heavy breakfast; according to a letter to one of his doctors, it was usually either tea with toast and butter or tea with a sweet biscuit. As he poured his tea, he expected July 31 to be a day like every other at Hampton Court during the Hanoverians' summer. "Of our occupations at Hampton Court," he wrote to a friend:

> No mill-horses ever went in a more constant, true or more unchanging circle, so that by the assistance of an almanack for the day of the week and a watch for the hour of the day, you may inform yourself fully, without any other intelligence but your memory, of every transaction within the verge of the Court. Walking, chaises, levees and audiences fill the morning. At night, the King plays commerce or backgammon. . . . At last the King comes up; the pool finishes, and everybody has their dismission. . . . Some [of the courtiers go to] supper and some to bed: and thus (to speak in Scripture style) the evening and the morning make the day.[40]

While there had always been etiquette and decorum in the royal household, it seemed that as the court's importance shrank, its adherence to protocol intensified. Other observers of the court, especially those with Jacobite leanings, were less inclined to identify long-term causes as responsible. According to them, this stultifying routine was the result of a Teutonic obsession with etiquette and order, imported by a minor German dynasty that should never have been given the throne and knew they could not appear great without ceremony. This characterization of the romantic and dramatic Stuarts against the rigidly dull Hanoverians was to endure for centuries, immortalized in the literature and songs inspired by the Stuarts' futile attempts to recapture the crown.

Hervey might not have agreed that the Hanoverians lacked a flair for the dramatic when his breakfast that morning was interrupted by news that the Prince of Wales had fled Hampton Court in the middle of the night. Prince Frederick's relationship with his parents had stumbled from bad to worse between 1733 and 1737. To slight them, he had withheld news of his wife's pregnancy and then decided to make sure they missed the birth of their first legitimate grandchild by smuggling his wife out of Hampton Court while King George II and Queen Caroline slept. Earlier that day,

Frederick, as one of the early patrons of cricket, had been playing the game on the Hampton Court lawns to give the impression that nothing was out of the ordinary.

Once he was sure his parents had gone to bed after their evening card game, the Prince and his new German wife, Augusta of Saxe-Gotha-Altenburg, had scurried down the stairs and through the quiet corridors. The Waleses clambered into a waiting carriage, which trundled fifteen miles to St. James's Palace in the capital. Eighteenth-century carriage rides were not noted for their comfort, and this one must have been particularly agonizing for Princess Augusta, whose contractions had started. She was squashed in with her husband, his equerry, her lady-in-waiting, and two of her maids. It took hours to reach St. James's, where Augusta was helped out of the carriage sobbing in agony.

The cause of the royal estrangement was, as it had been in the previous generation, a fusion of politics with personality. Where one ended and the other began with the Hanoverians was impossible to pinpoint. Lord Hervey's friendship with Queen Caroline had distressed Frederick on a personal level; nor did it help that his mother was close to a man who had come to detest him. Frederick retaliated by striking up a friendship with Hervey's estranged mother, the Countess of Bristol. Politically, Frederick had sided with the Tories in defiance of his parents' support for Walpole and the Whigs. To this disagreement had been added the combustible issue of money; acting with the full encouragement of Queen Caroline and Lord Hervey, who utilized his connections in Parliament to help their cause, Sir Robert Walpole had defeated Prince Frederick's appeal to the House of Commons to increase his annual income, as was hitherto traditional upon the marriage of an heir to the throne. Prince Frederick retaliated with the pre-labor dash from Hampton Court.

Hervey's day began not only with the news that Prince Frederick had gone, but that after her servants broke the news to her, an apoplectic Queen Caroline had followed the Prince and Princess of Wales into London. Members of the royal family were required to give birth with witnesses present to avoid another Warming Pan fiasco, a threat that was lively in

1737 on account of Queen Caroline herself. She left Hampton Court with the vow "I will be sure it is her child."[41] Had the baby born in the unoccupied chill of St. James's been a boy, Caroline might have made good on her threat to resurrect the Warming Pan blueprint in order to disinherit the new heir and replaced him with her favorite, Prince William. It did not prove necessary, as Hervey discovered when the Queen returned to Hampton Court that night and told him that the Princess of Wales had given birth to a "poor, ugly, little she-mouse." The girl was baptized Augusta in her mother's honor. Queen Caroline attended the fragile princess's christening and visited the new family a few times during the following weeks. She admitted to Lord Hervey that she did so only to put on "a good show for the public."[42]

The Queen never forgave her son for what he had done that night. Nor did the King, who refused to receive Frederick back at Hampton Court. Denied any chance of seeing his father, the Prince of Wales remained in residence at St. James's. He was keen to reconcile with his family, on the condition that they accepted they were entirely to blame for the discord and that he had done nothing wrong. Frederick's letter to his father, which arrived at the palace five days after the princess's birth, was, according to Hervey, a "desire earnestly to be re-admitted into the King's presence [but] protesting the uprightness of his intentions, and not owning himself in the wrong in any one step. Not a word *of* or *to* the Queen." The King told Frederick's equerry that he had no answer other "than what had been given": namely, that he would not receive or forgive the Prince for the way in which he had humiliated his family. Half the court sympathized with the Waleses; the other half with the King and Queen. Hervey, however, was a cocktail of boredom and disgust. "I am tired to death of hearing nothing but this," he wrote to the Whig Member of Parliament for Hindon, "over and over again; it *ennuies* me to a degree that is inconceivable. I shall see you tomorrow, and I suppose you, not being so tired of the subject as I am, will make me talk of it all over again."[43]

Hervey was soon provided with unwelcome distraction from the Wales scandal by the collapse of Queen Caroline's health. She stayed at Hampton

A painting believed to show Charles II departing from Hampton Court. He spent his honeymoon there in 1662, but later grew to dislike the palace.

"The curse of the nation": Charles II's most influential but unpopular mistress Barbara, Countess of Castlemaine, who treated Hampton Court as her own. Her other lovers included her cousin, a circus acrobat, and an actor who tried to poison her children.

The Right Honble Lady Barbara Countess of Castlemaine &c.

William III, king from 1689 until his death in 1702.
He ordered the demolition of half of Hampton Court.

An aerial view showing Hampton Court's Baroque wing constructed for
William III (*front*) that gives way to the surviving Tudor wing (*top and right*).

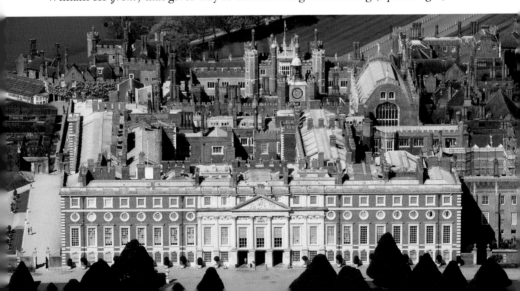

A crowned Queen Anne in *The Apotheosis of Queen Anne* on the ceiling of the Queen's Drawing Room.

Businesswoman and chocolatier Grace Tosier.

Frederick, Prince of Wales, having a music lesson at Hampton Court (which is visible through the windows). He is joined by his sisters, from left to right, the princesses Anne, Caroline, and Amelia.

"The darling pleasure of her soul was power": this eighteenth-century portrait of Queen Caroline is still on display at Hampton Court, her favorite home.

Camp, scathing, promiscuous, ferociously intelligent, and a fantastic dinner guest, Lord Hervey recorded in his memoirs the scandals of Georgian high society at Hampton Court.

One of the great minds of Victorian Britain, mathematician Michael Faraday with his wife, Sarah, who were often joined at their Hampton Court home by nieces and nephews after they moved there in 1861.

King George V places his personal wreath on the coffin of the Unknown Warrior in 1920. The coffin was made from an ancient oak, chosen specially from the Hampton Court estate.

Elizabeth II and her sister, Margaret, attending the Hampton Court coronation ball in 1953.

Tsar Nicholas II's sister Grand Duchess Xenia *(left)* at her Hampton Court home. From left to right after her are the Grand Duchess's daughter-in-law Princess Nadine, granddaughter Princess Olga, and the famously intimidating Mother Martha.

In 2016, Catherine, the Duchess of Cambridge, helped advertise and celebrate Hampton Court's new features. The cake, from Choccywoccydoodah, was a buttercream tribute to the palace's Tudor heraldry and founders.

Hampton Court, viewed from the restored Privy Gardens.

Court, as was customary for her and her family to do until October when they would return to London. In agony from her hernia, the Queen spent much of that summer and autumn either in the bath or praying in her oratory, once used for the symposiums she had chaired between various theologians and philosophers. She wept as she told Hervey one evening that she wished he was her son.[44] There were rallies and relapses throughout the autumn. In the second week of October, Hervey did not mention Caroline in a letter addressed from the palace to Stephen, who he seems to have worried had fallen into a depression.[45] Hervey left Hampton Court with Queen Caroline and the rest of the household thirteen days later on October 28, bound for St. James's, which Prince Frederick was ordered to vacate before his parents' arrival. Queen Caroline died there on November 20. Hervey had spent the last few nights of her life sleeping nearby on a couch, in case her breathing or pain caused her distress. Hearing the news that the Queen had died, Stephen asked if his brother, who had introduced them years earlier, would go to check on Hervey and was told that he was "as calm as ever I saw him, but afflicted to the greatest degree."[46] At the King's request, Hervey composed two of the epitaphs for Queen Caroline. When he felt capable of doing so, he wrote to Count Algarotti to express his thoughts on his late patron:

[T]hough real affection be a term as often lightly made use of, and as often prostituted as that of real friendship or real love, yet I assure you what I felt for her gave me a full right to express myself in those words. I know too the ridicule that generally attends an affectation of personal friendship for crowned heads; but you are so well acquainted with the manner in which I lived with her, that, if she had personal merit, you are sensible that I must have had the opportunities of finding it out; and if so, it would be a very hard fate indeed upon princes, if from those with whom they had lived in the same familiarity as if they had been private persons, they might not expect the same warmth of gratitude, which if they had been private persons they might have claimed in return. Upon my word, if I knew her, she was a thorough, wise, good and agreeable

woman; and the distinctions with which she always honored me, joined
to the satisfaction I had in her company, makes me look upon her death
to be as great a loss to my interest as to my pleasure, and makes my heart
regret the loss of her as much as my vanity or my ambition.[47]

When the Prime Minister heard that his greatest ally was dead, his reaction was somewhat less eloquent and nuanced. According to Lord Holland, Walpole looked up to the heavens to ask in theatrical self-pity, "My God, My God, why hast Thou forsaken me?" By the time of her death, Caroline had evidently regained her popularity in London, where the following graffiti was posted on the walls of a prominent London commercial building:

O DEATH, WHERE IS THY STING,
TO TAKE THE QUEEN, AND LEAVE THE KING?[48]

CHAPTER 22

GRACE AND FAVOR

A house of which one knew every room wasn't worth living in.

—Giuseppe Tomasi, Prince of Lampedusa,
The Leopard (1958)

Nearly all great buildings go through a period of obsolescence, a time when they seem out of date but not yet honorably antiquated. If they survive this period of their existence, and many—including most of Hampton Court's contemporaries—did not, they can become treasured symbols of the past. Hampton Court survived that treacherous stretch of her own history thanks to George III, king from 1760 until 1820, who became the first king since Henry VIII not to use the palace as a home. We know why, thanks to a comment made by the sixth of George's nine sons, Prince Augustus-Frederick, Duke of Sussex. As he wandered from room to room at Hampton Court during a visit as an adult, Augustus-Frederick wondered aloud which had been the spot where George II "struck my father. The blow so disgusted him that he could never afterwards be induced to think of it as a residence."[1]

Relations between George III's father, Prince Frederick, and Frederick's father, George II, had deteriorated further after Queen Caroline's death. They had not improved when, fourteen years later, Prince Frederick collapsed and died at the table while eating bread and butter with a cup of coffee. He had been caught in a downpour; then, upon returning home, had fallen asleep by an open window, which fatally aggravated preexisting health conditions, one of which may have been caused by a blow to the chest from a fast-bowled ball during a cricket match, or another sustained when he fell and hit his head during an altercation with the King.[2] After the Prince of Wales's death, the teenage Prince George's household was sometimes combined with his grandfather's, whose temper had grown no less foul as he aged.

Having endured so much unhappiness there in the nine years after his father's death, almost as soon as he came to the throne George III ordered the removal of many works of art and pieces of furniture from Hampton Court to decorate Windsor Castle, Kensington Palace, and Buckingham House.[3] As medical advances saw a progressive decline in the frequency and virulence of the once-annual outbreaks of plague in the capital, the royals had less need to bolt from the city at short notice, a factor that further decreased Hampton Court's utility. When George III developed an interest in reviving an antique palace as a place of convenient retreat from an increasingly industrialized London, his distressing memories of Hampton Court saw his attention settle instead on Windsor Castle.

George reigned through many momentous events in British history, including the mass mobilization of the abolitionist movement, which he supported, and calls for Catholic Emancipation, as well as American and Irish independence, which he did not.[4] The French Revolution occurred during his lifetime. Despite an earlier falling out over King Louis XVI's substantial support to the American revolutionaries in the 1770s and 1780s, George had privately admired Louis for his "sense of justice, candour, and rectitude [and the] simplicity and purity of his morals and private life," and he ordered mourning when the deposed French monarch was executed in 1793.[5] George III sheltered several surviving members of the French royal family by providing them with a country house in Buckinghamshire and use of the Palace of Holyroodhouse in Edinburgh. The French Revolution unintentionally also gave Hampton Court a new purpose when it was selected as a suitable home for another royal exile—George III's cousin Willem V, Prince of Orange—who sought asylum in Britain after his country was occupied by the French revolutionary armies. The exiled French royals were allegedly given homes elsewhere because Hampton Court was too close to London; George III distrusted Louis XVI's younger brother the Comte de Provence and "dreaded his intrigues."[6]

Despite his personal dislike of Hampton Court, George III was committed to preserving heritage; as a result, in the years since he had ceased to use it as a home, the King had set aside a suitable amount of money to ensure that the palace remained in good physical repair. He had authorized funds for much-needed conservation work to Verrio's murals on the King's Staircase in 1781.[7] The well-preserved palace was considered a perfectly decent venue for émigrés, and its residential program expanded. Since the reign of Edward II, Hampton Court had infrequently been used to provide rooms for favored royal servants in retirement, and George III had begun to do so more regularly. When the Prince of Orange moved into George II's former private apartments in 1793, it was not, therefore, the first time the estate had been used as a home for those with links to the royals, but the grant to an exiled prince of what had once been a king's suite marked a new phase in its utility. Piece by piece, rooms in the empty palace were turned into self-contained apartments that were awarded to those who had won the favor and received the grace of the sovereign. "Grace and favor" was, and is, the name usually given in conversation to this residential system.

When George III's long reign came to an end after sixty years, there was some discussion of Hampton Court being revived as a royal residence, but the march of technology and the passage of time ultimately made permanent his decision to withdraw the royal family from it. With the invention of the railways, Hampton Court offered no real attractions as a retreat. By the 1850s, the royals could travel greater distances when they wanted a holiday: Balmoral in Scotland, Osborne on the Isle of Wight, and Sandringham in Norfolk all eventually replaced Hampton Court's onetime appeal as a place to retreat, celebrate, or hunt. George's sons—kings George IV and William IV—and his granddaughter Queen Victoria continued his tradition of using Hampton Court as a boarding house for those judged worthy of the monarchy's largesse.

Tours of the palace had been taking place since at least the reign of

Elizabeth I, if not before, when the curious could, like Thomas Platter, supplement the caretakers' salaries with a bribe to let them in when the court was not in residence. George III had opened the palace's rooms to his relatives and retainers, and its grounds to his subjects. He spent a significant sum on renovating the overgrown gardens so that they could be enjoyed by visitors, even hiring Capability Brown—perhaps the greatest landscaper of the eighteenth century—to live and work at Hampton Court for a few years. After Brown left, the gardens were well cared for by a team headed by Thomas Haverfield, until he was indicted by a grand jury "on account of some fraudulent money concern" in the winter of 1804, at which point George III was still sufficiently interested in the gardens to involve himself in the royal household's response. Haverfield would have two months' salary, since, despite his fraud, the King pitied him: "[H]is health [is] so bad that his life has been almost daily in danger," advised a courtier. Care of the gardens was to pass to "William Padley, the foreman, [who is] assiduous and intelligent. . . . The Grape House and other material parts of the gardens seem to have been properly managed by him."[8]

A year after she succeeded to the throne in 1837, Queen Victoria extended her grandfather's policy by formally opening parts of Hampton Court's interiors to tourists. While the well-kept gardens remained popular, the early Victorian tourist experiment was haphazard. Most tours did not include the palace's run-down Great Hall; the omission was compared by one irked visitor to watching a performance of *Hamlet* that cut out the lead.

In 1844 the palace hosted more sovereigns than it had at any prior point in its history, when Queen Victoria visited her widowed aunt the Dowager Queen Adelaide, at her country retreat of Bushy House, which lay on the boundaries of the palace's estate. Joined by Queen Adelaide, who spent a great deal of her time at Bushy between her husband's death in 1837 and her own in 1849, Queen Victoria toured Hampton Court along with her husband, Prince Albert of Saxe-Coburg-Gotha, and their guests, the French king*

---

* The French monarchy was restored in 1814–15 and lasted under three kings until a revolution in 1848.

Louis-Philippe and his wife, Marie-Amélie of Naples and Sicily; Albert's uncle Léopold I, King of the Belgians, and his queen, Louise of Orléans; and Willem II and Anna of Russia, King and Queen of the Netherlands. King Louis-Philippe had turned Versailles into a museum to what he deemed the glories of French history. As with the British royals and Hampton Court, neither he nor any other member of the French royal house lived at Versailles.

The success of Louis-Philippe's transformation of Versailles into a repository of French history and a thriving tourist attraction may have inspired Queen Victoria and Prince Albert to consider the same for Hampton Court. Work was carried out on the Great Hall, which was reopened to visitors after a restoration that included ripping out the small private theater installed for George I and returning it to how it would have looked for earlier inhabitants. The bright floor tiles laid during Henry VIII's reign were long gone, so the Stuarts' timber boards stayed. Capitalizing on the visiting public's interest in Henry VIII and his half dozen wives, the Great Hall's west-facing windows were replaced with stained glass depicting their respective coats of arms, which was the first time that the heraldry of all seven had been on display together. Cardinal Wolsey's crests were added to the bay window in the alcove before the hall gives way to the Great Watching Chamber. There had been a remarkable discovery for the conservationists when they later found, carved in a corner of the hall, the intertwined initials of Anne Boleyn and Henry VIII, which had apparently escaped the stonemasons and carpenters sent in to remove every architectural trace of her following her downfall in 1536.

One man who benefited from the decision for the palace to be transformed into a museum, while also continuing to serve as a grace-and-favor compound, was the son of a blacksmith and a maid. By the summer of 1862, Michael Faraday had lived at Hampton Court for several years thanks to the grace-and-favor scheme. He and his wife had been granted a redbrick house on the estate, located on the opposite side of the bank and river to the palace itself. Following his retirement from public lectures, the seventy-year-old professor often took his wife from their house into the palace to enjoy the view from some benches over the gardens toward the Long

Water. His wife Sarah Faraday was sixty-two, a silversmith's daughter, and she and Michael had met many years earlier at church. Michael had petitioned the relevant authorities for permission to bring Sarah's wheelchair through the palace, as prior to that, it was not allowed.

Behind their bench were a grace-and-favor suite occupied by Robert Walpole's granddaughter, Lady Harriet Hoste, and another nearby granted to the Marquess of Donegall*'s widowed sister-in-law, Lady Honoria-Anastasia Chichester. Lady Honoria-Anastasia had won the proverbial lottery in room allocations by snagging one with a drawing room, master bedroom, servants' bedroom, private kitchen, pantry, lavatory, common room for her servants, and, detached from her suite and overlooking the interior of the Fountain Court, three rooms for entertaining. Some of the Faradays' neighbors had, however, moved to Hampton Court more through need than desire. Two floors above Lady Hoste's suite, the rooms originally created for William III's favorite Arnold van Keppel had been granted in 1861 to Mrs. Amelia-Maria Montagu-Villiers, the Bishop of Durham's widow, who had applied for rooms via the Church of England after her husband died deeply in debt. Her petition had made its way up to the Church's Supreme Governor, Queen Victoria, who approved it. The Queen had also allocated the apartments previously occupied by George II's daughters to Elizabeth Doherty, widow of a Lord Chief Justice who discovered, after her husband's funeral, that he had invested and lost all their money in failed railway companies.

Victorian Hampton Court still employed a staff of servants. Some also had part-time jobs elsewhere, which might explain, frustratingly, why so many of them are absent from the Hampton Court returns for the 1861 census. Thanks to the 1841 and 1881 censuses, we can see that they included carpenters, watchmen, plumbers, bricklayers, gas lamplighters, caretakers, turncocks, and a housekeeper, and that a school had been constructed on the grounds for the servants' children, some of whom caused quite a contre-

---

* Although Dhún na nGall, the Irish county it is named after, now spells its name in English as Donegal, the marquessate continues to use the antique spelling of Donegall dating from the time this aristocratic title was created in the seventeenth century.

temps when they were caught defacing three works by the great sixteenth-century German artist Hans Holbein and one by his contemporary and compatriot Albrecht Dürer. Grace-and-favor dwellers could be equally troublesome. Lord Henry and Lady Louisa Gordon, in particular, had been severely reprimanded by the royal household's representatives after a boozy picnic in the palace gardens, during which, as they drank and the sun sank, they had their servants light a fire dangerously close to three elms dating from the era of Henry VIII. Among the five of their eight children living with them was their son Augustus, an incorrigibly frequent graffitist of the palace's No Smoking signs, which were posted throughout for the two hundred thousand tourists who visited Hampton Court over the course of an average year by the middle of Victoria's reign.

The trains that bore the royals away from Hampton Court carried the people to it. The railway station was built on the other side of the river, next to the bridge, meaning that tourists had a very short walk to the palace. The nineteenth-century British reading public was obsessed with stories of Tudor and Stuart drama; Queen Victoria ordered the first official grave-stones to be placed over the sites where Anne Boleyn, Catherine Howard, and Jane Grey were buried, and millions of her subjects read some of the first best-selling popular histories, including Agnes and Elizabeth Strick-land's multivolume *Lives of the Queens of England*. Many of those readers then made their way to Hampton Court to see the nation's only surviving and accessible Tudor palace.[9] As Victorian Britain discovered its love of neo-Gothic and antique styles of architecture, many enthusiasts also made an excursion to Hampton Court a priority.

Hampton Court's healthy visitor numbers were partly a result of the Crown's decision not to charge admission. The choice was applauded by some of the first American tourists to visit the palace, one of whom, the novelist Nathaniel Hawthorne, noted:

> *Soldiers were standing sentinel at the exterior gateways, and at the various doors of the palace; but they admitted everybody without question, and without fee. Policemen, or other attendants, were in most of the*

rooms, but interfered with nobody; so that in this respect, it was one of the most pleasantest places to visit that I have found in England. A good many people of all classes, were strolling through the rooms. . . . The English Government [sic] keep it up, and to admit the people freely to it, for it is impossible for even a Republican not to feel something like awe—at least a profound respect—for all this state . . . and its permanence, too, enduring from age to age.[10]

The traffic was not appreciated by an admiral's widow Lady Jane Bourchier who, ensconced in what had once been Prince Frederick's private apartments, seethed with loathing of the day-trippers peering through her windows. She also resented their loud chatter and the cloud of tobacco smoke the tourists exhaled the second they were outside in the palace gardens, next to her windows, and could light up a cigarette.[11] She contacted the police and the Lord Chamberlain on the issue, to no avail.

Michael Faraday was more sanguine about the interruptions brought by the tourists. After he and Sarah had taken the air in the palace gardens, Michael would help his wife into her wheelchair, which he sometimes pushed back to their home by passing through the cloisters of the Fountain Court. It would be four more decades until the cloister lamps were converted to electricity, a development made possible in part by Faraday's genius and the career that had brought him to live in a palace from what he described as "a most ordinary" childhood in late Georgian London.[12]

His parents were both northerners—his father from Yorkshire, his mother from Westmorland—who had migrated south, leaving behind his family's smithy and her father's farm, in the hope of building a more af-

---

* The visit to Hampton Court made Hawthorne reflective about monarchy and history. On the one hand, as he wandered around the palace, he thought of "each royal generation adding new splendors to those accumulated by their predecessors. If one views the matter in another way, to be sure, we may feel indignant that such dolt-heads, rowdies, and every way mean people, as many of the English sovereigns have been, should inhabit these stately halls, contrasting its splendors with their littleness; but, on the whole, I readily consented within myself to be impressed for a moment with the feeling that royalty has its glorious side."

fluent life for their children. Michael went to a day school near their new home, where he recalled learning "the rudiments of reading, writing, and arithmetic." When he was not in school, he helped his mother around the house or played with friends in the neighborhood streets. When he was a little older, he got a part-time job as an errand boy before his father negotiated an apprenticeship for him with a bookseller. There Michael began to read some of his master's publications, such as *Conversations on Chemistry* by Jane Marcet and *Improvement of the Mind* by Isaac Watts. A love for science was born as he read everything he could find on the subject; he started to spend his spare time attending scientists' lectures at the Royal Institute, a recently founded London charitable educational trust set-up with the aim of increasing access to the sciences, where he made friends with young men of similar interests and formed his "desire to be engaged in scientific occupation, even though of the lowest kind."[13] His zeal, his regular attendance, and his intelligence caught the attention of the lecturers. One of them, Sir Humphry Davy, Professor of Chemistry, had sustained eye damage from a small explosion at his laboratory in 1812; he recruited Faraday as his amanuensis.

From amanuensis and laboratory assistant, Faraday had been invited to deliver lectures in the institutions he had visited as a teenager and to join committees dedicated to furthering scientific research. In his early thirties, Faraday discovered a new compound of hydrogen and carbon, which, after subsequent analysis by a fellow scientist, was called benzene. As his fame grew, among his correspondents were Ada King, Countess of Lovelace, whose work as a mathematician produced an algorithm so sophisticated and prescient that, years before computers were invented, she can now be regarded as one of the world's first "computer programmers." The Victorian era was one in which expertise was celebrated socially—particularly for scientific innovators, medical researchers, and engineers. In this environment, Faraday's career seemed unstoppable. For twenty-three years, beginning in 1829, he was a Professor of Chemistry at the Royal Military Academy, and, as with the Countess of Lovelace's algorithms, his research was to have implications long after his life. Faraday's discoveries of electromagnetic rotation later became the foundational principle behind the electric motor. He researched diamagnetism, the optic axis of crystals, terrestrial magnetism, the magnetic susceptibility of gases. Perhaps most famously, he proved electromagnetic induction, which laid the foundations for the practical, widespread use of electricity. His work with colleagues on electrochemical matters gave rise to nomenclature such as *anode, cathode, electrode, electrolyte, electrolysis*, and *ion*. He believed in the practical applicability of science, with some of his other work including proposals for the optical adjustment of lighthouse lenses and new designs for their chimneys.

In 1844 Faraday was called as an expert witness in the inquiry into the Haswell Colliery mining disaster. An explosion killed fourteen miners immediately and trapped eighty-one more inside the collapsed mine, where they suffocated to death. Only four men escaped with their lives. A member of the rescue party recorded:

> *The first body that was found was that of John Willis, a boy of 13. It was brought [up] at 9 o'clock and others followed. . . . Some [victims] had placed their caps in their mouths, no doubt with a view to preventing inhalation. . . . At one part of the mine, at the Brockley Flat, there were about [twenty] found who had been in the act of getting their clothes. Some were dressed, others nearly so. In the pit, it must be understood, the men worked nearly naked, their only dress being a small shirt and short trousers half down the thighs. These poor fellows were lying huddled together. As if they had felt what was coming, and had so clasped each other to die. Death from choke-damp is not instantaneous, and probably most of them lived for a quarter of an hour or more, and some much longer with the certainty of quick coming death.*[14]

The Haswell disaster shocked the British public, forcing many to confront the human cost of industrialization and, in particular, conditions in the mines. Coal, ubiquitous in powering everything from ships to factories to fireplaces in private homes, now formed the backbone of the British economy. The victims' relatives feared that the inquiry would be a whitewash for the mine's owners, so they asked a local lawyer, Mr. Mather, author of the previous statement, to help them. With "one or two friends of the pitmen," he went on their behalf to petition the Tory Prime Minister, Sir Robert Peel, to provide independent expert witnesses. As Mather notes, the Prime Minister agreed, with the result that "professor Leydell* [*sic*] and Faraday were appointed to attend and assist at the adjournment of the inquest."[15] Through his work for the Haswell inquiry, Faraday had made recommendations for better safety and ventilation in mines, which might have saved many lives, and a great deal of pain, in the decades ahead—if some influential mineowners had not waited until an election then successfully lobbied the new government to defer implementation. The public forgot about Faraday's proposals, and there were more mining disasters in the future.

Like the coal being used throughout the United Kingdom, the fuel brought to Hampton Court for use in the apartments' many private fireplaces was still mined in brutally dangerous conditions. The amount of sooty smoke pouring from the palace chimneys was considerable, since, even in summer, fires were still sometimes judged necessary to heat the rooms at night. There were some exceptions, for not all in the grace-and-favor community were permanent residents. The two fireplaces in the rooms allocated to Lady Sophia-Eliza Fox-Strangways, whose suite was above the eastern cloisters of the Fountain Court, were often unlit; she spent so much of her time at German spa towns that the Lord Chamberlain eventually threatened to terminate her lease, since there were others waiting for a chance to live at Hampton Court. Lady Sophia-Eliza's late husband had been the grandson of Lord Hervey's love, Stephen Fox; when Lord Hervey's heavily edited memoirs were published posthumously in the 1840s, his scorching observations helped stimulate interest in the era of George II, producing yet more footfall to Hampton Court.[16]

Many of those living at the palace in 1862 on a more frequent basis than Sophia-Eliza Fox-Strangways were entitled to bring their own servants or

---

* Sir Charles Lyell (1797-1875).

relatives with them, as courtiers had between Henry VIII and George II. The widowed Mrs. Sarah Pennycuick was joined by her unmarried daughter and five grandchildren, as well as their governess, a cook, a housemaid, and a coachman. Her neighbor, Mrs. Lucy Ellice, widow of the late Whig MP for Harwich, lived with her two daughters, a niece, and six servants.

Among the extra residents were the ghosts—at least according to many visitors, and to several grace-and-favor residents who hosted séances in their rooms to try to contact the palace's former inhabitants. It was during this period that visitors first mentioned sensing or seeing the ghosts of Queen Catherine Howard and Elizabeth I's lady-in-waiting Sybil Penne. Lady Jane Hildyard, who occupied the apartment between the Fountain and Clock courts, repeatedly felt unsettled by the presence of two ghosts. She wrote to the Lord Chamberlain's office about how unsatisfactory this was, to which she received the acerbic reply that Her Majesty's officials had much under their control, but, alas, the domestic tribulations of the unquiet dead were not one of them. Lady Hildyard considered herself vindicated when two skeletons were found buried beneath the Fountain Court's cloisters during digging there to install new drainpipes.[17] They were probably the remains of the two workmen killed by the collapse of the southern façade in 1689, which suggests strongly that the money entrusted by Queen Mary II to a courtier for their funerals and families was pocketed by the official, who then dumped their bodies beneath the cobblestones. Lady Hildyard felt vindicated that the "stupid Board of Works has at last found the two wretched men . . . who have been haunting me for years." However, rather than believe she had been communicating with workmen, dead or alive, she apparently accepted the wholly untrue story that Oliver Cromwell had murdered two dashing Royalist soldiers at Hampton Court during the civil war and that it was their specters that haunted her apartment.[18]

Spiritualism, the belief that the dead could be contacted through séances, was widespread and growing by the 1860s. Technology had rendered commonplace what had once been thought impossible, including messages through wires from one corner of the world to another. Why could it not do the same for other boundaries of geography, such as the one between the worlds? This development distressed Michael Faraday. Earlier in his career, he had been interested in, then researched and disproved, the eighteenth-century theory of Memerism, a belief that there was a natural force, or energy, surrounding all humans that could be used to cure them of many ailments, perhaps even of lethal diseases. Mesmerism had been as much a craze in the Georgian era as Spiritualism became in the Victorian, but if Faraday thought his investigations into the two would be similar, he was disabused of that mistake by the torrent of abuse he received after denouncing Spiritualism in a published letter, which left him "shocked at the flood of impious & irrational matter which has rolled before me in one form or another since I wrote my *Times* letter."[19] Faraday did not mock every Spiritualist or dismiss them as confidence tricksters; he concluded that some of Spiritualism's most impressive features, such as tables seemingly turning or levitating, were in fact likely the result of quasi-involuntary muscular actions on the part of believers, so sincere in their faith, or their desire to talk with their loved ones, that they were unaware that their body was unconsciously fulfilling for them what they needed or wanted to see. Nonetheless, the many abusive letters that he received after publishing his conclusions led him to suggest that the British education system must be "very greatly deficient in some very important principle," if so many of his fellow citizens believed in things like ectoplasm emanating from their Spiritualist guides.

Faraday's opposition to Spiritualism was both scientific and religious. "I cannot help thinking about these delusions of mind," he wrote, "& the credulity which makes many think that supernatural works are wrought where all is either fancy or knavery are related to that which is foretold of the latter days & the prevalence of unclean spirits."[20] The phrase "unclean spirits" is used twenty-one times in the New Testament, and for Faraday, Spiritualism was both scientifically disprovable and morally worrisome. He and Sarah were Sandemanians, an offshoot of Presbyterianism. Sandemanianism teaches that the crucifixion of Christ was a sacrifice so enormous as to be sufficient to atone for the sins of everyone, even those who did not believe in Christianity—an interpretation of salvation that prompted fierce disputes between Sandemanians and other Protestant denominations. When Faraday was offered an honorary doctorate from the University of Oxford, many high Anglicans teaching there tried to block it on the grounds that Faraday was a religious Dissenter, a sometimes pejorative term for a "Nonconformist," meaning a non-Anglican Protestant. Even within the Nonconformist Protestant sects, Sandemanian teachings on how non-Christians could go to Heaven were often considered heretical.

Faraday and his brother Robert became deacons in their church; from then on, Michael would, if necessary, cancel lectures to visit sick members of his congregation. He delivered free lectures to encourage children's love of science, became a benefactor-subscriber to the London Orphan Asylum, officiated at Sandemanian baptisms, preached sermons, and attended church twice weekly, on Sundays and Wednesdays. Despite his professorship at the Royal Military Academy, he declined on religious grounds to contribute his skills to the development of weaponry during the Crimean War of 1853–56. In his work, Faraday promoted a theistic view of the universe, since he believed that science did not disprove religion but rather that scientific research "conveys the gifts of God to man" by helping to uncover the inestimable majesty and complexity of the codes that God had woven into the fabric of creation, which Faraday argued was the universe, "things seen and unseen."[21]

The Faradays' religion prompted them to decline the offer of a reserved pew at weekly Anglican services in Hampton Court's chapel, with Michael replying, "We are dissenters and have our own place of worship in London."[22] As they walked beneath the archway of the Anne Boleyn Gate and into the Base Court, the Faradays passed the ground-floor apartment of Reverend Baily, Hampton Court's chaplain and a Fellow of Clare College, Cambridge, who may have wished there were more palace-dwelling Dissenters. The poor man was routinely plagued by complaints from the other residents about the allocation of pews in the chapel and ensuing rage at what those allocations reflected about precedence, as well as grace-and-favorites' dislike at the number of nonresidents who crowded into the Chapel Royal every Sunday. By the summer of 1862, the discontents most impressively regular and voluble in their complaints were the widowed Mrs. Fanny Pottinger, from the second floor of the Fountain Court, and Lady Maria Torrens, denizen of a third-floor apartment overlooking the Privy Gardens; the latter felt that subpar pews had been set aside for her, her niece, her housekeeper, her cook, and her maid. The servants were in a separate pew, of course, but theirs still needed to be a better spot than those occupied by other residents' staff.

The palace's entrance gate was two stories shorter than it had been when Cardinal Wolsey first had it installed. Its stability had given cause for concern in the reigns of Charles I, Charles II, James II, George I, and George II, and, under George III, the decision had been taken to reduce its stories from five to three.[23] As Michael pushed Sarah's chair through the entrance gate toward the gardens, they passed the quarters of the palace's redoubtable housekeeper, Mrs. Sarah Grundy, whose quest for moral rectitude was the reason why there was a room on one of the unused top floors in Hampton Court to which only she had the key. She stashed there any of the palace's treasures that she deemed unsuitable for Christian eyes. Among those she had shuttered away were Van Dyck's *Cupid and Psyche* and a nude Venus by Cariani, which she would only show upon receiving express written orders from the exasperated Lord Chamberlain. It is hard to believe that Sarah Grundy was thrilled with having rooms so close to two divorced grace-and-favor recipients: Augusta, Lady Paget, who had just about weathered the scandal caused by marrying her second husband only two days after she was divorced by her first, and Elizabeth Hamilton, former Marchioness of Abercorn, whose husband, one of the greatest landowners in the north of Ireland, was so famously polite that, when warned that his wife was about to leave him in the dead of night in a rented cab, he "sent a message begging her to take the family coach, as it ought never to be said that Lady Abercorn left her husband's roof in a hack."

Passing the quarters of Lady Paget, the former Lady Abercorn, and the fearsome Mrs. Grundy, the Faradays had no cause to go near the tennis courts, which lay to their right. An early professional tennis star, George Lambert, was another grace-and-favor resident, and Prince Albert had been an enthusiastic player. His locker's name plaque remained in the changing rooms, reading *H. R. H. Prince Albert*. The Faradays owed their favor to Prince Albert's grace. After attending some of Faraday's lectures, the Prince Consort was convinced that Michael was one of the best British minds of the century. A great patron of the sciences, Albert stepped in to help when Faraday began to falter. He had been struggling for a long time. The exhausting nature of Faraday's research into electricity had, in late 1839, caused a mental breakdown, the consequences of which, including debilitating vertigo, plagued Michael for the rest of his life. He frequently became dizzy, sometimes giddy, suffering excruciating migraines and, little by little, more frequent short-term memory loss. In August 1832 Faraday began to track his many projects by numbering each paragraph in his research journals. Paragraph 16,041, his last, was added on March 6, 1860. His final book, *Experimental Researches in Chemistry and Physics*, had been published the year before. In 1862 he gave his last lecture—the topic was gas furnaces—and after that he stepped back, as far as he could, to focus on his health and Sarah's.

From the mid-1840s, finding the city's pace and polluted air disagreeable, the Faradays had only lived in London by renting a house for a month or so each year. Otherwise they lived in the countryside, which Prince Albert helped make a permanent arrangement by offering them their grace-and-favor house at Hampton Court. Initially, Faraday declined the Prince's offer because both he and Sarah worried that they would be expected to pay for its maintenance and decoration. That, after all, was one of the main justifications for the whole grace-and-favor system. While some rooms were allocated to those in need, like the Bishop of Durham's widow, others were gifted to very wealthy individuals such as the aforementioned Honoria-Anastasia Chichester. As the Earl of Lincoln put it to a Parliamentary committee in 1842, it "was infinitely better that the apartments of the palace should be inhabited and kept in repair by those inhabitants, than that they should be allowed to go into decay, to be ultimately repaired at the public expense, or perhaps sold at auction. Would it not be revolting to every lover of this country to have a palace erected by Wolsey and restored by King William, sold at auction?"[24]

The Faradays were neither in the financial straits of some of the Hampton Court widows, who could therefore expect aid from the court, nor were they rich enough to easily accept the burden of a house like the one offered to them by Prince Albert. In recognition of his services to the country and the progress of science, Albert promised that the Faradays' bills at Hampton Court would be settled out of the royal household's budget, and the Crown would also foot the bill in decorating it for them. This meant a great deal to Faraday, not only in the obvious financial sense but also morally. As a Sandemanian, he was technically required to reject party politics, which he believed were divisive and corrupt. He had declined the honor of a knighthood on those grounds, since he believed the British honors system had become too political by being more in the gift of politicians than of kings and queens. He could, and did, however, accept royal patronage, as shown by his acceptance of the Prussian Order of Merit, awarded to him by an admiring King Friedrich-Wilhelm IV in 1842, and the Légion d'honneur from Emperor Napoleon III in 1855.* Faraday wrote to a friend, "We are now at Hampton Court, in the house which the Queen has given me. We shall use it in the summer months, and go into town in the cold weather and the Season. I believe it will be a comfortable pleasure for the years that remain of life."

The Queen and Prince Albert's help with the Hampton Court house also meant much to Faraday because the Prince Consort had continued to arrange things for him and Sarah, even as Albert struggled with two great problems of his own. The first was a diplomatic crisis called the Trent Affair, which was the closest Britain ever came to involvement in the American Civil War. Prince Albert had lobbied hard with his allies in the government to defeat those who wanted to exploit the affair to ensure

---

* Faraday may not always have been so firm in his political principles; in his younger days, he had been prepared to accept a pension from the British government until the Tories unexpectedly lost an election right before the Prime Minister authorized the payments to Faraday, who was then so mocked and belittled by the new Prime Minister, Lord Melbourne, that King William IV had stepped in to personally order the premier to apologize and then arranged Faraday's pension himself.

Britain entered the conflict on the side of the Confederacy. He had also been distressed around that time when his eldest son, the Prince of Wales, while serving with his regiment in Ireland, lost his virginity to an actress. The deeply religious Albert interpreted the liaison as a rejection by his son of every value he and his mother had tried to inculcate him with—and a worrying throwback to the indulgent womanizing of his great-uncles, which had shaken the monarchy's popularity in the previous decades. Albert was already ill from the typhoid that would kill him as he grappled with both political crisis and personal worries; he died at Windsor Castle in December 1861, aged forty-two, shortly before the Faradays spent Christmas in their Hampton Court home.

The Faradays' pretty redbrick house, with five bedrooms, a dining room, a kitchen, and a small garden, lay near the same bridge used by the tourists as they walked to and from the town's railway station. They accessed it by crossing the bridge that traversed the river Thames, which, in London, Michael had helped lead one of the first major campaigns to clean up after the Industrial Revolution. The Faradays had no children, and their nieces, Margery Ann Reid and Jane Barnard, stayed often with them at the Hampton Court house for extended periods. After six years of residence, Michael died there on August 25, 1867, and he was buried in the Sandemanian section of Highgate Cemetery in London. Queen Victoria had the lease at Hampton Court extended so that the invalided Sarah could stay there, cared for by her nieces and other family, until her death twelve years later.

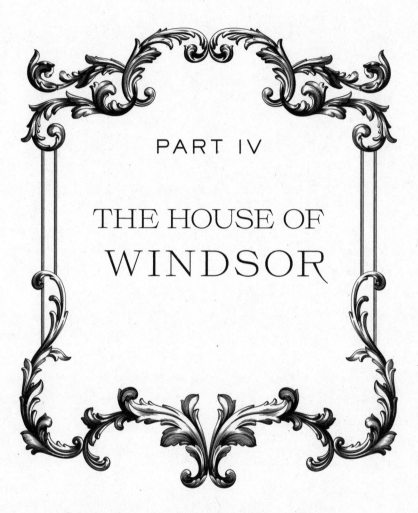

PART IV

THE HOUSE OF
WINDSOR

It is the silence that she hears, the silence of lost years.

—Rose Tremain, *Music and Silence* (1999)

CHAPTER 23

THE FALLEN OAK

Sir, I am informed there is to be a Funeral of a Brave Life at London on 11 of November. Will it be my dearest Boy? God knows who it will be as my youngest boy was killed on Oct. 2 of 1917 and I cannot get no information where he was buried or anything.

—Letter from Mrs. Rose Else to King George V (1920)

On leaving his grace-and-favor apartment—number 7 on the Royal Mews, which had once been the queen consort's stables before it was converted to use for staff accommodation—fifty-five-year-old Thomas Abnett walked across the Hampton Court cobblestones through the miserable autumn weather of 1920, which was sandwiched between one of the coldest summers in memory and a winter in which the south of England was battered by the worst snow it had seen since the blizzards of 1891.[1] Abnett checked on the palace's hundreds of lights, cleaning, maintaining, and repairing as he went. His wife, Ellen, remained at home, as wind and rain lashed the palace and the nearby town cemetery where their third son, twenty-three-year-old Herbert, had been buried the previous July. Herbert's lifelong struggles with poor health had been the reason he was excused from service in the First World War that had claimed the lives of his brothers Richard and Sidney. Both had served on the Western Front, where Richard was killed in action in September 1916, aged twenty-four;

twenty-year-old Sidney died seven months later in April 1917. Jack, who had enlisted in the Royal Navy when he was eighteen, was the only one of the four Abnett brothers still alive by 1920.

As Thomas went about his work inside Hampton Court, and Ellen welcomed Jack or his sisters, Elsie and Irene, for a visit, a "mighty" oak tree was cut down in the palace grounds. The United Kingdom was preparing to mark, a few weeks later, the second anniversary of the end of the Great War. Just over 846,000 citizens of the British Empire had lost their lives in the war: about 418,000 were, like Richard Abnett, killed in battle; 167,000, including Sidney Abnett, expired not long after battles from their wounds; 16,000 died as prisoners of war; and 113,000 died from disease, a category that included, but was not limited to, complications arising from their injuries. For the 161,000 declared "missing, presumed dead," even the faintest embers of hope had been extinguished after the war ended in 1918. Grief at this level of loss was widespread and deep, and was exacerbated by the fact that the majority of the dead had been buried in Belgium or France, where many of the British forces had been deployed to join their allies in the trenches dug to halt a German invasion.

Except for the comparatively small number who had been sent back to military hospitals in Britain, where they had subsequently died of their wounds, the approximately 850,000 bodies buried abroad fell broadly into two categories. The first were those who had been identified at the time of their deaths and whose graves were marked with headstones bearing their names, their regiment, and possibly some personal details. The second were the hundreds of thousands who had either been so disfigured or buried so quickly that they could not be identified and whose resting places were therefore capped after 1918 by gravestones identifying them as *Known unto God*. For many bereaved families, this meant they had no grave at which to mourn. To exhume and transport hundreds of thousands of bodies was not only logistically staggering but, from a health perspective, foolish. Something, however, had to be done. In preparation for a National Day of Mourning on November 11, 1920, the decision was reached to exhume the body of one of the unidentified dead, whose remains would be transported back to Britain in order for people to pay their respects at ceremonies in London, after which the body would be interred at Westminster Abbey, where it could offer a focal point for the bereaved. The term Unknown Soldier was replaced by that of Unknown Warrior, so as to ensure that all branches of the military and their families could mourn, and since naval personnel had first been deployed on land only after 1916, the order was given to select a body from those who had fallen in combat between 1916 and 1918.

The use of an oak from the Hampton Court estate to produce the Unknown Warrior's coffin was allegedly suggested by the King. George V, Queen Victoria's grandson, who had inherited the throne upon his father's death in 1910, had been dubious about the Unknown Warrior plan; his Private Secretary, Lord Stamfordham, informed Randall Davidson, Archbishop of Canterbury, that the King was "not sympathetic" to the proposal.[2] Davidson shared the King's misgivings—he disliked the designs for the war memorial under construction in Whitehall and due to be unveiled by the King on November 11, which was to be inscribed with a simple dedication to *The Glorious Dead*. Davidson worried that the veneration of veterans, and the memorialization of the fallen, would become something akin to a secular religion. Christianity's teachings were that the dead were not rendered glorious by military service, nor by anything on Earth, and Davidson criticized nearly every proposal leading up to the commemoration.

"The monument," he complained, "is pagan," and George V initially marched hand in hand with his archbishop's concerns. As late as the second week of October 1920, communications were still bouncing back and forth between the King's staff at Buckingham Palace, the Prime Minister's at Downing Street, and the Archbishop's in Lambeth Palace.[3] Hearing rumors of the King's reluctance, Maud Cazalet, a socialite whose twenty-two-year-old son Edward had been killed when an enemy shell struck his trench, took up her pen to write directly to Lord Stamfordham and inform him that "His Majesty's decision will be a great disappointment to many people who feel as I do, that as our sons gave their lives for their *King* and Country we would have liked the King to be the centre figure on the memorial day."[4]

Observing the public's growing enthusiasm for both the unveiling of the Cenotaph and the repatriation of an Unknown Warrior, the King reconsidered. In his ten years on the throne, George V had shown himself surprisingly attuned to the public mood and prepared to be flexible toward it, a tendency that explains why, in 1917, he had jettisoned his dynasty's German-sounding surname of Saxe-Coburg-Gotha to replace it with Windsor. In about the second week of October 1920, he admitted that he had been wrong about the Unknown Warrior. He encouraged Archbishop Davidson, as well as the leaders of other religious denominations, to send representatives to the Cenotaph and to a specifically Christian funeral for the Unknown Warrior at Westminster. Preparations proceeded more smoothly. On October 22, instructions were sent from the War Office in London to the British Department of Graves Registration and Enquiry (DGRE) in France "in connection with the internment of 'An Unknown Warrior' in Westminster Abbey on Armistice Day:—D.G.R.&E. will exercise its discretion as to the location from which the body is exhumed. . . . Under instructions to be issued later, the body will be conveyed to Calais and there placed in a full sized coffin, which will be sent out from England."[5]

The formerly reluctant George V became one of the most enthusiastic supporters of the Unknown Warrior's memorial. He ordered a crusader's sword to be removed from the armory at the Tower of London and sent to France, where he wanted it to rest on the Warrior's coffin until the funeral. At a time when the medieval crusades were still unambiguously presented by British historians as the apogee of chivalry, the message behind the sword's use for the 1920 memorials could not have been clearer to contemporaries. Victorian and Edwardian interest in Hampton Court had led to the palace being regarded as an ark of British history; hence George V's insistence that the Unknown Warrior's coffin should be made from one of Hampton Court's ancient oak trees. From the estate, the felled wood was sent to London, where it was crafted into a coffin that was lined with zinc. A lighter shell was sent ahead for the transportation of the Warrior's remains. The Hampton Court coffin, and the crusader's sword, were placed on a southbound train to be embarked upon a warship for its journey across the English Channel to France.

French gravediggers, working at night, extracted four cadavers from the graves of the unidentified British war dead in the military cemeteries, one from each of the main battle campaigns on the Western Front: the Aisne, the Somme, Arras, and Ypres. The gravedigging teams did not work together, nor were they told anything about why they had been hired.[6] The four sets of remains were then conveyed separately to a British Expeditionary Force base in St. Pol, on the outskirts of Dunkirk, where they were taken to the chapel, the entrance of which was guarded by British soldiers. Each set of remains was then individually draped in a British flag. At about midnight, General Louis Wyatt, a forty-six-year-old Londoner and General Commanding Officer of British troops still stationed in the region, entered the chapel, alone save for his adjutant, Colonel Gell. Neither Wyatt nor Gell knew which of the four had come from which battlefield. The lighter interior coffin shell from England was already waiting in the chapel. Wyatt wrote:

The four bodies lay on stretchers, each covered by a Union Jack. In front of the altar was the shell of the coffin which had been sent over from England to receive the remains. I selected one and with the assistance of Col. Gell placed it in the shell, we screwed down the lid. The other bodies were removed and reburied in the military cemetery outside my headquarters at St. Pol. I had no idea even of the area from which the body I had selected had come. The following morning the Church of England, the Roman Catholic, and the Non-Conformist chaplains held a service in the chapel. On the same day, at noon, the shell, under escort, was sent to Boulogne, where it was placed in a plain oak coffin.[7]

Before it left the base, Wyatt posted a notice for personnel to read: "The Camp Chapel will be open from 10.30 to 11.30 hours in order that all ranks who wish to do so may review the coffin containing the remains of The Unknown British Warrior." According to an officer's wife who paid her respects, "the hushed thrill in the camp all that day was marvellous. The Unknown Warrior was taken to Boulogne in an army ambulance with a bodyguard of eight sergeants." There it was placed in the "magnificent coffin" that had arrived from Hampton Court.[8]

In Boulogne, the Unknown Warrior lay overnight in state at the local château's Chapelle Ardente, where it was provided with a guard of honor by the French army. The next morning, officers arrived as pallbearers, while the coffin "was placed on a French military wagon and under the escort of the French troops taken to Boulogne Quay, where a British destroyer was waiting." As was the tall and lean figure of Major Samuel Fitz-Simon, a thirty-two-year-old survivor of the war in which he had served with the Royal Irish Rifles, and who had helped General Wyatt with the logistics of this latest mission. Known to his friends and family either by his middle name of Ernest or his nickname, Fitz, in the two years since the Great War ended, he had delayed returning to his home in south Belfast to stay in France and help with the DGRE's work.[9] As the coffin arrived, Fitz-Simon, whose youngest brother, Jack, had been killed a few hundred yards from him while they fought at the Battle of the Somme, broke protocol by losing his temper, and "there was quite a row at this point, as some French general had sent some apparently battered and ancient transport wagon to take the coffin."[10] The major's recollections are corroborated by photographs taken that day and held either in his family's collection or at the Imperial War Museum in London. Major Fitz-Simon, having been closely involved in the logistics surrounding the repatriation, was furious at the way in which specific instructions concerning the transportation of the remains had been ignored.

A minor diplomatic incident was avoided by the unexpected arrival on the quayside of Maréchal Ferdinand Foch, former French chief of the army staff and supreme allied commander, who had been the man to accept in person Imperial Germany's documents of surrender in 1918. He arrived at the harbor "to do honour to [the] body of an unknown British Soldier on its departure from France. I would suggest," wrote the British ambassador in Paris, "that His Majesty's government should send a message of thanks to Marshal Foch who has chosen to do this entirely of his own initiative."[11] Perhaps impressed rather than offended by Fitz-Simon's outburst, Foch gave the major his card to commemorate the occasion; Fitz-Simon kept it for the rest of his life.[12] The coffin then received its naval escort as it was maneuvered onto the warship HMS *Verdun* for its voyage to England.

A day later, the Unknown Warrior's coffin lay on a gun carriage in front of the Cenotaph, which was almost completely covered in an enormous British flag until the King pulled the cord, and it was unveiled to the people. But it was the coffin, apparently, in which the vast crowds were more interested, as noted by a journalist for *The Scotsman* newspaper, who himself became emotional at how the lone Warrior "was symbolical of the whole phantom host . . . Britain's exiled dead, scattered in graves known and unknown in every corner of the world."[13] George V, joined by his two eldest sons, the Prince of Wales and the Duke of York, wore military uniform with a black mourning band around his arm. At eleven o'clock in the morning, church bells tolled throughout the United Kingdom to commemorate the eleventh hour of the eleventh day of the eleventh month, when the war had ended and the guns had fallen silent. In memoriam, so would the people, in the first example of an annual tradition that endures to the present day. The silence of 1920, however, was more symbolic than actual. There was so much raw grief among the crowd that "many sobbed aloud."[14] After two minutes, a bugler played the Last Post, a military summons for soldiers to return to base at the end of the day and selected for the service to commemorate all those who now would never return. Wreaths were laid at the Cenotaph, the national anthem was played, hymns were sung, and the cortege moved off toward Westminster Abbey. The King placed a wreath on the coffin himself and then, accompanied by his sons, fell into step behind it as they followed the coffin in procession to the abbey. In the crowds who had come to pay their respects were many survivors of the war, some of them still in hospital clothes, some maimed or missing limbs, others permanently blinded by the poisoned gas unleashed against their trenches.

Dressed in mourning and watching from balconies in the Home Office, a government building, were King George's wife, Queen Mary; his mother, Queen Alexandra; his daughter, Princess Mary; his sisters Queen Maud of Norway and Princess Victoria; and his aunt Princess Beatrice, who, like her nephew, had shed a Teutonic name during the war. In her case, the change was her husband's patrimony of Battenberg, which was anglicized by most of the family to Mountbatten. Beatrice's twenty-three-year-old son, Prince Maurice, had been killed at the First Battle of Ypres, which she described as "one of those losses one can never get over . . . realising that one's dear child, who was like a ray of sunshine in the house, will never be amongst us again in this world."[15]

At the time of Maurice's death, Princess Beatrice had received an offer from the Secretary of State for War for her son's body to receive special exemption to be repatriated for burial in Britain. Feeling this would be an unforgivable exploitation of her privileges, especially in wartime, Princess Beatrice had declined, a decision approved of by the King. After the Armistice, Beatrice had, however, asked if she might be allowed to design Maurice's headstone herself, a request that the King, speaking through the Imperial War Graves Commission, personally vetoed with the stipulation that his cousin's grave was to be marked the same as every other combatant's. He had likewise rejected his aunt's request to lay a wreath at the unveiling of the Cenotaph, since no other soldier's mother was being allowed to do so.

From the Home Office, the three queens and three princesses were escorted to Westminster Abbey, arriving there before the cortege. As they were shown to their seats, the royal party could hear the congregation's "men sob, and the weeping of many of the women," and the wave of emotion affected them all; Queen Mary, in particular, struggled to maintain her composure.[16] Seats in the abbey had been allocated by lottery to those who had lost in the war loved ones now simply referred to as "The Missing." Buckingham Palace had been inundated with requests for tickets, far more than the abbey could hold, and so many pleas were posted to the King and Queen that facsimile responses were printed; household staff members worked through the night signing them to make sure every petitioner received some sort of answer. They came from middle-class widows such as Mrs. Newbold, who lived two miles from Hampton Court and who, having lost her only two children in service at the Front, "appeals to your

Gracious Majesty with every confidence that her appeal will be listened to and granted if possible."[17] There was a heart-breaking inquiry from a barely literate lady named Rose Else, a widowed factory worker whose "only Boy" had been killed aged nineteen in the trenches; she wrote to "ask his Magest the King if its true all mothers are to com to the Funeral?"[18] Neither Mrs. Else nor Mrs. Newbold was successful in the ticket lottery, and the King, aware of how many rejections there had been by force of necessity, took very seriously his role as "Chief Mourner," which is how he described himself several times in his diary entry. He wrote a letter to be placed on top of the coffin, accompanied by a wreath from himself and Queen Mary.

Many of those who have featured prominently in this history of Hampton Court are buried at Westminster. Giles Daubeney and his wife rest near Elizabeth of York and her husband, who are buried close to their grandchildren, Edward VI, Mary I, and Elizabeth I. Anne of Cleves, Margaret Douglas, James I, and Anna of Denmark are entombed there, as are Cromwell's daughter Betty Claypole and Charles I's son Henry, Duke of Gloucester, the youngest of the children to join the King at Hampton Court during his incarceration there. Another Duke of Gloucester who died young, Prince William, the son to whom the future Queen Anne gave birth at Hampton Court in 1689, is buried there, next to his mother and his father, George of Denmark, who are near the graves of Charles II, Mary II, William III, George II, Queen Caroline of Ansbach, Prince Frederick, and Princess Augusta. The Unknown Warrior was laid to rest in the western nave; after the sword was removed and the coffin lowered, George V scattered the first fistful of earth into the grave, which was then filled with one hundred sandbags of earth gathered from the different battlefields. It was then sealed and later covered with a tombstone that reads:

THUS ARE COMMEMORATED THE MANY
MULTITUDES WHO DURING THE GREAT
WAR OF 1914–1918 GAVE THE MOST THAT
MAN CAN GIVE, LIFE ITSELF
FOR GOD

FOR KING AND COUNTRY
FOR LOVED ONES, HOME AND EMPIRE
FOR THE SACRED CAUSE OF JUSTICE AND
THE FREEDOM OF THE WORLD.
THEY BURIED HIM AMONG THE KINGS BECAUSE
HE HAD DONE GOOD TOWARDS GOD AND TOWARD
HIS HOUSE.

After the funeral had concluded, the abbey doors were open to let in the first of the forty thousand who filed past the Tomb of the Unknown Warrior that day.

Two and a half years later, the Duke of York, youngest of the princes who had accompanied his father to that funeral and who, thirteen years later, succeeded to the throne as King George VI, returned to the abbey to become the first member of the royal family to be married in the dress uniform of the Royal Air Force, founded in the last months of the war as the newest branch of the British armed forces. Outside the abbey, rain fell on the crowds who had gathered to watch the first public wedding of a British prince since the sixteenth century, as the House of Windsor tentatively embraced the age of mass media. The Duke's twenty-two-year-old bride, Lady Elizabeth Bowes-Lyon, arrived on the arm of her Scottish father, Claude, Earl of Strathmore and Kinghorne, through the abbey's western door, where they were met by several members of the clergy who would escort them in procession to the altar. One of the clergymen fainted as the procession began, and, as they waited for him to be helped and the service to recommence, Elizabeth's eyes travelled up the nave, where she caught sight of the Tomb of the Unknown Warrior. Letting go of Claude's arm, she impulsively went over to the grave, on which she laid her bridal bouquet of roses and lily-of-the-valley. The organ then began to play as the wedding procession regrouped.[19]

This gesture on the part of Elizabeth, who was queen consort from 1936 to 1952 and Queen Mother from 1952 to 2002, became famous, although it is often misreported with the detail that she respectfully set the flowers on the grave as she and her husband left the abbey. The confusion perhaps arose from the fact that after every subsequent wedding in the House of Windsor, the bridal bouquet has been sent to the Unknown Warrior's grave.* Eyewitnesses from 1923 agree that Elizabeth's gesture was more impulsive, taking place during the unexpected delay caused by the cleric's fainting. Four of Elizabeth's brothers had served on the Western Front; one, Fergus, fell aged twenty-six during the Battle of Loos, during which about eighty-five thousand men were killed over the course of thirteen days. Some guests at the wedding felt that, as she waited with her father at the abbey door, Elizabeth's mind had turned to Fergus, prompting her to set her flowers on the grave.[20] Her parents' castle at Glamis in Scotland had been turned into a military convalescent home during the war, through which a teenage Elizabeth had seen many men come to be cured and then go back to a war from which they were not lucky enough to return a second time. Maybe it was one of them in the grave.

That was the point. As far as Elizabeth was concerned, whoever rested there might be one of their family friends, guests, or neighbors. It was equally likely to be the son, nephew, brother, father, uncle, cousin, lover, husband, or friend of those who cut down the tree at Hampton Court to make his coffin or of the carpenters who fashioned it. It might be Major Fitz-Simon's brother Jack or a former comrade of the Navy personnel who helped bring the coffin back across the Channel. It might be Mrs. Else's son, either of Mrs. Newbold's, or either of Thomas Abnett's. In being nobody, the Unknown Warrior could be everybody's.

Fourteen years later, as George and Elizabeth processed back up the nave for their coronation, they became the first king and queen crowned at Westminster who did not walk directly to the altar. The tomb lay directly in their path, and so they stepped to one side. At every royal wedding, cor-

---

* This tradition has been maintained by those, like the future Queen Elizabeth II, Princess Anne the Princess Royal, and Catherine, Princess of Wales, whose weddings took place at Westminster Abbey, as well as by royal brides Diana, Princess of Wales; Sarah, Duchess of York; Meghan, Duchess of Sussex; and the princesses Beatrice and Eugenie of York, who married in other locations and whose bouquets were taken later to Westminster.

onation, and funeral held at Westminster Abbey since 1920, the monarchy has deferred to the Unknown Warrior, a symbolic act apparently insisted upon by George V when deciding upon where to situate the grave. An English newspaper assured its readers in 1922 that "the tomb of the Unknown Warrior was carefully protected with rails, and no foot, whether King or Queen or bride stepped on the sacred spot."[21]

CHAPTER 24

WILDERNESS HOUSE

I have desired to go
Where springs not fail,
To fields where flies no sharp and sided hail
And a few lilies blow.
And I have asked to be,
Where no storms come.

—Father Gerard Manley Hopkins, "Heaven-Haven" (1918)

The Hampton Court ball of 1953 was Elizabeth II's last major public appearance before her coronation. "The Queen, dancing with the Duke of Edinburgh, looked as beautiful as the people imagined her to be," wrote Winston Churchill's Principal Private Secretary, Jock Colville.[1]

Thirty-eight, tall and slim, with his dark hair parted to the side, Colville's career and connections had left him equally well placed between monarchy and parliament. His six-month-old daughter Harriet had Elizabeth II and Winston Churchill for godparents; his wife, Margaret, had been a lady-in-waiting to Elizabeth II before her accession and would subsequently perform the same duty for the Queen Mother; his cousin and fellow Second World War veteran, Captain Terence O'Neill, later served as Prime Minister of Northern Ireland from 1963 to 1969; and, apart from Churchill, Colville had been assistant secretary to two other prime ministers, Neville Chamberlain and Clement Attlee. Colville knew how much heavy lifting Elizabeth II's coronation was expected to do, not just in improving public morale but also regarding Britain's international reputation. In the final seven years of her father's reign, a seemingly impotent Britain had sat back as her wartime allies in the Soviet Union imposed Communist satellite dictatorships in every European country east of Austria, with the exception of Finland and Greece, both of which were saved by the flexing of America's muscle and a massive injection of its cash. Two months before the ball, Hampton Court was briefly closed to the public to facilitate a private tour for Marshal Josip Broz, known as Tito, who at the start of the year had made himself President of Yugoslavia, a position which, along with his presidency of the country's League of Communists, he would hold until his death in 1980. Of all the new eastern European Communist heads of state, Tito was the one least obedient to Moscow, which explained the British government's enthusiasm for his official visit, since they hoped to entice Tito into greater cooperation with the Western powers. It did not say much, however, for Britain's position on the global stage that its Conservative Prime Minister had enthusiastically lobbied to host a Communist revolutionary who had just overthrown the Yugoslavian royal family, several of whom had supported the British during the war.[2] The British monarchy's symbols—old and new—were harnessed to create an impression of power that would hopefully generate prestige and influence that the country was struggling to sustain in the face of American and Soviet hegemony.

Despite his worries for the future, Colville was moved by what he saw at the Household Brigade ball—to him, it looked, for a moment, like it was 1939 again. Ballgowns spun across the wooden floors of the Great Hall in the arms of military uniforms, while tiaras and family heirlooms sparkled alongside medals and officers' boots polished to within an inch of their lives. At midnight, the Queen and the Duke of Edinburgh headed the guests as they were escorted from the Great Hall through lighted halls and palace chambers, passing the fountains wrapped with flowers, to enjoy a supper by candlelight in William III's Orangery. Among the guests was the elderly Mrs. Preston, a widow who did not have far to travel that evening. She had occupied a grace-and-favor apartment off the Fountain Court since

1928. She was joined by Lady Baden-Powell, widow of the Scouts' founder and hostess of regular séances at Hampton Court. There she reported feeling the spectral presence of Anne Boleyn in her suite of rooms; these were so spacious—she had a roof garden and room for twelve guests—that she nicknamed her grace-and-favor setup "Hampers Hotel."[3] In the weeks before the ball, Lady Baden-Powell had temporarily turned part of Hampers Hotel into dormitories for 120 visitors from overseas, all of whom were members of the Girl Guides invited to London for the Coronation.

Dining with them in the Orangery was Elizabeth II's glamorous aunt Princess Marina, accompanied by her seventeen-year-old son Prince Edward, Duke of Kent, and his sixteen-year-old sister, Princess Alexandra. Traditionally, a young lady such as Princess Alexandra would not have been invited to evening events like balls or banquets until she "came out" as a debutante, usually at the age of eighteen, but the rules had been bent for the coronation festivities and, in any case, the debutante system was on its last legs by 1953. Once endowed with almost spiritual significance by the British upper classes, after the Second World War its strictures, protocols, and parties went from being a rite of passage to an optional extra, then to a relic, and finally to a memory. There therefore seemed no good reason for Princess Alexandra of Kent not to accompany her brother and mother to the ball.

The Kents had won much sympathy from the public when Princess Marina's husband, George VI's youngest brother, was killed in a military airplane crash while on active service in the Second World War. Princess Marina, a granddaughter of Greece's King George I on her father's side and a great-granddaughter of Tsar Alexander II of Russia through her mother, had been celebrated by the British press for years for her elegance and sense of style. She was also capable of titanic snobbery, which she had shown in the 1930s by privately mocking the nonroyal ancestry of her Scottish sisters-in-law, Lady Elizabeth Bowes-Lyon and Lady Alice Douglas Montagu Scott—"the poor little Scotch girls," as Marina dubbed them.[4] The latter, by then Princess Alice, attended the Hampton Court ball accompanied by her husband, Prince Henry, Duke of Gloucester, the former Governor-General of Australia. He had an Edwardian moustache and a Hanoverian face ("flat at the back and rising to the real pineapple point of William IV," according to a rather honest dining companion), he was an enthusiast of whiskey, and he laughed so energetically that a dinner companion compared it to an orgasm. Another of the new Queen's uncles—far more dashing and far less popular than Uncle Henry—was present in the form of Louis, Lord Mountbatten, Elizabeth's uncle by marriage and the last Viceroy of India, which had gained independence from the British Empire six years earlier in 1947. Mountbatten was loathed by many on the British right wing, particularly by defenders of the empire, for the obvious enthusiasm with which he had regarded the end of imperial rule in India.[5] There were also accurate rumors that he secretly supported the abolition of Northern Ireland to enable the unification of Ireland into a single all-island republic, a position which makes the circumstances of his eventual assassination by those in favor of Irish unification even more ironic.[6]

After supper in the Orangery, there were fireworks and more dancing that carried on until a sunrise that prompted the normally conscientious Elizabeth to decide it was time to go home. As the Queen, Philip and Margaret were driven back up the Mall to Buckingham Palace, they saw other people ambling home from pre-coronation parties in their evening wear. When their Rolls-Royce reached the palace gates, they were spotted by a journalist and by people, "some in evening dress, hitch-hiking girls from the . . . villages of Scotland and Wales, still carrying their rucksacks, with early morning workers, [who] stood round the gates to cheer the Queen and her party home again."[7] Back at Hampton Court, the guests with grace-and-favor residences, like Mrs. Preston and Lady Baden-Powell, were already curled up in their beds. The next day, the task of dealing with the floral arrangements fell to the staff directed by the palace's new housekeeper, Gladys Pooley, who arranged for them to be arranged in bouquets that were sent to each of the grace-and-favor apartments, and to workers' families, local homes, and churches who used them for their Sunday displays or for forthcoming weddings.

Almost four years to the day after crowds had cheered Elizabeth II's car, a "little Ford" beetled over the same bridge on a warm afternoon in 1957. Its driver was half-Romanian, half-British socialite Irmgarde de Vaux, who made liberal use of the car's horn in her quest to outpace the heavy lorry traffic she had encountered since leaving London just after lunch.[8] In the passenger seat was the writer James Pope-Hennessy, forty years old, tall and elegant, with dark hair and brown eyes.[9] The two had been friends for years—Pope-Hennessy liked Irmgarde's chic confidence, while she admired his intelligence and wit. A family friend wrote, "Although physically attracted to his own sex, he loved the companionship of women to whom most of his enchanting correspondence was addressed."[10] Socialite and scholar were both enthusiastic smokers, and a succession of cigarettes had been clamped in Irmgarde's hand between London and Hampton Court, where she urged the car on over the bridge, passing the sightseers emerging from, or returning to, the nearby train station.

Irmgarde depressed the clutch as she showed their papers to a guard, who waved them through into the estate. The reason for James Pope-Hennessy's visit was the Dowager Queen Mary, who had died four years earlier and whose patronage had helped restore the palace's entrance.[11] After well-received biographies of the Victorian statesman Lord Houghton and then of the recently deceased Liberal politician the Marquess of Crewe, its author had, as much to his surprise as everybody else's, been contacted by the royal household with the news that Elizabeth II had been "pleased to place the writing of a book about Queen Mary in the hands of Mr. James Pope-Hennessy."[12] "In life, James was a poor judge of character," opined a relative, "and [he] had very little understanding of the motives even of people he knew well, but in dealing with the past, his understanding of the human personality was next door to infallible."[13] Since accepting the Queen's commission to write the official biography of her grandmother, Pope-Hennessy had spent much of the intervening two years travelling to see many of the places associated with his subject's life and to interview those who had known her. The palace itself was not on his itinerary. To have visited every site that had benefited from Queen

Mary's zeal for conservation would, as Pope-Hennessy grimaced, have taken decades.

Instead, Irmgarde steered the car onto a path that took them away from the palace and deeper into its estate, to an interview arranged for them by Queen Mary's daughter, the Dowager Countess of Harewood. An occupational hazard of writing a biography of the newly departed was that many of the living sources were themselves moving closer to mortality—a fact brought home a few months earlier by the death of the octogenarian Princess Marie-Louise of Schleswig-Holstein. A sharp-witted granddaughter of Queen Victoria, her memories of Queen Mary would likely have proved invaluable had Pope-Hennessy not repeatedly deferred to her staff's rescheduling of their interview—until, in the face of the princess's final illness, it was too late.[14] There were only three or four royals still alive from that generation who had known a younger Queen Mary well enough to be of use to her biographer, and one of them had been living in a house on the Hampton Court estate since the end of the Second World War. Her Imperial Highness the Grand Duchess Xenia of Russia, eldest sister of the last Tsar, was eighty-two years old, and, as with the late Princess Marie-Louise, Pope-Hennessy was convinced that the objections to his request for an audience emanated principally from her entourage.* They claimed the Grand Duchess's memory was failing and that she was, in any case, profoundly shy.

By 1957, Pope-Hennessy was used to the obfuscations of royalty and their well-intentioned flunkies. A year earlier, he had interviewed Pauline, Princess von Württemberg, who was completely unfazed by her family nickname of "fat cousin Pauline." She conducted the interview in a drawing room, with a bottle of Cointreau next to her, another bottle of a potent home-brewed plum liqueur, and a box of Virginia Slims; she pretended to have forgotten her English and spoke cautiously through her German trans-

---

* Often pronounced in English as "Zeenea," it can also be pronounced as "Kiz-enya" as it apparently was by several members of the Grand Duchess's family. It is sometimes translated into English with the spelling "Ksenia"; several surviving Westernized monograms from her marital home at the Yelagin Palace in Saint Petersburg show a *K* intertwined with her husband Alexander's *A*.

lator until she decided, halfway through the interview, that Pope-Hennessy was neither muckraker nor Communist, at which point she slipped into faultless English to ask him, "Please give my respects to Queen Elizabeth when you see her next, if she even knows who I am or that I exist, which she most probably doesn't."[15]

Xenia's reluctance to be interviewed was due in part to her natural shyness. She had also developed a particular fear of the press after their relentless pursuit of an interview with her on the subject of claims, made by a former patient of a German mental asylum, to be Xenia's youngest niece, the Grand Duchess Anastasia, missing with the rest of her immediate family since a Communist-led massacre in 1918.[16] Xenia had consistently refused to meet the woman, who launched one of the longest-running court cases in European history to force Xenia to recognize her as a Romanov. The bestowal of an Oscar that year on actress Ingrid Bergman for her depiction of the claimant in *Anastasia* had intensified Xenia's discomfort with publicity.*[17] It was only the reassuring letter from Queen Mary's daughter that had nudged Xenia's staff to finally contact Pope-Hennessy and offer a time to meet at her home in Hampton Court.[18]

Pope-Hennessy sympathized with Xenia's reluctance. He had been unenthusiastic about writing Queen Mary's biography in the first place, let alone conducting a seemingly endless round of interviews, all of which were governed by sensitivity to royal feelings and a relentlessly draining adherence to the relevant etiquette. He had initially drafted a letter to the royal household rejecting its offer and expressing his "deepest regret that I do not see how, at present, I can accept this flattering commission." That was until his mind was changed by his brother, director of the Victoria and Albert Museum in London, who urged him to think of it in a spirit of anthropology—"Royalty, I explained, were an endangered species, and this was an occasion to establish, through close inspection of a single life, the

---

* The character played so brilliantly by Bergman in the movie bore almost no resemblance, in terms of biography or personality, to the claimant. The script did, however, have her character at one point travel into Denmark under the name "Anna Anderson," which was one of the pseudonyms used by the pretender in reality.

nature of the phenomenon."[19] That appealed to Pope-Hennessy's view of the past as an interconnecting series of events caused by collisions between the personal and the political. He was skeptical of the idea of the tides of history, particularly of the theory that there was a dialectic to the past. "He was," wrote his brother, "unintellectual, not in the sense of being unintelligent (he was indeed extremely clever), but of being uninterested in criticism or in ideas."[20] It had been his strident contempt for a socialist or Marxist view of history that had helped convince courtiers that Pope-Hennessy was the man for the job, ameliorating concerns over the suitability of his character. The philanthropist Maud Russell, who knew him well, said that Pope-Hennessy was "two characters in one shell. The serious, hardworking, self-critical (as far as his writing was concerned), workmanlike being, and that other self—wild, careless, unheeding. A person might easily have known only one half of him and not had a clue to the other half."[21]

As they drove through the estate, Pope-Hennessy lit up another cigarette and admitted to an unfamiliar nervousness about interviewing the Grand Duchess. She was a witness to some of the greatest events in recent history. Xenia had made her first public appearance at her father's coronation in 1882 as an eight-year-old, mimicking her mother's wave and incline of the head to the crowd of thousands as they were driven through the streets of Moscow in a golden coach dating from the reign of Catherine the Great.[22] She had witnessed her grandfather's death after a bomb attack in Saint Petersburg; she had survived one herself when it ripped through her family's private train as she was eating pudding in the dining car. She watched the disintegration of one of the largest empires in human history; her son-in-law had allegedly been the chief instigator of the assassination of Rasputin, and she had been cast as the primary villain in the perplexing case of a pretender masquerading as her miraculously survived niece. If Pope-Hennessy was expecting reassurance for his nerves from Irmgarde, who counted among her closest friends the exiled Queen Mother of Romania and the *in-situ* Queen of Denmark, he was disappointed when she replied that she thoroughly understood his anxiousness. Xenia had not only seen much of history, but history would not see anyone like her again. The Romanov family's statutes, implemented by Xenia's late father, Alexander III, stipulated that only tsars' daughters and granddaughters in the male line were entitled to the honorific of Grand Duchess. An unintended consequence of that decision, following the downfall of the Russian monarchy, was that, after Xenia and her younger sister, there would be no more grand duchesses.[23] Irmgarde announced her intention to thus give Xenia the deepest curtsy, the kind she reserved for monarchs and their wives, rather than the "half inch to an inch" she deployed for minor German or British royalty.

Irmgarde brought the car to a halt by a wall encircling an early eighteenth-century dwelling originally built to house the gardener Charles Bridgeman after he was recruited to make the gardens suitable for William III. The two friends got out to stretch their legs while waiting, since they were seven minutes early for their audience at half past three. A small sign on the path announced the property's name, Wilderness House. Pope-Hennessy thought the residence "seemed entirely remote, in another world. It looked secret and quiet, like a house in a fairy story." The bustle of the town seemed far away. At 3:29 p.m., as Irmgarde put on her gloves and hat, Pope-Hennessy whispered to her, "There's someone looking at us out of the top window."

"So there is, dear," she replied. "Now, I wonder whose face that is? That is not a face I know."

Realizing they had been spotted by the new arrivals, the face disappeared behind hastily dropped blinds. Pope-Hennessy and Irmgarde opened a green-painted wooden door in the wall and walked through to the gravel path and "trim garden" of Wilderness House. After they rang the bell, the door was opened almost immediately by a tall and slightly gangly young man, Prince Alexander Romanoff,* accompanied by a Russian Orthodox

---

* In exile, the Romanovs changed the Western spelling of their name to Romanoff. Various reasons for this have been suggested, including the theory that it was done to prevent them being tracked by the KGB. It seems unlikely that the changing of a single consonant would have thrown the KGB off the scent, especially since the Romanovs/Romanoffs continued to style themselves as princes and princesses. It seems more likely that the spelling changed because phonetically Romanoff more closely correlated with its correct Russian pronunciation.

nun in a black habit and white mantle. Pope-Hennessy thought that Prince
Alexander, Grand Duchess Xenia's grandson, had the "permanent smile"
of the amiably stupid. He was more impressed by the nun, Mother Martha,
who, he thought, "has the face of a powerful elderly man, full-blooded and
not at all severe, and eyes which gaze straight into yours." The nun tended
to put her face very close to whomever she spoke to, a habit Pope-Hennessy
found faintly disconcerting.

The Grand Duchess Xenia had lived on the Hampton Court estate for
a dozen years, since returning to it from Balmoral, to which she had been
evacuated after a Nazi bomb had landed so close to Wilderness House that
it shattered all the windows and caused Xenia's daughter-in-law Princess
Elisabetta—already frail following a recent battle with cancer—to suffer
a fatal heart attack.[24] When Xenia first escaped the Russian Revolution in
1919, her cousin King George V had given her Frogmore Cottage, near
Windsor Castle, for her new home.[25] She had remained there until 1936
when George's son Edward VIII asked if Xenia would mind relocating so
that Frogmore could become a guest cottage for visiting American friends
of his mistress and future wife, Wallis Simpson.[26] Xenia had not had much
say in the matter, as King Edward had known when he made his politely
worded "request," but since moving to Hampton Court the Grand Duchess
had grown to love it, finding it a welcome retreat from a world that was
increasingly alien and frightening.

Mother Martha, a former Saint Petersburg debutante until her fiancé
was killed in a disastrous Russian cavalry charge in the opening weeks of
the First World War, had become the reclusive Grand Duchess's dietician,
nurse, lady-in-waiting, and guardian. Princess Margaret, when playing as
a child at Balmoral, had been so impressed by the size of Mother Martha's
sandal-sporting feet that she believed the nun was a man; it took quite a bit
of convincing by her mother, Queen Elizabeth, that she was incorrect, and
that Margaret really must not bring her observation up in conversation with
Mother Martha.[27]

As Mother Martha escorted Pope-Hennessy to the drawing room of
Wilderness House, she took his arm and leaned in to say: "Her Imperial

Highness expects you to ask her questions. Her Imperial Highness is very nervous, and otherwise she will not be able to speak."

Pope-Hennessy nodded and murmured words of polite obedience. The nun stopped again, "What a wonderful work you are having. My life, you know, has never been the same since Queen Mary died. Always so kind and always *the* Queen."

Surprised, Pope-Hennessy asked, "Queen Mary came here often?"

"Oh yes, constantly. And always so kind to Her Imperial Highness. But always *the* Queen. Nothing is the same since she died."

Pope-Hennessy had arrived with a list of questions pertaining to Xenia's and Queen Mary's shared holidays in the 1890s; he had no idea that his subject had continued to visit the family long after they sought asylum. Along with everybody else, he had assumed that the Windsors regarded the postrevolutionary Romanovs as embarrassments; poor cousins best kept out of sight and out of mind. How many times had Queen Mary's trips to oversee the conservation work at Hampton Court been an excuse for her to visit with Xenia?

On the threshold of the drawing room, Mother Martha stopped again to ask, "Now, what is your name? What is your name, again?"

"Pope-Hennessy."

"What?"

"Pope. Hennessy."

"Ah yes, I remember," nodded the nun, before she flung open the door, swept in, and announced, "Mr. Poke-Henderson to see Your Imperial Highness."

Pope-Hennessy walked in behind her and bowed from the neck. The first thing he noticed was the dozens of family pictures—the "mantelpiece and every available wall space crammed with photographs"—interspersed with religious icons and a bust of her cousin, the late King George V. There were several photographs of Xenia's murdered brother Tsar Nicholas II, including one with his wife and five children displayed on a table of its own. There were photographs of Xenia's other brothers—Michael, marched into a forest and shot by revolutionaries two weeks before Nicholas; and the

Grand Duke George, who had predeceased them all when he died in the arms of a passing peasant woman who found him after he collapsed on a Crimean mountain path while battling tuberculosis. Xenia's younger sister, Olga, was also in the photographs.* She no longer visited. Terrified of being kidnapped by the KGB or other Communist spies, Olga had emigrated to a farm in Canada. She had used her share of the proceeds from selling the last of their mother's jewelry to pay for it.[28]

Xenia rose from her small armchair to meet the historian. She was slender, with the beautiful dark eyes of her Danish mother and the narrow heart-shaped face of her aunt, Britain's Queen Alexandra. Her grey hair was curled in a style belonging to another generation. Given the depleted state of the Romanovs' finances, Pope-Hennessy suspected that the long ropes of pearls around Xenia's neck were artificial.[29] Nonetheless, in her dark dress he thought she appeared "beautifully made, like an exquisite little old doll." She absentmindedly waved Mother Martha from the room before extending her hand for Pope-Hennessy to bow over.

"It is so kind of Your Imperial Highness to let me come to see you," he said, before remembering that protocol required her to speak first.

"Yes," she said. "Princess Mary wrote, and I thought I must—I didn't want—I don't know how I can help you—now, you really must ask me the questions because—my poor old memory." At this, she tapped her head and smiled apologetically, "I don't know."

Pope-Hennessy felt a surge of sympathy for her. Her gestures were those of "an exceedingly nervous wild bird, which felt trapped. Her voice and hands fluttered, and her remarks trailed away nervously. It was as if she had been protected from strangers too stringently for too long, as if she were the member of an enclosed order suddenly brought face to face with a strange man."

She sat and then gestured that he could sit opposite her. Pope-Hennessy, keenly aware of the history sitting before him, began with questions about her and George V's Danish grandparents, and holidays they had shared in

---

* The Grand Duchess Olga Alexandrovna (1882–1960).

the 1890s. He steered away from anything too difficult or painful, largely avoiding discussion of the circumstances in which Xenia had left Russia. He noticed "the curious effect of the Grand Duchess Xenia's voice. It is somehow a *floating* voice, vague and in some curious way outside herself. It is as if she is trying to catch it and bring it back again to say something else. You could almost see the sentences trailing like thin smoke around the room." Just before the audience ended, Xenia said that she had set aside a book in the hope that Pope-Hennessy might like to see it.

"Is this," she began . . . "Well, there is one thing I wanted to ask *you*. Dame—Dame—Dame, uhm, Dame—"

"Dame Una?" he asked.

"Yes. Dame Una."

"She was my mother, Ma'am."

"I thought that, oh, your mother. I am so glad. You see, she came to see me when I was at Frogmore—that was many years ago now. But she came to see me because she was writing the Tsarina's story and then, we, well, I had the book here and I thought, here it is, that you might like to see it? I don't know."

Pope-Hennessy saw that Xenia had left out for him her copy of his mother's book *A Tsarina's Story*, a biography of Xenia's great-grandmother Princess Charlotte of Prussia, who had married the future Tsar Nicholas I in 1817.* *A Tsarina's Story* had been his mother's last published work before her death from cancer and, until that afternoon, he had no idea that she had interviewed Xenia while writing it. Xenia smiled nervously at him, which prompted Pope-Hennessy to thank her sincerely for her thoughtfulness, before he left with Irmgarde—and Prince Alexander—who had asked if they wouldn't mind giving him a lift to a party in London.

Pope-Hennessy's life of Queen Mary, published two years later, in 1959, was a great success and is still cited as an example of the ways an official biography can be interesting rather than hagiographically dull. He revealed

---

* Princess Charlotte of Prussia took the baptismal name of Alexandra Feodorovna upon her conversion to Russian Orthodoxy in preparation for her marriage to Tsar Nicholas I.

that Queen Mary had attended a memorial service in London for the murdered Tsar, which proved another of the few occasions when she was visibly upset in public, but he made no mention of the fact that Mary's husband, George V, had passed up the chance to offer Nicholas II political asylum in Britain.[30] Pope-Hennessy may not have known, for very few knew the truth at that time. Details of the 1917 proposal to give the Romanovs asylum in Britain emerged in the 1980s and it took until the 2010s for historians to uncover the less dramatic but no less tragic truth—that Britain had withdrawn its offer of asylum in the mistaken confidence that an alternative offer to relocate the deposed royals would be made by Norway, Sweden, Denmark, France, or Spain.[31] Not long after, the Communists took power in Russia, and it was too late.[32] The mistake made in not taking the Romanovs in the days immediately after Nicholas II's abdication may have helped save his sister Xenia's life two years later, in that it inspired a sense of urgency in the previously cautious George V.[33] When other Romanovs were subsequently threatened by the revolutionaries, King George sent a warship to evacuate them from Crimea under guard, and in 1919 he personally organized a secret mission to rescue the deposed Emperor of Austria and his immediate family, despite having been on the opposite side in the First World War.[34]

Xenia was struggling with chronic pain from fibrositis by the time *Queen Mary* was published. Her world shrank again; not only was it rare for her to leave Wilderness House, but also she could no longer manage its stairs. Another of her grandsons, Prince Nikita, moved in to help and to keep her company.[35] In the summer of 1959, during a visit to Canada, Elizabeth II and Prince Philip reunited with Xenia's sister, Olga, who joined them for lunch on the royal yacht *Britannia*. As Princess Marina told Xenia, "I saw Lilibet* . . . last week, and she told me all about seeing dear Aunt Olga. She loved her and said she was too sweet! She also said she was going to write and tell you."[36] Olga left the *Britannia* to go back to her small apartment above a barber's shop in Toronto, where she lived a quiet life centered

---

* Family nickname for Queen Elizabeth II (1926-2022).

on the local Russian Orthodox church and her love of painting. She had sold her Canadian farm after old age rendered its upkeep too difficult.

Along with letters from Elizabeth II, Princess Marina, and other relatives, Xenia also enjoyed visits from her grandson Alexander's ex-girlfriend, socialite Daphne Battine, who had become Daphne Dormer after ending her relationship with Alexander and marrying. Daphne remained on friendly terms with the Romanovs, and with Xenia in particular, whom she asked to stand as godmother to her first child Leanda.* Xenia accepted happily, and she and Daphne continued to exchange Christmas cards and, as long as Xenia's health permitted, visits. Early in 1960 that health gave way, and Xenia's only daughter, sixty-four-year-old Princess Irina Youssoupova, arrived at Hampton Court from Paris.† Helped by Mother Martha, Irina—a frequent guest at Wilderness House even before her mother's final illness—did her best to ease the back pain which caused Xenia such agony that her life shrank once more, this time to her bed. On April 20 Irina lit a candle in front of an icon of the Virgin and Child, and a Russian Orthodox priest, Father George, arrived to administer the last rites. With Irina sitting at one side of the bed and her eldest brother, Prince Andrei, on the other, they stayed with their mother until she passed away later that afternoon.[37] Mother Martha entered the room with a box labelled "Black Mourning Veils," a bulletin was released to the newspapers, the undertakers were contacted, and the funeral was held in Kensington at the Church of the Holy Assumption six days later. Prince Alexander married a Sicilian aristocrat and moved to New York; Mother Martha left royal service and vanished into anonymity immediately after Xenia's funeral; and James Pope-Hennessy was beaten to death in 1974 after he invited three men he thought he had befriended in a London pub to continue drinking with him

---

* Christened Leanda Xenia Sophia Stanhope Dormer, later the historian and author Leanda de Lisle.

† Described as one of the great beauties of Russian high society before the revolution, it was Irina's husband, Felix, who had allegedly masterminded the 1916 assassination of Rasputin in a last-ditch effort to save the monarchy.

in his apartment.[38] Having drunkenly if merrily told them about a generous advance he had received for his next book—a biography of Noël Coward—they attacked him, restrained and robbed him, tied him up, fled, and left him to choke to death while tied to a chair in his home.[39]

By the time of his murder, the Wilderness House drawing room where Pope-Hennessy had once interviewed the Grand Duchess Xenia was again unoccupied. From 1962 to 1969, it had been home to Major General Sir Charles Offley Harvey, a veteran of both world wars who, following his retirement from the army, went to Hampton Court to serve as its chief steward.[40] The same post had been held by Barbara Villiers in the days of Charles II; fortunately, Offley Harvey executed its duties of overseeing its maintenance with far greater conscientiousness.

CHAPTER 25

A HISTORIC
ROYAL PALACE

*Big houses that are begun in only glory were soon
maintained only by struggle.*

—Elizabeth Bowen, *Bowen's Court* (1942)

After the Offley Harveys, the next resident of Wilderness House was Charles "Chips" Fitzroy Maclean, Lord Maclean. Before arriving as Hampton Court's new chief steward in 1985, his varied career had included service in the Second World War and as Chief Scout for the British Boy Scouts Association from 1959 to 1971; he had succeeded his Scottish grandfather as Chief of Clan Maclean of Duart and served as Elizabeth II's Lord Chamberlain from 1971 to his retirement in 1984. His first duties in the latter role had been the organization of two difficult royal funerals—that of Elizabeth's estranged uncle, the ex-king Edward VIII, and then of her cousin Prince William of Gloucester, who, aged thirty, had been killed in front of thirty thousand spectators at an air show when his plane crashed. His body was burned so badly that he could be identified only by his dental records. Lord Maclean also had a central role in organizing the funerals of two of the guests from the 1953 Hampton Court ball—first, that of Prince William's father, Prince Henry, Duke of Gloucester, whose cognitive decline following a car crash meant that his wife could shield him from the

349

hideous details of their son's death, and then of Lord Mountbatten, following his assassination in a 1979 IRA bomb attack.* Lord Maclean had a hand, too, in happier royal events, including Princess Anne's 1973 wedding and Elizabeth II's Silver Jubilee of 1977. His last great task before stepping down to move to Hampton Court with his wife Jean was the organizing of the Prince of Wales's marriage to Lady Diana Spencer in July 1981, which attracted a global viewing audience of about 750 million.

At eleven in the morning on May 4, 2016, Charles and the late Diana's daughter-in-law Catherine, Duchess of Cambridge, stepped out of a car at Hampton Court. Wearing a boucle tweed, single-breasted dress coat by designer Michael Kors and nude heels from L. K. Bennett,[1] the thirty-four-year-old wife of the second in line to the British throne was greeted by the Queen's Lord Lieutenant of Greater London, Kenneth Olisa,[†] who presented to her the chairman of Historic Royal Palaces, Rupert Gavin. Both men escorted the Duchess of Cambridge on a walking tour of the palace's new Magic Garden, a children's playground that had been six years in the making. Appropriately, it had been installed on the grounds which, centuries earlier, had been the tiltyard, where Will Somers had paraded on a broom to entertain Edward VI. Like the set pieces for masques or great tourneys in the early modern royal households, the new playground had grottoes, battlements, towers, and play areas shaped like the heraldic beasts on the palace's bridge or the ones that had decorated Henry VIII's Privy Gardens.

Mothers and children had been invited into the Magic Garden, where the Duchess stopped to talk to some of those playing at a twenty-five-foot

---

* The other three killed in the attack were buried separately. They were the Irish aristocrat, the Dowager Baroness Brabourne (83); Northern Irish teenager Paul Maxwell (15), who had a summer job working on the local fishing boats; and Mountbatten's grandson Nicholas Knatchbull (14).

† At the time of writing, Sir Kenneth Olisa, following his knighthood in 2018.

slide shaped like the Tudor dragon. One of the eight-year-olds with whom she chatted, Olivia, had been given the day off from the local St. John the Baptist Church of England Junior School. Throughout her conversation with the Duchess, Olivia was sitting on top of the dragon with her classmate Elodie. She was later asked by a local journalist what they had talked about, replying, "She asked us what lessons we were missing, and we spoke about our school. She asked if we were having fun. She looked in the dragon's mouth, her legs got a bit wet. It was a surprise, they told us yesterday we would see her. We were all really excited. She's really pretty, and she looks like a very rich person. She was very nice."[2] Nine-year-old Darcey was also interviewed, with the revelation that he had learned that the Duchess's children, George and Charlotte, had just gotten a new pet hamster named Marvin. Another child at the playground, Gavin, was not quite sure what was going on and grabbed the chairman's sleeve as he went past to ask, "Who's that?"

"The Duchess of Cambridge," the chairman whispered.

"Oooh!" Gavin shouted, prompting the Duchess to stop and turn round to the question, "Are you the princess?"

"Just call me Kate," she replied, whereupon Gavin turned back to the playground to proclaim, "Guys! It's Princess Kate!"

The Duchess was introduced to Robert Myers, the landscape architect who had designed the garden and who had previously received awards from the Royal Horticultural Society for his designs at the annual Chelsea Flower Show, and she chatted with some of the gardeners who had helped plant the three thousand shrubs and seventeen thousand bulbs that had gone into beautifying the playground's surroundings.

It had been twenty-seven years since Hampton Court had become one of five British palaces entrusted into the care of the newly formed Historic Royal Palaces (HRP)—then an executive agency within the United Kingdom's Department of Environment—before it was transferred in 1995 to the remit of the Department of National Heritage, which in 1997 was renamed the Department for Digital, Culture, Media and Sport. A year later, HRP was registered as an independent charity, contracted to manage and maintain the palaces assigned to its portfolio and which received no sustained financial support, in that regard, from either the Crown or government agencies. Hampton Court was one of four palaces in HRP's care that are no longer lived in by members of the royal family, along with the Tower of London, Prince Frederick's former house at Kew Palace, and the Banqueting House, the sole surviving remnant of the immolated Palace of Whitehall. In 2014 the royal family's official residence in Northern Ireland, Hillsborough Castle, became one of the two, along with Kensington Palace, that still had royal residential quarters, while most of its public spaces were entrusted to HRP, who could open those sections to tourists. This arrangement gives the charity both a great deal of freedom when it comes to mounting exhibitions and an equal amount of pressure to stimulate the footfall and interest necessary to generate the revenue needed to maintain the six sites.

As the chairman explained to the Duchess of Cambridge while showing her the playground, the Magic Gardens was part of a deliberate strategy to entice more visitors while also embracing the spirit of the palace's past. With the amount of time and money that HRP had sunk into the Magic Garden, the charity was keen that the opening ceremony involve somebody in whom the press was interested, which was why the invitation had been issued to the Duchess of Cambridge's office at Kensington Palace two years earlier. As one of the historians working at Hampton Court reflected, "I remember how over the moon everyone was when she accepted. At a stroke, it raised the Magic Garden's profile as no amount of marketing could have achieved."

The Duchess of Cambridge's press following had been, for her, a double-edged sword. By 2016, it had generally, although not universally, settled into broadly favorable—and, in some sections of the press, adulatory—coverage. However, when she first came to public attention thanks to her university romance with her future husband, Prince William, there had been paparazzi intrusion and attempts to hack into her voicemails.[3] Photographs, taken with long-zoom cameras, of her sunbathing topless on a private balcony next to her husband on holiday in the Solomon Islands were sold to French tabloids, prompting criticism of her rather than of the photographers in some quarters.[4] Donald Trump, who later served as President of the United States from 2017 to 2021, suggested that "Kate Middleton is great—but she shouldn't be sunbathing in the nude—only herself to blame. Who wouldn't take Kate's picture and make lots of money if she does the nude sunbathing thing[?] Come on, Kate!"[5] When, during her first pregnancy, she suffered from hyperemesis gravidarum*, it was misleadingly described by some journalists as "morning sickness," and they nicknamed her "Duchess Do-Nothing" when she cancelled several public engagements due to hospitalization.[6]

This level of intrusion into royal privacy struck several members of the royal family, particularly her husband and her brother-in-law Prince Harry, as grotesque and—given the damage it had inflicted on the life of their late mother, Diana, Princess of Wales—dangerous, as well as a departure from the respect and consideration that had been shown in previous decades. That deferential treatment of royalty was however the product of a confluence of factors which, given the monarchy's longevity, could even be considered a short-term phenomenon. Between 1863 and 1923, Britain's future kings married a succession of women, in Alexandra of Denmark, Mary of Teck, and Elizabeth Bowes-Lyon, who all proved very popular while not having particularly scandalous private lives. This coincided with an era of intense patriotism in Britain that lasted well into the 1960s and a corresponding culture of deference to national institutions. The fact that the last of the trio, Elizabeth Bowes-Lyon, lived an exceptionally long life, dying aged 101 in 2002, ensured that to some degree this attitude endured in certain sections of the press. But even before she died, the mood had shifted with regard to the younger members of the royal family.

Looking to the more distant past, before the mid-nineteenth century, it is doubtful if consorts such as Henrietta Maria of France, Catherine of Braganza, or Caroline of Ansbach would have characterized the public's attitude as inherently deferential. What made the late-twentieth and twenty-first

---

* A sickness during pregnancy, which often lasts beyond the 16–20 week mark of a pregnancy and often requires hospitalization due to excessive nausea, vomiting, cramps, and dehydration.

centuries different was not that the period marked a break with traditional British scrutiny of the monarchy, but rather how all-encompassing and un-accountable that scrutiny could become, thanks to the rise in mass media and later to the speculation-rampant hinterlands of social media. It could, as the Duchess of Cambridge's case had seemingly exhibited by 2016, simul-taneously hinder and help an individual royal.

For HRP, the attention and popularity commanded by the Duchess of Cambridge could be utilized to their advantage. Like the monarchy, Hampton Court had left the age of divine right for one of modern mass appeal. The palace needs footfall, column inches, and social media posts to flourish as it enters its seventh century. The press coverage surrounding the Duchess of Cambridge's visit helped considerably in attracting visitors to Hampton Court, especially the "young families" demographic.

After touring the playground, the Duchess of Cambridge was escorted into an adjoining Garden Room, where she met several of those involved in turning the Magic Gardens into a reality. They included the charity's chief executive, Michael Day, who explained that the new playground was part of HRP's plans to make Hampton Court more enticing to families planning day trips, as well as more accessible with greater opportunities for differ-ent activities. Among those presented was Dr. Tracy Borman, a historian working with Historic Royal Palaces, whose previous publications included biographies of George II's mistress Henrietta Howard and Henry VIII's chief minister Thomas Cromwell, and who was preparing that year to pub-lish her book *The Private Lives of the Tudors*. Borman's daughter, six-year-old Eleanor, was also in the Garden Room to present the Duchess with a posy from the palace gardens; according to Eleanor's mother, the Duchess seemed to be "genuinely enjoying herself [and] . . . bending down to [Elea-nor's] level and chatting to her for way longer than I expected. Kate asked her who she was here with, what her favorite part of the Magic Garden was, how old she was, etc., and also complimented her on her dress." The Duchess unveiled a plaque, signed a special guest book to commemorate the occasion, and then cut into a colossus of a cake, which offered butter-cream tributes to Hampton Court's Tudor colors and motifs, produced for the occasion by a bakery with the fantastic name of Choccywoccydoodah. After that, the Duchess's driver took her back to London in time for her afternoon visit to the Anna Freud Centre for Children and Families, a charity and treatment facility for children with mental health concerns, of which the Duchess was patron.

The palace is better preserved and curated today than it has been at any point since George III's retreat. History seems to fall in on itself at Hampton Court, with Elizabethan red brick yielding suddenly to Baroque staircases, its Restoration-era canal halting at gravel pathways circling to Charles I's tennis court. The magnificent, the absurd, the tragic, and the important have interacted there over the course of its existence and their stories—perhaps more so than the architecture—continue to attract thousands of tourists every year. Purchasing a ticket for admission from a building that stands on the site of what was once the Cavalry Block—the outlines of the old hayracks are still visible on the walls—visitors enter over the drained moat, which faces quarters once occupied by Sarah Grundy, the Victorian housekeeper who waged a morality campaign by hiding the art collection's nudes in an upstairs room, and those allegedly haunted by Sybil Penne, the servant who died from the smallpox she caught caring for Elizabeth I at Hampton Court. They pass through the same gate accessed by Anne of Cleves and Lord William Howard as they rode in companionable awkwardness to the Christmas of 1540–41.

Much, of course, is gone thanks to William III and Mary II, yet much that is beautiful survives because of them. Among those to have vanished are the rooms where Catherine Howard suffered the first two weeks of her downfall, James I commissioned the Authorized Translation of the Bible, and Catherine of Braganza wept at the humiliation of being waited upon by the Countess of Castlemaine. The demolished rooms also included those where Oliver Cromwell mourned his daughter's death and Mary I quizzed her younger sister about her complicity in the 1554 rebellion. The Privy Gardens—on the original site where Elizabeth I feared for her life and through which Charles I left Hampton Court for the final time—were so altered by William III's designs that it is doubtful that they would recognize them. They are wonderful in summer, when the flowers—replanted in 1995 after the rediscovery of the Williamite plans—are in bloom. Inside, William's private rooms are often open, with his furniture and art collection returned, and his dining room set up by curators as if for a dinner party in 1699. His red velvet-covered commode and the yellow canopies of his bed can be seen, as can similarly intimate pieces like Queen Caroline's bath and her dressing table. Somewhere in those rooms must be the spot where George II hit his grandson with such cruel force that the future George III "could never afterwards be induced to think of it as a residence."[7]

The Tosiers' restored Chocolate Kitchens are located off the Fountain Court, which looks much as it did when Michael Faraday escorted his wife Sarah through it in her wheelchair. There are still some nameplates discreetly fastened onto walls, marking where the grace-and-favor residents live in a system which endured despite press criticism in 1986, after attention to it was stimulated by press coverage of a fire in Hampton Court's Baroque wing. The chapel is maintained as an Anglican place of worship—visitors are asked to remove their hats when they enter. In 2016, with Elizabeth II's permission, it became the first Chapel Royal to permit the celebration of a Roman Catholic Mass since the days of James II and the first to be held in that specific room since the residency of Mary I; the Archbishop of Westminster, Cardinal Vincent Nichols, was invited to celebrate Vespers in Latin, a moving gesture in light of the many ways in which Hampton Court has served as a launching pad for the sectarian divisions that caused so much suffering in British history.[8] The Privy Council chamber where major decisions regarding the Reformation were taken lies at the end of the Haunted Gallery, from which tourists can visit the room where Henry VIII married Katherine Parr, before walking around to peer into the restored Pages' Chamber that adjoins a Great Watching Chamber much more sedate than it was when James I's inebriated fellow revellers toasted the first Stuart Christmas in England. Visitors can stand in the Great Hall, where Anne Boleyn's initials interweaving with her husband's can be spotted by the curious, where Shakespeare premiered some of his plays and Elizabeth II danced in a pink ballgown to celebrate her forthcoming coronation. The Base Court has not changed much since the Bassett sisters entered it on their arrival to serve Queen Jane Seymour in the autumn of 1537; from there, doorways led to the narrow, cobblestoned walkways where servants and errand boys haggled over fish, meat, bread, and firewood. Lord Daubeney's kitchens, where wine was decanted for Henry VII and food cooked for Elizabeth of York, survive and, on cold days, the staff kindle fires in the original grates.

Between the Base and Clock Courts, in the Anne Boleyn Gate—and nobody is really sure of precisely when it was moved there—is the bell inscribed with a prayer to the Virgin Mary, the same bell from the vanished medieval chapel maintained under the terms of Lord Daubeney's lease in the 1490s. From there, it tolls to mark the passing of the hours and years at Hampton Court as it has done for centuries.

ACKNOWLEDGMENTS

I am grateful to my agent and friend Brettne Bloom, who first suggested I write a book about Hampton Court after a visit there together, and to my editors in Britain and America—Arabella Pike, Trish Todd, and Peter Borland—for their faith in this project and for their suggestions.

I would like to extend personal thanks to Dr. Tracy Borman, Leanda de Lisle, and Coryne Hall, who shared memories of their time at Hampton Court and answered questions about their relatives' or friends' experiences. The people who work at Hampton Court Palace today are wonderful—they have been helpful, warm, and welcoming, whether it be answering a question about a Georgian door or showing me what remains hidden of Wolsey's bricked-up chapel windows. My thanks to all of them, and especially to Sarah Slater and to James Harris, Clerk of the Chapel and Groom of the Vestry at His Majesty's Chapel Royal.

For encouragement, advice, and help, I would like to thank Olivia Auerbach, Dr. Lauren Browne, Dr. Ian Campbell, Dr. James Corke-Webster, Scott De Buitléir, Joanne and Dr. Mark Doody, Jake Douglas, Dr. Owen Emmerson, Peter Evangelista, Stewart Evans, Lydia Forte, Dr. Jonathan Foyle—whose lectures and conversations at Hever Castle in May 2022 on how Hampton Court looked to Anne Boleyn were inspirational—Ian Franklin, Steve Gove, Aoife Herity, Debra, Madeleine, and Eamon Hill,

Laura and Tom Hunniwood, Janice Hyndman, Darcy R. Keim, Philippa Lacey Brewell, Matt Lewis, Dr. Suzannah Lipscomb, Dr. Lauren Mackay, Dr. Miranda Malins, Kate McCaffrey, Aisleagh McConnell, Dr. Hannah McCormick, Ashley Montgomery, Molly O'Brien, Dr. Micheál Ó Siochrú, Dr. Estelle Paranque, Dr. Geoffrey Parker, Sheila Patterson, Darren Perks, Dr. John-Mark Philo, Dr. Linda Porter, Claire Ridgway, Kerry Rogan, Dr. David Ross, Dr. Valerie Schutte, Antonia and Archie Sebag-Montefiore, Octavia Seymour, Alexa and Colin Reid Smith, Dr. Lesley Smith, Nichelle Tramble Spellman, Eric, Susan, and Evelyn Spies, Beth Steer, Paul Storrs, Dr. James Taffe, Dr. Nicola Tallis, Kathryn Warner, Dr. Toby Wilkinson, Keith Williamson, and Dr. Elia Woodacre. My thanks too to the staff at the Bodleian Library, Oxford; the British Library; Castle Leslie, Monaghan; Hever Castle, Kent; Historic Royal Palaces; Saintfield Library, Co. Down; the Linen Hall, Lisburn Road, and McClay libraries, in Belfast, and at the National Archives. My family have my love and gratitude, as always.

My time on *The Palace* saw several farewells, of which the hardest to bear—my father's—has been mentioned in the introduction. Mike Ingram, a great historian who passed away in December 2021, kindly answered a question on the Wars of the Roses as I was researching the chapter on Lord Daubeney. Maura Kelly, who encouraged me so much in the early stages of *The Palace*, passed away halfway through the writing process. She endured her final illness with the passion and grace that were her main characteristics. Maura was a committed trade unionist, a champion of fairness, a lady, the best of company, and a true friend.

The Palace was my fourth and last book with my US editor Trish Todd, who retired as the final edits for this project were completed. Our friendship continues; however, I would be remiss if I did not say here what a wonderful editor Trish has been—to me, as to many others—and how grateful I am to her for everything she did in the eight years in which we worked together.

Gareth Russell
Rome, May 2023

NOTES

ABBREVIATIONS

BL—British Library (manuscripts)
BMC—British Museum Collection
Bod.—Bodleian Library

Cal. S. P. Dom.—*Calendar of State Papers Domestic: Edward VI, Mary and Elizabeth, 1547–80*, ed. Robert Lemon et al. (London: Longman, Brown, Green, Longman & Roberts, 1856–72)
Cal. S. P. Ireland—*Calendar of the State Papers Relating to Ireland, of the Reigns of Henry VIII, Edward VI, Mary, and Elizabeth*, ed. Ernest G. Atkinson et al. (London: Her Majesty's Stationery Office, 1860–1912)
Cal. S. P. Span., S.—*Calendar of State Papers, Spain (Simancas)*, vol. 1, *1558–1567*, ed. Martin A. S. Hume et al. (London: Her Majesty's Stationery Office, 1892)
Cal. S. P. Span.—*Calendar of Letters, Despatches, and State Papers Relating to the Negotiations Between England and Spain*, ed. G. Bergenroth et al. (London: Longman, Green, Longman & Roberts, 1862–1954)
Cal. S. P. Ven.—*Calendar of State Papers Relating to English Affairs in the Archives of Venice* (London: Her Majesty's Stationery Office, 1864)
FO—The National Archives—Foreign Office and Foreign and Commonwealth Office records from 1782
HMC Rutland—*The Manuscripts of His Grace the Duke of Rutland G. C. B., Preserved at Belvoir Castle* (London: Her Majesty's Stationery Office, 1888)
HMC Salisbury—*Calendar of the Manuscripts of the Most Honourable the Marquess of Salisbury Preserved at Hatfield House, Hertfordshire*, ed. Robert Gascoyne-Cecil, 3rd Marquess of Salisbury, et al. (London: Her Majesty's Stationery Office, 1883–1976)
INV—*The Inventory of Henry VIII*, ed. D. Starkey et al. (London: Society of Antiquaries of London, 1998–2012)
LC—The National Archives—Royal Household and Wardrobe files
Lisle Letters—*The Lisle Letters*, ed. Muriel St. Clare Byrne (Chicago: University of Chicago Press, 1981)
LP—*Letters and Papers, Foreign and Domestic of the Reign of Henry VIII*, ed. J. S. Brewer et al. (London: Her Majesty's Stationery Office, 1862–1932)
MS Ashmole—Bodleian Library (manuscripts)
ODNB—*Oxford Dictionary of National Biography* (Oxford: Oxford University Press, 2004)
RIA—Royal Irish Academy

RCIN—Royal Collection Identification Number
SP—*State Papers Domestics, 1547–1649* (The National Archives)
State Papers—State Papers, King Henry VIII (London, 1830–52)
WO—The National Archives—War Office and Successors: Registered Files

PROLOGUE

1. Interview given by Queen Camilla about Elizabeth II, BBC, September 18, 2022; *Sunday Dispatch* (UK), October 27, 1928; Ben Pimlott, *The Queen: Elizabeth II and the Monarchy* (London: HarperCollins, 2001), p. 31.
2. Elizabeth, Duchess of York, to Queen Mary, January 26, 1931, in William Shawcross, ed., *Counting One's Blessings: The Selected Letters of Queen Elizabeth The Queen Mother* (London: Macmillan, 2012), p. 185.
3. Angela Kelly, *The Other Side of the Coin: The Queen, the Dresser and the Wardrobe* (London: HarperCollins, 2019), p. 89.
4. The Court Circular, May 29, 1953.
5. *The Argus*, May 26 and June 1, 1953.
6. The court had ceased to use the palace as an official royal residence after the death of George II in 1760.
7. Christopher Hibbert, *George III: A Personal History* (London: Viking, 1998), pp. 57–58.
8. Gareth Russell, *Do Let's Have Another Drink: The Singular Wit and Double Measures of Queen Elizabeth the Queen Mother* (London: William Collins, 2022), p. 66.
9. Sarah Bradford, *Elizabeth: A Biography of Her Majesty The Queen,* rev. ed. (London: Heinemann, 1996), pp. 33, 41, 200.
10. "Monarchy Poll—December 2000," Ipsos online, last modified December 17, 2000; Nigel Nicolson, *The Queen and Us* (London: Weidenfeld & Nicolson, 2003), p. 109.
11. George Wedell, "Kurt Matthias Robert Martin Hahn (1886–1974)," in *ODNB*, 24:XXIV, pp. 451–53.
12. Under the terms of a 1705 Act of Parliament, direct-line descendants of Sophia, Electress of Hanover (d. 1714), were automatically British citizens, which made Philip's naturalization as a British citizen in 1947 "quite unnecessary"; see Pimlott, *The Queen*, p. 101. Neither Philip nor his family knew this until a friend informed Lord Mountbatten about the law twenty-five years later. Philip chose to adopt his uncle's anglicized surname of Mountbatten rather than his Greco-Danish dynastic name of Schleswig-Holstein-Sonderburg-Glücksburg.
13. Sarah Bradford, *George VI: The Dutiful King* (London: HarperCollins, 1991), p. 556.
14. Bradford, *Elizabeth*, p. 115.
15. British Film Institute, "TV in the 1950s," accessed online, December 22, 2022; Pimlott, *The Queen*, pp. 206–7.
16. Robert Lacey, *Monarch: The Life and Reign of Elizabeth II* (London: Simon & Schuster, 2003), p. 200.
17. Pimlott, *The Queen*, p. 285.
18. Although strongly disliked by the Conservative Party leadership, the League of Empire Loyalists was initially supported by several hard-line Conservatives. It was led by Arthur K. Chesterton, former director of press propaganda for the British Union

of Fascists. The league was disbanded in 1967, with many of its members gravitating toward the National Front.

19. Jeremy Paxman, *On Royalty* (London: Viking, 2006), p. 68.

20. Ernest Jones, "The Psychology of Constitutional Monarchy," in *Essays in Applied Psychoanalysis: a contribution to the psychology of politics and morals,* ed. R. E. Money-Kyrle (London: Hogarth Press, 1951), pp. 227–33.

21. C. S. Lewis, "Equality," *Spectator,* August 27, 1943.

22. Stephen Bates, "We Have To Be Seen To Be Believed: The Endurance Of The Royal Tour," *Guardian* (US edition) online, last modified March 29, 2022.

23. *Daily Mirror* (UK), May 30, 1953; *Argus,* June 1, 1953.

24. Sue Shephard, *The Surprising Life of Constance Spry* (London: Pan, 2011), p. 201.

25. James Pope-Hennessy, *Queen Mary* (London: George Allen & Unwin, 1959), pp. 482–84.

26. The Court Circular, May 29, 1953.

27. Ibid.

28. The Queen and the Duke of Edinburgh knew about the romance before Christmas 1952, when Townsend told "Tommy" Lascelles; despite Lascelles's urging that the Queen Mother be told as soon as possible, she did not find out until February 1953; see Sir Alan "Tommy" Lascelles, *King's Counsellor—Abdication and War: The Diaries of Sir Alan "Tommy" Lascelles,* ed. Duff Hart-Davis (London: Weidenfeld & Nicolson, 2007), p. 410.

29. Elizabeth II was descended from Edward III in several lines. His identification here as her nineteen-times great-grandfather is made by going back to Elizabeth's descent through Margaret of England, Queen of Scots (d. 1541), then through her paternal grandmother, Margaret (née Beaufort), Countess of Richmond and Derby (d. 1509), then back to her ancestor and Edward III's son John of Gaunt, Duke of Lancaster (d. 1399).

PART I: THE HOUSE OF TUDOR

CHAPTER 1: STAR OF THE SEA

1. Duncan Hawkins, "Anglo-Saxon Kingston: A Shifting Pattern of Settlement," *London Archaeologist* 8, no. 10 (Autumn 1998): pp. 271–72; Sarah Foot, *Athelstan: The First King of England* (New Haven, CT: Yale University Press, 2011), p. 74.

2. Hugh M. Thomas, *The English and the Normans: Ethnic Hostility, Assimilation, and Identity, 1066–c. 1220* (Oxford: Oxford University Press, 2003), pp. 105–6, 111–15.

3. Walter's grandmother was William the Conqueror's aunt; see G. Herbert Fowler, "De St Walery," *Genealogist* 30 (1914): pp. 1–17, and David C. Douglas, *William the Conqueror: The Norman Impact upon England* (New Haven, CT: Yale University Press, 1999), pp. 265–72.

4. The Knights Hospitaller was the father organization to today's Sovereign Military Hospitaller Order of St. John of Jerusalem, of Rhodes and of Malta, known more commonly as the Knights of Malta.

5. It is possible that an earlier king of England, Stephen (r. 1135–54), himself the son of a Crusader, had offered some early royal patronage to the order, which was interrupted or weakened by the civil war of the 1130s and 1140s.

6. Kathryn Warner, *Edward II: The Unconventional King* (Stroud, UK: Amberley, 2014), pp. 28–30, argues: "that Edward II loved Piers Gaveston is beyond all doubt. Precisely how he loved him, however, is a difficult question to answer." While the weight of evidence would support the theory that the king and the earl were lovers—see J. S. Hamilton, *Piers Gaveston, Earl of Cornwall, 1307–1312: Politics and Patronage in the Reign of Edward II* (Detroit: Wayne State University Press, 1988), pp. 13, 16–17—referring to Gaveston here simply as the man Edward II loved seems an acceptable erring on the side of caution without diluting the evidence. See, by way of comparison (abbreviated hereafter as *cf.*), Andrew Lumsden, "The fairy tale of Edward II," *Gay and Lesbian Review Worldwide* 11 (March/April 2004): n.p., and Pierre Chaplais, *Piers Gaveston: Edward II's adoptive brother* (Oxford: Oxford University Press, 1994).

7. Correspondence between this author and Kathryn Warner, May 29, 2020. I am grateful to Warner, biographer of Edward II, his queen, Isabella, and his last favorite, Hugh Despenser the Younger, for discussing with me the problems in locating any firm contemporary evidence that Byfleet was initially built as a gift for Gaveston. See also Hamilton, *Piers Gaveston*, pp. 41–42.

8. Warner, *Edward II*, p. 68; Ian Mortimer, *The Perfect King: The Life of Edward III, Father of the English Nation* (London: Vintage, 2008), pp. 17–25; Bryan Bevan, *Edward III: Monarch of Chivalry* (London: Rubicon Press, 1992), p. 17.

9. Both men were descended from King Edward III—Henry VI in the male line through the former's third son, John of Gaunt, Duke of Lancaster (d. 1399); his rival Richard, Duke of York, in the female line through Edward III's second son, Lionel, Duke of Clarence (d. 1368); and in the male line from Edward's fourth son, Edmund of Langley, Duke of York (d. 1402). The Lancastrians argued in favor of agnatic primogeniture and the Yorkists for cognatic primogeniture, although it is highly unlikely they would ever have done so had Henry VI's reign not been beset by so many difficulties. Richard, Duke of York, fell at the Battle of Wakefield in 1460, with the result that the first member of his line to take the crown was his son as Edward IV.

10. There is a long-standing debate over what precisely happened to Edward V and his brother. Thus far, none of the revisionist arguments have personally convinced me that either the ex-king or his younger brother lived beyond 1483. For a well-argued alternative interpretation, see Matthew Lewis, *The Survival of the Princes in the Tower: Murder, Mystery and Myth* (Stroud, UK: History Press, 2018).

11. Henry VII's late father, Edmund Tudor, 1st Earl of Richmond, had been Henry VI's half brother through their mother, the Dowager Queen Catherine of Valois. Henry VI was the son of Catherine's first husband, Henry V; Edmund was born from her second marriage to a former member of her household staff, Owen Tudor.

12. House of Commons, Parliamentary Information List, Briefing Paper 04637a, gives the surname as Wood.

13. J. L. Laynesmith, *The Last Medieval Queens: English Queenship, 1445–1503* (Oxford: Oxford University Press, 2006), p. 245.

14. The original, by Bernard André, Henry VII's poet laureate, reads *vir bonus, prudens, probus, et omnibus dilectus.* Cf. Dominic A. Luckett, "Crown Patronage and Political Morality in Early Tudor England: The Case of Giles, Lord Daubeney," *English Historical Review* (June 1995): pp. 578–79.

15. Michael Hicks, *Richard III: The Self-Made King* (New Haven, CT: Yale University Press, 2019), p. 313, puts the number of accompanying servants at four; S. J. Gunn, "Daubeney, Giles, First baron Daubeney," in *ODNB*, 15: pp. 236–37, gives six.

16. The Daubeneys were naturalized as English subjects by Edward I in 1295 and were granted livery by Edward II in 1326. Several previous Giles Daubeneys had served as MPs for Somerset in the fourteenth and fifteenth centuries.

17. For the ambassador's remark, see *Cal. S. P. Ven.*, I, 256; for Daubeney's career, see Gunn, "Daubeney, Giles," in *ODNB*, 15:pp. 236–37; the same author's *Early Tudor Government, 1485–1558* (London: Macmillan, 1995), pp. 33, 38; Dominic Luckett, "Daubeney family," in *ODNB*, 15:pp. 234–36; S. B. Chrimes, *Henry VII* (London: Eyre Methuen, 1972), pp. 111–12, 304. Chrimes queries Katherine of Aragon's assessment of Daubeney, suggesting that "it is not easy to see from his career why [she] should have described him in the terms that she did."

18. Desmond Seward, *The Last White Rose: The Secret Wars of the Tudors* (London: Constable, 2011), p. 101.

19. Ibid., p. 157.

20. Layer Marney was built c. 1520, two decades after the end of Daubeney's first building spree at Hampton, for Daubeney's brother-in-law Henry, 1st Baron Marney (d. 1523).

21. Luke 1:26–38.

22. Ruth Goodman, *How to Be a Tudor: A Dawn-to-Dusk Guide to Everyday Life* (London: Viking, 2015), pp. 6–8.

23. Ibid.

24. Ibid., pp. 18–20.

25. Ibid., p. 35.

26. This is John 1:1, as rendered in the Vulgate of Saint Jerome.

27. Eamon Duffy, *The Stripping of the Altars: Traditional Religion in England, c. 1400–c. 1580*, 2nd. ed. (New Haven, CT: Yale University Press, 2005), p. 183.

28. Ann Kussmaul, *Servants in Husbandry in Early Modern England* (Cambridge: Cambridge University Press, 1981), p. 3.

29. Prime was abolished by the liturgical reforms of the Second Vatican Council (1962–65).

30. This chapter's description of the physical layout of Hampton Court is based on Simon Thurley, *Hampton Court: A Social and Architectural History* (New Haven, CT: Yale University Press, 2003), pp. 1–13, and D. Batchelor, "Excavations at Hampton Court Palace," *Post Medieval Archaeology* 11, no. 1 (1977): pp. 36–49.

31. Exodus 27:20–21.

32. Duffy, *Stripping of the Altars*, p. 256; Christopher Allmand, *Henry V* (London: Methuen, 1992), pp. 275, 410.

33. As a previous leaseholder, Sir John Wode had been a vice admiral under King Richard III, it raises the possibility that Wode had installed the bell as part of his obligations to keep the chapel in working order and fully staffed, duties that had since fallen to Lord Daubeney.

34. These rooms were previously misidentified as having survived from Henry VIII's era. Recent excavations and research have established that much of the Great Kitchen at Hampton Court dates from Lord Daubeney's tenure, and he was quite possibly inspired by the King's kitchens at his new palace of Richmond; see also Thurley, *Hampton Court*, p. 45.

35. Historic Royal Palaces, "Hampton Court's Kitchens," accessed online, September 19, 2022.

36. *John Russell's Book of Nurture,* in *The Babees' Book: Medieval Manners for the Young: Done into Modern English from Dr. Furnivall's Texts*, ed. Edith Rickert and Israel Gollancz (New York: Cooper Square, 1966), p. 52.

37. Christopher Dyer, *Standards of Living in the Later Middle Ages: Social Change in England, c. 1200–1520* (Cambridge: Cambridge University Press, 1989), p. 55.

38. Sir Nicholas H. Nicolas, ed., *The Privy Purse Expenses of Elizabeth of York* (London: W. Pickering, 1830), pp. 2, 6–7, 12; Amy Licence, *Elizabeth of York: Forgotten Tudor Queen* (Stroud, UK: Amberley, 2014), p. 22.

39. Laynesmith, *Last Medieval Queens*, pp. 247–49. Elizabeth of York exerted similar influence over the early Tudor alterations to Greenwich Palace.

40. B. MacCarthy, ed., *Annála Uladh, Annals of Ulster from the Earliest Time to the Year 1541*, intro. Nollaig Ó Muraíle (Blackrock, Ire.: Éamonn de Búrca, 1998), 3:465, which also identifies Elizabeth as wife of the "king of the Saxons"; Laynesmith, *Last Medieval Queens*, p. 252.

41. Edward Hall, *Hall's Chronicle: Containing the History of England During the Reign of Henry IV and the Succeeding Monarchs to the End of the Reign of Henry VIII,* ed. Henry Ellis (London: J. Johnson et al., 1809), p. 264; Amy Licence, *Edward IV and Elizabeth Woodville: A True Romance* (Stroud, UK: Amberley, 2016), pp. 30, 105–7.

42. Nicola Tallis, *Uncrowned Queen: The Fateful Life of Margaret Beaufort, Tudor Matriarch* (London: Michael O'Mara, 2019), p. xxxv.

43. His wardship was granted in 1462 to William Herbert, 1st Earl of Pembroke, who was executed on July 27, 1469.

44. Celtic Sea was not bestowed as a name until delegates at a conference of British, Irish, and French fishery experts at Dublin in 1921 decided the sea had needed a proper designation for years. For the use of the secret tunnels to facilitate Henry and Jasper Tudor's escape during the siege, see Nathen Amin, "Tenby—the most important Tudor town?" *Tudor Places* (Summer 2022), pp. 22–25.

45. *Cal. S. P. Span.*, I, 177, 178; Henry was a refugee in the Duchy of Brittany (1471–84) and in France (1484–85). His father's maternal grandfather was King Charles VI of France.

46. Chrimes, app. D, "The Papal Dispensation for the Marriage of Henry VII and Elizabeth, 1486," in *Henry VII*, pp. 330–31.

47. Luke 1:42; F. Grose and T. Astle, eds., *Antiquarian Repertory: A Miscellaneous Assemblage of Topography, History, Biography, Customs, and Manners; Intended to Illustrate and Preserve Several Valuable Remains of Old Times* (London: E. Jeffrey, 1808), I, p. 218.

48. Licence, *Elizabeth of York*, p. 221.

49. *Cal. S. P. Ven.*, I, 298.

50. Giles Tremlett, *Catherine of Aragon: Henry's Spanish Queen* (London: Faber & Faber, 2010), 104.

51. John Leland, *De rebus Britannicus collectanea* (Oxford: Sheldonian Theatre, 1715), 5: pp. 373–74; Grose and Astle, *Antiquarian Repertory*, 2:pp. 322–23.

52. Licence, *Elizabeth of York*, p. 220.

53. Nicolas, *Privy Purse Expenses of Elizabeth of York*, p. 3.

54. Matthew 2:1–2.

55. Thomas Penn, *Winter King: The Dawn of Tudor England* (London: Penguin, 2011), p. 94.

CHAPTER 2: TURRETS AND TOWERS

1. James Butler's date of birth is contested. The year 1496 or 1497 seems the most likely, meaning that he was about seventeen when he received his wound at the siege of Thérouanne (1513). He was likely born in Kilkenny or, perhaps, in the neighboring county of Tipperary.

2. George Cavendish, *The Life of Cardinal Wolsey, by George Cavendish, His Gentleman Usher, and Metrical Visions*, ed. Samuel Weller Singer (Chiswick, UK: Harding, Triphook, and Lepard, 1825), p. 12.

3. Wolsey's pupils were Thomas Grey, later 2nd Marquess of Dorset, and Leonard Grey, later 1st Viscount Grane and Lord Deputy of Ireland (1536–40). They were sons of Thomas Grey, 1st Marquess of Dorset, Elizabeth of York's half brother as a son of Queen Elizabeth Woodville with her first husband, Sir John Grey, who fell in battle during the Wars of the Roses.

4. Sir Richard Nanfan died on January 7, 1507; the tomb of Giles, 1st Lord Daubeney, at Westminster Abbey gives his date of death as "the XII day of May in the yere of our Lord 1507."

5. It is not clear how Hampton Court was used between the 1st Lord Daubeney's death in 1507 and the 2nd Lord Daubeney's transfer of the lease to Cardinal Wolsey in 1515. Thurley, *Hampton Court*, p. 15, suggests that Giles Daubeney's widow, Elizabeth (née Arundell), may have sublet the estate until her son came of age, given the fact that her husband died in debt.

6. LP, II, 892.

7. Earlier in his political career, Wolsey had a riverside manor at Bridewell, closer to the City of London's boundaries, until his household and his ambition outgrew it. He also had and expanded several other magnificent properties.

8. Alden Gregory, "In his own image: Architectural patronage and self-symbolism in Archbishop Warham's motivations for rebuilding the palace at Otford (c. 1514–26)," in *The Intellectual Culture of the English Country House, 1500–1700,* ed. Matthew Dimmock, Andrew Hadfield, and Margareth Healy (Manchester, UK: Manchester University Press 2015), pp. 32–33, puts the commencement of Warham's work at Otford at c. 1514.

9. SP 1/26, f. 140; William Lambarde, *A Preambulation of Kent: Conteining the Description, Hystorie, and Customes of that Shire, Written in the yeere 1570* (Cheetham, UK: W. Burrill, 1826), p. 464.

10. Alden Gregory, "In his own image," p. 39.

11. Ibid., pp. 38–39 and fig. 2.7.
12. At the time of his visit to Hampton Court, Charles V was technically "emperor elect," his proper title from his election in 1520 until Pope Clement VII placed the imperial crown on his head at Bologna, Italy, in 1530, whereupon the latter word could be dropped from his title. However, most of Charles's contemporaries referred to him as emperor from 1520, and I have followed their lead, as the October 1520 ceremony in Aachen Cathedral ended with the proclamation that "the pope, having approved the election of Charles the Fifth, orders that henceforth he must take the title of 'emperor.'"
13. Frederick J. Furnivall, *Ballads from Manuscripts* (London: Taylor, 1868), 352.
14. Sophie Julien-Lees, Historic Royal Palaces Conservation Department Bulletin, November 25, 2005; Lucia Burgio et al., "The Hampton Court Terracotta Roundels Project," *Conservation Journal of the Victoria and Albert Museum* 57 (Spring 2009): online paper; Maev Kennedy, "Hampton Court Roundels Restored—and Their Humble Origins Revealed," *Guardian* (US edition) online, last modified September 28, 2011. The terracotta emperors were added to in number at a later date, and debate continues over which emperors were added and when.
15. My thanks to Professor Toby Wilkinson for confirming that the correct nomenclature for Cleopatra was that of pharaoh rather than queen regnant; correspondence with the author, November 2020.
16. It is unclear at what point Daubeney's entrance gate—between what is now the Clock Court and the Base Court—was demolished. It may have been during Wolsey's renovations or during Anne Boleyn's (1533–36). It was replaced by the gate now known as the Anne Boleyn Gate.
17. Eric Ives, *The Life and Death of Anne Boleyn: The Most Happy* (Oxford: Blackwell, 2004), p. 111.
18. Thurley, *Hampton Court*, p. 43.
19. Roger Bowers, "The cultivation and promotion of music in the household and orbit of Thomas Wolsey," in *Cardinal Wolsey: Church, state and art,* ed. S. J. Gunn and P. G. Lindley (Cambridge: Cambridge University Press, 1991), p. 179; SP1/16, fol. 174.
20. Matthew 16:13–19.
21. Hilary Wayment, "Wolsey and Stained Glass," in *Cardinal Wolsey*, Gunn and Lindley, pp. 119–20.
22. Ibid., p. 126; Peter Curnow, "The East Window of the Chapel at Hampton Court Palace," *Architectural History* 27 (1984): pp. 1–14.
23. This is based on the staff retained by Wolsey for the chapel in 1521; see BL, MS Harley 620, fols. 27v, 44v–45r.
24. Bowers, "Cultivation and Promotion of Music in Household and Orbit of Wolsey," pp. 185–86, 194.
25. 1 Timothy 3:1, 4–5.
26. Cavendish, *Life of Cardinal Wolsey*, pp. 67–68. Spelling modernized by this author.
27. Ibid., p. 68.
28. Ibid., in reference to the famous reception for the constable of France in 1527.
29. Ibid.

30. Jasper Ridley, *The Statesman and the Fanatic: Thomas Wolsey and Thomas More* (London: Constable, 1982), p. 115; LP, XI, 1358.

31. Lauren Mackay, *Among the Wolves of Court: The Untold Story of Thomas and George Boleyn* (London: I. B. Tauris, 2018), pp. 92–93.

32. Geoffrey Parker, *Emperor: A New Life of Charles V* (New Haven, CT: Yale University Press, 2019), p. 66.

33. Martyn Rady, *The Habsburgs: The Rise and Fall of a World Power* (London: Penguin Random House, 2020), p. 66.

34. Richard Pace to Thomas Wolsey, May 17, 1517, BL, Cotton MS. Vitellius B.XX/55.

35. Gilbert Burnet, *The History of the Reformation of the Church of England* (Oxford: Oxford University Press, 1829), 3:ii, pp. 11–12.

36. Geoffrey Parker, *Emperor*, p. 126.

37. Wolsey quite probably upped this display considerably for Charles V's visit. We know from a later diplomatic reception at Hampton Court—for the constable of France in 1527—that the impressed visitors guessed the gold plate on display to be worth around three hundred thousand ducats.

38. Sebastian Giustiniani, *Four Years at the Court of Henry VIII*, trans. R. L. Brown (Cambridge: Cambridge University Press, 2014), 2:314; Philippa Glanville, "Cardinal Wolsey and the goldsmiths," in *Cardinal Wolsey*, Gunn and Lindley, pp. 131–32.

39. Thurley, *Hampton Court*, 26.

40. LP, II (ii), 4662. S. J. Gunn and P. G. Lindley, introduction to *Cardinal Wolsey*, Gunn and Lindley, p. 35. Wolsey's Gallery now exists only as remains beneath the current Cartoon Gallery, dating from the reign of William III.

41. Geoffrey Parker, *Emperor*, p. 62.

42. This was the second Mary Tudor to whom Charles was betrothed—he had been engaged in infancy to her aunt, before that pact was broken so that the elder Mary could marry the widowed King Louis XII of France, during one of the transient moments of Anglo-French friendship.

43. Geoffrey Parker, *Emperor*, p. 83.

44. Ibid., pp. 397–98.

45. A. F. Pollard, *Wolsey* (London: Longmans Green, 1953), p. 306; Peter Gwyn, *The King's Cardinal: The Rise and Fall of Thomas Wolsey* (London: Pimlico, 2002), p. xv.

46. Geoffrey Parker, *Emperor*, p. 212.

47. LP, III, i, 432.

48. Geoffrey Parker, *Emperor*, p. 109.

49. Manuel Fernández Alvarez, *Charles V: Elected Emperor and Hereditary Ruler*, trans. J. A. Lalaguna (London: Thames and Hudson, 1975), p. 47.

50. Olivette Otele, *African Europeans: An Untold History* (London: C. Hurst, 2020), pp. 46–47.

51. Geoffrey Parker, *Emperor*, p. xv.

52. Andrés Reséndez, *The Other Slavery: The Uncovered Story of Indian Enslavement in America* (Boston: Mariner Books, 2016), p. 13.

53. James Walvin, *A World Transformed: Slavery in the Americas and the Origins of Global Power* (London: Robinson, 2022), pp. 20–22.

54. Ibid., p. 22.

55. James Alexander Williamson, *The Voyages of the Cabots and the Discovery of North America* (London: Argonauts Press, 1929), pp. 85, 244.

56. *Cal. S. P. Ven.*, III, 607.

57. Williamson, *Voyages of the Cabots*, p. 248.

58. John Julius Norwich, *Byzantium: The Early Centuries* (London: Guild, 1988), p. 147; Brian Moynahan, *The Faith: A History of Christianity* (London: Pimlico, 2003), pp. 125–27; Luigi Gambero, "Patristic Intuitions of Mary's Role as Mediatrix and Advocate: The Invocation of the Faithful for Her Help," *Marian Studies* 52 (2001): pp. 78–101.

59. Geoffrey Parker, *Emperor*, p. 122.

60. Rady, *Habsburgs*, p. 63; Hermann Wiesflecker, *Kaiser Maximilian I: Gründung des habsburgischen Weltreiches, Lebensabend und Tod, 1508–1519* (Vienna: Böhlau, 1981), 4: p. 424.

61. Rady, *Habsburgs*, p. 69.

62. Geoffrey Parker, *Emperor*, p. 122.

63. Gwyn, *King's Cardinal*, p. 480.

64. LP, III, 1656.

65. Thomas Stapleton, *The Life and Illustrious Martyrdom of Sir Thomas More* (Whitefish, MT: Kessinger, 2010), p. 34.

66. Jasper Ridley, *Statesman and the Fanatic*, pp. 132–35; Thomas More, *Responsio ad Lutherum* (New Haven, CT: Yale University Press, 1969), pp. 317, 499.

67. An early source for this information was George Cavendish. Had Cavendish been able to suggest a more "gentle" background for Wolsey, he would have. His father's likely occupation as a grazier may have been misread, explaining the much later claim that Wolsey was the son of a glazier. See also T. W. Cameron, "The Early Life of Thomas Wolsey," *English Historical Review* 3 (July 1888): pp. 458–61.

68. LP, III, i, 1114.

69. There is a debate over whether Skelton also studied at Oxford and that his degree from Cambridge was honorary; see H. L. R. Edwards, *Skelton: The Life and Times of an Early Tudor Poet* (London: Jonathan Cape, 1949), pp. 29–30, and Greg Walker, *John Skelton and the Politics of the 1520s* (Cambridge: Cambridge University Press, 1988), pp. 32–34.

70. John Skelton, *Poems by John Skelton,* intro. Richard Hughes (London: William Heinemann, 1924), pp. 39–61; Stanley Eugene Fish, *John Skelton's Poetry* (Yale University Press, 1965), pp. 44–46; John Scattergood, ed., *John Skelton: The Complete English Poems* (London: Penguin, 1983), p. 43.

71. Scattergood, *Complete English Poems*, p. 132; David Starkey, *Henry: The Prince who would turn Tyrant* (London: HarperCollins, 2009), pp. 120–24.

72. Gunn and Lindley, introduction, p. 38n.

73. Scattergood, *Complete English Poems*, pp. 289, 293–94.

74. Greg Walker, "Cardinal Wolsey and the satirists: the case of Godly Queen Hester re-opened," in *Cardinal Wolsey*, Gunn and Lindley, p. 241; Walker, *John Skelton and the Politics of the 1520s*, p. 52.

75. Walker, *John Skelton and the Politics of the 1520s*, pp. 188–90, argues convincingly that it was Wolsey's offer of patronage, rather than Skelton's alleged shifty loyalties to a

faction headed by the 2nd Duke of Norfolk, that led to the poet's change in tone. Cf. Edwards, *Skelton*, pp. 222–25.

76. Cavendish, *Life of Cardinal Wolsey*, pp. 5–6.

77. Wolsey may have recruited some of Buckingham's servants as informants. However, it seems unlikely that he plotted the duke's downfall; see Barbara J. Harris, *Edward Stafford, Third Duke of Buckingham* (Stanford, CA: Stanford University Press, 1986), pp. 188–89, 203–5.

78. Gunn and Lindley, introduction, p. 19.

79. Paul Slack, *Poverty and Policy in Tudor and Stuart England* (London: Longman, 1988), 116–17.

80. This was the predominant view of Cleopatra in the sixteenth century; it is not this author's. I am grateful to Sarah Slater for her generosity in discussing the roundels with me.

81. It is possible that Anne was at Hampton Court for the emperor's reception and all but certain that she attended other festivities during the visit.

82. LP, II, 1269.

83. Piers Butler had six daughters, all of whom have contested dates of birth. However, we can be relatively confident that at least four of them had made advantageous marriages by the early to mid-1520s: Margaret and Ailis to Fitzgeralds, Catherine to Lord Power, Eleanor to Lord Cahir, head of another collateral branch of the Butler dynasty. At some unspecified point during his feud with Thomas Boleyn, Piers's daughter Joan was also married to the head of a collateral Butler branch, the 10th Lord Dunboyne. The marriage of the youngest, Helen, to the future Earl of Thromond, head of the O'Brien dynasty, does not seem to have taken place until the early 1530s.

84. *Cal. S. P. Ireland,* Henry VIII, I, 8. The acts of Attainder passed against the earldom by the Dublin and London parliaments in 1461–62 were overturned for the Ormond title's restoration to John Butler, 6th Earl of Ormond, in 1475. However, the entailment was not restored in 1475, meaning that it was henceforth possible for the earldom to pass through an earl's daughter, such as Lady Margaret Boleyn, rather than solely through or to male-line descendants.

85. *Cal. S. P. Ireland,* Henry VIII, I, 7.

86. Ibid., 1:19.

87. The evidence remains circumstantial. Sir William Carey, Mary Boleyn's groom, was a somewhat odd choice for her, which could lend further credence to the idea that she was married quickly to preempt a firm proposal that she marry James, orchestrated by Cardinal Wolsey, the Earl of Surrey (then serving as Viceroy of Ireland) and Sir Piers Butler. When compared to the fact that her sister Anne seems only to have been linked to prospective earls before her betrothal to Henry VIII and that their brother George married a baron's daughter, Mary Boleyn's marriage to a wealthy court gentleman who was neither the son of a peer, nor in line to inherit a peerage, seems contextually to have been something of a step down for a Boleyn. In which case, speed may have been part of the marriage's motive. This remains speculative. Carey's position as a gentleman of the Privy Chamber may have made him an attractive candidate to the Boleyns when they needed to reaffirm their connections

to the Privy Chamber after Wolsey's reforms of the household had eroded their position there. It is possible that the marriage was arranged with both considerations in mind—outmaneuvering Piers Butler and building a valuable courtly connection for the family.

88. *Cal. S. P. Ireland,* Henry VIII, I, 18.

89. Both of Henry Percy's younger brothers, Sir Thomas Percy (executed in 1537) and Sir Ingram Percy (d. 1538), specifically identified their brother's generosity to Arundell as one of their major concerns about his mismanagement of their family's earldom. It is debatable whether this was simply extreme generosity to a friend or romantically motivated. See R. W. Hoyle, "Henry Percy, sixth earl of Northumberland, and the fall of the House of Percy, 1527–1537," in *The Tudor Nobility,* ed. G. W. Bernard (Manchester, UK: Manchester University Press, 1992), pp. 182–84, 205, and Gareth Russell, "His Dear Bedfellow: The debate over Harry Percy," *Tudor Life* (February 2016), pp. 2–5.

90. Hoyle, "Henry Percy," p. 184.

CHAPTER 3: THE ANNE BOLEYN GATE

1. Philippa of Hainault, Elizabeth of York, and Katherine of Aragon were the Queens consort who stayed at Hampton Court when it belonged to the Knights Hospitaller. Katherine, with Henry VIII, had stayed there in October 1518, June 1525, and January 1529. Queen Katherine also stayed there alone on several occasions.

2. Georges Ascoli, ed., *La Grande-Bretagne devant l'opinion française au XVIIe Siècle* (Geneva: Slatkine, 1971), p. 62; *Cal. S. P. Ven.,* IV, 824.

3. *Cal. S. P. Ireland,* I, 74.

4. LP, VI, 602.

5. LP, VI, 720.

6. Thurley, *Hampton Court,* p. 55.

7. LP, VI, 602.

8. LP, VI, 613.

9. Sir William Kingston to Lord Lisle, July 20, 1533, *The Lisle Letters: An Abridgement,* ed. Muriel St. Clare Byrne (Chicago: University of Chicago Press, 1983), p. 143.

10. Ibid.

11. Ives, *Life and Death of Anne Boleyn,* p. 182.

12. Margaret MacCurtain, "Women, Education and Learning in Early Modern Ireland," in *Women in Early Modern Ireland,* ed. Margaret MacCurtain and Mary O'Dowd (Edinburgh: Edinburgh University Press, 1991), p. 162.

13. Nicholas Sanders, *Rise and Growth of the Anglican Schism,* ed. and trans. David Lewis (London: Burns & Oates, 1877), p. 25.

14. Owen Emmerson and Claire Ridgway, *The Boleyns of Hever Castle* (Lúcar, Sp.: MadeGlobal, 2021), p. 101.

15. LP, V, 264, 285.

16. Thurley, *Hampton Court,* p. 53. This was the "real tennis," which is still played at the palace's tennis courts today.

17. Ibid., pp. 53–54.

18. Harold G. Leask, *Irish Castles and Castellated Houses* (Dundalk, Ire.: Dundalgan, 1964), pp. 57, 146–47; Jane Fenlon, "The Decorative Plasterwork at Ormond Cas-

tle: A Unique Survival," *Architectural History*, 44 (1998): pp. 67–69; Simon Thurley, "Tudor Ambition: Houses of the Boleyn family" lecture, Gresham College, London, September 16, 2020; available online.

19. Thurley, *Hampton Court*, p. 55; Simon Thurley, *The Royal Palaces of Tudor England: Architecture and Court Life, 1460–1547* (New Haven, CT: Yale University Press, 1993), pp. 50–51.

20. Thurley, *Hampton Court*, p. 49; Simon Thurley, *Houses of Power: The Places That Shaped the Tudor World* (London: TransWorld, 2017), pp. 172–73.

21. Retha M. Warnicke, *The Rise and Fall of Anne Boleyn: Family politics at the court of Henry VIII* (Cambridge: Cambridge University Press, 1989), pp. 56–58.

22. LP, IV, 824.

23. *Cal. S. P. Span.*, IV, ii, 584.

24. LP, VI, 918.

25. G. W. Bernard, "Anne Boleyn's Religion," *Historical Journal*, 36, no. 1 (March 1993): p. 18; Eric W. Ives, "Anne Boleyn and the Early Reformation in England: The Contemporary Evidence," *Historical Journal* 37, no. 2 (June 1994): pp. 389–400.

26. The griffin and the falcon were the two heraldic beasts of the Ormond earldom. See Michael Powell Siddons, *Heraldic Badges in England and Wales* (Woodbridge, UK: Society of Antiquaries of London, 2009), II, i, pp. 21–25, 132; James Fairbairn et al., *Fairbairn's Book of Crests of the Families of Great Britain and Ireland* (London: T. C. & E. C. Jack, 1905), 1:p. 424. It was also used in the decoration of the Butlers' Irish homes at Kilkenny Castle, Kilkenny, and Ormond Castle, Carrick-on-Suir.

27. Thurley, *Hampton Court*, p. 51.

28. LP, VII, 556, 888; Warnicke, *Rise and Fall of Anne Boleyn*, pp. 173–75.

29. LP, VII, 926, 937.

30. Ives, *Life and Death of Anne Boleyn*, p. 344; Cavendish, *Life of Cardinal Wolsey*, p. 34.

31. The most likely date for their wedding was November 14, 1532, with a second service held on January 25, 1533. See David Starkey, *Six Wives: The Queens of Henry VIII* (London: Chatto & Windus, 2003), pp. 462–64, 475–76.

32. Cavendish, *Life of Cardinal Wolsey*, p. 30. Weston, in his scaffold speech on May 17, 1536, alluded to his sexual promiscuity.

33. Brereton's wife was Lady Elizabeth Savage (née Somerset), widow of Sir John Savage the Younger and daughter of Charles Somerset, 1st Earl of Worcester; she outlived her second husband and died in 1545. Weston had married, aged about nineteen, Anne Pickering, heiress to a Cumberland landed family. She remarried after her first husband's execution.

34. John Husee to Honor, Lady Lisle, May 13, 1536, in *Lisle Letters*, 4:845.

35. James Orchard Halliwell-Phillips, ed., *Letters of the Kings of England* (London: H. Colborn, 1848), 1:p. 353.

36. Ives, *Life and Death of Anne Boleyn*, p. 345.

37. LP, X, 908; Amy Licence, *Anne Boleyn: Adultery, Heresy, Desire* (Stroud, UK: Amberley, 2017), p. 423.

38. Henry Ellis, ed., *Original Letters, illustrative of English History* (London: Harding, Triphook, and Lepard, 1824), I, ii, 121. For the debate on whether Queen Anne's sister-in-law Jane, Lady Rochford, committed perjury by testifying against her and

Lord Rochford, see Julia Fox, *Jane Boleyn: The Infamous Lady Rochford* (London: Weidenfeld & Nicolson, 2007), pp. 315–26; Nicola Clark, *Gender, Family, and Politics: The Howard Women, 1485–1558* (Oxford: Oxford University Press, 2018), pp. 126–27, and James Taffe, "Reconstructing the queen's household: a study in royal service, 1485–1547" (PhD thesis, Durham University, Durham, UK, 2022), pp. 233–34.

39. She was at Hampton Court, however, on the first alleged date of their adultery: December 3. She went to inspect work on her new apartments. See also Natalie Grueninger, app. 3, "The Alleged Offences," in *The Final Year of Anne Boleyn* (Stroud, UK: Pen & Sword, 2022).

40. Ives, *Life and Death of Anne Boleyn*, 343–45; cf. G. W. Bernard, *Anne Boleyn: Fatal Attractions* (New Haven, CT: Yale University Press, 2010), pp. 188–89.

41. Ives, *Life and Death of Anne Boleyn*, p. 326.

42. The notable exception is George Bernard, who does not believe the accusations of incest or of the adultery with Brereton but argues that the other three adulteries are plausible in varying degrees. See Bernard, *Anne Boleyn*, pp. 156–60, 188–92.

43. Starkey, *Six Wives*, pp. 556–62.

44. Warnicke, *Rise and Fall of Anne Boleyn*, pp. 191–93.

45. Ives, *Life and Death of Anne Boleyn*, pp. 322–23; Alison Weir, *The Lady in the Tower: The Fall of Anne Boleyn* (London: Jonathan Cape, 2009), pp. 320–23.

46. Greg Walker, "Rethinking the Fall of Anne Boleyn," *Historical Journal* 45, no. 1 (March 2002): especially pp. 19–26.

47. J. J. Scarisbrick, *Henry VIII*, 2nd ed. (New Haven, CT: Yale University Press), 1997, p. xii; Derek Wilson, *A Brief History of Henry VIII: Reformer and Tyrant* (London: Constable & Robinson, 2009), p. 275.

48. Ives, *Life and Death of Anne Boleyn*, p. 343.

49. The man—John ap Gruffydd Eyton—had previously been acquitted of complicity in a brawl that ended with the death of one of Brereton's servants. Brereton had him re-arrested and then interfered with his second trial, which condemned him to death.

50. J. Gwynfor Jones, *Wales and the Tudor State: Government, Religious Change and the Social Order, 1534–1603* (Cardiff: University of Wales Press, 1989), pp. 16, 18, 20–21; Philip Jenkins, *A History of Modern Wales, 1536–1990* (New York: Longman, 1992), pp. 81–83.

51. Ives, *Life and Death of Anne Boleyn*, pp. 347–48; E. W. Ives, ed., *The Letters and Accounts of William Brereton of Malpas* (Old Woking, UK: Record Society of Lancashire and Cheshire, 1976), pp. 34–36; E. W. Ives, "Court and Country Palatine in the Reign of Henry VIII: The Career of William Brereton of Malpas," *Transactions of the Historic Society of Lancashire and Cheshire* 123 (1972): p. 30; cf. Bernard, *Anne Boleyn*, pp. 148–49, and Warnicke, *Rise and Fall of Anne Boleyn*, pp. 218–19.

53. For Smeton/Smeyton's tenure at Hampton Court, see Thurley, *Hampton Court*, p. 16.

54. Richard K. Morris, "Architectural Terracotta at Sutton Place and Hampton Court," *British Brick Society Information* 44 (March 1988): pp. 3–8.

55. LP, X, 913, 914.

CHAPTER 4: THE MAIDENS' CHAMBER

1. Unless stated otherwise, this chapter's descriptions of Hampton Court in 1536–37 are based on Thurley, *Hampton Court*, pp. 65–70.

2. The Bassetts' land agent to Lady Lisle, June 4, 1535, *Lisle Letters*, 2:594.

3. John Husee to Arthur Plantagenet, Lord Lisle, October 2, 1537, *Lisle Letters*, 4:1022.

4. The identity of Arthur Plantagenet's mother remains unclear; Elizabeth Lucy seems most likely. Previous theories that Arthur was born to one of Edward IV's most famous lovers—either Lady Eleanor Butler or "Jane" Shore—have, however, been satisfactorily disproved.

5. St. Clare Byrne, *Lisle Letters: Abridgement*, p. 13.

6. Letters from Thybault, Sieur de Riou, and Peter Mewtas to Arthur Plantagenet, Lord Lisle, August 11, 1535, and October 9, 1537, respectively, *Lisle Letters*, 3:575, 4:899.

7. Marie Bassett to Honor Plantagenet, Lady Lisle, April 25, 1537, *Lisle Letters*, 3:619.

8. Marie Bassett to Philippa Bassett, March 13, 1536, *Lisle Letters*, 3:588.

9. Honor Plantagenet, Lady Lisle, to Madame de Bours, November 1535, *Lisle Letters*, 3:583a.

10. Sister Anthoinette de Saveuses to Honor Plantagenet, Lady Lisle, September 10, 1537, *Lisle Letters*, 3:605.

11. John Husee to Honor Plantagenet, Lady Lisle, June 18, 1536, *Lisle Letters*, 4:863.

12. Ibid., June 24, 1536, *Lisle Letters*, IV, 850, ii.

13. John Browne to Honor Plantagenet, Lady Lisle, May 12, 1534, *Lisle Letters*, 2:193.

14. LP, XIV, i, 762.

15. Sir John Russell to Arthur Plantagenet, Lord Lisle, May 20, 1537, *Lisle Letters*, 4:871.

16. John Husee to Honor Plantagenet, Lady Lisle, July 17, 1537, *Lisle Letters*, 4:887.

17. Ibid.

18. Wayment, "Wolsey and stained glass," p. 121.

19. Thurley, *Houses of Power*, pp. 220, 223–24.

20. Charles Wriothesley, *A Chronicle of England During the Reigns of the Tudors*, ed. William Douglas Hamilton (London: Camden Society, 1875), pp. 46–47; *Journal of the House of Lords*, vol. 1, *1509–1577* (London, s.n., 1771), 1: p. 84; LP, X, 901.

21. LP, X, 901.

22. Lauren Mackay, *Inside the Tudor Court: Henry VIII and his Six Wives through the writings of the Spanish Ambassador, Eustace Chapuys* (Stroud, UK: Amberley, 2014), p. 246.

23. *Cal. S. P. Span.*, V, ii, 71.

24. Victoria & Albert: MS 86.cc.49, f. 196b.

25. LP, X, 1134 (4); XI, 7.

26. *INV*, 2:94.

27. John Husee to Honor Plantagenet, Lady Lisle, September 17, 1537, *Lisle Letters*, 4:895.

28. Ibid.

29. Ibid., October 2, 1537, *Lisle Letters*, 4:896; LP, XVI, 41, 61, 62.

30. Husee to Plantagenet, September 17, 1537, *Lisle Letters*, 4:895.

31. Ibid.

32. Ibid.

33. John Husee's letter of September 17, 1537, mentions that Anne was going to be allocated the kind of room usually given to a yeoman-usher.

34. John Husee to Arthur Plantagenet, (?) September 17, 1537.

35. Marie Bassett to Honor Plantagenet, Lady Lisle, March 17, 1537, *Lisle Letters*, 3:615.

36. An exception to the rule was if a widowed king with several healthy sons remarried, as with Henry IV's wedding in 1403 to Joanna of Navarre, Dowager Duchess of Brittany. Henry IV had four sons from his first marriage.

37. Edward II and Henry VII were born in Wales when it was ruled by the Crown; Richard II and Edward IV were born in what is now France, but in territories then ruled by England.

38. LP, XI, 860.

39. R. W. Hoyle, *The Pilgrimage of Grace and the Politics of the 1530s* (Oxford: Oxford University Press, 2001), p. 204.

40. S. J. Connolly, *Contested Island: Ireland, 1460–1630* (Oxford: Oxford University Press, 2007), pp. 86–89.

41. Ibid., p. 239.

42. Ibid.

43. Constantia Maxwell, ed., *Irish History from Contemporary Sources, 1509–1610* (London: George Allen & Unwin, 1923), pp. 94–95.

44. Peter Mewtas to Arthur Plantagenet, Lord Lisle, October 9, 1537, *Lisle Letters*, 4:899.

45. LP, XI, 8.

46. Luke 1:5–25; LP, XII, ii, 947.

47. *State Papers*, 1:570; LP, XII (ii), 905.

48. Steven J. Gunn, "War, dynasty and public opinion in Early Tudor England," in *Authority and Consent in Tudor England: Essays Presented to C. S. L. Davies*, ed. G. W. Bernard and Steven J. Gunn (Burlington, VT: Ashgate, 2002), p. 139.

49. Wriothesley, *Chronicle of England*, 1:pp. 65–67.

50. Gunn, "War," p. 139.

51. Ibid., p. 142.

52. LP, XII, ii, 988 (2); *Lisle Letters*, 4: 428.

53. A formal investiture ceremony is traditionally required before the heir to the throne may be known as Prince of Wales, whereas the heir's lesser titles, the dukedom of Cornwall and the earldom of Chester, can be awarded at birth. Although no such ceremony was ever conducted for Edward Tudor, he was referred to as the Prince of Wales throughout most of his childhood.

54. The first recorded use of fireworks in England had been to celebrate the wedding of Edward's paternal grandparents in 1486.

55. LP, XII, ii, 970.

56. LP, XII, ii, 1004.

57. Jennifer Loach, *Edward VI*, ed. George Bernard and Penry Williams (New Haven, CT: Yale University Press, 1999), p. 7.

58. Loach, *Edward VI*, pp. 6–7, argues for the "retention in her womb of parts of the placenta [that] led to a catastrophic haemorrhage several days after labour." Cf. Richard L. DeMolen, "The Birth Of Edward VI And The Death Of Queen Jane: The Arguments For And Against Caesarean Section," *Renaissance Studies* (December 1990): pp. 388–91. Alison Weir, "Why Did Jane Seymour Die in Childbed?," Tudor Times, last modified May 3, 2018, argues "that anaemia, possible postpartum blood

loss after a long labour, dehydration from diarrhoea, and extended bed rest and in-activity caused an embolism, and probably more than one—not enough to trigger instant death, but enough to put Jane gradually into cardio-respiratory failure, shock, and death."

59. LP, XII, ii, 970.
60. Ibid., 977.
61. Ibid., 971.
62. Ibid., 1060.

CHAPTER 5: THE GREAT WATCHING CHAMBER

1. LP, XVI, 60, 311.
2. Dyer, *Standards of Living*, pp. 58–63.
3. William Dugdale, *The Baronage of England, or An Historical Account of the Lives and most Memorable Actions of Our English Nobility in the Saxons' time, to the Norman Conquest; And from thence, of those who had their rise before the end of King Henry the Third's Reign* (London: Thomas Newcomb, 1675), 2:p. 278.
4. Gareth Russell, *Young and Damned and Fair: The Life and Tragedy of Catherine Howard at the Court of King Henry VIII* (London: HarperCollins, 2017), p. xxv. Margaret (née Gamage) had previously been a maid of honor to Queen Anne Boleyn, who may have arranged her marriage to Lord William, who was also Anne's uncle. See Clark, *Gender, Family, and Politics*, pp. 102–3.
5. Russell, *Young and Damned and Fair*, pp. 181–82.
6. *Cal S. P. Span.*, VI, i, 149.
7. Jennifer Ward, *English Noblewomen in the Later Middle Ages* (London: Longman, 1992), p. 86.
8. LP, XIV, i, 490.
9. Thanks to the research project conducted by Daphne Ford at Hampton Court between 1973 and 1996, we can estimate that about twenty-six million bricks were used at the palace during Henry VIII's reign. See also Thurley, *Houses of Power*, pp. 150–51.
10. Mackay, *Inside the Tudor Court*, pp. 18–19, 202–3.
11. LP, XV, 161, 662, 665. Chapuys's most frequent communications were to Charles V and Maria of Austria, Dowager Queen of Hungary; the latter also served as her brother the emperor's governor of the Netherlands for a quarter century beginning in 1553.
12. HMC Rutland, 1:p. 27.
13. LP, XVI, 374.
14. *Cal S. P. Span.*, VI, i, 148.
15. Ibid., 144.
16. On Queen Catherine's appearance, see William Thomas, *The Pilgrim: A Dialogue on the Life and Actions of King Henry the Eighth*, ed. J. A. Froude (London: Parker, Son, and Bourn, 1861), p. 58. Catherine Howard's date of birth cannot credibly have been later than 1523; see Russell, *Young and Damned and Fair*, pp. 16–19, and LP, XVI, 1426. In the 1990s and 2000s, a theory gained popularity that Catherine was born around 1525, making her fourteen or fifteen at the time of her marriage to the forty-

nine-year-old Henry VIII; see Joanna Denny, *Katherine Howard: A Tudor Conspiracy* (London: Portrait, 2005), pp. 5, 8–9, and Alison Weir, *The Six Wives of Henry VIII* (London: Pimlico, 1991), pp. 413–14. In the author's note to her 2020 novel about Catherine Howard, *The Tainted Queen,* Weir argued that new evidence from the 1520s has shifted the date back to c. 1522.

17. BL, Stowe MS 559, f. 55r; LP, XVI, 1389.
18. *Cal S. P. Span.*, VI, i, 149.
19. MS Ashmole, f. 92.
20. LP, XVI, 60.
21. *Cal S. P. Span.*, VI, i, 155.
22. Burnet, *History of the Reformation*, 1:pp. 691–92; LP, XVI, 1067, grant 16.
23. *A collection of Ordinances and Regulations for the government of the Royal Household, made in divers reigns: from King Edward III to King William and Queen Mary, also receipts in ancient cooking* (London: Society of Antiquaries, 1790), p. 155.
24. Burnet, *History of the Reformation*, 5:276.
25. LP, XVI, 379, grant 34.
26. Mary's late husband, Henry Fitzroy, had been Duke of Richmond and Somerset and Earl of Nottingham. Later in the reign, when the Seymour match was once again suggested, the Dowager Duchess's brother, the Earl of Surrey, allegedly claimed that marriage to a Seymour was beneath a Howard. With its implication that such a marriage had not, apparently, been beneath the Tudors, the remark may have helped intensify Henry VIII's hatred for Lord Surrey. See also Clark, *Gender, Family and Politics*, pp. 161–64.
27. LP, XVI, 41; Susan E. James, *Kateryn Parr: The Making of a Queen* (Brookfield, VT: Ashgate, 1999), p. 298.
28. LP, IX, 576–77; Clark, *Gender, Family, and Politics*, pp. 77–79.
29. *INV,* 2:118.
30. LP, XVI, 541; *Cal S. P. Span.*, VI, i, 155.
31. LP, XVI, 597.
32. *Cal S. P. Span.*, VI, i, 150; LP, XVI, 482, 534.
33. Burnet, *History of the Reformation*, 1:623; LP, XVI, 511, 517.

CHAPTER 6: THE HAUNTED GALLERY

1. Denny, *Katherine Howard*, pp. 261–62; David Keane, "Ghost of Henry VIII's Wife Caught on Camera," *Mirror (UK)* online, last modified December 29, 2015; Historic Royal Palaces, "Historic Hauntings at Hampton Court Palace," accessible online, 2021.
2. LP, XVI, 1278.
3. Ibid., 1297; Linda Porter, *Crown of Thistles: The Fatal Inheritance of Mary, Queen of Scots* (London: Macmillan, 2013), p. 278.
4. Morgan Ring, *So High a Blood: The Life of Margaret, Countess of Lennox* (London: Bloomsbury, 2017), pp. 40–41.
5. LP, XI, 147.
6. Henry Ellis, *Original Letters*, III, iii, 208.
7. For a debate on the authorship, see Ring, *So High a Blood*, pp. 60–62.

8. LP, XVI, 1389; Ring, *So High a Blood*, p. 68.
9. Charles Howard's father, Sir Edmund Howard, was an elder half brother of Thomas Howard the Younger. Edmund was born c. 1478, and Thomas the Younger, c. 1511.
10. SP 1/167, f. 127; Burnet, *History of the Reformation*, 1:pp. 623–24.
11. Russell, *Young and Damned and Fair*, pp. 305, 457. Agnes Howard (née Tilney), Duchess of Norfolk, was technically the Queen's step-grandmother, and her guardian c. 1531–39.
12. Edward Herbert, 1st Baron Herbert of Cherbury, *The Life and Raigne of Henry the Eighth* (London: M. Clark, 1683), p. 534.
13. LP, XVI, 1339.
14. Mary O'Dowd, "Gaelic Economy and Society," in *Natives and Newcomers: Essays on the Making of Irish Colonial Society, 1534–1641*, ed. Ciarán Brady and Raymond Gillespie (Dublin: Irish Academic Press, 1986), pp. 120–47; Colm Lennon, *The Lords of Dublin in the Age of Reformation* (Dublin: Irish Academic Press, 1989), pp. 105, 195.
15. Russell, app. 2, "The Ladies of Catherine Howard's Household," in *Young and Damned and Fair*.
16. LP, XVI, 1332.
17. Ibid.
18. Ibid.
19. Herbert, *Life and Raigne*, p. 534.
20. Russell, *Young and Damned and Fair*, p. 309; Thurley, *Hampton Court*, p. 74.
21. *State Papers,* 1:p. 689.
22. Burnet, *History of the Reformation*, 6:document 72.
23. Herbert, *Life and Raigne*, p. 535.
24. *Cal. S. P. Span.*, VI, I, 209.
25. LP, XVI, 1334.
26. For the debate on the letter, see this author's views that the letter is not credibly one that suggests blackmail by either party in Russell, *Young and Damned and Fair*, pp. 271–73, 289–90, and cf. Conor Byrne, *Katherine Howard: A New History* (Lúcar, Sp.: MadeGlobal, 2014), pp. 161–65.
27. *State Papers,* 1:pp. 692–95.
28. Ibid., pp. 694–95.
29. *Cal. S. P. Ven.*, V, 284.
30. Frederic Madden, ed., *Narrative of the Visit of the Duke of Najera to England, in the Year 1543–4, Written by his Secretary, Pedro de Gante* (London: Society of Antiquaries, 1831), p. 353.
31. James, *Kateryn Parr*, pp. 39, 39–40n; Madden, *Visit of the Duke of Najera*, p. 353.
32. James, *Kateryn Parr*, pp. 127–28.
33. Katherine Parr, Queen of England and Ireland, *The Lamentation of a Sinner,* ed. and trans. Ollie Lansdowne (accessed online, via the New Whitchurch Press, 2022).
34. LP, XIX, i, 487.
35. *Cal. S. P. Span.*, VII, 266; LP, XIX, i, 730.
36. George Buchanan, ed., *The History of Scotland,* trans. James Aiken (Charleston, SC: Nabu, 2010), 2:p. 343.

CHAPTER 7: THE TILTYARD

1. Loach, *Edward VI*, p. 89.
2. David Loades, *Intrigue and Treason: The Tudor Court, 1547–1558* (London: Pearson, 2004), p. 97.
3. Loach, *Edward VI*, p. 90.
4. W. K. Jordan, ed., *The Chronicle and Political Papers of King Edward VI* (Ithaca, NY: Cornell University Press, 1966), p. 17.
5. Colonel Sir Reginald Hennell, *The History of the King's Body Guard of the Yeomen of the Guard* (Westminster, UK: Archibald Constantine, 1904), p. 59.
6. The earldom of Northumberland had been in abeyance since the death without sons in 1537 of Henry Percy, the 6th Earl. His brother Thomas was executed for complicity in the Pilgrimage of Grace, for which another brother, Ingram, died attainted as a prisoner. The earldom was restored to the Percy family—the 6th Earl's nephew—by Queen Mary I in 1557.
7. James Ludovic Lindsay, 26th Earl of Crawford, and Robert Steele, eds., *Tudor and Stuart Proclamations, 1485–1714,* vol. 1, *England and Wales* (Oxford: Clarendon Press, 1910), 5; Ed. VI. 24/18 July, No. 403.
8. See the proclamations from Hampton Court for July 17 and August 16, 1551, from Westminster on September 9, and Farnham on September 11. It was still a matter of concern when they returned to Hampton Court in October; see Crawford and Steele, *Tudor and Stuart Proclamations,* 1:5; Ed. VI, nos. 402, 404–7.
9. W. K. Jordan, *The Chronicle*, p. 75.
10. Loach, *Edward VI*, pp. 138–39.
11. J. G. Nichols, ed., *Literary Remains of King Edward the Sixth* (London: B. Franklin, 1857), 1:81.
12. Osraí in modern Irish and Osraighe in classical, Ossory covered land in what is now the counties of Kilkenny and Laois, the barony of Upper Ossory comprising mostly the former territories in Laois. The ruling family traced its ancestry back to a first-century king named Óengus Osrithe, a semilegendary leader regarded as the founding father of the region and the tribes of Osraí.
13. *Cal. S. P. Ireland,* I, 41.
14. Leanda de Lisle, "Truthiness, Fake History and the Story of the Whipping Boy," *Aspects of History* online, accessed October 14, 2020; cf. Philip Wilson, *The Beginnings of Modern Ireland* (Dublin: Maunsel, 1912), p. 384.
15. *Cal. S. P. Dom., Edward VI,* 950.
16. Loach, *Edward VI*, pp. 152–53.
17. The Suffolk dukedom fell into abeyance with the death of the 3rd Duke in 1551. It was revived for the 3rd Duke's brother-in-law Henry Grey, 3rd Marquess of Dorset, whose wife, Frances, was next in line. As the family line had thus technically changed from Brandon to Grey, it was revived with Grey as the new 1st Duke of Suffolk.
18. 2 Chronicles 34:1.
19. Ibid., 34:3–7.
20. HMC Salisbury, 1:p. 131.

21. Chris Skidmore, *Edward VI: The Lost King of England* (London: Weidenfeld & Nicolson, 2008), p. 164.

22. Ibid., p. 230.

23. Ibid., p. 164.

24. Stephen Alford, *Kingship and Politics in the Reign of Edward VI* (Cambridge: Cambridge University Press, 2002), pp. 39–40.

25. Diarmaid MacCulloch, *Thomas Cranmer: A Life* (New Haven, CT: Yale University Press, 1996), p. 474.

26. Peter Marshall, *Heretics and Believers: A History of the English Reformation* (New Haven, CT: Yale University Press, 2017), p. 342.

27. There was a theoretically strong candidate in Princess Katarina of Sweden, who was both Protestant and only eighteen months Edward's junior; this meant they could have married sooner than he could Catholic Elisabeth, who was seven years younger. However, Katarina's father, King Gustav I (r. 1523–60), had been elected to his throne, a detail that potentially reduced her dynastic credibility. It raises the possibility that, when it came to his marriage, snobbery outranked spirituality in Edward's criteria. Gustav I transformed the Swedish monarchy into a hereditary one and was regarded, then and subsequently, as responsible for turning Sweden into a significant power in Europe.

28. James O. Halliwell-Philips, ed., *Letters of the Kings of England* (London: H. Colborn, 1848), 2:p. 49.

29. It was headed by the Lord High Admiral, Lord Clinton, who acted as Barnaby's sponsor to formally introduce him to King Henri II of France.

30. Nichols, *Literary Remains*, I, pp. 69–70. Barnaby, perhaps mindful of how his position had been weakened by his lack of Protestant zeal, made fun of Catholic religious art in some of his replies.

31. Halliwell-Philips, *Letters of the Kings of England*, 2:p. 54.

32. Skidmore, *Edward VI*, p. 235.

33. A variety of theories have been put forward as to the causes of Edward VI's death. Loach, *Edward VI*, pp. 160–62, suggests renal failure; Frederick Holmes, Grace Holmes, and Julia McMorrough, "The Death of Young King Edward VI," *New England Journal of Medicine* 45, no. 1 (July 5, 2001): 60–62, argue for tuberculosis; Linda Porter, *Mary Tudor: The First Queen* (London: Piatkus, 2009), pp. 184–86, suggests a bacterial pulmonary infection that left Edward defenseless against secondary infections.

34. Loades, *Intrigue and Treason*, p. 131.

35. His father had visited court on several occasions during Barnaby's tenure there, for instance see *Cal. S. P. Ireland,* Henry VIII, I, 64. For Barnaby's life after Edward VI's death, see John O'Donovan, trans., *Annala Rioghachta Eireann: Annals of the Kingdom of Ireland, by the Four Masters, from the Earliest Period to the Year 1616* (Dublin: Royal Irish Academy, 1856), 5:1531; *Cal. S. P. Ireland,* Mary I, I, 8; Jon G. Crawford, *Anglicizing the Government of Ireland: The Irish Privy Council and the Expansion of Tudor Rule, 1556–1578* (Blackrock, Ire.: Irish Academic Press, 1993), p. 207; RIA, MS 24, F 17, f. 28v. Fitzpatrick seems to have served at the siege of Leith (1558).

36. Sir John T. Gilbert and Sir Edward Sullivan, eds., *National Manuscripts of Ireland* (London: Her Majesty's Stationery Office, 1879), p. 172.

37. Ciarán Brady, *The Chief Governors: The rise and fall of reform government in Tudor Ireland, 1536–1558* (Cambridge: Cambridge University Press, 1994), pp. 287–88.
38. *Cal. S. P. Ireland,* Elizabeth I, XII, 95; XVII, 8; XXV, 12; XLIII, 14.

CHAPTER 8: THE PRIVY GARDENS

1. The English weather in 1554–55 was severe enough to cause two consecutive bad harvests, and food shortages occurred in 1555; see David Loades, *Mary Tudor: A Life* (Oxford: Blackwell, 1989), pp. 260–61.
2. Legally known as Jane Dudley following her marriage to the Duke of Northumberland's son Guildford, she is still referred to more often by her maiden name.
3. Leanda de Lisle, *The Sisters Who Would Be Queen: The Tragedy of Mary, Katherine and Lady Jane Grey* (London: HarperPress, 2009), p. 234.
4. Gunn, "War," p. 136.
5. Ibid., p. 133.
6. "Saint Peter in Chains." Also the burial site of, among others, Elizabeth's uncle Lord Rochford, her stepmother Catherine Howard, Jane Grey, and Robert Dudley's father, John.
7. Thurley, *Houses of Power,* pp. 173–74. It is almost certainly from this more private wharf that Queen Catherine Howard and her reduced entourage left Hampton Court during her downfall in 1541.
8. Jean Baptiste Louis Kaulek, ed., *Correspondance politique de mm. de Castillon et de Marillac, ambassadeurs de France en Angleterre (1537–1542)* (Paris: Félix Aclan, 1885), p. 347.
9. Ibid.
10. Aysha Pollnitz, "Religion and Translation at the Court of Henry VIII: Princess Mary, Katherine Parr and the *Paraphrases of Erasmus,*" in *Mary Tudor: Old and New Perspectives,* ed. Susan Doran and Thomas S. Freeman (London: Palgrave Macmillan, 2011), pp. 132–36.
11. By the time Foxe was writing, Mary I and Henry Bedingfeld were dead, Elizabeth was queen—with better things to do than reminisce about the time she had been suspected of treason by her sister—and Susan Clarencieux had emigrated to Spain.
12. Matthew 3:16; John 1:32.
13. Miles Huggarde, *The displaying of the Protestants, sondry their practises* (London: Robert Caly, 1556), p. 64; George Townsend, ed., *The Acts and Monuments of John Foxe* (London: R. B. Seeley and W. Burnside, 1837), 6:pp. 611–12, 641–42; Jasper Ridley, *Bloody Mary's Martyrs: The Story of England's Terror* (London: Constable, 2001), pp. 65–67.
14. D. M. Loades, *The Oxford Martyrs* (London: B. T. Batsford, 1970), pp. 151–52.
15. The sobriquet seems to have been an attempt to draw a comparison between Mary and Henrietta Maria, Catholic queen consort between 1625 and 1649.
16. See in particular Porter, *Mary Tudor,* and Anna Whitelock, *Mary Tudor: England's First Queen* (London: Bloomsbury, 2010).
17. For the revisionist assessment of Mary's religious policy, see Eamon Duffy, *Fires of Faith: Catholic England Under Mary* (New Haven, CT: Yale University Press, 2010). Kent, however, is a significant counterexample, where the burnings increased respect

for Protestantism; see Patrick Collinson, "The Persecution in Kent," in *The Church of Mary Tudor,* ed. Eamon Duffy and David Loades (Burlington, VT: Ashgate, 2006), p. 332.

18. Collinson, "Persecution in Kent," pp. 309–10, 325–28, 332–33.

19. *Cal. S. P. Span.,* XIII, 71.

20. Porter, *Mary Tudor,* pp. 333–34.

21. S. M. Thorpe, "Strelley, Robert," in *The History of Parliament: The House of Commons, 1509–1558,* ed. S. B. Bindoff (London: History of Parliament Trust, 1982), 3:pp. 397–98. Strelley, MP for Leicestershire, died on January 23, 1554.

22. *Cal. S. P. Span.,* XIII, 193.

23. Porter, *Mary Tudor,* pp. 334–35.

24. The royal household also introduced much tighter restrictions on who could attend court and ordered taverns near Hampton Court to cease providing accommodation for servants unless they had written proof regarding which courtier employed them. See M. S. Giuseppi, A. C. Wood, and A. E. Stamp, eds., *Calendar of the Patent Rolls Preserved in the Public Record Office: Philip and Mary,* vol. 2, *A.D. 1554–1555* (London: His Majesty's Stationery Office, 1936), Proclamation of October 15, 1554, p. 103; Henry Kamen, *Philip of Spain* (New Haven, CT: Yale University Press, 1997), pp. 57–59; Thurley, *Houses of Power,* p. 307.

25. She was also queen of two more kingdoms of imagination. Ever since Edward III—the son of a French princess—had failed to make good on his claims to the French throne after his uncle's death, his English successors maintained at their coronations that they were the rightful kings and queens of France. Mary had been crowned as such in 1553, as all her successors would be until George III abolished the claim in the early nineteenth century. Similarly, she was styled Queen of Jerusalem after her father-in-law's abdication, since the Hapsburgs claimed to be the rightful heirs to the crusader-kingdom of Jerusalem, which had ceased legally to exist in 1291. The spectral Jerusalem title was used for the final time at the funeral of Zita, the last Dowager Empress of Austria, in 1989.

26. *Cal. S. P. Span.,* XIII, 229.

27. Porter, *Mary Tudor,* p. 338.

28. Ibid., p. 337; Warnicke, *Rise and Fall of Anne Boleyn,* pp. 158–59.

29. Starkey, *Six Wives,* pp. 114–18.

30. This author was previously convinced of the cancer misdiagnosis as an explanation for what happened in 1555. However, Porter, *Mary Tudor,* pp. 402–4, argues convincingly that Mary was most likely killed by influenza during the epidemic of 1558 rather than by cancer.

31. *Cal. S. P. Span.,* XIII, 230.

32. Ibid.

CHAPTER 9: THE PARADISE

1. William Brenchley Rye, ed., *England as Seen by Foreigners in the Days of Elizabeth and James the First* (London: John Russell Smith, 1865), pp. 18, 204; Thurley, *Hampton Court,* p. 87; Ernest Law, *The History of Hampton Court Palace in Tudor Times* (London: George Bell, 1885), pp. 205, 328–29, 334–35.

2. J. E. Neale, *Queen Elizabeth* (London: Jonathan Cape, 1934), pp. 25–26, 75, 130; Anne Somerset, *Elizabeth I* (London: Phoenix Giant, 1997), pp. 14–15; Mark Stoyle, *West Britons: Cornish Identities and the Early Modern British State* (Exeter, UK: University of Exeter Press, 2002), p. 220; Huw Thomas, "Blanche Parry's Life at the Side of Queen Elizabeth I," BBC News online, last modified January 25, 2018; A. N. Wilson, *The Elizabethans* (London: Hutchinson, 2011), pp. 45–46; Denis Casey, "Elizabeth I spoke language of Irish warlords," *Irish Examiner*, May 17, 2011; Jessica Crown, "A 'rare and marvellous' guest: Elizabeth I samples life in Cambridge 450 years ago," Department of History, University of Cambridge online, last modified September 5, 2014; "On the occasion of the visit of Queen Elizabeth II to Ireland, Dr. Denis Casey asks whether she will speak Irish, as her predecessor Elizabeth I would have done," the Department of Anglo-Saxon, Norse, and Celtic, Cambridge University (accessed online, July 14, 2020).

3. *Cal. S. P. Span. S.*, I, 62.

4. E. M. Tenison, *Elizabethan England: Being the History of This Country in Relation to All Foreign Princes* (Royal Leamington Spa, UK: printed privately for subscribers, 1933), I, pp. 164, 212.

5. Also known as Charles II, Archduke of Inner Austria, or Archduke Karl Franz.

6. The conflict in which England lost Calais—known as the Hapsburg-Valois War or the Last Italian War—was later presented as an unambiguous disaster by Mary I's posthumous critics, one of whom may have invented the apocryphal quote from Mary that Calais would be found imprinted on her heart. The Tudor-Hapsburg armies, in fact, won a significant victory at the Battle of Saint-Quentin, arguably one of the greatest military triumphs of the sixteenth century. As regards the fall of Calais, neither Mary I nor Elizabeth I ever made any serious efforts to reconquer it, which makes sense in light of the cost and difficulty of defending it during the reigns of their brother, father, and grandfather. Its loss was an embarrassment rather than a catastrophe.

7. Philip II's third wife was the same Elisabeth of Valois once considered a potential bride for Edward VI.

8. The Earl of Arundel in question was Henry Fitzalan, 12th Earl (1512–80). His second wife, Mary, died the year before Elizabeth's accession, as had the 4th Duke of Norfolk's first wife, Lady Mary Fitzalan. By the time of Elizabeth's smallpox scare in 1562, Norfolk had remarried to Lady Mary Dudley, but he was again suggested as a potential bridegroom for the Queen after the duchess's death in 1564.

9. Report from Caspar, Baron Breuner, to Emperor Ferdinand I, June 7, 1559, in *Queen Elizabeth and Some Foreigners: Being a series of hitherto unpublished letters from the archives of the Hapsburg family,* ed. Victor von Klarwill (London: John Lane, 1928), p. 81.

10. The same point was made by France's Queen Mother, Catherine de' Medici, with the remark that sexual scandals were always concocted to insult powerful women like Elizabeth; see Estelle Paranque, *Blood, Fire and Gold: The Story of Elizabeth I and Catherine de Medici* (London: Penguin, 2022), pp. 74-76, 95-96.

11. Somerset, *Elizabeth I*, p. 195.

12. Joseph Bain, ed., *Calendar of State Papers relating to Scotland and Mary, Queen of Scots, 1547–1603* (Edinburgh: H. M. General, 1898), 1:1146.

13. BL, Cotton MS Caligula B 10 fol. 350v.

14. F. E. Halliday, "Queen Elizabeth I and Dr. Burcot," *History Today* (1955): pp. 542–44; Anna Whitelock, *Elizabeth's Bedfellows: An Intimate History of the Queen's Court* (London: Bloomsbury, 2013), p. 72.

15. Mortimer Levine, *The Early Elizabeth Succession Question, 1558–1568* (Stanford, CA: Stanford University Press, 1966), p. 46.

16. According to de la Quadra, the councillors who supported Huntingdon included the Duke of Norfolk and Robert Dudley. See also Levine, *Early Elizabeth Succession Question*, pp. 7–8, 45–48.

17. *Cal. S. P. Span. S.*, I, 189.

18. Henry Carey, 1st Baron Hunsdon (1526–96), was Elizabeth I's maternal cousin, son of her late aunt Lady Mary Boleyn and her first husband, Sir William Carey.

19. *Cal. S. P. Span. S.*, I, 187.

20. Ibid., 189.

21. Ibid.

22. "Queen Elizabeth's Answer to the Commons' Petition that she Marry, 28 January 1563," in *Elizabeth I: Collected Works,* ed. Leah S. Marcus, Janel Mueller, and Mary Beth Rose (Chicago: University of Chicago Press, 2000), p. 71.

23. *Cal. S. P. Span. S.*, I, 189.

24. Whitelock, *Elizabeth's Bedfellows*, p. 69.

25. Tenison, *Elizabethan England*, "Note B," p. 246.

26. Marcus Selden Goldman, "Sir Philip Sidney and Arcadia" (PhD thesis, University of Illinois, 1931), p. 173.

27. Sara C. Nelson, "Ghost of the Grey Lady of Hampton Court Photographed," *Huffington Post,* last modified February 25, 2015; cf. Andrew Griffin, "Ghost of the Grey Lady at Hampton Court: How 'image aliasing' allows iPhone cameras to capture 'spectres,'" *Independent* (UK), last modified February 25, 2015.

28. She stayed there, briefly, from necessity in 1563, when she had to flee an outbreak of the plague at Whitehall; no more long-term stays are recorded until 1567. See Thurley, *Hampton Court*, p. 83.

29. Paul Johnson, *Elizabeth: A Study in Power and Intellect* (London: Weidenfeld & Nicolson, 1974), pp. 400–401.

30. For an excellent assessment of this, see Kate Maltby, "Why is Elizabeth I, the Most Powerful Woman In Our History, Always Depicted as a Grotesque?," *Guardian* (US edition) online, last modified May 25, 2015.

31. The most famous claim that Elizabeth was an imposter is the "Bisley Boy" theory, which originated with the novelist Bram Stoker (1847–1912) in his nonfiction book *Famous Impostors* [sic] (New York: Sturgis & Walton, 1910). Cf. Dr. Kit Heyman's article "It Was Necessary" (accessed online, August 8, 2022), in which they argue that Elizabeth I was potentially nonbinary. The use of Elizabethan political rhetoric—praising Elizabeth in both masculine and feminine terms—is fascinating. It was common, however, rather than unique to Elizabeth, to use gender-nonconfirming rhetoric to extol female rulers in the sixteenth century. As their political authority was held to be anomalous to their gender, many of their panegyrists praised them in both masculine and feminine terminology. Dr. Heyman's article is available via the Shakespeare's Globe website.

CHAPTER 10: EMPTY ROOMS

1. Unless stated otherwise, the following descriptions of Elizabethan London are taken from Thomas Platter the Younger, *Thomas Platter's Travels in England, 1599,* intro. and ed. Clare Williams (London: Jonathan Cape, 1937), pp. 169, 181–83, 189, 199.
2. The following description of Platter the Younger's visit is based on his testimony in *Travels,* pp. 199–205.
3. This was the device of Elizabeth I's great-grandmother Margaret, Countess of Richmond and Derby, and used frequently by her descendants.
4. The life of Tobias is contained in the Book of Tobit, part of the Deuterocanonical Apocrypha. For its continued inclusion in most Protestant translations of the Bible at this stage in Christian history, please see chapter 12.

PART II: THE HOUSE OF STUART & CROMWELL

CHAPTER 11: THE PAGES' CHAMBER

1. Robert Parker Sorlien, ed., *The Diary of John Manningham of the Middle Temple, 1602–1603* (Hanover, NH: University Press of New England, 1976), fol. 111b.
2. Thomas Dekker, *The Wonderfull yeare, 1603,* ed. G. B. Harrison (London: Bodley Head, 1924), p. 86.
3. James was doubly descended from the first Tudor king through the latter's daughter Margaret, Queen of Scots (d. 1541). Her son from her first marriage, King James V (d. 1542), was the father of Mary, Queen of Scots (ex. 1587), while her daughter from her second marriage, Margaret Douglas, Countess of Lennox (d. 1578), was the mother of Henry Stuart, Lord Darnley (murdered 1567), James VI's father. See Family Tree 1, "The House of Tudor."
4. John Ashton, intro., *A Ballade of the Scottyshe Kynge, Written by John Skelton, Poet Laureate to King Henry the Eighth* (London: Elliot Stock, 1882), p. 81; Ross Cowan, "Flodden: Scotland's Greatest Defeat," *Military History Monthly,* October 2013.
5. Jim Sharpe, "Social strain and social dislocation, 1585–1603," in *The Reign of Elizabeth I: Court and culture in the last decade,* ed. John Guy (Cambridge: Cambridge University Press, 1995), pp. 208–9.
6. Victoria de la Torre, "'We Few of an Infinite Multitude': John Hales, Parliament, and the Gendered Politics of the Early Elizabethan Succession," *Albion* 33, no. 4 (Winter 2001), p. 561.
7. Sarah Fraser, *The Prince Who Would Be King: The Life and Death of Henry Stuart* (London: William Collins, 2017), p. 44.
8. Sir Philip was also a maternal grandson of Lady Mary Sidney, the lady-in-waiting who had been disfigured by smallpox while caring for Elizabeth I at Hampton Court in 1562.
9. Leanda de Lisle, *After Elizabeth: The Death of Elizabeth and the Coming of King James* (London: Harper Perennial, 2006), p. 305.
10. Ethel Carleton Williams, *Anne of Denmark* (London: Longman, 1970), p. 73.

11. Elizabeth, whose maternal grandmother, the Countess of Ormond, had been a Howard, had begged Philip to publicly attend only one Protestant service, after which she promised to restore him to his wealth and royal favor. Philip felt he could not in good conscience do what she asked. He was canonized as Saint Philip Howard by Pope Paul VI in 1970.

12. The Main Plot, as it was known, had aimed to oust James I in favor of Lady Arbella Stuart, who seems to have been unaware of her role as figurehead to a potential coup. Arbella was a guest at Hampton Court during Christmas 1603–04, indicating that King James did not hold her culpable for the plotters' aims; see the letters from Lady Arbella Stuart to Mary Talbot, Countess of Shrewsbury, August 23 and c. September 16, 1603, and to Gilbert Talbot, 7th Earl of Shrewsbury, December 18, 1603, in *The Letters of Lady Arbella Stuart,* ed. Sara Jayne Steen (Oxford: Oxford University Press, 1994), pp. 181, 185, 197.

13. Fynes Morrison, *An history of Ireland, from the year 1599 to 1603: With a short narration of the state of the kingdom from the year 1169. To which is added, A description of Ireland* (Dublin: S. Powell, 1735), 1:pp. 16–17.

14. Cyril Falls, *Elizabeth's Irish Wars* (London: Methuen, 1950), p. 334.

15. The Tuscan and Savoyard ambassadors created such a fuss over who between them had the higher rank "that to displease neither, it was thought best to let both alone," so they were disinvited to one of the Queen's masques. See Dudley Carleton's letter of January 15, 1604, to John Chamberlain, in *Dudley Carleton to John Chamberlain, 1603–1624: Jacobean Letters,* ed. Maurice Lee Jr. (New Brunswick, NJ: Rutgers University Press, 1972), p. 55.

16. There is a lively set of debates on Shakespearean authorship, which again falls beyond the purview of this book. I include him here because it is my opinion that Shakespeare was the author of the works traditionally attributed to him, and, in particular, I disagree very much with the suggestion that they must have been secretly written by a member of the aristocracy, since Shakespeare did not come from the "right" class to pen such intellectual pieces.

17. Peter Ackroyd, *Shakespeare: The Biography* (London: Chatto & Windus, 2005), pp. 374–76.

18. Lee Jr., *Dudley Carleton to John Chamberlain,* p. 53.

19. De Lisle, *After Elizabeth,* p. 243; Lady Arbella Stuart to Gilbert Talbot, 7th Earl of Shrewsbury, September 16, 1603, in *Letters of Lady Arbella Stuart,* p. 184.

20. Lee Jr., *Dudley Carleton to John Chamberlain,* pp. 53–54.

21. Clare MacManus, *Women on the Renaissance Stage: Anna of Denmark and Female Masquing in the Stuart Court, 1590–1619* (New York: Manchester University Press, 2002), p. 100.

22. Lee Jr., *Dudley Carleton to John Chamberlain,* p. 55.

23. The two were grandchildren of Lady Margaret Douglas—James through her eldest son, Henry Stuart, Lord Darnley, who was murdered in 1567, and Arbella through her younger son Charles Stuart, 5th Earl of Lennox (d. 1576). See Family Tree 2, "The House of Stuart."

24. Lady Arbella Stuart to Gilbert Talbot, 7th Earl of Shrewsbury, December 18, 1603, in *Letters of Lady Arbella Stuart,* p. 197; Leeds Barroll, *Anna of Denmark, Queen of England: A Cultural Biography* (Philadelphia: University of Pennsylvania Press, 2001), p. 91.

25. The masque had the character of the goddess Iris refer to "mighty Brittany," meaning here the British Isles rather than the French duchy; Venus had the lines about "strange nations" uniting "with affections true." See MacManus, *Women on the Renaissance Stage*, pp. 102, 110.
26. Thurley, *Hampton Court*, p. 107.
27. Lee Jr., *Dudley Carleton to John Chamberlain*, pp. 53–57.

CHAPTER 12: THE HAMPTON COURT CONFERENCE

1. Thurley, *Hampton Court*, p. 108.
2. Sir James Melville, *Memoirs of his Own Life by Sir James Melville of Halhill,* ed. T. Thomson (Edinburgh: Bannatyne Club, 1827), p. 134; Antonia Fraser, *Mary Queen of Scots* (London: Weidenfeld & Nicolson, 1976), p. 89.
3. In her book *After Elizabeth* (2003), Leanda de Lisle argues that King James may have suffered from attention deficit hyperactivity disorder (ADHD). It has also been suggested that the King may have had mild cerebral palsy or suffered from perinatal brain damage.
4. Harris D. Wilson, *King James VI and I* (Oxford: Oxford University Press, 1967), p. 165.
5. For the original scriptural citation for Harington's comment, see Matthew 12:43; for the comment itself, see Sir John Harington, *Nugae antiquae: being a miscellaneous collection of original papers in prose and verse: written in the reigns of Henry VIII, Queen Mary, Elizabeth, King James, &c,* ed. Rev. Henry Harington (Bath, UK: T. Shrimpeton, 1779), 1:pp. 181–82.
6. Peter Lake, *Moderate Puritans and the Elizabethan Church* (Cambridge: Cambridge University Press, 1982), p. 30.
7. Sir Roger Wilbraham et al., *The Journal of Sir Roger Wilbraham, Solicitor-General in Ireland and Master of Requests for the Years 1593–1616, Together with Notes in Another Hand for the Years 1642–1649* (Cambridge, UK: Royal Historical Society and the Camden Society, 2009), p. 62.
8. Edward Cardwell, ed., *Documentary Annals of the Reformed Church of England* (Oxford: Oxford University Press, 1844), 2:pp. 80–84.
9. John 19:26–27; 1 Corinthians 3:1–4.
10. Sarah Fraser, *Prince Who Would Be King*, p. 54.
11. Adam Nicolson, *When God Spoke English: The Making of the King James Bible* (London: HarperPress, 2004), pp. 52–53.
12. Ibid., p. 57.
13. Preface to the King James Authorized Translation of the Bible (1611).
14. Philippians 1:1.
15. This was to remain controversial even in modern-day Christianity. For instance, the Good News Bible of 1976 translates Philippians 1:1 as "church leaders and helpers," while 1978's New International Version prefers "overseers and deacons."
16. Genesis 19:4–5.
17. In the fourteenth century, there was a theological proposition that, on this basis, sodomy could be used as analogous to the mortal sin of bestiality.
18. Mark D. Jordan, *The Invention of Sodomy in Christian Theology* (Chicago: University of Chicago Press, 1997), p. 29.

19. This is based on a debate over Christ's words on Sodom and Gomorrah, recorded in Hebrews 13:12.

20. He also excluded sodomy from the terms of a general pardon; see his letter to Robert Cecil, July 1610, in *Letters of King James VI & I*, ed. G. P. V. Akrigg (Berkeley: University of California Press, 1984), 148.

21. George Villiers, 1st Duke of Buckingham, to King James I, September 1, 1623, in David M. Bergeron, *King James and Letters of Homoerotic Desire* (Iowa City: University of Iowa Press, 1999), B19, p. 198.

22. For further discussion of James's sexuality, see David M. Bergeron, "King James and Robert Carr: Letters and Desire," in *Explorations in Renaissance Culture* 22, no. 1 (1996): pp. 1–30; Michael B. Young, *King James VI and I and the History of Homosexuality* (London: Macmillan, 2000), pp. 13–15, 29–35; De Lisle, *After Elizabeth*, pp. 54–56; and Andrea Zuvich, *Sex and Sexuality in Stuart Britain* (Barnsley, UK: Pen & Sword, 2020), pp. 150–54. Cf. Maurice Lee Jr., *Great Britain's Solomon: James VI and I in His Three Kingdoms* (Chicago: University of Illinois Press, 1990), pp. 247–48.

23. Young, *James VI and I and the History of Homosexuality*, p. 42.

24. De Lisle, *After Elizabeth*, p. 200.

25. Ephraim J. Burford, *Bawds and Lodgings: A history of the London Bankside brothels, c. 1000–1675* (London: Peter Owen, 1976), p. 175.

26. De Lisle, *After Elizabeth*, p. 55.

27. Carleton Williams, *Anne of Denmark*, p. 134.

28. Young, *James VI and I and the History of Homosexuality*, p. 42.

29. Ibid.

30. Bergeron, "King James and Robert Carr," p. 1.

31. Preface to the King James Authorized Translation of the Bible.

32. It remains in most Catholic editions of the Bible, despite the ruling in 1927 by Pope Pius XI that the Johannine Comma's validity is open to debate and scrutiny. Biblical literalism is far less prevalent in Catholicism than in Protestantism, which meant that the question of the Comma's continued inclusion in Catholic translations of the New Testament remains less controversial.

33. For example, when the KJV translation of 1 Kings 19:12, referring to the "still small voice" of the Prophet Elijah, was rendered instead as the "low murmuring sound," this was mocked by some traditionalists, when, in fact, it was a far closer match to the Hebrew expression *qol demamah daqqah*.

34. John Barton, *A History of the Bible: The Book and Its Faiths* (London: Allen Lane, 2019), p. 5.

35. Alister E. McGrath, *In the Beginning: The Story of the King James Bible and How It Changed a Nation, a Language, and a Culture* (New York: Doubleday, 2001), pp. 254–56; Richard Dawkins, "Why I Want All Our Children to Read the King James Bible," *Guardian* (US edition) online, last modified May 19, 2012; Hannah Furness, "Modern Bible Is Too Dull, Says Philip Pullman," *Daily Telegraph* (UK), January 14, 2015.

CHAPTER 13: THE QUEEN'S BEDCHAMBER

1. *Cal. S. P. Ven.*, X, 102.

2. Mark 5:25–34.

3. Kenneth F. Kiple, ed., *The Cambridge World History of Human Disease* (Cambridge: Cambridge University Press, 2008), 8: pp. 689–93.

4. Leanda de Lisle, *White King: Traitor, Murderer, Martyr* (London: Chatto & Windus, 2018), p. x.

5. Carleton Williams, *Anne of Denmark*, p. 193.

6. Ibid., pp. 197–98.

7. *Cal. S. P. Ven.*, XIV, 393.

8. Ernest Philip Alphonse Law, *A History of Hampton Court: Stuart Times* (London: George Bell & Sons, 1898), pp. 85–86.

9. This was principally due to the implementation of tolls on trading ships, the income from which was tripled by Frederick II's decision to increase it from 1 percent to 2 percent of every ship's cargo; see also Knud J. V. Jespersen, *A History of Denmark*, trans. Ivan Hill (London: Palgrave, 2004), pp. 116–17, and Karen Larsen, *A History of Norway* (Princeton, NJ: Princeton University Press, 1948), pp. 251–52.

10. Ackroyd, *Shakespeare*, p. 418.

11. Jacobo Fitz-James Stuart y Falcó, 17th Duke of Alba, ed., *Documentos inéditos para la historia de España: Correspondencia oficial de don Diego Sarmiento de Acuña, conde de Gondomar* (Madrid: s. n., 1944), 3:58.

12. *Acts and Proceedings of the General Assemblies of the Kirk of Scotland, 1560–1618* (Edinburgh: s. n., 1839), minutes for session 13 of the General Assembly, March 31, 1596.

13. David Calderwood, *The History of the Church of Scotland* (Edinburgh: Wicklow Society, 1844), 5:460.

14. *Cal. S. P. Ven.*, X, 739.

15. Anne Somerset, *Unnatural Murder: Poison at the Court of James I* (London: Weidenfeld & Nicolson, 1997), p. 121.

16. James Bliss, ed., *The Works of the Most Reverend Father in God William Laud, D. D., Sometime Archbishop of Canterbury* (Oxford: John Henry Parker, 1838), 3:170.

17. Barroll, *Anna of Denmark*, pp. 136–37.

18. BL, MS Cotton Titus B.vii, fol. 483v.

19. Somerset, *Unnatural Murder*, pp. 333–34.

20. Carleton Williams, *Anne of Denmark*, p. 202.

21. Ibid., p. 200.

22. *Cal. S. P. Ven.*, X, 40. For Anna's matrimonial policy being reflective of Danish diplomatic precedent rather than religious interests, see Barroll, *Anna of Denmark*, pp. 164–67.

23. Carleton Williams, *Anne of Denmark*, p. 200.

24. Barroll, *Anna of Denmark*, pp. 162–72.

25. Pauline Gregg, *King Charles I* (Toronto: J. M. Dent, 1981), p. 60.

26. Carleton Williams, *Anne of Denmark*, p. 201.

CHAPTER 14: THE WHARF

1. Dominic Pearce, *Henrietta Maria* (Stroud, UK: Amberley, 2015), p. 210.

2. Ibid., p. 211.

3. De Lisle, *White King*, p. 149.

4. Ibid.

5. Ibid.

6. Rye, *England as Seen by Foreigners*, p. 133.

7. De Lisle, *White King*, p. 150.

8. Charles I's two youngest daughters, the princesses Anne and Catherine, had died in infancy. Anne passed away aged three and Catherine on the day after her birth, shortly after her baptism. Alison Plowden, *The Stuart Princesses* (Stroud, UK: Alan Sutton, 1996), pp. 71–73.

9. Alison Plowden, *Henrietta Maria: Charles I's Indomitable Queen* (Stroud, UK: Sutton, 2001), p. 259.

10. Plowden, *Henrietta Maria*, p. 155.

11. Robert Armstrong, *Protestant War: The "British" of Ireland and the Wars of the Three Kingdoms* (Manchester, UK: Manchester University Press, 2005), pp. 223, 231–35. For the difficulty in estimating the casualty figures in 1641, and how the definition of what a casualty was shifted depending on contemporary perspectives, see Aidan Clarke, "The '1641 Massacres,'" in *Ireland, 1641: Contexts and Reactions,* ed. Micheál Ó Siochrú and Jane Ohlmeyer (Manchester, UK: Manchester University Press, 2013), pp. 37–51.

12. Hilary Simms, "Violence in County Armagh, 1641," in *Ulster 1641: Aspects of the Rising,* ed. Brian Mac Cuarta (Belfast: Institute of Irish Studies, 1993), pp. 124–25.

13. Jonathan Bardon, *The Plantation of Ulster: The British Colonisation of the North of Ireland in the Seventeenth Century* (Dublin: Gill & Macmillan, 2011), p. 281.

14. Also known as Saint Patrick's Purgatory, or Baisleac Naomh Pádraig, on Lough Derg in County Donegal. See the Sermon of Most Rev. William Conway Bishop of Neve: At St. Patrick's Purgatory, Lough Derg, 20 August 1961, in *Seanchas Ardmhacha: Journal of the Armagh Diocesan Historical Society* 4, no. 2 (1961–62): p. 151.

15. *Cal. S. P. Ven.*, XXV, 275.

16. Gregg, *King Charles I*, p. 416.

17. De Lisle, *White King*, p. 224.

18. Before the Reformation, it had been the site of Syon Abbey, where both Lady Margaret Douglas and Queen Catherine Howard were detained.

19. Edward Hyde, 1st Earl of Clarendon, *The History of the Rebellion and the Civil Wars in England* (Sacramento, CA: Franklin Classics, 2018), 5:p. 264.

20. James Butler (1610–88) moved through three rungs of the aristocracy, inheriting the title from his grandfather as 12th Earl of Ormond in 1634. It was elevated to a marquessate by Charles I in 1642 and then to a dukedom by Charles II in 1661.

21. Thurley, *Hampton Court*, p. 113.

22. De Lisle, *White King*, p. 233.

23. John Lilburne, "To the Honourable Judges of the King's Bench: The Humble Petition of Lieut. Col. John Lilburne," in *Tracts on Liberty by the Levellers and Their Critics,* ed. David M. Hart and Ross Kenyon (Indianapolis: Liberty Fund, 2014), p. v.

CHAPTER 15: THE TEMPORARY PALISADE

1. Although Greenwich had been called the Palace of Placentia when it was first built for the court of Henry VI in the fifteenth century, it was hardly ever referred to as such during the Tudor or Stuart eras. Its dilapidated remnants were demolished in the reign of Charles II.

2. Simon Thurley, *Palaces of Revolution: Life, Death and Art at the Stuart Court* (London: William Collins, 2021), p. 257.

3. *Cal. S. P. Ven.*, XXXI, 49.

4. The Hapsburgs and the Bourbons wrung their hands in horror at Charles I's execution but raised them with equal vigor at the auctions for his treasure. For instance, the presence of Hans Holbein's famous portraits of queens Jane Seymour and Anne of Cleves at respective museums in Vienna and Paris was a consequence of the interregnum auctions.

5. Thurley, *Hampton Court*, p. 112.

6. Wayment, "Wolsey and Stained Glass," p. 121.

7. *Cal. S. P. Ven.*, XXX, 110.

8. R. Scrope and T. Monkhouse, eds., *State Papers collected by Edward, Earl of Clarendon, Commencing from the year 1621* (Oxford: Clarendon Press, 1767–86), 3:p. 327.

9. Lucy Hutchinson, *Memoirs of the Life of Colonel Hutchinson*, ed. N. H. Keeble (London: J. M. Dent, 1913), p. 256.

10. Samuel Carrington, *The History of the Life and Death of His Most Serene Highness, Oliver, late Lord Protector wherein, from his cradle to his tomb, are impartially transmitted to posterity, the most weighty transactions foreign or domestique that have happened in his time, either in matters of law, proceeddings in Parliament, or other affairs in Church or state* (London: Nath. Brook at the Sign of the Angel, 1659), p. 218.

11. W. C. Abbott and C. D. Crane, eds., *The Writings and Speeches of Oliver Cromwell* (Oxford: Clarendon Press, 1987), 1:416.

12. There is a debate over the extent of Lady Claypole's intercession for royalist prisoners during the interregnum. It seems unlikely, however, that her lobbying for them indicates that she personally harbored monarchist sympathies.

13. Scrope and Monkhouse, *State Papers,* 3:p. 239.

14. Royalist writers, either unaware of her child's death or indifferent to it, seem guilty of projection in attributing her decline to grief at failing to prevent her father's execution of Reverend Hewett earlier that year.

15. Under the monarchy, these rooms had been granted to the king's Master of the Horse, one of the highest-ranking court officials.

16. Thomas Birch, *A Collection of the State Papers of John Thurloe* (London: Fletcher Gyles, 1742), 7:171.

17. Antonia Fraser, *Cromwell: Our Chief of Men* (London: Weidenfeld & Nicholson, 2008), 830.

18. Birch, *State Papers,* 7:262.

19. Bridget Cromwell's marriage to General Henry Ireton ended with his death during a plague epidemic in Ireland. She subsequently married another general, Charles Fleetwood, who was inducted to the peerage by her father. This title was retrospectively annulled upon the restoration of the monarchy in 1660; however, she was still Lady Fleetwood at the time of her younger sister's funeral, hence the use of the title here. The year 1658 was particularly painful for her sister Frances, whose husband, Robert Rich, had died of tuberculosis that February. I am grateful to Miranda Malins for discussing with me which forms of address were used for the Protector's daughters, specifically Frances, who does not seem to have acquired a courtesy title

through her marriage but rather through being Cromwell's daughter. See also Lee Prosser, "Writings and Sources: The Inventory of 1659," *Cromwelliana: The Journal of the Cromwell Association* 2, no. 6 (2009): p. 66.

20. Antonia Fraser, *Cromwell*, pp. 45–47; cf. Ronald Hutton, *The Making of Oliver Cromwell* (New Haven, CT: Yale University Press, 2021), pp. 20–21.

21. *Cal. S. P. Ven.*, XXXI, 57.

22. It killed a higher percentage of the population than did the First World War.

23. Barbara Coulton, "Cromwell and the Readmission of the Jews to England, 1656," The Cromwell Association (accessed online, June 19, 2021), p. 18.

24. Ibid., p. 14.

25. Jack Malvern, "We've Been Looking at the Wrong 'Warts and All' Painting of Cromwell," *The Times* (London) online, last modified November 18, 2013.

26. Winifred, Lady Burghclere, *The Life of James, First Duke of Ormonde* (London: John Murray, 1912), 1:pp. 343–44; Micheál Ó Siochrú, *Confederate Ireland, 1642–1649: A Constitutional and Political Analysis* (Dublin: Four Courts Press, 1999), pp. 171–72.

27. Pope Innocent X's offer had been negotiated with, and conveyed through, the Queen's confidant Kenelm Digby; see Ó Siochrú, *Confederate Ireland*, p. 100.

28. Ibid., p. 167.

29. Micheál Ó Siochrú, *God's Executioner: Oliver Cromwell and the Conquest of Ireland* (London: Faber and Faber, 2008), p. 82.

30. Sean O'Callaghan, *To Hell or Barbados: The Ethnic Cleansing of Ireland* (Dublin: Brandon, 2013), p. 27.

31. Ó Siochrú, *God's Executioner*, p. 84.

32. Ibid.

33. Éamonn an Dúna, "Mo lá leóin go deo go n-éagad," in *Five Seventeenth-Century Political Poems,* ed. Cecile O'Rahilly (Dublin: Institiúid Árd-Léinn Bhaile Átha Cliath, 1977), p. 90.

34. Bardon, *Plantation of Ulster*, pp. 285–86.

35. James Butler, 1st Marquess and later 1st Duke of Ormond, to Prince Rupert of the Rhine, September 18, 1649, in Ó Siochrú, *God's Executioner*, p. 84.

36. Ó Siochrú, *God's Executioner*, p. 85. Cf. Tom Reilly, *Cromwell: An Honourable Enemy: The Untold Story of the Cromwellian Invasion of Ireland* (Dingle, Ire: Brandon, 1999), pp. 232–33.

37. Ó Siochrú, *God's Executioner*, p. 77.

38. Peter Berresford Ellis, *Hell or Connaught!: The Cromwellian Colonisation of Ireland, 1652–1660* (London: Hamish Hamilton, 1975), p. 91.

39. Bardon, *Plantation of Ulster*, p. 287.

40. Cromwell's cartographer, William Petty, estimated that his employer had sent nearly 100,000 from Ireland to the colonies in the Caribbean or in northeastern America, which seems unfeasibly high in light of other data available. His claim that just over a half million Irish Catholics and 112,000 Irish Protestants died in consequence of the 1640s is harder to refute. See Bardon, *Plantation of Ulster*, pp. 286–87.

41. Ó Siochru, *God's Executioner*, p. 230.

42. Bardon, *Plantation of Ulster*, p. 286.

43. John P. Prendergast, *The Cromwellian Settlement of Ireland* (London: Longman, Green, Roberts & Green, 1865), pp. 180–82.

44. O'Callaghan, *Hell or Barbados*, p. 15.

45. Antonia Fraser, *Cromwell*, p. 835.

46. Philippians 4:8–9.

47. George Fox, *The Journal of George Fox,* ed. John L. Nickalls (London: Religious Society of Friends, 1975), pp. 347–48.

48. Ibid., p. 350.

49. Ó Siochrú, *God's Executioner*, pp. 246–63.

50. Antonia Fraser, *Cromwell*, p. 851.

CHAPTER 16: THE COUNTESS OF CASTLEMAINE'S QUARTERS

1. For Henrietta Maria being referred to by the title of queen mother during her widowhood, see entry for Christmas Eve 1666 in Samuel Pepys, *The Diary of Samuel Pepys,* ed. Robert Latham and William G. Matthews (University of California Press, 2000), and Pearce, *Henrietta Maria*, p. 290.

2. Thurley, *Palaces of Revolution*, pp. 295–96.

3. Sarah-Beth Watkins, *Catherine of Braganza: Charles II's Restoration Queen* (Winchester, UK: Chronos, 2017), p. 22.

4. John Evelyn, *The Diary of John Evelyn,* ed. William Bray (Washington, DC: M. Walter Dunne, 1901), 1:p. 358; Pen Vogler, *Scoff: A History of Food and Class in Britain* (London: Atlantic Books, 2020), pp. 45–46.

5. Vogler, *Scoff*, pp. 237–38.

6. Pepys, diary entry, July 26, 1662, in *Diary of Samuel Pepys,* 3:p. 147.

7. Edward Hyde, 1st Earl of Clarendon, *The Life of Edward, Earl of Clarendon* (Oxford: Clarendon Press, 1761), 3:pp. 184–85.

8. Pearce, *Henrietta Maria*, p. 290.

9. Mary Spongberg, "*La Reine malheureuse*: Stuart History, Sympathetic History and the Stricklands' History of Henrietta Maria," *Women's History Review* 20, no. 5 (2011), pp. 745–64.

10. Queen Henrietta Maria, the Queen Mother, to Christine of France, Dowager Duchess of Savoy, in Hermann Ferrero, ed., *Lettres de Henriette-Marie de France, Reine d'Angleterre, et sa Soeur Christine, Duchesse de Savoie* (London: Wentworth Press, 2018), p. 126.

11. Jenny Uglow, *A Gambling Man: Charles II and the Restoration, 1660–1670* (London: Faber and Faber, 2009), p. 149.

12. Bryan Bevan, *Charles the Second's French Mistress: A Biography of Louise de Kéroualle, Duchess of Portsmouth* (London: R. Hale, 1972), p. 72.

13. Pepys, diary entry, March 25, 1668, in *Diary of Samuel Pepys*, 8:pp. 131–33.

14. *The Poor-Whores Petition: To the most Splendid, Illustrious, Serene and Eminent Lady of Pleasure, the Countess of Castlemayne*, Bod. MS Don b.8, 190–93.

15. Zuvich, *Sex and Sexuality*, p. 164.

16. The last to do so was King Henry I, who reigned from 1100 to 1135.

17. Linda Porter, *Mistresses: Sex and scandal at the court of Charles II* (London: Picador, 2020), pp. 162–63.

18. Zuvich, *Sex and Sexuality*, p. 169.

19. Porter, *Mistresses*, pp. 41–42.

20. Anne was later acknowledged by the King as his child, at which point her surname was changed to Fitzroy, a medieval term to denote a king's bastard. It was quite some time after her marriage to Thomas Lennard, 1st Earl of Sussex, that Anne became Hortense Mancini's lover, with 1678 being the most probable date. The Countess of Sussex would have been about seventeen and Hortense about thirty-one. The Sussexes subsequently quit court and moved to Paris, where Anne later left Lord Sussex during her affair with the English ambassador, Ralph Montagu, subsequently 1st Duke of Montagu and formerly Queen Catherine of Braganza's Master of the Horse. The Earl of Sussex squandered much of his fortune on a gambling addiction. The Sussexes later reconciled and remained married until the Earl's death in 1715; Anne died six years later.

21. Pepys, diary entry, Christmas Eve and Christmas Day, 1667, in *Diary of Samuel Pepys*, 7:pp. 588–89.

22. Ibid.

23. Thurley, *Hampton Court*, p. 140.

24. Uglow, *A Gambling Man*, p. 268.

25. Zuvich, *Sex and Sexuality*, p. 122.

26. Pepys, diary entry, May 15, 1668, in *Diary of Samuel Pepys*, 8:p. 201.

27. Uglow, *A Gambling Man*, p. 269.

28. Eilish Gregory, "Catherine of Braganza's Relationship with Her Catholic Household," in *Forgotten Queens in Medieval and Early Modern Europe,* ed. Estelle Paranque and Valerie Schutte (London: Routledge, 2018), pp. 133–34.

29. Pepys, diary entry, August 19, 1662, in *Diary of Samuel Pepys*, 3:pp. 170–71.

30. For a convincing rebuttal of the rumors concerning Jermyn and the Duchess of York, see Uglow, *A Gambling Man*, pp. 98–99.

31. Plowden, *Henrietta Maria*, pp. 256–57.

32. Eilish Gregory, "Catherine of Braganza," p. 136.

33. The Archbishop of Armagh became Saint Oliver Plunket after being canonized in 1975 by Pope Paul VI, who, five years earlier, had also canonized five priests executed during the Popish Plot. Lord Stafford was beatified as Blessed William Howard the Martyr by Pope Pius XI in 1929.

CHAPTER 17: THE ORANGERY

1. Maureen Waller, *Ungrateful Daughters: The Stuart Princesses Who Stole Their Father's Crown* (London: Hodder & Stoughton, 2002), p. 47; Anne Somerset, *Queen Anne: The Politics of Passion* (London: Harper Press, 2012), p. 81.

2. Waller, *Ungrateful Daughters*, p. 39.

3. Somerset, *Queen Anne*, p. 84.

4. Most prominently, the reforms prompted in reaction to the 1798 uprising included the third Act of Union that created the United Kingdom; it came into legal effect on January 1, 1801.

5. Jonathan Bardon, *A History of Ulster* (Dundonald, UK: Blackstaff Press, 1992), p. 168; W. N. Osborough, "The ailure to enact an Irish Bill of Rights: A gap in Irish constitutional history," *Irish Jurist* 33 (1998): p. 405.

6. Neither the Bill of Rights (1689) nor the Act of Settlement (1701) was recognized as legal by James II and VII's supporters, the Jacobites.

7. The accessions of Harold II (1066), William I (1066), Henry I (1100), Stephen (1135), Henry II (1154), John (1199), Edward III (1327), Henry IV (1399), Edward IV (1461 and 1470), Henry VI (1471), Richard III (1483), Henry VII (1485), and James I (1603) had all, to varying degrees, seen primogeniture sublimated to, or used in conjunction with, either acclamation, conquest, diplomacy, and/or legislative endorsement.

8. Supplemented by the Act of Settlement in 1701, the Bill of Rights' provisions regarding the civil rights of British subjects remain intact at the time of writing, as does the requirement for a British monarch to be an Anglican. However, the monarch and those in line for the throne may now marry a Roman Catholic without losing their place as heirs to the throne, thanks to legislation enacted between 2011 and 2015, which also revised the previous provision whereby the throne passed to the eldest son. It now passes in order of birth, with no preference accorded with regard to gender.

9. The House of Lords' right to veto was repealed by the Parliament Act of 1911.

10. This was dismantled by a series of reforms, collectively known as Catholic Emancipation, enacted between 1766 and 1829.

11. A case could be made that there had been a pair of coruling monarchs before in England between 1035 and 1040, with King Harold I and his half brother, Harthacanute, King of Denmark, whose authority in England was exercised by a regent, his mother, Emma of Normandy.

12. Thurley, *Palaces of Revolution*, p. 391.

13. Gibbons was born in Rotterdam to two English royalist parents who had sought refuge in the Netherlands during the civil war.

14. William Whiston, *Memoirs of the Life and Writings of Mr. William Whiston* (London: Whiston and White, 1753), p. 100.

15. Zuvich, *Sex and Sexuality*, pp. 185–86.

16. Respectively, the dates of the Save Ulster from Sodomy campaign in opposition to the decriminalization of homosexuality and the end of the filibustering against the legalization of same-sex marriage. See also Martin Wainwright, "Tatchell Recruits Unionist Hero for Gay Rights Cause," *Guardian* (US edition) online, last modified July 27, 2008; Brian Lacey, *Terrible Queer Creatures: Homosexuality in Irish history* (Dublin: Wordwell, 2008), p. 74; David Young, "Orange Order Historian Disputes Gay Rights Campaigner Peter Tatchell's Claim That King Billy Was Bisexual," *Belfast Telegraph*, August 21, 2015.

17. Bryan Bevan, *King William III: Prince of Orange, the first European* (London: Rubicon Press, 1997), p. 160.

18. Zuvich, *Sex and Sexuality*, p. 271.

19. Jane Ridley, *George V: Never a Dull Moment* (London: Chatto & Windus, 2021), p. 17.

20. F. M. G. Higham, *King James the Second* (London: Hamish Hamilton, 1934), pp. 307–9.

21. Ethan H. Shagan, "Early modern violence from memory to history: a historiographical essay," in Ó Siochrú and Ohlmeyer, *Ireland, 1641*, p. 17.

CHAPTER 18: THE APOTHEOSIS OF QUEEN ANNE

1. Anne's parental grandfather, Edward Hyde was ennobled by Charles II, first as Baron Hyde (1660) and then as 1st Earl of Clarendon (1661). However, at the time his daughter and Anne's mother was born (1637), Hyde was working as a lawyer and had not yet even been knighted.
2. Claire Tomalin, *Samuel Pepys: The Unequalled Self* (London: Penguin, 2002), p. 114.
3. Matthew Dennison, *The First Iron Lady: A Life of Caroline of Ansbach* (London: William Collins, 2018), p. 117.
4. Zuvich, *Sex and Sexuality*, p. 188.
5. *The Favourite* (Fox Searchlight Studios, 2018), directed by Yorgos Lanthimos, written by Deborah Davis and Tony McNamara, starring Olivia Colman (Queen Anne), Rachel Weisz (Sarah Churchill, Duchess of Marlborough), Emma Stone (Abigail Hill, Baroness Masham), and Nicholas Hoult (Robert Harley, 1st Earl of Oxford).
6. Somerset, *Queen Anne*, pp. 360–61.
7. I am grateful to Emrys Kein for our discussion on the correspondence between Queen Anne and the Duchess of Marlborough. For a further discussion, see Somerset, *Queen Anne*, pp. 53–55, and cf. Zuvich, *Sex and Sexuality*, pp. 187–95, for the argument that the relationship was probably neither sexual nor romantic.
8. Somerset, *Queen Anne*, p. 145.
9. Élisabeth-Charlotte, Dowager Duchess of Orléans, to Sophia, Dowager Electress of Hanover, April 17, 1701, in Elisabeth Charlotte, Duchess of Orléans, *A Woman's Life in the Court of the Sun King: Letters of Liselotte von der Pfalz, Elisabeth Charlotte, Duchesse d'Orléans,* ed. and trans. Elborg Forster (Baltimore: Johns Hopkins University Press, 1997), p. 130.
10. She also had a sister, Princess Louise-Marie-Thérèse (see Family Tree 2), whose birth in France four years after the Glorious Revolution disproved Anne's assertion that her stepmother had been incapable of bearing a healthy child—a charge that had many a major plank of the "Warming Pan" scandal.
11. Jock Haswell, *James II: Soldier and Sailor* (London: Hamish Hamilton, 1972), p. 307.

PART III: THE HOUSE OF HANOVER

CHAPTER 19: THE CHOCOLATE KITCHENS

1. Studia Rosenthaliana, *Notarial Records Relating to the Portuguese Jews in Amsterdam up to 1639* (1996), 30, ii, pp. 304–18.
2. Zuvich, *Sex and Sexuality*, pp. 117–18.
3. Polly Putnam, "The Wife of the King's Chocolate Maker," for Historic Royal Palaces and University of Reading blog, accessed March 14, 2021.
4. *Gentleman's Journal*, June 1721.
5. Vogler, *Scoff*, p. 309.
6. Élisabeth-Charlotte, Dowager Duchess of Orléans, to Sophia, Dowager Electress of Hanover, July 10, 1704, in Orléans, *A Woman's Life*, p. 156.

7. Sarah Murden, "18th-Century Drinking Chocolate," *Recipes of the Georgian Era* (blog), All Things Georgian, January 6, 2015.
8. Eleri Lynn, "Georgian Celebrity and Gossip," Historic Royal Palaces, July 2, 2014.
9. Élisabeth-Charlotte, Dowager Duchess of Orléans, to Luise von Degenfeld, October 14, 1714, in Orléans, *A Woman's Life*, p. 196.
10. This was not Charles II's sister but her widower's second wife. Élisabeth-Charlotte, Dowager Duchess of Orléans, to Sophia, Dowager Electress of Hanover, October 26, 1704, in Orléans, *A Woman's Life*, p. 156.
11. Élisabeth-Charlotte, Dowager Duchess of Orléans, to Luise von Degenfeld, January 22, 1715, in Orléans, *A Woman's Life*, p. 197. Even the Duchess's use of the title Princess of Wales is revealing, given that, officially, the French government did not recognize that a prince of Wales had existed since James II's death in 1701, when the previous Jacobite incumbent became James III and VIII.
12. Thurley, *Hampton Court*, p. 248.

CHAPTER 20: QUEEN CAROLINE'S APARTMENTS

1. The second of her three sons, Prince George, had died in infancy in 1718.
2. Brian W. Hill, *Sir Robert Walpole: "Sole and Prime Minister"* (London: Hamish Hamilton, 1989), p. 175.
3. Dennison, *First Iron Lady*, p. 310.
4. Ibid., p. 33.
5. Stephen Taylor, "Caroline, Queen of Great Britain and Ireland," *ODNB*, 10:p. 202.
6. David Price, ed., *Letters on England by Voltaire* (London: Cassell, 1894), p. 55.
7. G. R. Stirling Taylor, *Robert Walpole and His Age* (London: Jonathan Cape, 1931), p. 76.
8. Tracy Borman, *King's Mistress, Queen's Servant: The Life and Times of Henrietta Howard* (London: Vintage, 2010), p. 109.
9. As with all arbitrary designations in history, this has been queried, both by those who argue credibly that Walpole was de facto prime minister for eight or nine years before Lord Townshend's downfall—which, as an event, only formalized an existing reality—and by those who counter that the term *prime minister* did not formally enter Britain's political lexicon until the careers of Walpole's two successors, the Earl of Wilmington and Henry Pelham, both of whom have been described by various biographers as the country's "real" first prime minister. To all practical intents, Robert Walpole was the first, and he is usually regarded as such.
10. Dennison, *First Iron Lady*, p. 229.
11. BMC1921, "The Noble Stand of the Glorious," published March/April 1733; see Paul Langford, *Walpole and the Robinocracy* (Cambridge, UK: Chadwyck-Healey, 1986), print 26, pp. 86–87.
12. BMC1936, "Britannia Excisa; Britain Excis'd," published March/April 1733; see Langford, *Walpole and the Robinocracy*, print 23, pp. 80–81.
13. Hill, *Sir Robert Walpole*, p. 175.
14. Lord Hervey to Henry Fox, February 6, 1733, in Giles Fox-Strangways, 6th Earl of Ilchester, ed., *Lord Hervey and His Friends, 1726–38* (London: John Murray, 1950), p. 158.
15. The comparison to Wolsey also appeared in anti-Walpole and anti-Excise pamphlets;

see BMC1925, published 1733, in Langford, *Walpole and the Robinocracy*, plate 29, pp. 92–93.

16. John Hervey, 2nd Baron Hervey, *Lord Hervey's Memoir,* ed. Romney Sedgwick (London: B. T. Batsford, 1963), p. 254.

CHAPTER 21: THE QUEEN'S STAIRS

1. RCIN405746. It is listed as decorating the Hall at Hampton Court during Charles II's reign.

2. Lord Hervey to Dr. Cheyne, December 9, 1732, in Ilchester, *Lord Hervey and His Friends*, pp. 151–52.

3. Robert Halsband, *Lord Hervey: Eighteenth-Century Courtier* (Oxford: Clarendon Press, 1973), pp. 66.

4. Lord Hervey to the Bishop of Salisbury, August 14, 1733, in Ilchester, *Lord Hervey and His Friends*, p. 171.

5. Lord Hervey to Stephen Fox, October 26, 1733, in ibid., p. 171.

6. Ilchester, *Lord Hervey and His Friends*, p. 145n.

7. Lord Hervey to Henry Fox, February 6, 1733, in ibid., p. 158.

8. Lord Hervey to the Bishop of Salisbury, August 14, 1733, and to Rev. Conyers Middleton, October 15, 1733, in ibid., pp. 171, 176.

9. Lord Hervey to the Duke of Richmond, July 18, 1733, in ibid., pp. 151–52.

10. Lucy Moore, *Amphibious Thing: The Life of Lord Hervey* (London: Viking, 2000), p. 286.

11. Lord Hervey to Stephen Fox, November 4, 1732, and January 25, 1733, in Ilchester, *Lord Hervey and His Friends*, pp. 145, 156–57.

12. Lord Hervey to Stephen Fox, November 11, 1732, in ibid., p. 149. Ilchester seems to have mistranscribed "old" for "own."

13. Lord Hervey to Stephen Fox, September 18, 1731, in ibid., p. 90.

14. Lord Hervey to Stephen Fox, December 21, 1731, in ibid., p. 124.

15. John Hervey, 2nd Baron Hervey, *Memoirs of the Reign of George II,* ed. John Wilson Croker (London: John Murray, 1848), 3:p. 832.

16. Halsband, *Lord Hervey*, pp. 88–92.

17. Moore, *Amphibious Thing*, pp. 22–23.

18. Ibid., pp. 51–56, 59–60.

19. Lord Hervey to Stephen Fox, December 15, 1729, and September 2, 1731, in Ilchester, *Lord Hervey and His Friends*, p. 83.

20. Halsband, *Lord Hervey*, pp. 122–23.

21. Lord Hervey to Stephen Fox, day unspecified, August 1730.

22. Halsband, *Lord Hervey*, p. 58.

23. Lord Hervey to Stephen Fox, August 23, 1731, in Ilchester, *Lord Hervey and His Friends*, p. 80.

24. Halsband, *Lord Hervey*, p. 90; Moore, *Amphibious Thing*, pp. 38–39.

25. Maynard Mack, *Alexander Pope: A Life* (New Haven, CT: Yale University Press, 1985), pp. 644–46.

26. Dennison, *First Iron Lady*, p. 317.

27. Lord Hervey to Queen Caroline, date unknown, c. 1736, in Ilchester, *Lord Hervey and His Friends*, pp. 245–47.

28. Moore, *Amphibious Thing*, pp. 103–5, 134–35.

29. There were also far less credible rumors that Lord Hervey had slept with Frederick's sister Princess Caroline. Beyond idle gossip, there is nothing in Hervey's or the princess's behavior that supports the theory of a romance between them. Nor, given the value still then attached to the virginity of unmarried princesses, does it seem likely that an ambitious person like Hervey would have risked so much for Princess Caroline. His surviving papers indicate a detached fondness for her rather than any obvious romantic or sexual interest. See Halsband, *Lord Hervey*, p. 149, and Moore, *Amphibious Thing*, p. 180.

30. Moore, *Amphibious Thing*, pp. 140–42.

31. Stephen Taylor and Hannah Smith, "Hephaestion and Alexander: Lord Hervey, Frederick, Prince of Wales, and the Royal Favourite in England in the 1730s," *English Historical Review* 124, no. 507 (April 2009): p. 99.

32. John Van der Kiste, *King George II and Queen Caroline* (Stroud, UK: History Press, 2013), p. 115.

33. Stephen and his wife, Elizabeth, had their first child, Susannah—who was conceived two or three months after they began cohabiting—eight years after their wedding. George II later made the couple aristocrats as Earl and Countess of Ilchester, and Stephen hyphenated his surname to Fox-Strangways to preserve both his surname and his wife's.

34. Moore, *Amphibious Thing*, pp. 242–43, 248–49.

35. Lord Hervey to Stephen Fox, June 25, 1737, in Ilchester, *Lord Hervey and His Friends*, p. 266.

36. Lord Hervey to Henry Fox, June 13, 1737, in ibid., pp. 264–66.

37. Despite being a Whig, Lord Bristol loathed the Prime Minister for his character; see Halsband, *Lord Hervey*, p. 148.

38. In the event, this did not happen, as Hervey predeceased his father by eight years. The earldom passed to Hervey's eldest son, George (1721–55). For the Hervey title, see Moore, *Amphibious Thing*, pp. 166–67, and Halsband, *Lord Hervey*, pp. 147–8.

39. Hervey, *Reign of George II*, 3:p. 475.

40. Lord Hervey to Charlotte Clayton, January 31, 1733, in Ilchester, *Lord Hervey and His Friends*, p. 169.

41. Dennison, *First Iron Lady*, p. 326.

42. Hervey records Queen Caroline's words as "*une bonne grimace pour le publique.*"

43. Lord Hervey to Henry Fox, August 5, 1737, in Ilchester, *Lord Hervey and His Friends*, p. 267.

44. Halsband, *Lord Hervey*, p. 222.

45. Lord Hervey to Stephen Fox, October 15, 1737, in Ilchester, *Lord Hervey and His Friends*, pp. 274–75.

46. Ibid., p. 275n.

47. Lord Hervey to Count Francesco Algarotti, January 26, 1738, in ibid. pp. 274–75.

48. Halsband, *Lord Hervey*, p. 229.

CHAPTER 22: GRACE AND FAVOR

1. J. H. Jesse, *Memoirs of the Life and Reign of King George the Third* (London: Tinsley Brothers, 1867), 3:pp. 10–11.

2. Andrew Roberts, *George III: The Life and Reign of Britain's Most Misunderstood Monarch* (London: Allen Lane, 2021), p. 18.

3. A. Aspinall, ed., *The Later Correspondence of George III* (Cambridge: Cambridge University Press, 1968), 4:2972, 2992.

4. J. C. Long, *George III* (London: Macdonald, 1960), pp. 295–96; John L. Bullion, "George III on Empire, 1783," *William and Mary Quarterly* 51, no. 2 (April 1994): pp. 305–10; E. A. Smith, *George IV* (New Haven, CT: Yale University Press, 1999), pp. 82–84; John Bew, *Castlereagh: Enlightenment, War and Tyranny* (London: Quercus, 2011), pp. 172–74, 187; Richard Bourke, *Empire and Revolution: The Political Life of Edmund Burke* (Princeton, NJ: Princeton University Press, 2015), pp. 403, 420–21, 477; Roberts, *George III*, pp. 499, 581.

5. John Hardman, *The Life of Louis XVI* (New Haven, CT: Yale University Press, 2016), p. 168.

6. Aspinall, *Later Correspondence of George III*, 3:892; Philip Mansel, *Louis XVIII* (London: Blond & Briggs, 1981), p. 140.

7. A second set of conservation projects on the same staircase was authorized by his son William IV in 1836.

8. Aspinall, *Later Correspondence of George III*, 4:2975.

9. St. James's Palace survived but, then as now, it was not frequently open to the public.

10. Nathaniel Hawthorne, *The English Notebooks of Nathaniel Hawthorne,* ed. Randall Stewart (New York: Modern Language Association of America, 1941), p. 284.

11. Sarah E. Parker, *Grace and Favour: A Handbook of Who Lived Where in Hampton Court Palace from 1750 to 1950* (Historic Royal Palaces: Hampton Court Palace, 2005), p. 42.

12. The conversion to electricity at Hampton Court took place between 1904 and 1907. I am grateful to Sarah Slater for her discussions with me about the palace in Faraday's era and immediately after.

13. Frank A. J. L. James, "Faraday, Michael," in *ODNB*, 19:pp. 28–30.

14. Testimony of Mr. Mather, courtesy of the Northern Mine Research Society.

15. Ibid.

16. Moore, *Amphibious Thing*, p. 39n.

17. "Discovery of human skeletons," *Times* (UK), November 4, 1871.

18. Correspondence between the author and Sarah Slater, February 21, 2023. The story of the murdered Cavalier spies was reported in the *Times* after historical enthusiasts mistook the source—a novel called *Captain Dangerous*—for a work of fact; see letters to the editor, the *Times*, November 7 and 9, 1871. The novel's author, G. A. Sala, wrote to the paper to offer a correction a few days later; see letter to the editor, the *Times*, November 10, 1871. The *Times* ran its own correction on November 13, 1871. See also Andrea Zuvich, "Hampton Court's Cavalier Ghosts," *The Seventeenth Century Lady* (blog), February 20, 2013.

19. Frank A. J. L. James, *Michael Faraday* (Oxford: Oxford University Press, 2010), p. 100.

20. Ibid.

21. Ian H. Hutchinson, "The Genius and Faith of Faraday and Maxwell," *New Atlantis* (Winter 2014), p. 89.

22. Sarah E. Parker, *Grace and Favour*, p. 143.

23. Thurley, *Hampton Court*, p. 18 and fig. 16.

24. Ibid., p. 328.

PART IV: THE HOUSE OF WINDSOR

CHAPTER 23: THE FALLEN OAK

1. The Meteorological Office of the United Kingdom, Archives for the Daily Weather Report, 1911–20, and the 1901 Census for the United Kingdom, "Abnett, Thomas Robert." Sidney's obituary in April 1917 described Ellen incorrectly as a widow. His date of death is given on his gravestone as February 26, 1921.

2. Arthur Bigge, 1st Baron Stamfordham, to Randall Davidson, Archbishop of Canterbury, October 7, 1920.

3. Heather Jones, *For King and Country: The British Monarchy and the First World War* (Cambridge: Cambridge University Press, 2021), pp. 372–73.

4. Maud Cazalet to Arthur Bigge, 1st Baron Stamfordham, June 16, 1920; for Edward Cazalet's death, see Peter Martin, "A Very Brief Life," *Guards Magazine: Journal of the Household Division* online, accessed November 12, 2021.

5. Commonwealth War Graves Commission Archive NADD 6/1/16, 1/11/1920-22/10/2009.

6. Mark Scott, *Among the Kings: The Unknown Warrior, an Untold Story* (Newtownards, UK: Colourpoint House, 2020), p. 133.

7. *Daily Telegraph* (UK), November 11, 1939.

8. Vera Brodie, *Tea and Talk* (unpublished memoirs), the National Army Museum Collection.

9. WO 339/54634.

10. Scott, *Among the Kings*, pp. 137–39.

11. WO32/3000.

12. Scott, *Among the Kings*, pp. 138–39.

13. *Scotsman* (Edinburgh), November 12, 1920.

14. Ibid.

15. Jones, *For King and Country*, p. 344.

16. *Scotsman* (Edinburgh), November 12, 1920.

17. Jones, *For King and Country*, p. 381.

18. LC/LCO/Special/Unknown Warrior, 1920: Application for Seats, in a letter from Rose Else to King George V, n. d. 1920. The original author's spelling is preserved here.

19. It has been stated that the tradition started with Elizabeth's future sister-in-law, Princess Mary, at her wedding the previous year to Henry Lascelles, Viscount Lascelles, and that Elizabeth's was simply the more famous gesture. Princess Mary,

however, did not send her bouquet to the Tomb of the Unknown Warrior, rather her carriage stopped en route back from the ceremony to allow her to give her bouquet to a soldier who laid it at the cenotaph, while Lord Lascelles saluted.

20. William Shawcross, *Queen Elizabeth The Queen Mother* (London: Macmillan, 2009), p. 177.

21. Juliet Nicolson, *The Great Silence, 1918–20: Living in the Shadow of the Great War* (London: John Murray, 2010), p. 342; *Sheffield (UK) Daily Telegraph*, March 4, 1922.

CHAPTER 24: WILDERNESS HOUSE

1. Shephard, *The Surprising Life*, p. 201.

2. FO 371/102179, Anthony Eden to Winston Churchill, July 14, 1952.

3. Sarah E. Parker, *Grace and Favour*, p. 26.

4. Hugo Vickers, *Elizabeth the Queen Mother* (London: Arrow Books, 2006), p. 123.

5. Gyles Brandreth, *Philip and Elizabeth: Portrait of a Marriage* (London: Random House, 2004), 300; Philip Ziegler, *Mountbatten* (London: Orion, 2001), pp. 313–14.

6. That Mountbatten supported a united Ireland was confirmed by the declassification of the relevant papers in the Irish National Archives in 2008. See Henry McDonald, "Royal blown up by IRA backed united Ireland," *Guardian* online (US edition), last modified December 29, 2007, and Harry Keaney, "Mountbatten Wished for a United Ireland," *Irish Independent* online, last modified January 3, 2008.

7. *The Argus*, June 1, 1953.

8. Unless stated otherwise, the following account of James Pope-Hennessy's interview with the Grand Duchess Xenia Alexandrovna of Russia is based upon Pope-Hennessy's notes and diary entry for May 14, 1957; see James Pope-Hennessy, *The Quest for Queen Mary*, ed. Hugo Vickers (London: Zuleika, 2018), pp. 170–79.

9. This physical description of Pope-Hennessy is based upon the photograph taken of him by Cecil Beaton, which is currently kept in the Cecil Beaton Studio Archive at the venerable auction house Sotheby's.

10. James Lees-Milne, "Hennessy, [Richard] James Arthur Pope-," *ODNB* 26 (2004), p. 378.

11. Unlike her daughter-in-law, Queen Mary was referred to as Queen Mother only infrequently in widowhood, although her granddaughter's governess, Marion Crawford, did call her that in her biography of her, *The Queen Mother* (London: George Newnes, 1951).

12. *The Times* (UK), July 8, 1955. The initial invitation came through a letter from Sir Owen Morshead to James Pope-Hennessy, June 13, 1955.

13. Sir John Pope-Hennessy, *Learning to Look* (London: Heinemann, 1991), p. 83.

14. Pope-Hennessy, *Quest for Queen Mary*, p. 83.

15. James Pope-Hennessy's interview notes for Pauline, Furstin zu Wied and Princess von Württemberg, July 21, 1956.

16. John Klier and Helen Mingay, *The Quest for Anastasia: Solving the Mystery of the Lost Romanovs* (London: Birch Lane, 1997), p. 95.

17. *Anastasia* (20th Century-Fox, 1956), directed by Anatole Litvak and adapted by Arthur Laurents from the play by Marcelle Maurette, starring Ingrid Bergman (Anna

Anderson/the Grand Duchess Anastasia), Helen Hayes (the Dowager Empress Marie), Yul Brynner (General Bounine), and Martita Hunt (Baroness von Lievenbaum).

18. Her Royal Highness Princess Mary the Princess Royal to James Pope-Hennessy, April 22, 1957, Getty Collection.

19. Pope-Hennessy, *Learning to Look*, p. 83.

20. Ibid.

21. Ibid., pp. 81–82.

22. Coryne Hall, *Little Mother of Russia: A Biography of the Empress Marie Feodorovna* (London: Shepheard-Walwyn, 1999), p. 99.

23. This was the assumption in 1957. There has since been a contested revival of the title by Grand Duchess Maria Vladimirovna, granddaughter of Xenia's cousin the Grand Duke Cyril, who claimed headship of the imperial family in exile. The surviving Romanovs have been divided about the Grand Duchess Maria's revival of the title, as well as claims that it invalidates the Pauline Succession Laws of 1797, whereby Tsar Paul banned the imperial family from being headed by a woman ever again. Supporters of Maria Vladimirovna argue that the extraordinary circumstances of the revolution have required a pragmatic reevaluation of the succession edicts of tsars Paul and Alexander III.

24. Princess Elisabetta Romanoff (1886–1940), a daughter of the Duke of Sasso-Ruffo, had been recovering from cancer when Hampton Court was targeted during the Blitz. Sadly, she was too fragile to weather the shock of the air raid. The house at Balmoral loaned to Xenia by George VI during the Second World War was Craigowan. See John van der Kiste and Coryne Hall, *Once a Grand Duchess: Xenia, Sister of Nicholas II* (Stroud, UK: Sutton, 2004), pp. 215–16.

25. Jane Ridley, *George V*, pp. 369–70.

26. Van der Kiste and Hall, *Once a Grand Duchess*, p. 202.

27. My thanks to author Coryne Hall for sharing with me this anecdote, which she herself was told by Queen Elizabeth the Queen Mother during their audience in December 2001.

28. Other Romanovs suspected for years that the reason the KGB never captured Xenia was because she was being protected by her British relatives on royal estates. See HH Princess Olga Romanoff with Coryne Hall, *A Wild and Barefoot Romanov* (London: Shepheard-Walwyn, 2017), pp. 28–29.

29. He was correct. In 1922 a con artist had tricked Xenia out of the pearls she had taken with her from Russia; see Van der Kiste and Hall, *Once a Grand Duchess*, pp. 164–66.

30. Pope-Hennessy, *Queen Mary*, p. 506.

31. For a full discussion of the negotiations of the Romanov rescue, see Coryne Hall, *To Free the Romanovs: Royal Kinship and Betrayal in Europe, 1917–1919* (Stroud, UK: Amberley, 2018), and Helen Rappaport, *The Race to Save the Romanovs: The Truth Behind the Secret Plans to Rescue the Russian Imperial Family* (London: St. Martin's Press, 2018).

32. Pavel Bykov, *The Last Days of Tsardom,* trans. Arthur Rostein (London: M. Lawrence, 1934), p. 33; Princess Olga with Hall, *Princess Olga*, pp. 7–8.

33. Hall, *To Free the Romanovs*, p. 62.

34. Gordon Brook-Shepherd, *The Last Empress: The Life and Times of Zita of Austria-Hungary, 1892–1989* (London: HarperCollins, 1991), p. 137.

35. Prince Alexander's elder brother; both were sons of Prince Nikita Alexandrovich (1900–74) and his wife, Countess Maria Vorontsova-Dashkova (1903–97).

36. Van der Kiste and Hall, *Once a Grand Duchess*, p. 238.

37. Also known by the English variant of his name, Andrew; see Princess Olga and Hall, *Princess Olga*, pp. 2, 62.

38. For Mother Martha's departure, see ibid., p. 41.

39. Tom Tullett and John Penrose, "Top Author Murdered," *Daily Mirror* (UK), January 26, 1974, 1; Lees-Milne, "Hennessy, [Richard] James Arthur Pope-," p. 379; Pope-Hennessy, *Learning to Look*, pp. 228–29.

40. In 1970 his widow, Lady Lily Offley Harvey, left Wilderness House, as she hoped to live somewhere smaller. She was granted one of the grace-and-favor apartments near the palace tennis courts, which she kept until her death in 1975.

CHAPTER 25: A HISTORIC ROYAL PALACE

1. My thanks to Antonia Sebag-Montefiore, of Montague Ede tailoring, for gamely answering my very dim questions about the proper clothing terminology.

2. This chapter's account of the future Princess of Wales's visit to Hampton Court in May 2016 is based on the recollections of Dr. Tracy Borman—who attended the ceremony—related through her correspondence with this author, May 11, 2021, for which I am profoundly grateful; Court Circular, May 4, 2016; "The Duchess of Cambridge Open[s] the Magic Garden at Hampton Court Palace," British Royal Family (Royal.UK), last modified May 4, 2016; "Kate Reveals Royal Hamster News on Garden Visit," BBC News online, last modified May 4, 2016; Bethan Holt, "A thrifty £6.16 per wear: The Duchess of Cambridge recycling her trusty LK Bennett heels is paying off," *Daily Telegraph* (UK), May 5, 2016; "Kate in Kors & Ilincic Repeats for Engagements, Tells Child, 'You Can Call Me Kate,'" *What Kate Wore* (blog), last modified October 31, 2016; Ellie Cambridge, "Duchess of Cambridge Opens Magic Garden at Hampton Court Palace," *Surrey (UK) Comet* online, last modified May 4, 2016; and Gordon Rayner, "The Duchess of Cambridge welcomes pitter patter of (very) tiny feet," *Daily Telegraph* (UK), May 5, 2016.

3. Stephen Brook, "Kate Middleton wins apology and damages from Rex Features," *Guardian* (US edition) online, last modified March 11, 2010; Lisa O'Carroll, "Prince William's messages for Kate Middleton were hacked, court told," *Guardian* (US edition) online, last modified December 19, 2013.

4. Anna Kretschmer, "Royal fury: How Donald Trump sparked outrage with 'creepy' Kate jibe," *Daily Express* (UK) online, last modified November 1, 2019.

5. Donald J. Trump, tweet, September 19, 2012.

6. Marie-Claire Dorking, "Work-Shy or Working Mum? Duchess of Cambridge Shrugs Off 'Lazy' Label," Yahoo Life, last modified March 21, 2016.

7. Jesse, *Life and Reign of King George the Third*, pp. 101–2.

8. Harrier Sherwood, "Hampton Court's Chapel Royal Stages First Catholic Service for 450 Years," *Guardian* (US edition) online, last modified February 9, 2016.

BIBLIOGRAPHY

Abbott, W. C., and C. D. Crane, eds. *The Writings and Speeches of Oliver Cromwell*. Oxford: Clarendon Press, 1987.

Ackroyd, Peter. *Shakespeare: The Biography*. London: Chatto & Windus, 2005.

Acts and Proceedings of the General Assemblies of the Kirk of Scotland, 1560–1618. Edinburgh: s. n., 1839.

Akrigg, G. P. V., ed. *Letters of King James VI & I*. Berkeley: University of California Press, 1984.

Alba, Jacobo Fitz-James Stuart y Falcó, 17th Duke of, ed. *Documentos inéditos para la historia de España: Correspondencia oficial de don Diego Sarmiento de Acuña, conde de Gondomar*. Madrid: s. n., 1944.

Alford, Stephen. *Kingship and Politics in the Reign of Edward VI*. Cambridge: Cambridge University Press, 2002.

Allmand, Christopher. *Henry V*. London: Methuen, 1992.

Alvarez, Manuel Fernández. *Charles V: Elected Emperor and Hereditary Ruler*. Translated by J. A. Lalaguna. London: Thames & Hudson, 1975.

Amin, Nathen. "Tenby—The Most Important Tudor Town?" *Tudor Places*, Summer 2022.

Armstrong, Robert. *Protestant War: The "British" of Ireland and the Wars of the Three Kingdoms*. Manchester, UK: Manchester University Press, 2005.

Aronson, Theo. *Royal Family: Years of Transition*. London: John Murray, 1983.

Arthurson, Ian. "Nanfan, Sir Richard." *Oxford Dictionary of National Biography*. Vol. 40 (2004).

Ascoli, Georges, ed. *La Grande-Bretagne devant l'opinion française au XVIIe Siècle*. Geneva: Slatkine, 1971.

Ashton, John, intro. *A Ballade of the Scottyshe Kynge, Written by John Skelton, Poet Laureate to King Henry the Eighth*. London: Elliot Stock, 1882.

Aspinall, A., ed. *The Later Correspondence of George III*. Cambridge: Cambridge University Press, 1968.

Atkinson, Ernest G., et al., eds. *Calendar of the State Papers Relating to Ireland, of the Reigns of Henry VIII, Edward VI, Mary, and Elizabeth*. London: Her Majesty's Stationery Office, 1860–1912.

Aungier, George James. *The History and Antiquities of Syon Monastery, the Parish of Isleworth and the Chapel of Hounslow*. London: J. B. Nichols and Sons, 1840.

Bain, Joseph, ed. *Calendar of State Papers Relating to Scotland and Mary, Queen of Scots, 1547–1603*. Edinburgh: H. M. General, 1898.

Baker-Smith, Veronica. *Royal Discord: The Family of George II.* Twickenham, UK: Athena Press, 2008.

Baldwin, David. *Elizabeth Woodville: Mother of the Princes in the Tower.* Stroud, UK: History Press, 2012.

Bardon, Jonathan. *A History of Ulster.* Dundonald, UK: Blackstaff, 1992.

———. *The Plantation of Ulster: The British Colonisation of the North of Ireland in the Seventeenth Century.* Dublin: Gill & Macmillan, 2011.

Barnes, A. W. "Constructing the Sexual Subject of John Skelton." *English Literary History* 71, no. 1 (Spring 2004): 29–51.

Barroll, Leeds. *Anna of Denmark, Queen of England: A Cultural Biography.* Philadelphia: University of Pennsylvania Press, 2001.

Barton, John. *A History of the Bible: The Book and Its Faiths.* London: Allen Lane, 2019.

Batchelor, D. "Excavations at Hampton Court Palace." *Post-Medieval Archaeology* 11, no. 1 (1977): 36–49.

Beresford, David. "Butler, Thomas (c. 1424–1515)." In *Dictionary of Irish Biography.* Vol. 2. Cambridge: Royal Irish Academy and Cambridge University Press, 2009.

Bergenroth, G., et al., eds. *Calendar of Letters, Despatches, and State Papers Relating to the Negotiations Between England and Spain.* London: Longman, Green, Longman & Roberts, 1862–1954.

Bergeron, David M. *King James and Letters of Homoerotic Desire.* Iowa City: University of Iowa Press, 1999.

———. "King James and Robert Carr: Letters and Desire." *Explorations in Renaissance Culture* 22, no. 1 (1996): 1–30.

Bernard, G. W. *Anne Boleyn: Fatal Attractions.* New Haven, CT: Yale University Press, 2011.

———. "Anne Boleyn's Religion." *Historical Journal* 36, no. 1 (March 1993): 1–20.

———. "The Fall of Anne Boleyn." *English Historical Review* (July 1990).

———, ed. *The Tudor Nobility.* Manchester, UK: Manchester University Press, 1992.

Bernard, G. W., and S. J. Gunn, eds. *Authority and Consent in Tudor England: Essays Presented to C. S. L. Davies.* Burlington, VT: Ashgate, 2002.

Bevan, Bryan. *Charles the Second's French Mistress: A Biography of Louise de Kéroualle, Duchess of Portsmouth.* London: R. Hale, 1972.

———. *Edward III: Monarch of Chivalry.* London: Rubicon Press, 1992.

———. *King William III: Prince of Orange, the First European.* London: Rubicon Press, 1997.

Bew, John. *Castlereagh: Enlightenment, War and Tyranny.* London: Quercus, 2011.

Bindoff, S. T., ed. *The House of Commons, 1509–1558.* London: Secker & Warburg, 1982.

Bingham, Caroline. *James V, King of Scots: 1512–1542.* London: Collins, 1971.

Birch, Thomas, ed. *A Collection of the State Papers of John Thurloe.* London: Fletcher Gyles, 1742.

Bliss, James, ed. *The Works of the Most Reverend Father in God William Laud, D. D., Sometime Archbishop of Canterbury.* Oxford: John Henry Parker, 1838.

Boase, C. W., ed. *Register of the University of Oxford,* Vol. 1, *1449–63; 1505–71.* Oxford: Clarendon Press, 1885.

Borman, Tracy. *Henry VIII and the Men Who Made Him.* London: Hodder & Stoughton, 2018.

———. *King's Mistress, Queen's Servant: The Life and Times of Henrietta Howard.* London: Vintage, 2010.

———. *Thomas Cromwell: The Untold Story of Henry VIII's Most Faithful Servant.* London: Hodder and Stoughton, 2014.

Bourke, Richard. *Empire and Revolution: The Political Life of Edmund Burke.* Princeton, NJ: Princeton University Press, 2015.

Bullion, John L. "George III on Empire, 1783." *William and Mary Quarterly* 51, no. 2 (April 1994): 305–10.

Bradford, Sarah. *Elizabeth: A Biography of Her Majesty the Queen.* Revised edition, London: Penguin, 2002.

———. *George VI: The Dutiful King.* London: HarperCollins, 1991.

Brady, Ciarán. *The Chief Governors: The Rise and Fall of Reform Government in Tudor Ireland, 1536–1558.* Cambridge: Cambridge University Press, 1994.

———. "The O'Reillys of East Breifne and the Problem of Surrender and Regrant." *Breifne* 6 (1985).

Brady, Ciáran, and Raymond Gillespie, eds. *Natives and Newcomers: Essays on the Making of Irish Colonial Society, 1534–1641.* Dublin: Irish Academic Press, 1986.

Brandreth, Gyles. *Charles and Camilla: Portrait of a Love Affair.* London: Century, 2005.

———. *Philip and Elizabeth: Portrait of a Marriage.* London: Random House, 2004.

Brewer, J. S., et al., eds. *Letters and Papers, Foreign and Domestic of the Reign of Henry VIII.* London: Her Majesty's Stationery Office, 1862–1932.

Bridgeford, Andrew. *1066: The Hidden History of the Bayeux Tapestry.* New York: Fourth Estate, 2004.

Brodie, Vera. *Tea and Talk* (unpublished memoirs, The National Army Museum Collection).

Brook-Shepherd, Gordon. *The Last Empress: The Life and Times of Zita of Austria-Hungary, 1892–1989.* London: HarperCollins, 1991.

Brown, R. Allen. *The Normans.* Woodbridge, UK: Boydell Press, 1984.

Buchanan, George, ed. *The History of Scotland.* Translated by James Aiken. Glasgow: Blackie, Fullerton, 1827.

Buchanan, Patricia Hill. *Margaret Tudor, Queen of Scots.* Edinburgh: Scottish Academic Press, 1985.

Burford, Ephraim J. *Bawds and Lodgings: A History of the London Bankside Brothels, c. 100–1675.* London: Peter Owen, 1976.

Burgess, Colin, with Paul Carter. *Behind Palace Doors: My Service as the Queen Mother's Equerry.* London: John Blake, 2006.

Burgess, Glenn, Rowland Wymer, and Jason Lawrence, eds. *The Accession of James I: Historical and Cultural Consequences.* New York: Palgrave Macmillan, 2006.

Burghclere, Winifred Gardner, Lady. *The Life of James, First Duke of Ormonde.* London: John Murray, 1912.

Burgio, Lucia, et al. "The Hampton Court Terracotta Roundels Project." *Conservation Journal of the Victoria and Albert Museum* 57 (Spring 2009).

Burnet, Gilbert. *The History of the Reformation of the Church of England.* Oxford: Oxford University Press, 1829.

Bush, M. L. "The Lisle-Seymour Disputes: A Study of Power and Influence in the 1530s." *Historical Journal* (1966).

Bykov, Pavel. *The Last Days of Tsardom*. Translated by Arthur Rostein. London: M. Lawrence, 1934.

Byrne, Conor. *Katherine Howard: A New History*. Lúcar, Sp: MadeGlobal, 2014.

Calderwood, David. *The History of the Church of Scotland*. Edinburgh: Wicklow Society, 1844.

Calendar of State Papers Relating to English Affairs in the Archives of Venice. London: Her Majesty's Stationery Office, 1864.

Cameron, T. W. "The Early Life of Thomas Wolsey." *English Historical Review* 3 (July 1888): 458–61.

Canny, Nicholas. *From Reformation to Restoration: Ireland, 1534–1660*. Dublin: Helicon, 1987.

———. *Making Ireland British, 1580–1650*. Oxford: Oxford University Press, 2001.

Cardwell, Edward, ed. *Documentary Annals of the Reformed Church of England*. Oxford: Oxford University Press, 1844.

Carleton Williams, Ethel. *Anne of Denmark*. London: Longman, 1970.

Carrington, Samuel. *The History of the Life and Death of His Most Serene Highness, Oliver, Late Lord Protector*. London: Nath. Brook at the Sign of the Angel, 1659.

Carson, Annette. *Richard III: The Maligned King*. Stroud, UK: History Press, 2012.

Cavendish, George. *The Life of Cardinal Wolsey, by George Cavendish, His Gentleman Usher, and Metrical Visions*. Edited by Samuel Weller Singer. Chiswick, UK: Harding, Triphook, and Lepard, 1825.

Chaplais, Pierre. *Piers Gaveston: Edward II's Adoptive Brother*. Oxford: Oxford University Press, 1994.

Cheetham, Anthony. *The Wars of the Roses*. London: Cassell, 2000.

Chibnall, Marjorie. *The Debate on the Norman Conquest*. Manchester, UK: Manchester University Press, 1999.

Childs, Jessie. *Henry VIII's Last Victim: The Life and Times of Henry Howard, Earl of Surrey*. London: Vintage, 2008.

Chrimes, S. B. *Henry VII*. London: Eyre Methuen, 1972.

Clarendon, Edward Hyde, 1st Earl of. *The History of the Rebellion and the Civil Wars in England*. Sacramento, CA: Franklin Classics, 2018.

Clark, Nicola. *Gender, Family, and Politics: The Howard Women, 1485–1558*. Oxford: Oxford University Press, 2018.

A Collection of Ordinances and Regulations for the Government of the Royal Household, Made in Divers Reigns: From King Edward III to King William and Queen Mary, Also Receipts in Ancient Cooking. London: Society of Antiquaries, 1790.

Connolly, S. J. *Contested Island: Ireland, 1460–1630*. Oxford: Oxford University Press, 2007.

Considine, John. "Overbury, Thomas." In *Oxford Dictionary of National Biography*. Vol. 64 (2004).

Conway, William. "The Sermon of Most Rev. William Conway, Bishop of Neve: At St. Patrick's Purgatory, Lough Derg, 20 August 1961." *Seanchas Ardmhacha: Journal of the Armagh Diocesan Historical Society* 4, no. 2 (1961–62).

Cooper, David. "On the Twelfth of July in the Morning . . . (Or the Man Who Mistook His Sash for a Hat)." *Folk Music Journal* 8, no. 1 (2001).

Cooper, Nicholas. "Sutton Place Re-Examined." *Antiquaries Journal* 94 (September 2014): pp. 173–210.

Coulton, Barbara. "Cromwell and the Readmission of the Jews to England, 1656." Cromwell Association online. Accessed June 19, 2021.

Cowan, Ross. "Flodden: Scotland's Greatest Defeat." *Military History Monthly,* October 2013.

Crawford, Anne, ed. *Letters of the Queens of England, 1100–1547.* Stroud, UK: Sutton, 1997.

Crawford, James Ludovic Lindsay, 26th Earl of, and Robert Steele, eds. *Tudor and Stuart Proclamations, 1485–1714.* Vol. 1: *England and Wales.* Oxford: Clarendon Press, 1910.

Crawford, Jon G. *Anglicizing the Government of Ireland: The Irish Privy Council and the Expansion of Tudor Rule, 1556–1578.* Blackrock, Ire.: Irish Academic Press, 1993.

Crawford, Marion. *The Queen Mother.* London: George Newnes, 1951.

Crown, Jessica. "A 'Rare and Marvellous' Guest: Elizabeth I Samples Life in Cambridge 450 Years Ago." University of Cambridge Department of History online. Last modified September 5, 2014.

Cuddy, Neil. "The Anglo-Scottish Union and the Court of James I, 1603–1625." *Transactions of the Royal Historical Society* (March 1991): 107–24.

Cunningham, Sean. "Guildford, Sir Richard." In *Oxford Dictionary of National Biography.* Vol. 24 (2004).

Curl, James Stevens. *The Londonderry Plantation, 1609–1914.* Chichester, UK: Phillimore, 1986.

Curnow, Peter. "The East Window of the Chapel at Hampton Court Palace." *Architectural History* 27 (1984): 1–14.

Dekker, Thomas. *The Wonderfull Yeare, 1603.* Edited by G. B. Harrison. London: Bodley Head, 1924.

DeMolen, Richard L. "The Birth of Edward VI and the Death of Queen Jane: The Arguments for and Against Caesarean Section." *Renaissance Studies* (December 1990): 388–91.

Denholm-Young, Noël, ed. *Vita Edwardi Secundi Monachi Cuiusdam Malmesberiensis.* London: Thomas Nelson & Sons, 1957.

Dennison, Matthew. *The First Iron Lady: A Life of Caroline of Ansbach.* London: William Collins, 2018.

Denny, Joanna. *Katherine Howard: A Tudor Conspiracy.* London: Portrait, 2005.

Dimmock, Matthew, Andrew Hadfield, and Margaret Healy, eds. *The Intellectual Culture of the English Country House, 1500–1700.* Manchester, UK: Manchester University Press, 2015.

Dodd, A. H. *The Elizabethans.* Scarborough, UK: Book Club Associates, 1973.

Dodd, G., and A. Musson, eds. *The Reign of Edward II: New Perspectives.* London: Boydell and Brewer, 2006.

Doran, Susan, and Thomas S. Freeman, eds. *Mary Tudor: Old and New Perspectives.* London: Palgrave Macmillan, 2011.

Douglas, David C. *William the Conqueror: The Norman Impact upon England.* New Haven, CT: Yale University Press, 1999.

Duffy, Eamon. *Fires of Faith: Catholic England Under Mary.* New Haven, CT: Yale University Press, 2010.

———. *Saints, Sacrilege and Sedition: Religion and Conflict in the Tudor Reformations.* London: Bloomsbury, 2012.

———. *The Stripping of the Altars: Traditional Religion in England, c. 1400–c. 1580.* 2nd ed. New Haven, CT: Yale University Press, 2005.

Duffy, Eamon, and David Loades, eds. *The Church of Mary Tudor.* Burlington, VT: Ashgate, 2006.

Dugdale, William. *The Baronage of England, or An Historical Account of the Lives and Most Memorable Actions of Our English Nobility in the Saxons' Time, to the Norman Conquest; and from Thence, of Those Who Had Their Rise Before the End of King Henry the Third's Reign.* London: Thomas Newcomb, 1675.

Dunn, Jane. *Elizabeth and Mary: Cousins, Rivals, Queens.* London: HarperCollins, 2003.

Dyer, Christopher. *Standards of Living in the Later Middle Ages: Social Change in England, c. 1200–1520.* Cambridge: Cambridge University Press, 1989.

Edwards, A. S. G. "Cavendish, George." In *Oxford Dictionary of National Biography.* Vol. 10 (2004).

———. *Skelton: The Critical Heritage.* London: Routledge & Kegan Paul, 1981.

Edwards, David. "Butler [Bocach], James, Ninth Earl of Ormond and Second Earl of Ossory." In *Oxford Dictionary of National Biography.* Vol. 9 (2004).

———. *The Ormond Lordship in County Kilkenny, 1515–1642: The Rise and Fall of Butler Feudal Power.* Dublin: Four Courts Press, 2003.

Edwards, H. L. R. *Skelton: The Life and Times of an Early Tudor Poet.* London: Jonathan Cape, 1949.

Ellis, Henry, ed. *Original Letters, Illustrative of English History.* London: Harding, Triphook, and Lepard, 1824.

Ellis, Peter Berresford. *Hell or Connaught!: The Cromwellian Colonisation of Ireland, 1652–1660.* London: Hamish Hamilton, 1975.

Emmerson, Owen, and Claire Ridgway. *The Boleyns of Hever Castle.* Lúcar, Sp: MadeGlobal, 2021.

Evelyn, John. *The Diary of John Evelyn.* Edited by William Bray. Washington, DC: M. Walter Dunne, 1901.

Falls, Cyril. *Elizabeth's Irish Wars.* London: Methuen, 1950.

Feehan, John. *The Landscape of Slieve Bloom: A Study of Its Natural and Human Heritage.* Dublin: Blackwater Press, 1979.

Fenlon, Jane. "The Decorative Plasterwork at Ormond Castle: A Unique Survival." *Architectural History* 44 (1998): 67–69.

Ferguson, Charles. *Naked to Mine Enemies: The Life of Cardinal Wolsey.* London: Longmans, Green, 1958.

Ferrero, Hermann, ed. *Lettres de Henriette-Marie de France, Reine d'Angleterre, et sa Soeur Christine, Duchesse de Savoie.* London: Wentworth Press, 2018.

Finney, Arthur F. *John Skelton: Priest as Poet.* Chapel Hill: University of North Carolina Press, 1987.

Fish, Stanley Eugene. *John Skelton's Poetry.* New Haven, CT: Yale University Press, 1965.

FitzGerald, Brian. *The Geraldines: An Experiment in Irish Government, 1169–1601.* New York: Staples Press, 1951.

Fitzgerald, Teri, and Claire Ridgway. "Henry Norris and William Brereton: The Knighthood Confusion." The Anne Boleyn Files, online (February 1, 2013).

Fitzpatrick, David. *Descendancy: Irish Protestant Histories Since 1795.* Cambridge: Cambridge University Press, 2014.

Foot, Sarah. *Athelstan: The First King of England.* New Haven, CT: Yale University Press, 2011.

Forge, J. W. Lindus. *Oatlands Palace*. Walton-on-Thames, UK: Walton and Weybridge Local History Society, 1982.

Foster, Joseph, ed. *Alumni Oxonienses: The Members of the University of Oxford, 1500–1714: Their Parentage, Birthplace, and Year of Birth, with a Record of Their Degrees*. Vol. 4. Oxford: James Parker, 1891.

Fowler, G. Herbert. "De St Walery." *Genealogist* 30 (1914): 1–17.

Fox, George. *The Journal of George Fox*. Edited by John L. Nickalls. London: Religious Society of Friends, 1975.

Fraser, Antonia. *Cromwell: Our Chief of Men*. London: Weidenfeld & Nicolson, 2008.

———. *King James*. London: Weidenfeld & Nicolson, 1974.

———, ed. *The Lives of the Kings and Queens of England*. London: Book Club Associates, 1975.

———. *Mary Queen of Scots*. London: Weidenfeld & Nicolson, 1976.

Fraser, Sarah. *The Prince Who Would Be King: The Life and Death of Henry Stuart*. London: William Collins, 2017.

Furnivall, Frederick J. *Ballads from Manuscripts*. London: Taylor, 1868.

Fyre, Susan. *Elizabeth I: The Competition of Representation*. New York: Oxford University Press, 1993.

Gambero, Luigi. "Patristic Intuitions of Mary's Role as Mediatrix and Advocate: The Invocation of the Faithful for Her Help." *Marian Studies* 52 (2001): 78–101.

Gébler, Carlo. *The Siege of Derry: A History*. London: Time Warner Books, 2005.

Gilbert, John T., and Edward Sullivan, eds. *National Manuscripts of Ireland*. London: Her Majesty's Stationery Office, 1879.

Giuseppi, M. S., A. C. Wood, and A. E. Stamp, eds. *Calendar of the Patent Rolls Preserved in the Public Record Office: Philip and Mary*. Vol. 2, *A. D. 1554–1555*. London: His Majesty's Stationery Office, 1936.

Giustiniani, Sebastian. *Four Years at the Court of Henry VIII*. Translated by R. L. Brown. Cambridge: Cambridge University Press, 2014.

Given-Wilson, Christopher. *Edward II: The Terrors of Kingship*. London: Allen Lane, 2016.

Goldman, Marcus Selden. "Sir Philip Sidney and Arcadia." PhD thesis, University of Illinois, 1931.

Goodall, John. "The Last Royal Hall." *Country Life,* October 7, 2020.

———. "Playing at Chequers: Chequers Court, Buckinghamshire." *Country Life,* May 6, 2020.

Goodman, Ruth. *How to Be a Tudor: A Dawn-to-Dusk Guide to Everyday Life*. London: Viking, 2015.

Graves, James. "The Ancient Tribes and Territories of Ossory. No. 1." *Transactions of the Kilkenny Archaeological Society* 1, no. 2 (1850): 230–47.

Gray, Annie. *At Christmas We Feast: Festive Food Through the Ages*. London: Profile, 2021.

Gregg, Pauline. *King Charles I*. Toronto: J. M. Dent, 1981.

Grose, Francis, and Thomas Astle, eds. *The Antiquarian Repository*. London: Edward Jeffery, 1807.

Grueninger, Natalie. *The Final Year of Anne Boleyn*. Stroud, UK: Pen & Sword, 2022.

Gunn, S. J. *Early Tudor Government, 1485–1558*. London: Macmillan, 1995.

————. "Daubeney, Giles, First Baron Daubeney." In *Oxford Dictionary of National Biography*. Vol. 15 (2004).

————. "King, Oliver." In *Oxford Dictionary of National Biography*. Vol. 31 (2004).

Gunn, S. J., and P. G. Lindley, eds. *Cardinal Wolsey: Church, State and Art*. Cambridge: Cambridge University Press, 1991.

Guy, John, ed. *The Reign of Elizabeth I: Court and Culture in the Last Decade*. Cambridge: Cambridge University Press, 1995.

Gwyn, Peter. *The King's Cardinal: The Rise and Fall of Thomas Wolsey*. London: Pimlico, 2002.

Hall, Coryne. *Little Mother of Russia: A Biography of the Empress Marie Feodorovna*. London: Shepheard-Walwyn, 1999.

————. *To Free the Romanovs: Royal Kinship and Betrayal in Europe, 1917–1919*. Stroud, UK: Amberley, 2018.

Hall, Edward. *Hall's Chronicle: Containing the History of England During the Reign of Henry IV and the Succeeding Monarchs to the End of the Reign of Henry VIII*. Edited by Henry Ellis. London: J. Johnson et al., 1809.

Halliday, F. E. "Queen Elizabeth I and Dr. Burcot." *History Today,* August 1955, 542–44.

Halliwell-Philips, James O., ed. *Letters of the Kings of England*. Vol. 2. London: H. Colborn, 1848.

Halsband, Robert. *Lord Hervey: Eighteenth-Century Courtier*. Oxford: Clarendon Press, 1973.

Hamilton, J. S. *Piers Gaveston, Earl of Cornwall, 1307–1312: Politics and Patronage in the Reign of Edward II*. Detroit: Wayne State University Press, 1988.

Hardman, John. *The Life of Louis XVI*. New Haven, CT: Yale University Press, 2016.

Hardwicke, Philip York, 2nd Earl of, ed. *Miscellaneous State Papers from 1501 to 1726*. London: Stratham and Caddell, 1778.

Harington, Sir John. *Nugae Antiquae: Being a Miscellaneous Collection of Original Papers in Prose and Verse: Written in the Reigns of Henry VIII, Queen Mary, Elizabeth, King James, &c*. Edited by Rev. Harry Harington. Bath, UK: T. Shrimpeton, 1779.

Harper-Bill, Christopher. "Morton, John." In *Oxford Dictionary of National Biography*. Vol. 39 (2004).

Harris, Barbara J. *Edward Stafford, Third Duke of Buckingham*. Stanford, CA: Stanford University Press, 1986.

Harris, G. B., ed. *The Letters of Queen Elizabeth*. London: Cassell, 1935.

Harris, John, Geoffrey de Bellaigue, and Oliver Millar. *Buckingham Palace*. London: Thomas Nelson & Sons, 1968.

Hart, David M., and Ross Kenyon, eds. *Tracts on Liberty by the Levellers and Their Critics*. Indianapolis: Liberty Fund, 2014.

Haswell, Jock. *James II: Soldier and Sailor*. London: Hamish Hamilton, 1972.

Hatton, Ragnhild. *George I: Elector and King*. London: Thames and Hudson, 1978.

Hawkins, Duncan. "Anglo-Saxon Kingston: A Shifting Pattern of Settlement." *London Archaeologist* 8, no. 10 (Autumn 1998): 271–78.

Hawthorne, Nathaniel. *The English Notebooks of Nathaniel Hawthorne*. Edited by Randall Stewart. New York: Modern Language Association of America, 1941.

Head, David M. "'Beyng Ledde and Seduced by the Devyll': The Attainder of Lord

Thomas Howard and the Tudor Law of Treason." *Sixteenth Century Journal* 14, no. 4 (Winter 1982): 3–16.

———. *The Ebbs and Flows of Fortune: The Life of Thomas Howard, Third Duke of Norfolk.* Athens: University of Georgia Press, 2009.

Heal, Felicity. "The Archbishops of Canterbury and the Practice of Hospitality." *Journal of Ecclesiastical History* 33, no. 4 (October 1982): 544–63.

———. *Hospitality in Early Modern England.* Oxford: Clarendon, 1990.

Hennell, Colonel Sir Reginald. *The History of the King's Body Guard of the Yeomen of the Guard.* Westminster, UK: Archibald Constantine, 1904.

Herbert of Cherbury, Edward Herbert, 1st Baron. *The Life and Raigne of Henry the Eighth.* London: M. Clark, 1683.

Hernán, Enrique García. *Ireland and Spain in the Reign of Philip II.* Translated by Liam Liddy. Dublin: Four Courts Press, 2009.

Hervey, John Hervey, 2nd Baron. *Memoirs of the Reign of George II.* Edited by John Wilson Croker. London: John Murray, 1848.

Hervey, John Hervey, 2nd Baron. *Lord Hervey's Memoirs.* Edited by Romney Sedgwick. London: B. T. Batsford, 1963.

Heyam, Kit. "It Was Necessary: Taking Joan of Arc on Their Own Terms." Shakespeare's Globe online. Last modified August 8, 2022.

Hibbert, Christopher. *The English: A Social History, 1066–1945.* London: Guild, 1987.

———. *George III: A Personal History.* London: Viking, 1998.

———. *The Marlboroughs: John and Sarah Churchill, 1650–1714.* London: Viking, 2001.

Hicks, Michael. *Richard III: The Man Behind the Myth.* London: Collins & Brown, 1991.

———. *Richard III: The Self-Made King.* New Haven, CT: Yale University Press, 2019.

Higginbotham, Susan. *Margaret Pole: The Countess in the Tower.* Stroud, UK: Amberley, 2016.

Higham, F. M. G. *King James the Second.* London: Hamish Hamilton, 1934.

Hill, Brian W. *Sir Robert Walpole: "Sole and Prime Minister."* London: Hamish Hamilton, 1989.

Hilton, Lisa. *Queens Consort: England's Medieval Queens.* London: Phoenix, 2008.

Hodgkin, Thomas. *George Fox.* London: Methuen & Co., 1896.

Holmes, Frederick, Grace Holmes, and Julia McMurrough. "The Death of the Young King Edward VI." *New England Journal of Medicine* 345, no. 1 (July 5, 2001): 60–62.

Holt, J. C. *Colonial England, 1066–1215.* London: Hambledon Press, 1997.

Horrox, Rosemary. "Elizabeth [Elizabeth of York]." In *Oxford Dictionary of National Biography.* Vol. 18 (2004).

Hoyle, R. W. *The Pilgrimage of Grace and the Politics of the 1530s.* Oxford: Oxford University Press, 2001.

Huggarde, Miles. *The Displaying of the Protestants, Sondry Their Practices.* London: Robert Caly, 1556.

Hume, Martin A. S., et al., eds. *Calendar of State Papers, Spain (Simancas).* Vol. 1, *1558–1567.* London: Her Majesty's Stationery Office, 1892.

Hunneyball, Paul. "Archbishop Laud's Secret 'Misfortunes': Decoding Sexual Identity in the Seventeenth Century." The History of Parliament (accessed online, August 3, 2021).

Hutchinson, Ian H. "The Genius and Faith of Faraday and Maxwell." *New Atlantis*, Winter 2014.

Hutchinson, Lucy. *Memoirs of the Life of Colonel Hutchinson*. Edited by N. H. Keeble. London: J. M. Dent, 1913.

Hutchinson, Robert. *The Last Days of Henry VIII: Conspiracy, Treason and Heresy at the Court of the Dying Tyrant*. London: Phoenix, 2006.

Hutton, Ronald. *The Making of Oliver Cromwell* (New Haven, CT: Yale University Press, 2021).

Ilchester, Giles Fox-Strangways, 6th Earl of, ed. *Lord Hervey and His Friends, 1726–38*. London: John Murray, 1950.

Irwin, Liam, and Gearóid Ó Tuathaigh, eds. *Limerick: History and Society—Interdisciplinary Essays on the History of an Irish County*. Dublin: Geography, 2009.

Ives, Eric W. "Anne Boleyn and the Early Reformation in England: The Contemporary Evidence." *Historical Journal* 37, no. 2 (June 1994): 389–400.

———. "Court and County Palatine in the reign of Henry VIII: The career of William Brereton of Malpas." *Transactions of the Historic Society of Lancashire and Cheshire* (1972): 1–38.

———, ed. *The Letters and Accounts of William Brereton of Malpas*. Old Woking, UK: Record Society of Lancashire and Cheshire, 1976.

———. *The Life and Death of Anne Boleyn: The Most Happy*. Oxford: Blackwell, 2004.

Jack, Sybil M. "Wolsey, Thomas." In *Oxford Dictionary of National Biography*. Vol. 60 (2004).

Jackson, Daniel. "A Russian Royal Resident: Grand Duchess Xenia Romanov and Hampton Court Palace." *Historic Royal Palaces* (blog), April 6, 2017.

James, Frank A. J. L. "Faraday, Michael." In *Oxford Dictionary of National Biography*. Vol. 19 (2004).

———. *Michael Faraday*. Oxford: Oxford University Press, 2004.

James, Susan E. *Kateryn Parr: The Making of a Queen*. Burlington, VT: Ashgate, 1999.

Jenkins, Philip. *A History of Modern Wales, 1536–1990*. New York: Longman, 1992.

Jespersen, Knud J. V. *A History of Denmark*. Translated by Ivan Hill. London: Palgrave, 2004.

Jesse, J. H. *Memoirs of the Life and Reign of King George the Third*. London: Tinsley Brothers, 1867.

Johnson, Paul. *Elizabeth I: A Study in Power and Intellect*. London: Weidenfeld & Nicolson, 1974.

Jones, Heather. *For King and Country: The British Monarchy and the First World War*. Cambridge: Cambridge University Press, 2021.

Jones, J. Gwynfor. *Wales and the Tudor State: Government, Religious Change and the Social Order, 1534–1603*. Cardiff: University of Wales Press, 1989.

Jordan, Mark D. *The Invention of Sodomy in Christian Theology*. Chicago: University of Chicago Press, 1997.

Jordan, W. K., ed. *The Chronicle and Political Papers of King Edward VI*. Ithaca, NY: Cornell University Press, 1966.

Journal of the House of Lords. Vol. 1, *1509–1577*. London: s.n., 1771.

Junor, Penny. *The Firm: The Troubled Life of the House of Windsor*. London: HarperCollins, 2005.

Kamen, Henry. *Philip of Spain*. New Haven, CT: Yale University Press, 1997.

Kann, Robert A. *A History of the Habsburg Empire, 1526–1918*. London: University of California Press, 1974.

Kaulek, Jean Baptiste Louis, ed. *Correspondance politique de mm. de Castillon et de Marillac, ambassadeurs de France en Angleterre*. Paris: Félix Alcan, 1885.

Keay, Anna. *The Last Royal Rebel: The Life and Death of James, Duke of Monmouth*. London: Bloomsbury, 2016.

Kelly, Angela. *The Other Side of the Coin: The Queen, the Dresser and the Wardrobe*. London: HarperCollins, 2019.

Kieckhefer, Richard. *European Witch Trials: Their Foundations in Popular and Learned Culture, 1300–1500*. London: Routledge & Kegan Paul, 1976.

King, Edmund. *King Stephen*. New Haven, CT: Yale University Press, 2010.

King, Greg. *The Murder of Rasputin: The Truth About Prince Felix Youssoupov and the Mad Monk Who Helped Bring Down the Romanovs*. London: Century, 1996.

Kiple, Kenneth F., ed. *The Cambridge World History of Human Disease*. Cambridge: Cambridge University Press, 2008.

Klarwill, Victor von, ed. *Queen Elizabeth and Some Foreigners: Being a Series of Hitherto Unpublished Letters from the Archives of the Hapsburg Family*. London: John Lane, 1928.

Klier, John, and Helen Mingay. *The Quest for Anastasia: Solving the Mystery of the Lost Romanovs*. London: Birch Lane, 1997.

Kussmaul, Ann. *Servants in Husbandry in Early Modern England*. Cambridge: Cambridge University Press, 1981.

Lacey, Brian. *Terrible Queer Creatures: Homosexuality in Irish History*. Dublin: Wordwell, 2008.

Lacey, Robert. *Monarch: The Life and Reign of Elizabeth II*. London: Simon & Schuster, 2003.

Lake, Peter. *Moderate Puritans and the Elizabethan Church*. Cambridge: Cambridge University Press, 1982.

Lambarde, William. *A Preambulation of Kent: Conteining the Description, Hystorie, and Customes of That Shire, Written in the Yeere 1570*. Cheetham, UK: W. Burrill, 1826.

Lane, Pádraig G., and William Nolan, eds. *Laois, History and Society: Interdisciplinary Essays on the History of an Irish County*. Dublin: Geography, 1999.

Langford, Peter. *Walpole and the Robinocracy*. Cambridge, UK: Chadwyck-Healey, 1986.

Larsen, Karen. *A History of Norway*. Princeton, NJ: Princeton University Press, 1948.

Lascelles, Alan. *King's Counsellor—Abdication and War: The Diaries of Sir Alan "Tommy" Lascelles*. Edited by Duff Hart-Davis. London: Weidenfeld & Nicolson, 2007.

Law, Ernest P. A. *A History of Hampton Court: Stuart Times*. London: George Bell & Sons, 1898.

———. *The History of Hampton Court Palace: Tudor Times*. London: George Bell, 1885.

Lay, Paul. *Providence Lost: The Rise and Fall of Cromwell's Protectorate*. London: Head of Zeus, 2020.

Laynesmith, J. L. *The Last Medieval Queens: English Queenship, 1445–1503*. Oxford: Oxford University Press, 2006.

Leask, Harold G. *Irish Castles and Castellated Houses*. Dundalk, Ire.: Dundalgan, 1964.

Lee, Jr., Maurice. *Dudley Carleton to John Chamberlain, 1603–1624.* New Brunswick, NJ: Rutgers University Press, 1972.

———, ed. *Great Britain's Solomon: James VI and I in His Three Kingdoms.* Chicago: University of Illinois Press, 1990.

Lees-Milne, James. "Hennessy, [Richard] James Arthur Pope-" In *Oxford Dictionary of National Biography.* Vol. 26 (2004).

Leighton, Cadoc D. A. *Catholicism in a Protestant Kingdom: A Study of the Irish Ancien Régime.* Dublin: Gill & Macmillan, 1994.

Leland, John. *De rebus Britannicus collectanea* (Oxford: Sheldonian Theatre, 1715).

Lemon, Robert, et al., eds. *Calendar of State Papers Domestic: Edward VI, Mary and Elizabeth, 1547–80.* London: Longman, Brown, Green, Longman & Roberts, 1856–72.

Lennon, Colm. *The Lords of Dublin in the Age of Reformation.* Dublin: Irish Academic Press, 1989.

Levine, Mortimer. *The Early Elizabethan Succession Question, 1558–1568.* Stanford, CA: Stanford University Press, 1966.

Lewis, C. S. "Equality," *Spectator,* August 27, 1943.

Lewis, Matthew. *The Survival of the Princes in the Tower: Murder, Mystery and Myth.* Stroud, UK: History Press, 2018.

Licence, Amy. *Anne Boleyn: Adultery, Heresy, Desire.* Stroud, UK: Amberley, 2017.

———. *Edward IV and Elizabeth Woodville: A True Romance.* Stroud, UK: Amberley, 2016.

———. *Elizabeth of York: Forgotten Tudor Queen.* Stroud, UK: Amberley, 2014.

Lincoln, Margarette. *London and the Seventeenth Century: The Making of the World's Greatest City.* New Haven, CT: Yale University Press, 2021.

Lisle, Leanda de. *After Elizabeth: The Death of Elizabeth and the Coming of King James.* London: Harper Perennial, 2006.

———. "Truthiness, Fake History and the Story of the Whipping Boy." *Aspects of History* online. Accessed October 14, 2020.

———. *The Sisters Who Would Be Queen: The Tragedy of Mary, Katherine and Lady Jane.* London: HarperPress, 2009.

———. *White King: Traitor, Murderer, Martyr.* London: Chatto & Windus, 2018.

Loach, Jennifer. *Edward VI.* Edited by G. W. Bernard and Penry Williams. New Haven, CT: Yale University Press, 1999.

Loades, David. *Intrigue and Treason: The Tudor Court, 1547–1558.* Edinburgh: Pearson, 2004.

———. *Mary Tudor: A Life.* Oxford: Blackwell, 1989.

———. *The Mid-Tudor Crisis, 1545–1565.* Basingstoke, UK: Palgrave, 1992.

———. *The Oxford Martyrs.* London: B. T. Batsford, 1970.

Lock, Julian. "Wynter, Thomas." In *Oxford Dictionary of National Biography.* Vol. 60 (2004).

Long, J. C. *George III.* London: Macdonald, 1960.

Luckett, Dominic. "Crown Patronage and Political Morality in Early Tudor England: The Case of Giles, Lord Daubeney." *English Historical Review* 110, no. 437 (June 1995): 578–95.

———. "Daubeney Family." In *Oxford Dictionary of National Biography.* Vol. 15 (2004).

Lumsden, Andrew. "The Fairy Tale of Edward II." *Gay and Lesbian Review Worldwide* 11, no. 2 (March/April 2004): n.p.

Lynn, Eleri. "Georgian Celebrity and Gossip." *Historic Royal Palaces* (blog), July 2, 2014.

Lyons, Mary Ann. "FitzGerald, Thomas "Silken Thomas."" In *Dictionary of Irish Biography*. Vol. 3. Cambridge: Royal Irish Academy and Cambridge University Press, 2009.

Mac Carthy, B., ed. *Annála Uladh, Annals of Ulster from the Earliest Time to the Year 1541*. Introduction by Nollaig Ó Muraíle. Blackrock, Ire.: Éamonn de Búrca, 1998.

Mac Cuarta, Brian, ed. *Ulster 1641: Aspects of the Rising*. Belfast: Institute of Irish Studies, 1993.

MacCulloch, Diarmaid. *The Boy King: Edward VI and the Protestant Reformation*. Berkeley: University of California Press, 2002.

———. *Thomas Cranmer: A Life*. New Haven, CT: Yale University Press, 1996.

———. *Tudor Church Militant: Edward VI and the Protestant Reformation*. London: Penguin, 2001.

MacCurtain, Margaret, and Mary O'Dowd, eds. *Women in Early Modern Ireland*. New York: Edinburgh University Press, 1991.

MacDougall, Norman. *James IV*. Edinburgh: John Donald, 1989.

Mack, Maynard. *Alexander Pope: A Life*. New Haven, CT: Yale University Press, 1985.

Mackay, James. *In the End Is My Beginning: A Life of Mary, Queen of Scots*. Edinburgh: Mainstream, 1999.

Mackay, Lauren. *Among the Wolves of Court: The Untold Story of Thomas and George Boleyn*. New York: I. B. Tauris, 2018.

———. *Inside the Tudor Court: Henry VIII and His Six Wives Through the Writings of the Spanish Ambassador, Eustace Chapuys*. Stroud, UK: Amberley, 2014.

Madden, Frederic, ed. *Narrative of the Visit of the Duke of Najera to England, in the Year 1543–4, Written by his Secretary, Pedro de Gante*. London: Society of Antiquaries, 1831.

Mansel, Philip. *Louis XVIII*. London: Blond & Briggs, 1981.

The Manuscripts of His Grace the Duke of Rutland G. C. B., Preserved at Belvoir Castle. London: Her Majesty's Stationery Office, 1888.

Marcus, Leah S., Janel Mueller, and Mary Beth Rose, eds. *Elizabeth I: Collected Works*. Chicago: University of Chicago Press, 2000.

Marshall, Peter. *Heretics and Believers: A History of the English Reformation*. New Haven, CT: Yale University Press, 2017.

Marshall, Rosalind K. *Mary I*. London: Her Majesty's Stationery Office, 1993.

Maxwell, Constantia, ed. *Irish History from Contemporary Sources, 1509–1610*. London: George Allen & Unwin, 1923.

McGrath, Alister E. *In the Beginning: The Story of the King James Bible and How It Changed a Nation, a Language, and a Culture*. New York: Doubleday, 2001.

McLynn, Frank. *Lionheart and Lackland: King Richard, King John and the Wars of Conquest*. London: Vintage, 2007.

McManus, Clare. *Women on the Renaissance Stage: Anna of Denmark and Female Masquing in the Stuart Court, 1590–1619*. New York: Manchester University Press, 2002.

Mears, Natalie. *Queenship and Political Discourse in the Elizabethan Realms*. Cambridge: Cambridge University Press, 2005.

Melville, James. *Memoirs of his Own Life by Sir James Melville of Halhill*. Edited by T. Thomson. Edinburgh: Bannatyne Club, 1827.

Mertes, Kate. *The English Noble Household, 1250–1600: Good Governance and Political Rule*. Oxford: Blackwell, 1998.

Money-Kyrle, R. E., ed. *Essays in Applied Psychoanalysis: A Contribution to the Psychology of Politics and Morals.* London: Hogarth Press, 1951.

Moore, Lucy. *Amphibious Thing: The Life of Lord Hervey.* London: Viking, 2000.

Moorhouse, Geoffrey. *The Last Office: 1539 and the Dissolution of a Monastery.* London: Weidenfeld & Nicolson, 2008.

More, Thomas. *Responsio ad Lutherum.* New Haven, CT: Yale University Press, 1969.

Morgan, Hiram. "Extradition and Treason-Trial of a Gaelic Lord: The Case of Brian O'Rourke." *Irish Jurist* 22, no. 2 (January 1987): 285–301.

———. "Hugh O'Neill, 2nd Earl of Tyrone." In *Dictionary of Irish Biography.* Vol. 7. Cambridge: Royal Irish Academy and Cambridge University Press, 2009.

———. *Tyrone's Rebellion: The Outbreak of the Nine Years Wars in Tudor Ireland.* Woodbridge, UK: Royal Historical Society, 1993.

Morris, Marc. *The Anglo-Saxons: A History of the Beginnings of England.* London: Hutchinson, 2021.

Morris, Richard K. "Architectural Terracotta at Sutton Place and Hampton Court." *British Brick Society Information,* no. 44 (March 1988): 3–8.

Morris, Sarah, and Natalie Grueninger. *In the Footsteps of Anne Boleyn.* Stroud, UK: Amberley, 2015.

Morrison, Fynes. *A History of Ireland, from the Year 1599 to 1603.* Dublin: S. Powell, 1753.

Mortimer, Ian. *The Perfect King: The Life of Edward III, Father of the English Nation.* London: Vintage, 2008.

Morton, Andrew. *Elizabeth and Margaret: The Intimate World of the Windsor Sisters.* London: Michael O'Mara, 2021.

Moynahan, Brian. *The Faith: A History of Christianity.* London: Pimlico, 2003.

Muir, Kenneth. *Life and Letters of Sir Thomas Wyatt.* Liverpool, UK: Liverpool University Press, 1963.

Murden, Sarah. "18th-Century Drinking Chocolate." *Recipes of the Georgian Era* (blog). All Things Georgian, January 6, 2015.

Murphy, Beverley A. *Bastard Prince: Henry VIII's Lost Son.* Stroud, UK: History Press, 2010.

Neale, John E. *Queen Elizabeth.* London: Jonathan Cape, 1934.

Neillands, Robin. *The Wars of the Roses.* London: Cassell, 1992.

Newitt, Malyn. *The Braganzas: The Rise and Fall of the Ruling Dynasties of Portugal and Brazil, 1640–1910.* London: Reaktion Books, 2019.

Nicholl, Katie. *Kate: The Future Queen.* London: Hachette, 2015.

Nichols, J. G., ed. *Literary Remains of King Edward the Sixth.* Vol. 1. London: B. Franklin, 1857.

Nicolas, Nicholas Harris. *The Privy Purse Expenses of Elizabeth of York.* London: W. Pickering, 1830.

Nicolson, Adam. *When God Spoke English: The Making of the King James Bible.* London: HarperCollins, 2011.

Nicolson, Juliet. *The Great Silence, 1918–20: Living in the Shadow of the Great War.* London: John Murray, 2010.

Nicolson, Nigel. *The Queen and Us.* London: Weidenfeld & Nicolson, 2003.

Norton, Elizabeth. *The Boleyn Women.* Stroud, UK: Amberley, 2014.

Norwich, John Julius. *Byzantium: The Early Centuries*. London: Guild, 1988.

"Notarial Records Relating to the Portuguese Jews in Amsterdam up to 1639." *Studia Rosenthaliana* 25, no. 1 (Spring 1991).

Ó Siochrú, Micheál. *Confederate Ireland, 1642–1649: A Constitutional and Political Analysis.* Dublin: Four Courts Press, 1999.

———. *God's Executioner: Oliver Cromwell and the Conquest of Ireland.* London: Faber and Faber, 2008.

Ó Siochrú, Micheál, and Jane Ohlmeyer, eds. *Ireland, 1641: Contexts and Reactions.* Manchester, UK: Manchester University Press, 2013.

O'Callaghan, Sean. *To Hell or Barbados: The Ethnic Cleansing of Ireland.* Dublin: Brandon, 2013.

O'Donovan, John, trans. *Annala Rioghachta Eireann: Annals of the Kingdom of Ireland, by the Four Masters, from the Earliest Period to the Year 1616.* Dublin: Royal Irish Academy, 1856.

O'Neill, Brendan, ed. *Irish Castles and Historic Houses.* Translated by James Stevens Curl. London: Caxton, 2002.

O'Rahilly, Cecile, ed. *Five Seventeenth-Century Political Poems.* Dublin: Institiúid Árd-Léinn Bhaile Átha Cliath, 1977.

Okerlund, Arlene. *Elizabeth: England's Slandered Queen.* Stroud, UK: Tempus, 2006.

Orléans, Élisabeth-Charlotte, Duchess of. *A Woman's Life in the Court of the Sun King: Letters of Liselotte von der Pfalz, Elisabeth Charlotte, Duchesse d'Orléans.* Translated and introduction by Elborg Forster. Baltimore: Johns Hopkins University Press, 1997.

Osborough, W. N. "The Failure to Enact an Irish Bill of Rights: A Gap in Irish Constitutional History." *Irish Jurist* 33 (1998): 392–416.

Otele, Olivette. *African Europeans: An Untold History.* London: C. Hurst, 2020.

Oxford Dictionary of National Biography. Oxford: Oxford University Press, 2004.

Palmer, William. *The Problem of Ireland in Tudor Foreign Policy, 1485–1603.* London: Boydell Press, 1994.

Paranque, Estelle. *Blood, Fire and Gold: The Story of Elizabeth I and Catherine de Medici.* London: Penguin, 2022.

Paranque, Estelle, and Valerie Schutte, eds. *Forgotten Queens in Medieval and Early Modern Europe: Political Agency, Myth Making, and Patronage.* London: Routledge, 2018.

Parker, Geoffrey. *Emperor: A New Life of Charles V.* New Haven, CT: Yale University Press, 2019.

Parker, Sarah E. *Grace and Favour: A Handbook of Who Lived Where in Hampton Court Palace from 1750 to 1950.* Historic Royal Palaces, Hampton Court Palace, 2005.

Parr, Queen Katherine. *Lamentations of a Sinner.* Edited and translated by Ollie Lansdowne. London: New Whitchurch Press, 2022.

Patterson, Orlando. "Slavery and Slave Revolts: A Socio-Historical Analysis of the First Maroon War, Jamaica, 1655–1740, Part 1." *Social and Economic Studies* 19, no. 3 (September 1970): 289–325.

Paxman, Jeremy. *On Royalty.* London: Viking, 2006.

Peal, Robert. *Meet the Georgians: Epic Tales from Britain's Wildest Century.* London: William Collins, 2021.

Pearce, Dominic. *Henrietta Maria.* Stroud, UK: Amberley, 2015.

Penn, Thomas. *Winter King: The Dawn of Tudor England.* London: Penguin, 2012.

Pepys, Samuel. *The Diary of Samuel Pepys.* Edited by Robert Latham and William G. Matthews. London: G. Bell & Sons, 1971.

Perceval-Maxwell, Michael. "Butler, James, 12th Earl and 1st Duke of Ormond." In *Dictionary of Irish Biography.* Vol. 2. Cambridge: Royal Irish Academy and Cambridge University Press, 2007.

Pimlott, Ben. *The Queen: Elizabeth II and the Monarchy.* London: HarperCollins, 2001.

Platter the Younger, Thomas. *Thomas Platter's Travels in England 1599: Rendered from the German and with Introductory Matter.* Introduction and edited by Clare Williams. London: Jonathan Cape, 1937.

Plowden, Alison. *Henrietta Maria: Charles I's Indomitable Queen.* Stroud, UK: Sutton, 2001.

———. *The Stuart Princesses.* Stroud, UK: Alan Sutton, 1996.

Pollard, A. F. *Wolsey.* London: Longmans Green, 1953.

Pope-Hennessy, James. *Queen Mary.* London: George Allen and Unwin, 1959.

———. *The Quest for Queen Mary.* Edited by Hugo Vickers. London: Zuleika, 2018.

Pope-Hennessy, John. *Learning to Look.* London: Heinemann, 1991.

Porter, Linda. *Crown of Thistles: The Fatal Inheritance of Mary, Queen of Scots.* London: Macmillan, 2013.

———. *Katherine the Queen: The Remarkable Life of Katherine Parr.* London: Macmillan, 2010.

———. *Mary Tudor: The First Queen.* London: Piatkus, 2009.

———. *Mistresses: Sex and Scandal at the Court of Charles II.* London: Picador, 2020.

———. *Royal Renegades: The Children of Charles I and the English Civil Wars.* London: St. Martin's Press, 2018.

Prendergast, John P. *The Cromwellian Settlement of Ireland.* London: Longman, Green, Roberts & Green, 1865.

Prescott, H. F. M. *Mary Tudor: The Spanish Tudor.* London: Eyre & Spottiswoode, 1952.

Price, David, ed. *Letters on England by Voltaire.* London: Cassell, 1894.

Price, Munro. *The Fall of the French Monarchy: Louis XVI, Marie-Antoinette and the Baron de Breteuil.* London: Macmillan, 2002.

Prosser, Lee. "Cromwellian Britain: Hampton Court Palace." *Cromwelliana: The Journal of the Cromwell Association* (2009).

———. "Writings and Sources: The Inventory of 1659." *Cromwelliana: The Journal of the Cromwell Association* 2, no. 6 (2009): 66.

Putnam, Polly. "The Wife of the King's Chocolate Maker," for Historic Royal Palaces and University of Reading blog (accessed online, March 14, 2021).

Rady, Martyn. *The Habsburgs: The Rise and Fall of a World Power.* London: Penguin Random House, 2020.

Rappaport, Helen. *The Race to Save the Romanovs: The Truth Behind the Secret Plans to Rescue the Russian Imperial Family.* London: St. Martin's Press, 2018.

Reilly, Tom. *Cromwell. An Honourable Enemy: The Untold Story of the Cromwellian Invasion of Ireland.* Dingle, Ire.: Brandon, 1999.

Reséndez, Andrés. *The Other Slavery: The Uncovered Story of Indian Enslavement in America.* Boston: Mariner Books, 2016.

Rickert, Edith, and Israel Gollancz, eds. *The Babees' Book: Medieval Manners for the Young: Done into Modern English from Dr. Furnivall's Texts.* New York: Cooper Square, 1966.

Ridley, Jane. *George V: Never a Dull Moment.* London: Chatto & Windus, 2021.

Ridley, Jasper. *Bloody Mary's Martyrs: The Story of England's Terror.* London: Constable, 2001.

———. *The Statesman and the Fanatic: Thomas Wolsey and Thomas More.* London: Constable, 1982.

Ring, Morgan. *So High a Blood: The Life of Margaret, Countess of Lennox.* London: Bloomsbury, 2017.

Roberts, Andrew. *George III: The Life and Reign of Britain's Most Misunderstood Monarch.* London: Allen Lane, 2021.

Robinson, Peter, and Ian Paisley. *Their Cry Was "No Surrender."* Belfast: Crown, 1988.

Romanoff, HH Princess Olga, with Coryne Hall. *A Wild and Barefoot Romanov.* London: Shepheard-Walwyn, 2017.

Russell, Gareth. *Do Let's Have Another Drink: The Singular Wit and Double Measures of Queen Elizabeth the Queen Mother.* London: William Collins, 2022.

———. "His Dear Bedfellow: The Debate over Harry Percy." *Tudor Life,* February 2016.

———. *Young and Damned and Fair: The Life and Tragedy of Catherine Howard at the Court of King Henry VIII.* London: HarperCollins, 2017.

Rye, William Benchley, ed. *England as Seen by Foreigners.* Charleston, SC: BiblioLife, 2009.

Salisbury, Robert Gascoyne-Cecil, 3rd Marquess of, et al., eds. *Calendar of the Manuscripts of the Most Honourable the Marquess of Salisbury Preserved at Hatfield House, Hertfordshire.* London: Her Majesty's Stationery Office, 1883–1976.

Sanders, Nicholas. *Rise and Growth of the Anglican Schism.* Edited and translated by David Lewis. London: Burns & Oates, 1877.

Sanghera, Sathnam. *Empireland: How Imperialism Has Shaped Modern Britain.* London: Viking, 2021.

Scarisbrick, J. J. *Henry VIII.* 2nd ed. New Haven, CT: Yale University Press, 1997.

Scattergood, John. "Skelton, John." In *Oxford Dictionary of National Biography,* Vol. 50 (2004).

———, ed. *John Skelton: The Complete English Poems.* London: Penguin, 1983.

Schauer, Margery S., and Frederick Schauer. "Law as the Engine of State: The Trial of Anne Boleyn." *William and Mary Law Review* 22, no. 1 (1980): 49–84.

Scofield, Cora L. *The Life and Reign of Edward the Fourth, King of England and of France and Lord of Ireland.* London: Frank Cass, 1967.

Scott, Mark. *Among the Kings: The Unknown Warrior, an Untold Story.* Newtownards, UK: Colourpoint House, 2020.

Scrope, R., and T. Monkhouse, eds. *State Papers Collected by Edward, Earl of Clarendon, Commencing from the Year 1621.* Oxford: Clarendon Press, 1767–86.

Seward, Desmond. *The Last White Rose: The Secret Wars of the Tudors.* London: Constable, 2011.

Seward, Ingrid. *Prince Philip Revealed: A Man of His Century.* London: Simon & Schuster, 2020.

Sharpe, Kevin. *Selling the Tudor Monarchy: Authority and Image in Sixteenth-Century England.* New Haven, CT: Yale University Press, 2009.

Shawcross, William, ed. *Counting One's Blessings: The Selected Letters of Queen Elizabeth the Queen Mother.* London: Macmillan, 2012.

———. *Queen Elizabeth The Queen Mother: The Official Biography.* London: Macmillan, 2009.

Shephard, Sue. *The Surprising Life of Constance Spry.* London: Pan, 2011.

Shepherd, Robert. *Ireland's Fate: The Boyne and After.* London: Aurum Press, 1990.

Siddons, Michael Powell. *Heraldic Badges in England and Wales.* Woodbridge, UK: Society of Antiquaries of London, 2009.

Siemann, Wolfram. *Metternich: Strategist and Visionary.* Translated by Daniel Steuer. Cambridge, MA: Harvard University Press, 2019.

Skelton, John. *Poems by John Skelton.* Introduction by Richard Hughes. London: William Heinemann, 1924.

Skidmore, Chris. *Death and the Virgin: Elizabeth, Dudley and the Mysterious Fate of Amy Robsart.* London: Phoenix, 2010.

———. *Edward VI: The Lost King of England.* London: Weidenfeld & Nicolson, 2007.

Slack, Paul. *Poverty and Policy in Tudor and Stuart England.* London: Longman, 1988.

Smith, E. A. *George IV.* New Haven, CT: Yale University Press, 1999.

Smith, Lesley. "Childbirth in the Late Sixteenth Century." *Family Planning Reproductive Health Care* 33, no. 1 (January 2007): 63–64.

Somerset, Anne. *Elizabeth I.* London: Phoenix Giant, 1997.

———. *Unnatural Murder: Poison at the Court of James I.* London: Weidenfeld & Nicolson, 1997.

———. *Queen Anne: The Politics of Passion.* London: Harper Press, 2012.

Sorlien, Robert Parker, ed. *The Diary of John Manningham of the Middle Temple, 1602–1603.* Hanover, NH: University Press of New England, 1976.

Spongberg, Mary. "*La Reine malheureuse*: Stuart History, Sympathetic History and the Stricklands' History of Henrietta Maria." *Women's History Review* 20, no. 5 (2011): 745–64.

St. Clare Byrne, Muriel, ed. *The Letters of King Henry VIII: A Selection, with a Few Other Documents.* London: Cassell, 1936.

———, ed. *The Lisle Letters.* Chicago: University of Chicago Press, 1981.

———, ed. *The Lisle Letters: An Abridgement.* Chicago: University of Chicago Press, 1983.

Stanford, Peter. *Martin Luther: Catholic Dissident.* London: Hodder & Stoughton, 2017.

Stapleton, Thomas. *The Life and Illustrious Martyrdom of Sir Thomas More.* Whitefish, MT: Kessinger, 2010.

Starkey, D., et al., eds. *The Inventory of Henry VIII.* London: Society of Antiquaries of London, 1998–2012.

Starkey, David. *Henry: The Prince Who Would Turn Tyrant.* London: HarperCollins, 2009.

———. *Six Wives: The Queens of Henry VIII.* London: Vintage, 2004.

Stater, Victor. *High Life, Low Morals: The Duel That Shook Stuart Society.* London: John Murray, 1999.

Stoker, Bram. *Famous Impostors.* New York: Sturgis & Walton, 1910.

Stoyle, Mark. *West Britons: Cornish Identities and the Early Modern British State.* Exeter, UK: University of Exeter Press, 2002.

Stuart, Arbella. *The Letters of Lady Arbella Stuart.* Edited by Sara Jayne Steen. Oxford: Oxford University Press, 1994.

Taffe, James. "Anne Boleyn and Her Gentlewomen in the Tower of London" (online lecture, July 2021).

———. "Reconstructing the Queen's Household: A Study in Royal Service, 1485–1547." PhD thesis, Durham University, Durham, UK, 2022.

Tallis, Nicola. "All the Queen's Jewels, 1445–1548." PhD thesis, University of Winchester, Winchester, UK, 2018.

———. *Uncrowned Queen: The Fateful Life of Margaret Beaufort, Tudor Matriarch.* London: Michael O'Mara, 2019.

Taylor, G. R. Stirling. *Robert Walpole and His Age.* London: Jonathan Cape, 1931.

Taylor, Stephen. "Caroline, Queen of Great Britain and Ireland." In *Oxford Dictionary of National Biography.* Vol. 10 (2004).

Taylor, Stephen, and Hannah Smith. "Hephaestion and Alexander: Lord Hervey, Frederick, Prince of Wales, and the Royal Favourite in England in the 1730s." *English Historical Review,* 124, no. 507 (April 2009): 283–312.

Tenison, E. M. *Elizabethan England: Being the History of This Country in Relation to All Foreign Princes.* Royal Lemington Spa, UK: printed privately for subscribers, 1933.

Thomas, Hugh M. *The English and the Normans: Ethnic Hostility, Assimilation, and Identity, 1066–c. 1220.* Oxford: Oxford University Press, 2003.

Thomas, Melita. *The House of Grey: Friends and Foes of Kings.* Stroud, UK: Amberley, 2019.

Thomas, William. *The Pilgrim: A Dialogue on the Life and Actions of King Henry the Eighth.* Edited by J. A. Froude. London: Parker, Son, and Bourn, 1861.

Thurley, Simon. *Hampton Court: A Social and Architectural History.* New Haven, CT: Yale University Press, 2003.

———. *Houses of Power: The Places That Shaped the Tudor World.* London: Transworld, 2017.

———. *Palaces of Revolution: Life, Death and Art at the Stuart Court.* London: William Collins, 2021.

———. *The Royal Palaces of Tudor England: Architecture and Court Life, 1460–1547.* New Haven, CT: Yale University Press, 1993.

———. "Tudor Ambition: Houses of the Boleyn Family." Lecture presented at Gresham College, London, September 16, 2020.

Tomalin, Claire. *Samuel Pepys: The Unequalled Self.* London: Penguin, 2002.

Torre, Victoria de la. "'We Few of an Infinite Multitude': John Hales, Parliament, and the Gendered Politics of the Early Elizabethan Succession." *Albion* 33, no. 4 (Winter 2001): 557–82.

Tostado, Igor Pérez. *Irish Influence at the Court of Spain in the Seventeenth Century.* Dublin: Four Courts Press, 2008.

Townsend, George, ed. *The Acts and Monuments of John Foxe.* London: R. B. Seeley and W. Burnside, 1837.

Tremlett, Giles. *Catherine of Aragon: Henry's Spanish Queen.* London: Faber and Faber, 2010.

Uglow, Jenny. *A Gambling Man: Charles II and the Restoration, 1660–1670.* London: Faber and Faber, 2009.

Van der Kiste, John. *King George II and Queen Caroline.* Stroud, UK: History Press, 2013.

Van der Kiste, John, and Coryne Hall. *Once a Grand Duchess: Xenia, Sister of Nicholas II.* Stroud, UK: Sutton, 2004.

Vickers, Hugo. *Elizabeth the Queen Mother.* London: Arrow Books, 2006.

Visser, Margaret. *The Rituals of Dinner: The Origins, Evolution, Eccentricities, and Meaning of Table Manners.* London: Viking, 1992.

Vogler, Pen. *Scoff: A History of Food and Class in Britain.* London: Atlantic Books, 2020.

Walford, Edward. *The County Families of the United Kingdom; or, Royal Manual of the Titled and Untitled Aristocracy of Great Britain and Ireland.* London: Robert Hardwicke, 1860.

Walker, Greg. *John Skelton and the Politics of the 1520s.* Cambridge: Cambridge University Press, 1988.

———. "Rethinking the Fall of Anne Boleyn." *Historical Journal* 45, no. 1 (March 2002): 1–29.

Waller, Maureen. *Sovereign Ladies: The Six Reigning Queens of England.* London: John Murray, 2006.

———. *Ungrateful Daughters: The Stuart Princesses Who Stole Their Father's Crown.* London: Hodder & Stoughton, 2002.

Walvin, James. *A World Transformed: Slavery in the Americas and the Origins of Global Power.* London: Robinson, 2022.

Ward, Jennifer. *English Noblewomen in the Later Middle Ages.* London: Longman, 1992.

Warner, Kathryn. *Edward II: The Unconventional King.* Stroud, UK: Amberley, 2014.

Warnicke, Retha M. *The Rise and Fall of Anne Boleyn: Family Politics at the Court of Henry VIII.* Cambridge: Cambridge University Press, 1989.

———. "Sexual Heresy at the Court of Henry VIII." *Historical Journal* 30, no. 2 (June 1987): 247–68.

Watkins, Sarah-Beth. *Catherine of Braganza: Charles II's Restoration Queen.* Alresford, UK: Chronos, 2017.

Watson, Constance. "The Secrets of Oxburgh Hall." *Catholic Herald,* September 2020.

Webb, Diana. *Privacy and Solitude in the Middle Ages.* New York: Continuum, 2007.

Wedell, George. "Hahn, Kurt Matthias Robert Martin." In *Oxford Dictionary of National Biography.* Vol. 24 (2004).

Wedgwood, C. V. *Oliver Cromwell.* London: Gerald Duckworth, 1973.

Weir, Alison. *The Lady in the Tower: The Fall of Anne Boleyn.* London: Jonathan Cape, 2009.

———. *The Six Wives of Henry VIII.* London: Pimlico, 1991.

———. "Why Did Jane Seymour Die in Childbed?" Tudor Times. Last modified May 3, 2018.

Welch, Frances. *A Romanov Fantasy: Life at the Court of Anna Anderson.* London: Short, 2007.

Wheeler, James Scott. *Cromwell in Ireland.* Dublin: Gill & Macmillan, 1999.

Whiston, William. *Memoirs of the Life and Writings of Mr. William Whiston.* London: Whiston and White, 1753.

Whitelock, Anna. *Elizabeth's Bedfellows: An Intimate History of the Queen's Court.* London: Bloomsbury, 2013.

———. *Mary Tudor: England's First Queen.* London: Bloomsbury, 2010.

Whyte, Catherine. "Hampton Court Palace Opens Royal Chocolate Kitchen." *Essential Surrey & South-West London* (February 25, 2014).

Wiesflecker, Hermann. *Kaiser Maximilian I: Gründung des habsburgischen Weltreiches, Lebensabend und Tod, 1508–1519.* Vienna: Böhlau, 1981.

Wilbraham, John, et al. *The Journal of Sir Roger Wilbraham, Solicitor-General in Ireland and Master of Requests for the Years 1593–1616, Together with Notes in Another Hand for the Years 1642–1649.* Cambridge, UK: Royal Historical Society and the Camden Society, 2009.

Williams, Kate. *Rival Queens: The Betrayal of Mary, Queen of Scots.* London: Penguin Random House, 2018.

———. *Young Elizabeth: The Making of Our Queen.* London: Weidenfeld & Nicolson, 2012.

Williams, Neville. *The Life and Times of Henry VII.* London: George Weidenfeld and Nicolson, 1973.

Williamson, James A. *The Voyages of the Cabots and the Discovery of North America.* London: Argonauts Press, 1929.

Wilson, A. N. *The Elizabethans.* London: Hutchinson, 2011.

Wilson, Derek. *A Brief History of Henry VIII: Reformer and Tyrant.* London: Constable & Robinson, 2009.

———. *In the Lion's Court: Power, Ambition, and Sudden Death in the Reign of Henry VIII.* New York: St. Martin's Griffin, 2003.

———. *Uncrowned Kings of England: The Black Legend of the Dudleys.* London: Constable & Robinson, 2005.

Wilson, Harris D. *King James VI and I.* Oxford: Oxford University Press, 1967.

Wilson, Philip. *The Beginnings of Modern Ireland.* Dublin: Maunsel, 1912.

Winter, Jay. *Sites of Memory, Sites of Mourning: The Great War in European Cultural Memory.* Cambridge: Cambridge University Press, 2017.

Wriothesley, Charles. *A Chronicle of England During the Reigns of the Tudors.* Edited by William Douglas Hamilton. London: Camden Society, 1875.

Wyatt, Thomas. *Sir Thomas Wyatt: The Complete Poems.* Edited by R. A. Rebholz. London: Penguin, 1978.

Young, Michael B. *King James VI and I and the History of Homosexuality.* London: Macmillan, 2000.

Ziegler, Philip. *Mountbatten.* London: Orion, 2001.

Zuvich, Andrea. *Sex and Sexuality in Stuart Britain.* Barnsley, UK: Pen & Sword, 2020.

INDEX

A

Abbott, George (archbishop), 194, 197

Abercorn, Cecil-Frances Hamilton, Marchioness of, 315

Abercorn, James Hamilton, 6th Earl of, 295

Abercorn, John Hamilton, 1st Marquess of, 315

Abnett, Ellen, 321

Abnett, Elsie, 322

Abnett, Herbert, 321

Abnett, Irene, 322

Abnett, Jack, 322

Abnett, Richard, 321–2

Abnett, Sidney, 321–2

Abnett, Thomas, 321, 331

Abolitionism (slavery), see Anti-slavery

Abraham (patriarch), 152

Acre, siege of, 18

Act of Settlement (1701), 282

Act of Union (1536), 71

Act of Union (1707), 262

Act of Union (1800), 262

Acts and Monuments (book), 125

Adelaide of Saxe-Meiningen, Queen of the United Kingdom and Hanover, 304

Adrian VI, pope, 42

Advent, 34

Æthelstan, King of England, 17

Agincourt, battle of, 24

Aisne, battle of, 325

Albany, Henry Stuart, 1st Duke of, see Darnley

Albemarle, Arnold van Keppel, 1st Earl of, 255, 256, 306

Albert of Saxe-Coburg-Gotha, Prince Consort of the United Kingdom, 304, 315–16, 317

Alexander ("the Great"), King of Macedonia, 252, 261, 293

Alexander II, Tsar of Russia, 340

Alexander III, Tsar of Russia, 340–1

Alexander Michaelovich, Grand Duke of Russia, 338n

Alexander VI, pope, 43

Alexandra of Denmark, Queen of the United Kingdom, 327, 328, 344, 353

Alexandra of Kent, the Hon. Lady Ogilvy, 335

Algarotti, Francesco, 294, 299

Alice, Duchess of Gloucester, 335

Amadas, Robert, 40

Amelia of Great Britain, princess, 288

American Civil War, 317–18

American Revolution, 302

Amsterdam, 273

Anastasia (movie), 339

Anastasia Nikolaevna, Grand Duchess of Russia, 339, 343

Angelus, 28, 28n

Angus, Archibald Douglas, 6th Earl of, 98, 107

Anna (Danish maid), 189–90, 196

Anna Freud Centre for Children and Families, 355

Anna of Denmark, Queen of England, Scotland, and Ireland

alleged conversion to Catholicism, 196

as alleged target of witchcraft, 170, 191

appearance, 187, 188

bereavements, 160, 187, 191

and Charles I, 187–97